WITHDRAWN

Maenads dressed as Wild Women attack the poet-musician Orpheus to silence his harmonious music with their discord. From Ovid, *Metamorphoses* (Antwerp: Christopher Plantin, 1591). Reprinted by permission of the Folger Shakespeare Library (PA 6519 M2 1591 Cage).

Myth, Emblem, and Music
in Shakespeare's *Cymbeline*

Myth, Emblem, and Music in Shakespeare's *Cymbeline*

An Iconographic Reconstruction

Peggy Muñoz Simonds

DELAWARE

Newark: University of Delaware Press
London and Toronto: Associated University Presses

Associated University Presses
440 Forsgate Drive
Cranbury, NJ 08512

Associated University Presses
25 Sicilian Avenue
London WC1A 2QH, England

Associated University Presses
P.O. Box 39, Clarkson Pstl. Stn.
Mississauga, Ontario,
L5J 3X9 Canada

The paper used in this publication meets the requirements of the American National Standard for Permanence of Paper for Printed Library Materials Z39.48-1984.

Library of Congress Cataloging-in-Publication Data

Simonds, Peggy Muñoz, 1928–
    Myth, emblem, and music in Shakespeare's Cymbeline : an iconographic reconstruction / Peggy Muñoz Simonds.
        p.   cm.
    Includes bibliographical references and index.
    ISBN 0-87413-429-3 (alk. paper)
    1. Shakespeare, William, 1564–1616.   Cymbeline.   2. Art and literature—England—History—17th century.   3. Emblems in literature.   4. Music and literature.   5. Myth in literature.
    6. Figures of speech.   7. Tragicomedy.   I. Title.
PR2806.S56   1992
822.3'3—dc20   90-50930
                                                              CIP

For
Roger Tyrrell Simonds

This book is dedicated to the memory of my brother
Chief Petty Officer Frank J. Muñoz, USN

—From *Sonnets to Orpheus* by Rainer Maria Rilke—

26

But you, divine one, you, till the end still sounding,
when beset by the swarm of disdained maenads,
you outsounded their cries with order, beautiful one,
from among the destroyers arose your upbuilding music.

None of them there could destroy your head or your lyre,
however they wrestled and raged; and all the sharp
stones they flung at your heart
turned soft on touching you and gifted with hearing.

In the end they battered and broke you, harried by
                                                vengeance
the while your resonance lingered in lions and rocks
and in the trees and birds. There you are singing still.

O you lost god! You unending trace!
Only because at last enmity rent and scattered you
are we now the hearers and a mouth of Nature.

*   *   *

Contents

University of Delaware Press
Manuscript Competition Winners

Shakespearean Literature
John W. Blanpied, *Time and the Artist in Shakespeare's English Histories*
Robert Ornstein, *Shakespeare's Comedies: From Roman Farce to Romantic Mystery*
Donald W. Foster, *Elegy by W.S.: A Study in Attribution*
David Hoeniger, *Medicine and Shakespeare in the English Renaissance*
Peggy Muñoz Simonds, *Myth, Emblem, and Music in Shakespeare's Cymbeline*

Early American Culture to 1840
Daniel D. Reiff, *Small Georgian Houses in England and Virginia: Origins and Development Through the 1750s*

Military, Naval, and Diplomatic History
Richard J. Hargrove, Jr., *General John Burgoyne*

Eighteenth-Century Studies
Donald T. Siebert, *The Moral Animus of David Hume*

American Art
Rowland Elzea, *John Sloan's Oil Paintings: A Catalogue Raisonné*

Acknowledgments

Much of the research for this study was supported by a National Endowment for the Humanities Fellowship for College Teachers in 1982.

I am especially grateful for the continuing support of my husband Roger Tyrrell Simonds, Professor of Philosophy at the American University, without whose help this book could not have taken shape. His translations of emblems and commentaries from Neo-Latin, Italian, and French sources have been invaluable, and his mastery of our shared and often uncooperative computer have saved the day on more occasions than I like to admit. His help with proofreading and advice on the philosophical sections of the book have been equally important.

I am indebted as well to Virginia W. Callahan, Professor Emerita of Classics, Howard University, who first introduced me to emblem books, then generously shared her translations of Andrea Alciati's emblems before they were published and her personal notes on Alciati's sources. Having taught me most of what I know about emblem literature during a 1980 Folger Institute Seminar on The Renaissance Emblem, she has since been a constant source of information and inspiration, as has Mary D. Garrard, Professor of Art History at the American University, who trained me in the iconographic method and first taught me how to read Renaissance art works. I am grateful for Professor Garrard's willingness to review and offer many helpful comments on my chapter "The Iconography of Imogen's Bedroom."

The intriguing question of how to define "tragicomedy" has remained with me as a challenge ever since I took a graduate course in the genre offered some years ago by Jeanne A. Roberts at the American University. I first tackled the problem of Shakespeare's use of the deus ex machina in *Cymbeline* in Muriel C. Bradbrook's Folger Institute Seminar on "Dramatic Conventions of the English Renaissance" in 1978. I remain very grateful to Professor Bradbrook for her introduction to the English Faculty at Cambridge University, where I spent a one semester leave, and for her encouragement of this project. I am indebted as well to Inga-Stina Ewbanks for reviewing an early paper of mine on Shakespeare's Wild Men that I wrote for her 1987 Folger Institute Seminar on "Jacobean Tragic Styles."

I particularly wish to express my thanks to Ann Thompson of the

University of Liverpool and to R. Chris Hassel, Jr., of Vanderbilt University for their very helpful comments on the manuscript as a whole. Last, but not least, I want to thank Jay Halio, Director of the University of Delaware Press, for gently nagging me into completing the book.

Valuable assistance in my research was also provided by the librarians, curators, and staff of the Folger Shakespeare Library, Washington, D.C., where most of my work was done, the American University Library, Beinecke Rare Book Library, Bodleian Library, British Library, University Library and English Faculty Library at Cambridge University, Huntington Library, Library of Congress, J. Pierpont Morgan Library, Library of the National Gallery of Art, and the Warburg Institute of the University of London.

Portions of the section on Eros and Anteros in chapter 3 have previously appeared in my essay "Eros and Anteros in Shakespeare's Sonnets 153 and 154" in *Spenser Studies* 7 (1986): 261–286. Most of chapter 4 on "The Iconography of Primitivism" has also appeared earlier as an article in *Renaissance Drama* 16 (1985): 95–120, and three sections of chapter 5 have been published previously as "Some Emblematic Courtier *Topoi* in *Cymbeline*" in *Renaissance Papers* (1981): 97–112. The final section of chapter 7 on the elm and the vine has appeared as an article entitled "The Marriage Topos in *Cymbeline:* Shakespeare's Variations on a Classical Theme" in *English Literary Renaissance* 19 (Winter 1989): 94–117. The sections on hearing in Chapter 9 have previously appeared as an essay entitled " 'No more . . . offend our hearing': Aural Imagery in *Cymbeline*" in *Texas Studies in Literature and Language* 24 (Summer 1982): 137–54: the material on Jupiter as the Christian deity descending was first published as "Jupiter, His Eagle, and BBC-TV," in *Shakespeare on Film Newsletter* 10 (December 1985): 3; and part of chapter 10 has appeared in revised form as " 'Killing care and grief of heart': Orpheus and Shakespeare" in *Renaissance Papers* (1990): 79–90. I am very grateful to the editors of all the above journals for permission to reprint this material.

Parts of this book have also been delivered as papers at meetings of the Shakespeare Association of America, Renaissance Society of America, Southeastern Renaissance Society, South Central Renaissance Society, Folger Institute Colloquia, Twentieth International Congress on Medieval Studies in Kalamazoo, South Atlantic Modern Language Association, Community College Humanities Association, and the Modern Language Assocation.

The epigraph for this study is Sonnet 26 from Rainer Maria Rilke's *Sonnets to Orpheus,* translated by M. D. Herter Norton, and published by W. W. Norton & Company, Inc., New York, 1942. I am indebted to Penguin Books, Ltd., for permission to reprint approximately 310 words from *The Travels of Sir John Mandeville,* translated by C. W. R. D.

Moseley (Penguin Classics, 1983), translation copyright © C. W. R. D. Moseley, 1983. I am also grateful to Farrar, Straus & Giroux, Inc., for permission to use an excerpt from *The White Goddess,* by Robert Graves, copyright © 1948 by Robert Graves, renewal copyright © 1975 by Robert Graves. Reprinted by permission of Farrar, Straus & Giroux, Inc.

Throughout this book I have quoted lines from the Arden edition of Shakespeare's *Cymbeline,* edited by J. M. Nosworthy, (London, Methuen & Co. Ltd., 1955). All references to other plays by William Shakespeare are from *The Riverside Shakespeare,* edited by G. Blakemore Evans (Boston, Houghton-Mifflin Company, 1974).

Introduction

The past is a foreign country:
They do things differently there.
—L. P. Hartley

The purpose of this book is to reconstruct a Renaissance *Cymbeline* in much the same way that Roland Mushat Frye attempted to recover a Renaissance *Hamlet*.[1] I shall approach this objective through iconography, or the study of the conventional imagery and symbolic representations of standard Renaissance themes that appear in the art of the period—and even later, if the truth be known. This means that I shall be examining the basic materials of Renaissance poetry—the *topoi* (traditional tropes or topics of invention), which the poet first chooses to use and then later varies or combines with other *topoi* in order to make a personal statement about a given theme. While art historians study the visual image and identify its visual sources and the literary texts that lie behind it, I shall look at verbal dialogue and stage imagery and then search for both visual and literary precursors in an effort to interpret the mythological and symbolic structure of Shakespeare's *Cymbeline*.

The Importance of Commonplaces and Classical *Topoi*

It seems significant to me that if the art historian can find a given topic of invention in a Shakespearean play or poem, he or she is usually convinced at once that the same *topos* in the painting under study is an authentic Renaissance idea since it is still giving off lively sparks by the end of the cultural period. We Shakespearean scholars should be equally interested in the way our dramatist sums up Renaissance high culture within a popular art form and so skillfully passes it forward to us, although our different cosmology and philosophical beliefs often tend to blind us to its meaning.

How often have we heard modern undergraduates complain that Shakespeare's plays are very "hard" to read today, despite the fact that they were once considered to be "pop art"? I would complain even further that we

13

scholars—as well as our students—no longer know how to read Shakespeare as accurately as we should, despite the aid of the *Oxford English
Dictionary* and multiple editorial footnotes. We do not think as he did; we
never learned the poetic trade by keeping a commonplace book in which
to write down standard tropes and their meanings; we do not read emblem
books or even the Bible very much; most of us have not studied the
classics in sufficient detail; and we are often unfamiliar with the majority
of the traditional *topoi* to which the dramatist so frequently refers. The
latter include the comparison of the microcosm and the macrocosm to a
world lyre that must be kept in tune, and such recurring images as a
ravished tree, a caged bird, a stricken deer and its search for a cure, a pine
tree struck by lightning, an old hag with snakes coming out of her mouth,
etc., etc. Images of this sort actually constitute the shared poetic language
of the Renaissance, a language that is not generally being taught these
days in our colleges and universities, despite the availability of many fine
studies of individual *topoi*. But, without a knowledge of this strange
language of images and metaphors based on classical and biblical sources,
modern readers are bound to find Shakespeare's texts very difficult indeed
to "understand."

The results of this lack of knowledge in serious scholarship are often
impressionistic interpretations like the following by an otherwise sensible
critic:

> Belarius's preference for the "safer hold" of the "sharded beetle" over the
> domain of the "full-wing'd eagle" . . . suggests pastoral reverence for quietness
> and humility as well as pastoral aversion to expansive acquisitiveness. The
> reference to the "eagle" appropriately evokes Rome, about to invade Britain
> once again.[2]

Aside from the fact that *Cymbeline* is not really a pastoral at all, as I shall
demonstrate later, the author of the above passage has misread the significance of both the eagle and the beetle in a Shakespearean context. The
emblematic beetle is anything but humble when it invades the eagle's nest
and destroys its offspring, as we shall see in chapter 4; while the eagle is
hardly ever used as a symbol of Rome in this play, except by the Roman
Soothsayer. I will show here that its meanings are more often Christian
and derive from *Physiologus* and from the Bible, or that the eagle simply
refers to kingship, as is the case in the above quotation from Belarius, a
Renaissance courtier who had obviously read his Erasmus. The critic I
have quoted is probably unfamiliar with an explanation of the eagle and
beetle trope that appeared some years ago in *Notes & Queries*.[3]

An even more famous Shakespearean scholar made a similar error of
interpretation in an important book that has profoundly influenced our

reading of the plays in the light of seasonal folk rituals. C. L. Barber tells us that in *A Midsummer Night's Dream,*

> Titania, embracing Bottom, describes herself in terms that fit her surroundings and uses the association of ivy with women of the songs traditional at Christmas:
>
> So doth the Woodbine the sweet honeysuckle
> Gently entwist; the female ivy so
> Enrings the barky fingers of the elm.[4]
>
> (4.1.45–47)

This image has nothing to do with Christmas carols; it is an inversion of the classical commonplace and visual emblem of the elm and the vine, a widely used marriage *topos* in the Renaissance to be fully discussed in chapter 7. Although the fruitful vine gives life to the dying elm, ivy actually kills the tree about which it twines and thus symbolizes an illicit and unnatural love.

As a stranger in the foreign land of the past, I too shall undoubtedly make my own share of such mistakes. However, the point here is that Renaissance poets usually did not make up new and original metaphors. Instead they employed conventional *topoi* appropriately and often varied them to suggest new meanings, or they combined them with others in a new way. The basic material or clay of poetry was always the commonplace, which every educated person had been trained to understand in that distant past. In the words of S. K. Heninger, Jr., for Renaissance poets, "The creative act rests more in selecting the prefabricated metaphor which is most expressive, rather than in devising with uniqueness or even with novelty. For the poet, therefore, the framing of metaphors is an act of discovery and choice more than of creating *ex nihilo.*"[5] Modern artists such as Pablo Picasso, Paul Klee, John Fowles, Tom Stoppard, and D. M. Thomas also make use of traditional iconography to carry meanings that are unfortunately lost on viewers and readers who do not recognize the ancient language of commonplaces.[6]

John Hollander, to take just one example, recently published a poem called "Summer Day" in *The New Yorker,* wherein he refers to his discomfort at using such *topoi* as a form of modern expression.

> Tinged with false promise, edged with polychrome,
> The sunset's red drips up along its dome;
>   Tuning the corded jib sheet to the strum
> Of evening air we make a run for home.
> Twilight and meaning, darkness and rising hope
> Stretched out across my path a twisted rope.
>   Last night, in simple truth, I fell asleep.
> Today I trip over last evening's trope.[7]

The poet sees his jib sheet, a rope on a sailboat, as a string on the World Lyre representing both the microcosm and the macrocosm, and this taut rope sings in perfect harmony with the cosmos as he sails his boat toward home. The metaphor derives from a familiar harmonist *topos* about which Hollander, the scholar, has written extensively.[8] Yet in a less enchanted moment the next morning, the rope ironically becomes no more than an object for the poet to trip over. His subconscious intuitive sense of universal harmony is lost in the probing light of present day rational skepticism and science.

The Iconographic Method and Its Dangers

Essentially then, my approach to *Cymbeline* is through a study of the once believable and popular Renaissance *topoi* to be found in the play through analogy with the same *topoi* as they appear in emblem books and other artifacts. There are, of course, some dangers in this method. First, one must keep in mind that every *topos* can be inverted to mean its opposite. An example of this might be the image of a courtier in stocks, which can imply that the courtier has given away his freedom of speech and action in exchange for a gold chain and advancement, or—as in *King Lear* when Kent is put in stocks for speaking the truth—it might mean the reverse, that the only free man in sight is the outspoken prisoner of the oppressors. This doubleness requires the critic to ask him- or herself in every case if he has missed irony in his analysis. Second, since there are usually multiple variations of a given *topos,* the scholar must either choose the most likely significance in the context of the poem or play or admit that in this particular case one cannot be sure which meaning is correct without further information. We must always remember that the poet may be deliberately ambiguous in his use of some *topoi,* for poetic, political, or religious reasons.

Third, just as different combinations of words have a different significance, different combinations of images have different meanings. For example, the eagle and the beetle *topos* has no conceptual relation to the eagle flying into the sun, or to the eagle and the fountain, the eagle and the rock, the eagle and the serpent, etc. A quick glance at Henkel and Schöne's thematic encyclopedia of emblems will immediately illustrate this point to those in search of stable icons.[9] Fourth, it is essential to notice the cultural context of an image if we are to understand its meaning properly. In the West an owl symbolizes wisdom because it can see in the dark and is associated with Athena; in the East the same owl means foolishness because it cannot see in the daytime like everyone else. In Renaissance studies especially it also helps to know whether the *topos* is being employed by a Catholic or a Protestant poet or painter.

A fifth danger lies in wait for the critic who overemphasizes the significance of a minor *topos* in a given work and thus misses the more important *topos* it reinforces. One must always keep the work as a whole in mind. In addition, one must analyze the image in terms of the time period when the poem or play was written. The eagle was indeed an imperial symbol for Roman writers, but it was often used as a symbol of monastic contemplation by Christians during the Middle Ages, as John Steadman has shown,[10] and we will discover in this book that it had even more complex meanings in the context of the Renaissance and its period of religious Reformation. If the sixth danger is thus one of ignoring historical context, the seventh and most serious danger of the iconographic method for literary scholars is the mistake of looking through emblem books for apparently relevant pictures and failing to translate the Latin texts, which often give rather contrary or unexpected meanings to the pictures. As far as emblems are concerned, their significance can often be found in the relationship between text and picture, with the text usually, but not always, the most important aspect. Many scholars are not aware, it would seem, that emblematists often had no choice of and no control over the pictures utilized by their publishers to accompany the verses.[11] In some cases, the publisher employed old woodcuts he happened to have on hand to illustrate a new book of emblematic verses, so that the pictures can sometimes be more misleading than helpful.

Nevertheless, I have found Renaissance emblem books, which usually combine a motto, a picture, and a verse on each page or two, and which were widely disseminated and widely read in Shakespeare's lifetime, to be particularly helpful tools in this study of *Cymbeline*. They tell us that a given idea or attitude was current at the time and often suggest how the *topos* might be interpreted. But emblems can seldom be claimed as direct sources for poetic metaphors. Their content can always be found elsewhere: in the work of other poets and their sources, which could include the poetry of antiquity, the hieroglyphs of Horapollo, the adages of Erasmus, *Physiologus,* the Bible, and so forth. In the words of Steadman, "Except in rare instances the attempt to establish specific literary or iconographical indebtedness [to an emblem] can be misleading. In most cases the parallels are valuable chiefly as parallels and nothing more; the commonplaces as commonplaces, and precisely because they *are* such; the tradition as tradition."[12] Unfortunately, Henry Green, the first important modern student of emblematics in the nineteenth century, did cite emblems as Shakespearean sources, and ever since, scholars who consider emblems to be valuable doors into the world of Renaissance *topoi* have had to apologize for him.[13] In spite of this, his pioneer book called *Shakespeare and the Emblem Writers* remains an important resource for contemporary iconographers who do not need to accept his critical conclusions.

In any event, the references to or uses of emblematic ideas in the dramatic dialogue of the Renaissance are clearly ubiquitous. To take only one example in *Cymbeline,* the character Pisanio provides us with a powerful verbal emblem of slander:

> No. 'tis slander,
> Whose edge is sharper than the sword, whose tongue
> Outvenoms all the worms of Nile, whose breath
> Rides on the posting winds, and doth belie
> All corners of the world. Kings, queens, and states,
> Maids, matrons, nay, the secrets of the grave
> This viperous slander enters.

(3.4.34–40)

This complex image is analogous to similar statements in Ovid's *Metamorphoses,* Ripa's *Iconologia,* and above all, to Geffrey Whitney's emblem on Envy in *A Choice of Emblemes.* Here, under the *inscriptio* "Invidiae descriptio" and the *pictura* of a hag with snakes in her mouth and sagging breasts, a hag who seems to be ripping her heart out of her own body as she strides through the world with her walking stick, Whitney writes the following explanatory *subscriptio:*

> What hideous hagge with visage sterne appeares?
>   Whose feeble limmes, can scarce the bodie staie:
> This, Enuie is: leane, pale, and full of years,
> Who with the blisse of other pines awaie.
>   And what declares, her eating vipers broode?
>   That poysoned thoughtes, bee euermore her foode.
>
> What meanes her eies? so bleared, sore, and redd:
> Her mourninge still, to see an others gaine.
> And what is mente by snakes vpon her head?
> The fruit that springes, of such a venomed braine.
>   But whie, her harte shee rentes within her brest?
>   It shewes her self, doth worke her owne vnrest.
>
> Whie lookes shee wronge? because shee woulde not see,
> An happie wight, which is to her a hell:
> What other partes within this furie bee?
> Her harte, with gall: her tonge, with stinges doth swell.
>   And laste of all, her staffe with prickes aboundes:
>   Which showes her wordes, wherewith the good shee
>   woundes.[14]

Needless to say, Shakespeare's version of the *topos* is somewhat different. It is more concise and more poetic in that it extends the reach of slander into the grave, and thus is more effective; but it is, nevertheless, simply one more variation on the theme of *Invidia* or Envy that leads to slander. Above all, it is immediately reminiscent of Whitney's familiar woodcut of slander in action.

Inuidiæ defcriptio.

Ad Ra. W.

Inuidiam Ouid. defcribit. 2. Metamorph.

WHAT hideous hagge with vifage fterne appeares?
  Whofe feeble limmes, can fcarce the bodie ftaie:
This, Enuie is: leane, pale, and full of yeares,
Who with the bliffe of other pines awaie.
    And what declares, Her eating vipers broode?
    That poyfoned thoughtes, bee euermore her foode.

Lucret. 3.
Macerat Inuidia ante oculos illu effe potētem,
Illum adfpectari, claro qui incedit honore:
Ipfi fe in tenebrù volui,
œrúq́ue queruntur.

What meanes her eies? fo bleared, fore, and redd:
Her mourninge ftill, to fee an others gaine.
And what is mente by fnakes vpon her head?
The fruite that fpringes, of fuch a venomed braine.
    But whie, her harte fhee rentes within her breft?
    It fhewes her felfe, doth worke her owne vnreft.

Whie lookes fnee wronge? bicaufe fhee woulde not fee,
An happie wight, which is to her a hell:
What other partes within this furie bee?
Her harte, with gall: her tonge, with ftinges doth fwell.
    And lafte of all, her ftaffe with prickes aboundes:
    Which fhowes her wordes, wherewith the good fhee woundes.

Ouid. lib. 1. De Arte Amandi.

Fertilior feges eft aliènis femper in agris,
Vicinúmq́ pecus grandius vber habet.

De In.

A personification of Envy that leads to Slander. From Geffrey Whitney, *A Choice of Emblems* **(Leiden: Christopher Plantin, 1586), 94. Reprinted by permission of the Folger Shakespeare Library (STC 254378).**

Agreeing that Renaissance literary comments on slander derive from the Envy *topos,* Joyce H. Sexton surveys the tradition from the classics, through the Church Fathers, the late medieval tradition, and the Renaissance in her chapter entitled "Slander's Venom'd Spear."[15] She concludes that viperous Envy can be ultimately summarized in western culture as "the opposition to love, the alignment against humanity out of sheer indiscriminate spite, the enmity to the Holy Ghost" (1978, 22). Emblematist Otto van Veen insists even further that envy always follows in the footsteps of love. In his emblem "Enuy is loue's shadow," van Veen depicts Cupid walking along a country path with Envy literally portrayed as his shadow. She is a Medusa-like figure, with snakes in place of hair and snakes in her hands, while her mouth is wide open to scream forth slander. The verse states that

> The more the Sunne shynes cleer the darker shadows bee,
> The more loue doth appeer the more is enuy seen,
> And loue securest lyes within dark secresie.[16]

In other words, lovers who boast of their beloveds, as do Collatine and Posthumus, will invariably awaken envy in the hearts of others. Love, like diplomatic negotiations, must be kept secret until the wedding day, or the day when a treaty between governments is actually signed.

Envy following Amor as his shadow. From Otto van Veen, *Emblemes of Loue* (Antwerp, 1608), 51. Reprinted by permission of the Folger Shakespeare Library (STC 24627a.5 copy 1).

Dieter Mehl has enumerated three different ways that poets utilized emblems in Renaissance drama: (1) the "direct borrow or quotation," (2) "the insertion of allegorical scenes or tableaux" that provide "a pictorial commentary on the action of the play," and (3) "emblematic images in the course of a scene, as a significant combination of verbal and visual expression."[17] To this list we should add (4) the even more common practice of providing a new verbal variation of the theme, as schoolboys were trained to do in connection with Alciati's emblems.[18] In any case, the emblem books can still serve us today as fascinating guidebooks to the metaphorical language and visual imagery peculiar to that foreign country known as the past, where we must patiently engage in literary and visual archaeology if we wish to understand *Cymbeline* in its historical context.

Political Iconography and Irony

Most recent studies of the iconography perceived in the play have been concerned primarily with the imagery of royalty. But, as I have suggested, we must also always keep an ear tuned for irony in Shakespeare's echoing of emblems, even in his allusions to the political emblems of his patron, James I. For example, *Cymbeline* appears to celebrate the Jacobean propaganda theme of peace as a "means of preserving the commonwealth,"[19] although the peace referred to in the play is actually the historical *pax romana* necessary for the birth of Christ to occur during Cymbeline's reign. The last word in the text is "peace," since the king is now a ratifier of Augustus's *pax romana,* and only the deceased wicked Queen and her loutish son had wanted war against Rome in the first place.

It is true that on his accession to the throne, James did take the motto *Beati pacifici* for his own, as we can see written on the tapestry behind the throne in the emblematic portrait of the king engraved by Simon Van de Passe as a frontispiece to James's printed *Workes* (1616). Yet there is more to be seen in this portrait, which contains all three of the usual parts of an emblem: motto, picture and verse. *Beati pacifici* (Blessed are the peacemakers) appears at the top of the emblem. To the king's right in this engraving is the usual combination of the sword and the book in Protestant iconography—a sword marked *Justicia* lying across a Bible entitled *Verbum Dei.*[20] To the king's left is the cushion of sovereignty on which the crown would rest when not being worn. The verse beneath the picture reads:

Crounes have their compasse, length of dayes their date,
Triumphes their tombes, felicitie her fate;
Of more then earth, can earth make none partaker,
But knowledge makes the KING most like his maker.[21]

It is significant that the absolutist notion here that kings have something approaching divine knowledge is of course thoroughly undermined by Shakespeare in *Cymbeline,* a tragicomedy in which the player king is easily led astray by outward beauty and practiced flattery. Unlike this portrait, the play seems to suggest that a royal commitment to peace is praiseworthy, but that a royal claim to godlike omniscience is absurd.

Similar iconography appears on the title page of *The Workes* of King James, with the important addition of a pictorial version of the new sovereign's commitment to Queen Elizabeth's Protestantism. Within an elaborately decorated architectural framework, we see a winged personification of *Religio* in a niche to the left of the title. She leans her right arm on a wooden cross, the base of which rests on a skeleton and symbolizes the overcoming of Death by Christianity, a theme to be repeated in *Cymbeline* (although in pagan terms). We know that she represents Protestantism because she holds an open copy of the Scriptures in her left hand to indicate the importance of the Word of God to her followers and its immediate availability to all readers. In contrast, Cesare Ripa's *Religione* in his *Iconologia* is veiled to indicate mystery; she holds a closed copy of the Bible under her right arm along with the cross, and displays the Counter-Reformation symbol of the flame of devotion in her uplifted left hand.[22] Behind her is an elephant that represents the virtues of the good Catholic worshipper. Returning to James's title page engraved by Renold Elstrack, the figure of *Pax* stands on a pile of military arms in a niche to the left of the title. She upholds the olive branch of Peace in her right hand and the cornucopia of Plenty in her left hand. This propaganda promise of peace and plenty under James I is very likely echoed in Shakespeare's *Cymbeline* when the player king freely chooses peace over continued war with Rome.[23]

In addition, as many scholars have noticed, we do find a definite allusion to the Brutus myth of English history in *Cymbeline* through the heroine's name, Imogen, which is now thought to be a misprint of the name of Brute's wife, Innogen. James I found the story of the legendary Trojan king of Britain particularly appropriate for propaganda purposes, since Brute had foolishly divided the island between his three sons, while James, as the second Brute, was attempting to reunite the three kingdoms once again. Shakespeare refers to the tragedy of division in *King Lear;* in contrast, his *Cymbeline* celebrates the happy reunion of three loving royal siblings. The Brute myth had already served a major propaganda purpose for the monarch in Anthony Munday's Lord Mayor's pageant of 1605 entitled *The Triumphs of Re-United Britannia.*

Despite these open allusions to certain Jacobean propaganda themes, we shall discover that *Cymbeline* is also a play filled with subtle satire on the exalted claims of the British royal family, which it seems on the surface

BEATI PACIFICI

Crounes haue their compasse, length of dayes their date,
Triumphes their tombes, felicitie ßee fate :
Of more then earth, can earth make none partaker,
But knowledge makes the KING most like his maker.

Simon Passaeus sculp:Lond.   Ioh: Bill excudit.

**An emblematic portrait of King James I, complete with motto and verse, serves as
the frontispiece to the king's *Workes* (London, 1616). Reprinted by permission of the
Folger Shakespeare Library (STC 14344 copy 1).**

Personifications of Religion and Peace dominate the title page of King James's *Workes* (London, 1616). Reprinted by permission of the Folger Shakespeare Library (STC 14344 copy 1).

to flatter. At one point the player king is so powerless that he has to be saved by shaggy Wild Men from capture by the Roman army. A king, after all, is nothing without the support of his people. Even the grace so triumphantly celebrated in the play is that of Jupiter and not that of the royal presence, and the king must, in fact, humble himself at the end to learn his own grace from his once despised son-in-law Posthumus. Actions witnessed onstage also must have some subliminal effect on an audience. In *Cymbeline* we see a "silly" peasant easily disarm the elegant courtier Iachimo, and although we know that the peasant is really Posthumus, the fact remains that we have witnessed the easy defeat of a nobleman by an apparently common person in hand to hand combat. This dumb-show battle parallels the earlier defeat of the princely Cloten by the Wild Boy Guiderius. Such repetition is in itself often a sign of satire. Although, if called to account, Shakespeare could easily defend himself by saying that the Wild Boy was really a prince. Nevertheless, the ironic theatrical scene is still vibrant in our mind's eye, and we have learned that the lowest element in society has no difficulty in disarming and killing an unreformed prince. The Cromwellian revolution was soon to prove the truth of this satirical warning to the established monarchy.

I shall say no more here about royal iconography, which has been so amply discussed by others, but instead concentrate the main body of this study on the peculiar genre of *Cymbeline,* the philosophical myths dramatized in the play, and the traditional *topoi* that Shakespeare has woven so skillfully into the visual and verbal imagery of its action and its dialogue. From here on, I shall examine *Cymbeline* primarily in search of what Ben Jonson has called the "remou'd mysteries" of dramatic art in the Renaissance.

Notes

1. See Roland Mushat Frye, *The Renaissance Hamlet: Issues and Responses in 1600* (Princeton, N.J.: Princeton University Press, 1984).

2. See Robert S. Miola, *Shakespeare's Rome* (Cambridge: Cambridge University Press, 1983), 219.

3. See H. W. Crundell, "Shakespeare, Lyly, and Aesop," *Notes and Queries* 168 (1935): 312.

4. C. L. Barber, *Shakespeare's Festive Comedy: A Study of Dramatic Form and Its Relation to Social Custom* (Princeton, N.J.: Princeton University Press, 1959), 136. References are to act, scene, and line(s).

5. S. K. Heninger, Jr., *Touches of Sweet Harmony: Pythagorean Cosmology and Renaissance Poetics* (San Marino, Calif.: The Huntington Library, 1974), 338.

6. For examples in D. M. Thomas, see Peggy Muñoz Simonds, "*The White Hotel:* A Sexual Satire," *Critique* 27 (Fall 1985): 51–63.

7. John Hollander, "Summer Day," *The New Yorker* (14 August 1989): 28.

8. See Hollander, *The Untuning of the Sky: Ideas of Music in English Poetry, 1500–1700* (Princeton, N.J.: Princeton University Press, 1961).

9. See Arthur Henkel and Albrecht Schöne, eds., *Emblemata* (Stuttgart: J. B. Metzlersche Verlagsbuchandlung, 1967).

10. John Steadman, "Chaucer's Eagle: A Contemplative Symbol," *PMLA* 75 (1960): 153–59.

11. Daniel Russell does not consider this serious iconographical problem in his otherwise interesting article "Alciati's Emblems in Renaissance France," *Renaissance Quarterly* 34 (Winter 1981): 534–54; nor does Huston Diehl in her "Graven Images: Protestant Emblem Books in England," *Renaissance Quarterly* 39 (Spring 1968): 49–66.

12. See John Steadman, "The Iconographical Approach," in *Nature into Myth: Medieval and Renaissance Moral Symbols* (Pittsburgh: Duquesne University Press, 1979), 32. For an important study of methodology in the use of emblems, see Peter M. Daly, "Shakespeare and the Emblem: The Use of Evidence and Analogy in Establishing Iconographic and Emblematic Effects in the Plays," in *Shakespeare and the Emblem: Studies in Renaissance Iconography and Iconology,* ed. Tibor Fabiny (Szeged: Attila Jószef University Press, 1984), 117–86.

13. Henry Green, *Shakespeare and the Emblem Writers* (London: Trübner & Co., 1870).

14. Geffrey Whitney, *A Choice of Emblemes* (Leiden: Christopher Plantin, 1586), 94. In the private library of Peter Blayney, I have seen a tattered copy of Whitney that had been used as a pattern book for some kind of household decorations. A number of the pictures have pinholes pricked into the designs and show evidence of lead having been rubbed over the page to reproduce the design on another piece of paper placed behind the picture.

15. See Joyce H. Sexton, *The Slandered Woman in Shakespeare* (Victoria, B.C.: University of Victoria Press, 1978), 11–38. For her discussion of *Cymbeline,* see pp. 61–76.

16. Otto van Veen, *Amorvm emblemata, or Emblemes of Loue* (Antwerp, 1608), 50–51.

17. See Dieter Mehl, "Emblems in Renaissance Drama," *Renaissance Drama* n.s. 2 (1969): 43–51.

18. See T. W. Baldwin, *William Shakspere's Small Latine & lesse Greeke,* 2 vols. (Urbana: University of Illinois Press, 1944), vol. 2, 322–23.

19. See David Bergeron, *English Civic Pageantry 1558–1642* (London: Edward Arnold, 1971), 300. Other politically oriented studies include Jonathan Goldberg, *James I and the Politics of Literature* (Baltimore: Johns Hopkins University Press, 1983); David Bergeron, *Shakespeare's Romances and the Royal Family* (Lawrence, Kansas: University Press of Kansas, 1985); and Leah S. Marcus, *Puzzling Shakespeare: Local Reading and Its Discontents* (Berkeley: University of California Press, 1988).

20. For a discussion of this iconographical tradition, see John N. King, *Tudor Royal Iconography: Literature and Art in an Age of Religious Crisis* (Princeton, N.J.: Princeton University Press, 1989), 54–115.

21. James I, *The Workes of the Most High and Mightie, Prince Iames* (London: Robert Barker and Iohn Bill, 1616), frontispiece.

22. See Cesare Ripa, *Iconologia* (1611; reprint New York: Garland Publishing, Inc., 1976), 456.

23. See Goldberg, 240–41.

Myth, Emblem, and Music in Shakespeare's *Cymbeline*

1

Cymbeline as a Renaissance Tragicomedy

Yet, with my nobler reason, 'gainst my fury
Do I take part. The rarer action is
In virtue than in vengeance.

—*The Tempest*

As E. D. Hirsch, Jr., has argued, we cannot hope to interpret a literary work with any degree of accuracy, much less criticize it fairly, until we have established its genre with a high degree of certainty,[1] and Ernst Gombrich has extended this same warning to the study of art history and iconography.[2] The problem of genre is particularly relevant to Shakespeare's *Cymbeline,* a play that is still considered to be "unsuccessful" or merely "experimental" by many literary critics. A misunderstanding of its genre lies, for example, at the heart of Samuel Johnson's scornful criticism of the play in the eighteenth century. Finding the work to be neither an emotionally cathartic tragedy nor an amusing comedy, and in no way Aristotelian, Johnson summarily dismissed it as a failure:

> This play has many just sentiments, some natural dialogues, and some pleasing scenes, but they are obtained at the expense of much incongruity. To remark the folly of the fiction, the absurdity of the conduct, the confusion of the names, and manners of different times, and the impossibility of the events in any system of life, were to waste criticism upon unresisting imbecility, upon faults too evident for detection, and too gross for aggravation.[3]

More recently Arthur C. Kirsch insisted that *Cymbeline* "is resistant to any coherent interpretation" because of these very incongruities.[4]

However, in a later study, *Shakespeare and the Experience of Love,* Kirsch modified his criticism by explaining the incongruities of the play in terms of Freudian dream theory and then admitting that *Cymbeline* is extraordinarily powerful as a work of dramatic art. In this tragicomedy, he says,

> Time is simultaneously condensed and dilated, as it is both in the mystery drama and dreams, and the play returns us more directly, as those forms do, to

29

the transcendental and primal processes of transformation. In *Cymbeline* as in the mystery drama, one world literally is ransomed and another destroyed, and the epiphany of that movement is confirmed in the actual manifestation of a god; and in the psychic drama of *Cymbeline* the resolution of erotic guilt is achieved through the "senseless speaking such / As sense cannot untie" of an actual dream within a play as well as through the style of dream-work in the whole of the drama. I think it is the return to these primal and sacred forms in *Cymbeline* that makes its theatrical self-consciousness seem finally so numinous and that enables the play as a whole to represent so great a range of erotic experience.[5]

This change of attitude, I believe, comes not only through Kirsch's preoccupation with Freud and modern psychology as a way of coming to terms with the unrealistic elements of tragicomedy but also through his simultaneous work with Christian ideas of redemption: the suffering caused by the "Fortunate Fall," which made the redeemer necessary, and the spiritual purification that results from the marriage bond, a Pauline analogy to the redemptive bond between Christ and His Church.

Once we cease looking for the realism and unities of Aristotelian comedy or tragedy in its structure, as did Kirsch, *Cymbeline* does indeed begin to reveal its true dramatic value. In recognition of this fact, Northrop Frye, Barbara Mowat, and others have preferred to call the play a "Romance," since some elements of its plot and its pervasive fairy-tale quality certainly derive from the romance tradition.[6] But, as Caesarea Abartis has insisted, "romance is a narrative genre; its sprawling structure and episodic action are not immediately suitable for the two hours' traffic of the stage."[7] More importantly, there is no suggestion in the play of a narrative voice controlling the events, as in the more experimental and earlier tragicomedy *Pericles*. On the other hand, most narrative romances describe an extended journey of initiation, and *Cymbeline* does in fact have two such journeys: one for the hero to Rome and back again, and one for the heroine to the periphery of her kingdom and to a primitive existence based on virtue rather than on social level before she is restored to her father and finally to her husband. At the same time, the overall treatment of this story material is strikingly dramatic, often ritualistic, and even ceremonial in effect. Such ceremonial scenes include the exchange of love tokens between Posthumus and Imogen, the state meeting with the Roman ambassador, the funeral scene, and the famous series of reconciliations in act 5. Occasionally the play is pure spectacle for the theater, as in the scene of Imogen's resurrection from the dead only to discover a headless corpse lying by her side, and as in the even more theatrical scene of Jupiter's descent from the "heavens" to the sleeping Posthumus. All this is far more than narrative romance—it is the deliberate theatrical magic of a Jacobean court masque brought into the public playhouse to excite and influence the imagination of an audience. Yet the play is not strictly a masque either since there is no final dance to unite the audience with the players.

Joan Hartwig has demonstrated that *Cymbeline,* despite its admittedly romantic elements, is best characterized as a tragicomedy.[8] More specifically, I will argue here that it is a Renaissance tragicomedy, which we can compare to other sixteenth-and seventeenth-century plays of the same genre and recognize as a masterpiece of its kind. Indeed those who have been privileged to witness a serious, rather than a farcical, production of *Cymbeline* have reported it to be a more deeply moving experience in the theater than it could possibly be in the study where so much of its inherent theatricality must be imagined.

I emphasize that the play's genre is *Renaissance* tragicomedy in order to distinguish it clearly from the many modern experiments with tragicomic form that have emerged out of a very different philosophical matrix from that of Shakespeare's time. Content does determine form. There was indeed such a self-conscious genre as Renaissance tragicomedy during the sixteenth and seventeenth centuries, a form invented by Italian poets to represent in drama the essential optimism of Christian Platonism more organically than was possible through either comedy or tragedy. This new genre was thoroughly discussed in *The Compendium of Tragicomic Poetry* by Giambattista Guarini, who asked the rhetorical question, "what need have we today to purge terror and pity with tragic sights, since we have the precepts of our most holy religion, which teaches us with the word of the gospel? Hence these horrible and savage spectacles are superfluous, nor does it seem to me that today we should introduce a tragic action for any other reason than to get delight from it."[9] Thus for the Renaissance, tragicomedy transcends tragedy, which is a reenactment of human sacrifice for the good of the community. Tragicomedy, in contrast, dramatizes personal reform and a redeeming act of faith as part of a spiritual initiation rite. This new genre, combining both tragic and comic elements, was imitated with enthusiasm throughout Europe with varying degrees of success.

In any discussion of Renaissance tragicomedy, however, we must recognize that the presence of comic or visionary scenes within a tragedy does not automatically transform it into a tragicomedy, as has been claimed for both *Coriolanus* and *Antony and Cleopatra,*[10] any more than the reminder of death at the end of *Love's Labor's Lost* changes its basic comic genre in the least. Shakespeare was never a simplistic playwright. Moreover, one of the commonly accepted characteristics of Elizabethan drama in general is just this tendency to place parodic comic scenes in tragedies, as in Christopher Marlowe's *Doctor Faustus,* and serious scenes in comedies. To take one obvious example of the latter, old Egeon is condemned to death by the duke in the very first scene of Shakespeare's early *Comedy of Errors,* but the play remains recognizably a comedy based on a classical model.

Renaissance tragicomedy can be defined broadly as a theatrical mixed-form that becomes something completely new, although it derives from at least four major literary ancestors. The first two ancestors are medieval and Christian: (1) the miracle play or saint's tale with its exceptionally virtuous hero or heroine, its central bloody martyrdom, and its climax of wonder,[11] and (2) the morality play with its testing pattern, which usually ends with gratuitous divine forgiveness for the erring hero.[12] The second two generic ancestors are classical and pagan and often overtly Neo-platonic: (1) the classical tragicomedies by Euripides, Plautus, and Terence, which were studied by Renaissance schoolboys, and (2) the esoteric romances of the Greeks and of the later Latin author Apuleius, all works that contain disguised information on the mystery cults of antiquity. The fusion of these traditions was first attempted in Italy through a pastoral play by Poliziano called *Orfeo* (c.1480). Concerned with the violent death of Orpheus, this pastoral entertainment was structurally based on the native *sacra rappresentazione,* which indicates the spiritual focus of the genre from its Renaissance inception.

As we know, Poliziano's hero Orpheus was the leader of the Muses, the priest of a mystery cult, and a poet-musician who attempted to combine sensory experience with divine harmony and intelligence in art by rescuing Eurydice (earthly beauty) from death and decay. The myth of his final sacrificial death as the subject of the first Italian pastoral tragicomedy is highly significant. According to Richard Cody, Renaissance Neoplatonists understood the Orpheus myth to be "an allegory of the death and new life of the rational soul, lost and found again in the flames of intellectual love,"[13] and the *Orfeo* specifically made "the Orpheus myth an allegory of the cosmos and the human soul according to Plato."[14] The many Italian pastoral tragicomedies that followed Poliziano's *Orfeo*[15] intermingled echoes of the language and rituals of Christianity, properly seen as a mystery religion itself, with the Orphic rites of antiquity recently discovered or "invented" by Ficino and his Florentine academy. Such plays concerned the implications for courtiers or "lovers," as well as for professional poets, of the Platonic theology expressed in the *Phaedrus,* the *Symposium,* and later in the writings of Ficino, Pico, Lorenzo de Medici, and others, including Michelangelo as sonneteer. Thus Renaissance tragicomedy is from its beginnings a courtly, a philosophical, and a highly ritualistic form of theater requiring considerable sophistication and learning from its audience.

Fundamentally tragicomedy became for the Renaissance what the famous emblematic title page, engraved by William Hole for *The Workes of*

Ben Jonson, visually suggests that it is: the most inclusive and the most sacred dramatic form of the period. Published in 1616, the engraving, based on an "architectural design," bears an inscription from the *Ars Poetica* of Horace (line 92), "SI[N]GVLA QVAEQVE LOCVM TEN-EANT S[O]RITITA DECEN[T]ER," which was translated by Jonson himself as "Each subject should retaine / The place allotted it, with decent praise," according to Margery Corbett and R. W. Lightbown.[16] It depicts the muses of the five dramatic genres utilized by Renaissance playwrights: tragicomedy, satire, pastoral, tragedy, and comedy. The dominant figure of TRAGI COMOEDIA, wearing a crown and holding a sceptre, appears at the center of the upper level of the engraving, hovering—like an ancient tutelary deity—over the cartouche of a Roman theater. She is dressed like the figure of COMOEDIA (below on the right) in the tunic and chiton of an ordinary person, and she wears the slippers or *socci* proper to classical comedy. In keeping with her crown and sceptre, the tragicomic muse partially covers her humble costume with a richly jeweled robe like that worn by TRAGOEDIA below on the left, thus indicating her dependence on the social levels depicted in both primary dramatic genres.

In small niches on either side of her, we can just make out the figures of the true patron gods of the theater: Dionysos on her right and Apollo on her left. Dionysos is portrayed as a Wild Man,[17] wearing nothing but two wreathes of grapevine or ivy—one on his head and one about his waist. In his left hand he brandishes a thyrsus, which is also entwined with leaves, while his right hand holds what is most probably a drinking cup. Apollo, whose head radiates light, has his left hand on his familiar attribute the lyre, and he carries what appears to be a scroll or prophecy in his right hand. He represents a shepherd, having served Admetus in that capacity on earth; in contrast, Dionysos is, of course, the wildest of Wild Men in classical mythology. These tiny figures tell us that either the shepherd or the Wild Man was considered to be a proper character in the mixed genre of tragicomedy. Both may also appear together in the same play with propriety, but they are not at all similar figures in iconography.[18]

This distinction between the two gods of the theater is further emphasized in Hole's engraving by the large personifications of Satire and Pastoral on the next architectural level below Tragicomedy. Satire is represented by an Italianate satyr (or possibly Pan himself), who holds a set of reed pipes and balances between his legs an elongated club or a defoliated sapling, the traditional weapon of wildness. The satyr is one of many forms in European art of the Wild Man, who may also be depicted as a sylvan hunter or a green man.[19] In contrast, the personification of Pastoral drama to the lower left of Tragicomedy in the engraving is a well-dressed and obviously civilized or courtly shepherd. He holds the musical instrument called a recorder and balances between his legs a long shep-

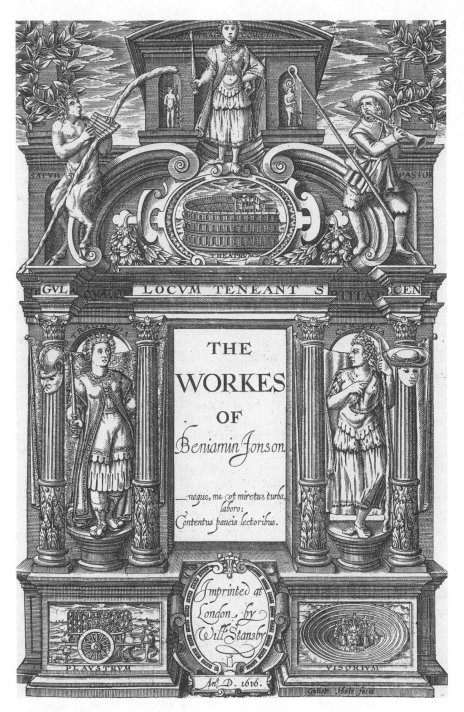

Emblematic title page to *The Workes of Benjamin Jonson* (London, 1616). Reprinted by permission of the Folger Shakespeare Library (STC 14751 copy 1).

herd's crook. Such a figure could never be confused with Shakespeare's most famous Wild Man, Caliban, or with the cannibalistic Bremo in *Mucedorus.*

Wild Men and shepherds may, of course, appear together in tragicomedy, as in fact they do in Tasso's *Aminta,* Guarini's *Il pastor fido,* and Shakespeare's *The Winter's Tale* when satyrs perform a fertility dance during the shepherds' springtime festival, but the shepherds are usually predominant in the Italian tragicomedies, which are essentially pastorals. In *Cymbeline,* however, there are no shepherds, only warriors and hunters, and here the alternative world to the court is distinctly primitive, although Imogen does indeed wistfully yearn for a pastoral setting: "Would I were / A neat-herd's daughter, and my Leonatus / Our neighbour-shepherd's son!" (1.2.79–81). Instead Imogen, a royal princess, must learn to cook for three Wild Men in the rough mountains of Wales. This in turn may suggest a predominantly satiric or ironic social purpose underlying the events of Shakespeare's play (see Waith, 1952, 50–59), since wildness always symbolizes the lowest level of Renaissance society or the extreme opposite from the king and his court. If the Wild Man in a play is lustful, drunken, and violent like Caliban in *The Tempest,* the court—even when it is exiled to the green world—is correspondingly civilized and often carefully controlled by a magician ruler. If the Wild Men are honest, courageous, and courteous, as are Arviragus, Guiderius, and Belarius in *Cymbeline,* the court in contrast is lustful, greedy, violent, and essentially uncivilized. Such a court is satirized by the playwright, and *reform* then becomes the primary motif of the tragicomedy.

In the following discussion of Renaissance tragicomedy, I shall limit my observations to the shared characteristics we find in three major examples of the genre: Torquato Tasso's *Aminta* (1573),[20] Giambattista Guarini's *Il pastor fido* (1590),[21] and William Shakespeare's *Cymbeline* (1609–10), the primary object of this study. These plays have at least nine specific characteristics in common, aside from the obvious traits of a peculiar mixture of genres, gratuitous happy endings after terrible dangers, and either the presence of both noble and apparently ordinary characters in *Il pastor fido* and *Cymbeline* or the stylistic technique of having simple shepherds speak elegant poetry in *Aminta.* The nine characteristics, with no hierarchical order implied, include (1) a strong emphasis on either pastoralism or primitivism; (2) the use of satyrs or Wild Men as the primary instruments of satire; (3) allusions to well-known literary sources and especially to previous tragicomedies, which remind the audience of the artificialities of the genre; (4) heroic self sacrifice; (5) formal commentaries on the nature and power of love and on the fortunate workings of providence; (6) provocative social equalizing achieved through love; (7) the setting of a wilderness cave as the place of psychic transformation and as a symbol of both womb and tomb; (8) the celebration of one or more blood rituals reflecting Platonic theology in order to make possible the required happy finale through a change in human perspective; and (9) an interest in the Orphic art of poetry itself and the problem of transforming sense into intelligence or images into Platonic Ideas.

1. Pastoralism or Primitivism

The first specific characteristic of Renaissance tragicomedy is an emphasis either on pastoralism, which is concerned with Apollonian Orpheus and courtly poetry, or on primitivism, which leads us into the irrational and savage world of Dionysos where Orpheus met his death. In pastoral plays the satyr will appear only in forest scenes. Plays accentuating primitivism, however, may not have a single shepherd in the *dramatis personae,* although his lack is subconsciously felt by the audience. In *Cymbeline,* for example, the world of the play is undergoing a psychological and spiritual preparation for the birth of the Good Shepherd or Christ, as many scholars have noted.[22] This means that the main characters must mature as human lovers and learn *caritas* (sacrificial divine love and forgiveness) before the appearance of the true God of Love on earth and the beginning of the New Dispensation in sacred history. Tasso more openly symbolizes the advent of the Good Shepherd into Arcadia by the figure of Amor dressed as a shepherd in the prologue to his *Aminta.* Guarini's main characters are all shepherds and nymphs except for one large, hairy satyr.

2. Satyrs as Instruments of Satire

Second, satyrs or Wild Men are the primary instruments of satire within such plays. As Eugene M. Waith has pointed out in his discussion of the relationship between satyr and satire, "It was not so offensive to hear harsh or coarse abuse from the lips of an outlandish creature who was known in legend to be harsh and coarse by nature. The satire could be accepted, like the licensed insults and ribaldry of the Feast of Fools, as part of a ritual or game" (1952, 51). In Tasso's *Aminta* the satyr attacks Sylvia, a personification of Platonic Beauty, while she is bathing nude in a forest pool. After tying the chaste nymph by her hair to a tree, he then attempts to rape her. However, the good shepherd (and poet) Aminta arrives just in time to save her from violation, although he too longs to see and understand the secret of Sylvia's beauty. This crucial scene of *gazing on beauty bare* by both the satyr and the shepherd-poet is narrated in the play rather than dramatized; but a graphic version of it in oils, emphasizing the sharp contrast between the dark woods inhabited by the satyr and the golden meadows where the shepherds pasture their flocks, was later painted for the court of Ferrara by Domenichino, possibly to help those in the audience who had trouble seeing Platonically with the mind's eye.[23] It is significant that the only satiric lines in Tasso's tragicomedy are placed in the mouth of the rapacious satyr, who comments bitterly after the famous nostalgic chorus "O bella età de l'oro" ["The Golden Age"] that love itself is now only a commodity to be bought and sold:

> E veramente il secol d'oro è questo,
> Poiche sol vince l'oro, e regna l'oro.
> O chiunque tu fosti, che insegnasti
> Primo a vender l'amor, sia maledetto.

(Tasso 257)

> (This is indeed the age of gold; for gold
> Is conquered of all, and gold is king.
> Oh thou, whoe'er thou wert, that first did shew
> The way to make love venal, be thou accursed.)

(Hunt 165)

The love of gold also dominates Cymbeline's court in Shakespeare's tragicomedy, and we hear similar lines from Cloten, the doomed satyr dressed as a prince:

>   'Tis gold
> Which buys admittance (oft it doth) yea, and makes
> Diana's rangers false themselves, yield up
> Their deer to the stand o' th' stealer: and 'tis gold
> Which makes the true man kill'd, and saves the thief.

(2.3.66–70)

In fact the sharpest satirical barb in *Cymbeline* seems to be that the Wild Men bred in nature are true and pure, while the artificial court harbors slanderers and rapists and routinely banishes civilized counselors such as Belarius. Furthermore, since *Cymbeline* celebrates primitivism rather than pastoralism, satire is probably the major political thrust of the play rather than the flattery of a purified court that we see in *Aminta* and in Shakespeare's wedding tragicomedy, *The Tempest,* where savagery exists but is always under the control of Prospero's white magic, perhaps as a theatrical example of how reason must control the passions in Plato's ideal society.

The Satyr (now capitalized in the *dramatis personae*) is once again the vehicle of satire in Guarini's *Il pastor fido*. Emerging from the edge of the forest, he grabs the false nymph Corisca—Guarini's artistic *imitatio* of a lady of the court—by her hair and announces that he intends to rape her. But in this comic allusion by way of the nymph's luxuriant hair to the central incident in Tasso's *Aminta,* Corisca's hair turns out to be nothing but an artificial wig. It comes off in the Satyr's hand, and she escapes her attacker with ease. In John Dymock's 1602 translation or adaptation, which Shakespeare might well have read,[24] the Satyr—left holding Corisca's wig—cries out in frustration,

> O me my head, my backe, my side. Oh what
> A fall is this? I scarce can turne myselfe,
> And she is gone and left her head behind?
> Vnusuall wonder. Nimphs and shepheards come,
> Behold a witchcraft tricke of one that's fled
> And liues without a head! How light it is?
> It hath no braines, there commeth out no blood.

(Dymock 1602, sig. G^v)

> (Oimè il capo! Oimè il fianco! Oimè la schiena!
> Oh che fiera caduta! A pena i'posso
> movermi e rilevarmene. E pur vero
> é ch'ella fugga e qui rimanga il teschio?
> Oh maraviglia inusitata! O ninfe,
> o pastori, accorrete e rimirate
> il magico stupor di chi sen fugge
> e vive senza capo. Oh come è lieve!
> Quanto ha poco cervello e come il sangue
> fuor non ne spiccia!)

(Guarini 170)

We are to understand from this speech that the beauty of courtly ladies is often artificial, unlike intellectual beauty in the realm of Ideas. Guiderius makes similar comments over the dismembered head of Cloten in *Cymbeline,* once again observing that the head in question has no brains (4.2.113–15). The source of this peculiar anticourtier trope is a fable by Aesop and an emblem by Andrea Alciati to be discussed later in this study.

3. Obvious Allusions to Previous Tragicomedies

Such forthright allusions to previous tragicomedies constitute the third characteristic of the form. For example, Guarini takes the name of Tasso's hero Aminta (deriving from Amor) and uses it in *Il pastor fido* as his name for the first faithful shepherd who died in Arcadia's distant past to save a sinful nymph. In *Cymbeline,* Shakespeare may also be alluding to the bloody vcil that falsely signifies Sylvia's death in Tasso's *Aminta,* when the

English playwright has Pisanio send a bloody cloth to Posthumus as proof of Imogen's death. On the other hand, a common source of the bloody veil for both plays could also have been Ovid's tale of Pyramus and Thisbe in the *Metamorphoses*. Both allusions are very likely intended by Shakespeare. In addition, J. H. Whitfield sees a number of striking references to Guarini's *Il pastor fido* in the later Shakespearean tragicomedy, including the ultimate repentance and forgiveness of the slanderers Corisca and Iachimo, the use of oracles in both plays, and the device of lost babies eventually found.[25] Such allusions remind the audience of the generic type they are watching and of all its many artifices.

We can find other important allusions to *Il pastor fido* in Shakespeare's text as well. After Guarini's Silvio has wounded the nymph Dorinda, having mistaken her for a beast hiding in the woods, he begs her to shoot an arrow of revenge into his breast.

> Ecco gli stali e l'arco;
> ma non ferir già tu gli occhi o le mani,
> colpevoli ministri
> d'innocente voler; ferisci il petto,
> ferisci questo mostro,
> de pietade e d'amore aspro nemico;
> ferisci questo cor che ti fu crudo:
> eccoti il petto ignudo.

(Guarini 314–16)

> (Wound not mine eyes or handes, th'are innocent;
> But wound my brest, monster to pittie, foe
> To loue: wound me this hart, that cruel was
> To thee: behold, my brest is bare.)

(Dymock sig. N)

In *Cymbeline,* Imogen, hearing that Posthumus believes her sexually false and thus beastly, offers her heart to Pisanio's knife in a like manner:

> Come, here's my heart,
> . . . . Prithee, dispatch:
> The lamb entreats the butcher. Where's thy knife?
> Thou art too slow to do thy master's bidding
> When I desire it too.

(3.4.79–99)

The male-pursuing women, Dorinda in *Il pastor fido* and Imogen in *Cymbeline,* are considered to be no better than wild animals by the men they love and thus easy prey—because of their weak feminine nature—to the temptations of material lust and self-indulgence, unlike the more rational male of the species. However, both authors clearly intend this sexist aspersion to be recognized as false, as the plots amply demonstrate.

Allusions to other famous literary works actually abound in these tragicomedies, suggesting the assumed presence of a very sophisticated audience. Shakespeare even alludes through his plot based on sexual
jealousy and through the similarities between the characters of the stage
slanderers, Iago and Iachimo, to his own tragedy *Othello,* as many commentators have noticed.

4. Heroic Self-sacrifice as the Sign of True Love

Heroic self-sacrifice, portrayed as a type of Erasmian folly leading to joy
in the end, is a fourth common factor in the Christian tragicomedy of the
Renaissance. Aminta flings himself off a cliff in Tasso's play when he is
told that Sylvia has been devoured by wolves. Yet the act is a "Fortunate
Fall" since the shepherd is not killed, and his minor injuries excite pity and
then love in the breast of the previously cold Sylvia. In *Il pastor fido,*
Nuntio informs Titiro of the shepherd Mirtillo's offer to die as a sacrifice to
Diana in place of the condemned nymph Amarillis, whom he loves:

> Già con l'ordine sacro,
> per condur la tua figlia a cruda morte,
> il sacerdote s'inviava, quando,
> vedendola Mirtillo (oh, che stupendo
> caso udirai!), s'offerse
> di dar con la sua morte a lei la vita.
>
> (Guarini 340)

> (And now with sacred order goes the Priest
> To bring thy daughter to her bloodied ende,
> The whilst *Mirtillo* (wondrous thing to tell)
> Offer'd by his owne death, to giue her life.
>
> (Dymock sig. O)

Mirtillo's willingness to die for her convinces Amarillis at last that her
natural love for the shepherd is a true love. In a similar fashion, Shakespeare's Posthumus, believing Imogen to be already dead by his own
order, offers himself as a sacrificial atonement for his crime: "so I'll die /
For thee, O Imogen, even for whom my life / Is, every breath, a death"
(5.1.24–26).

5. The Nature of Love and the Workings of Providence

Fifth, we discover similar commentaries on the theme of love and the
workings of divine providence, or God's love, in all three of these Renais-

sance tragicomedies. Although various kinds of human love are dramatized, discussed, and criticized in these plays, the main focus is ultimately
on *caritas,* which was the type of love most highly regarded by Christianity. Tasso, for instance, opens his *Aminta* with a prologue delivered by
the little love god Amor, disguised here as a shepherd. As I have previously mentioned, this allusion to Christ as the Good Shepherd and God
of Love would have been unmistakable to an alert Renaissance audience.
Amor pretends, however, to be only a naughty Cupid hiding from his
mother Venus, or Nature, so that he—rather than Nature—should determine the targets for his divine arrows. He thus mingles with the "lowly
populace," as did Christ, where the goddess will never think to look for
him. Amor promises that during the play he will cause the chaste nymph
Sylvia to love Aminta at last through her feelings of "pity," feelings that
have little to do with sexuality. He also promises that the dramatic form
and language of the play will be new:

Queste selue hoggi ragionar d'Amore
S'udranno in nuoua guisa: e ben parrassi,
Che la mia Deità sia qui presente
In se medesma, e non ne suoi ministri.
Spirerò nobil sensi a rozi petti;
Raddolciro de le lor lingue il suono;
Perche, ouunque i mi sia, io sono Amore,
Ne pastori non men, che ne gli heroi;
E la disagguaglianza de soggetti,
Come a me piace, agguagliore questa è pure
Suprema gloria, e gran miracol mio,
Render simili a le piu dotte cetre
Le rustiche sampogne.

(Tasso 233)

(After new fashion shall these woods today
Hear love discoursed; and it shall well be seen,
That my divinity is present here
In its own person, not its ministers.
I will inbreathe high fancies in rude hearts;
I will refine and render dulcet sweet
Their tongues; because, wherever I may be
Whether with rustic or heroic men,
There am I, Love; and inequality,
As it may please me, do I equalize;
And 'tis my crowning glory and great miracle,
To make the rural pipe as eloquent
Even as the subtlest harp.)

(Hunt 150)

Thus Amor warns that tragicomedy will not be realistic because lowly
shepherds will speak the poetry and dream the dreams of epic heroes. The

subtle political point of this courtly play will then be the equalizing of the social classes in poetry, or an evocation of the Christian brotherhood of man, since love is common to all men and women and all are loved equally by God. Tasso does not bring the lovers Aminta and Sylvia onstage in the last scene of his play, preferring instead to have Elpino describe their ecstatic reunion in his hermit's cave. Aminta has been transformed through his "Fortunate Fall" from the unrequited lover to the beloved, while Sylvia is metamorphosed through her feelings of pity from a cold follower of Diana to a "wild Bacchante" or a priestess of Dionysos. All this is clearly not to be misunderstood as the story of an ordinary love, as the Chorus reminds us at the end of the play.

Il pastor fido echoes the same spiritual motif of "the faithful shepherd" who, like Christ, is willing to sacrifice himself for love. Guarini's variation on Tasso's reunion of the lovers in a cave is to have his lovers Amarilli and Mirtillo imprisoned by the Satyr in a cave, where they are later found by the shepherds and accused of adultery. The familiar classical plot device of "the lost one found" ultimately saves Mirtillo from becoming a sacrifice in place of Amarilli to the moon goddess Diana. He is neither a stranger in Arcadia nor a lowly shepherd at all but the lost descendant of Hercules to whom Amarilli was originally promised. The final Chorus expresses Guarini's basic Christian-humanist message: "Quello è vero gioire / che nasce da virtù dopo il soffrire" ("True joy is a thing / That springs from Vertue after suffering"). The same idea is reinforced by the Silvio–Dorinda plot in which the hunter Silvio does not know how much he loves his pursuer Dorinda until he mistakenly wounds her with an arrow and witnesses her suffering—at which point the hunter becomes the hunted: the beloved becomes the lover.

Although the God of Love does not actually appear in *Il pastor fido,* his impending birth as a monster within nature (that is, as an immortal deity imprisoned within the body of a mortal man) is referred to in the text as an expected outcome of Arcadia's long years of suffering in a fallen state after a nymph betrayed her lover. Carino, the foster father of Mirtillo, exclaims,

O provvidenza eterna,
con qual alto consiglio
tanti accidenti hai fin a qui sospesi,
per farli poi cader tutti in un punto!
Gran cosa hai tu concetta,
gravida se' di *mostruoso parto:*
o gran bene o gran male
partotirai tu certo.

(Guarini 370; italics added)

(Eternall prouidence which with thy counsell hast
Brought all these occurents to this onely point,

Th'art great with childe of some huge monstrous birth,
Either great good or ill thou wilt bring forth.)

(Dymock sigs. P2 and P2ᵛ)

To prepare for such an event, Guarini has all his characters (except for the incorrigible Satyr) put aside their desires for revenge, which are proper only to tragedy, in favor of a tragicomic and Christian act of charitable forgiveness. For example, although he has been betrayed by Corisca, the shepherd Coridone refuses to be excited to vengeance against her by the angry Satyr:

Ma non ho già sì basso cor che basti
mobilità di femmina a turbarlo.
Troppo felice e onorata fora
la femminil perfidia, se con pena
di cor virile, e con turbar la pace
e la felicitá d'alma bennata,
s'avesse a vendicar. Oggi Corisca
per me dunque si viva, o, per dir meglio,
per me non moia e per altrui si viva;
sarà la vita sua vendetta mia.
Viva a l'infamia sua, viva al suo drudo,
poich'è tal ch'io non l'odio, e ho più tosto
pietà di lei che gelosia di lui.

(Guarini 298)

(What shall I doe? Shall I attir'd with spleene,
Seeke with outragious furie for reuenge?
Fie no, I honour her too much: so bee
The case with reason waighed; it rather would
Haue pittie and compassion, then reuenge.)

(Dymock sig. M2)

In act 5, Amarilli and Mirtillo also forgive the lustful Corisca, whose plots have actually misfired and brought the true lovers together. As James J. Yoch, Jr., has observed,

Guarini made compassion, not passion, the most important psychological effect of the drama, and his exemplary discussion of feeling is emphatically moral. He saw compassion as the principal difference "between the continent and the incontinent, who can be called the soldiers of virtue, except that one does not have pity for his body and afflicts it that he may not have torment in his spirit, while the other is so tender of his body that he permits himself to fall into an offense of the spirit, which causes him the anxiety of repentence."[26]

Guarini's strong emphasis on repentance and forgiveness is anything but pagan, and it provides us with unmistakable evidence of the basic Christian purposes of Renaissance tragicomedy. Such purposes are not sectarian or doctrinal but are common to both the Catholic and Protestant cultures of the time and are always highly self-conscious in this new genre specifically designed by and for dramatic poets of the Christian era.

For example, Shakespeare apparently chose the undistinguished reign of Cymbeline as the period of his play because this was the very time when Christ was born in Bethlehem, as historian John Speed noted in his discussion of the many coins stamped to honor "Cunobeline."[27] Posthumus repents his orders for Imogen's death and, like Guarini's Coridon in respect to Corisca, freely forgives Imogen's supposed adulterous behavior. She, in turn, forgives the unforgivable—his lack of faith in her chastity and his attempt to have her killed. Cymbeline forgives them all, including Belarius who has kidnapped the king's sons, and after Cymbeline submits to Caesar, Rome forgives the British revolt against the rule of Augustus in order to establish the *pax romana* so important to the Gospel accounts of the Nativity.

In the examination of love, however, Tasso sings of Amor in the Platonic sense as the desire for Beauty and exalts the poetry of Orphic passion to spur the human soul to gain knowledge of Ideal Beauty; while Guarini is careful to distinguish between the two opposing love gods or Cupids of Plato, an echo of which also appears in Shakespeare's *Cymbeline*. Indeed Tasso considers Eros to be simple lust and worthy only of the satyr in his tragicomedy. His love god from the beginning is Anteros, or the love of virtue, who hides under the garments of a shepherd in this play. The Chorus at the end of act 2 in *Aminta* praises this hidden god, or sacred love, as the true inspiration of poetry:

> Amore, in quale scola,
> Da qual maestro s'apprende
> La tua sì lunga, e dubbia arte d'amare?
> Chi n'insegna aspiegare
> Cio che la menta intende,
> Mentre con l'ali tue soura il Ciel vola?
> Non gia la dotta Athene,
> Ne'l Liceo nel dimostra,
> Non Febo in Helicona,
> Che sì d'Amor ragiona,
> Come colá s'mpara
> Freddo ne parla, e poco,
> Non alza i suoi pensieri
> A par de tuoi mestieri
> Amor degno maestro
> Sol tu sei di te stesso,
> E sol tu sei da te medesmo espresso.

> (Tasso 269)

> (Tell us, O Love, what school,
> What mighty master's rule,

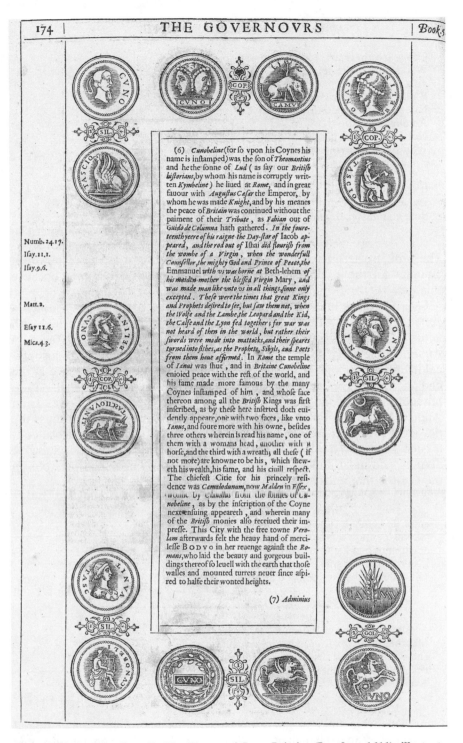

(6) Cunobeline (for ſo vpon his Coynes his name is inſtamped) was the ſon of Theomantius and he the ſonne of Lud (as ſay our Britiſh biſtorians, by whom his name is corruptly written Kymbeline) he liued at Rome, and in great fauour with Auguſtus Cæſar the Emperor, by whom he was made Knight, and by his meanes the peace of Britain was continued without the paiment of their Tribute, as Fabian out of Guido de Columna hath gathered. In the foureteenth yeere of his raigne the Day-ſtar of Iacob appeared, and the rod out of Iſhai did flouriſh from the wombe of a Virgin, when the wonderfull Counſellor, the mighty God and Prince of Peace, the Emmanuel with vs was borne at Beth-lehem of his maiden-mother the bleſſed Virgin Mary, and was made man like vnto vs in all things, ſinne only excepted. Theſe were the times that great Kings and Prophets deſired to ſee, but ſaw them not, when the Wolfe and the Lambe, the Leopard and the Kid, the Calfe and the Lyon fed together; for war was not heard of then in the world, but rather their ſwords were made into mattocks, and their ſpeares turned into ſithes, as the Prophets, Sibyls, and Poets from them haue affirmed. In Rome the temple of Ianus was ſhut, and in Britaine Cunobeline enioied peace with the reſt of the world, and his fame made more famous by the many Coynes inſtamped of him, and whoſe face thereon among all the Britiſh Kings was firſt inſcribed, as by theſe here inſerted doth euidently appeare, one with two faces, like vnto Ianus, and foure more with his owne, beſides three others wherein is read his name, one of them with a womans head, another with a horſe, and the third with a wreath; all theſe (if not more) are knowne to be his, which ſheweth his wealth, his fame, and his ciuill reſpect. The chiefeſt Citie for his princely reſidence was Camalodunum, now Malden in Eſſex, wonne by Claudius from the ſonnes of Cunobeline, as by the inſcription of the Coyne next enſuing appeareth, and wherein many of the Britiſh monies alſo receiued their impreſſe. This City with the free towne Verolam afterwards felt the heauy hand of mercileſſe B O D V O in her reuenge againſt the Romans, who laid the beauty and gorgeous buildings thereof ſo leuell with the earth that thoſe walles and mounted turrets neuer ſince aſpired to halfe their wonted heights.

(7) Adminius

Numb. 24. 17.
Iſay. 11. 1.
Iſay. 9. 6.

Matt. 2.

Eſay 11. 6.
Mica. 4. 3.

Page 174 from John Speed's *The History of Great Britaine* (London, 1611), illustrating coins from the reign of King Cymbeline or Cunobeline. Reprinted by permission of the Folger Shakespeare Library (STC 23045).

Can teach thine art, so doubtful and so long?
Who shall enable sense
To know the intelligence
Which takes us heavenward on thy pinions strong?
Not all that learned throng
Among the Attic trees,
Nor Phoebus on his hill
Who sings of loving still,
Could truly tell us of thy mysteries.

. . . .
It is thyself alone
By whom thou canst be shewn,
Sole manifester thou of all thy sense.)

(Hunt 174)

The broken rhetoric of love, Tasso then claims, is a far more powerful stimulus for the ascending soul than the writing of learned men because this rude rhetoric can be understood by everyone.

Guarini is less interested in discussing poetics or aesthetics through a series of eclogues within his play *Il pastor fido* and more concerned with actually dramatizing various kinds of love in action than is Tasso in *Aminta*. He openly displays his own classical learning and his philosophical intentions by way of a Platonic choral ode on the nature of love at the end of act 3. The ode begins "Come se' grande, Amore, / di natura miràcolo è del mondo!" (244), a passage that apparently derives from Andrea Alciati's Emblems 106, 107, and 108, all three of which discuss the power of love over heaven and earth alike. Previously Guarini has contrasted Eros—or the love of earthly beauty (which is only a shadow of divinity and must die)—with Anteros, the love of virtue and the soul, in the Chorus that ends act 2:

Il vero e vivo
amor de l'alma è l'alma: ogn'altro oggetto,
perché d'amare è privo,
degno non è el l'amoroso affetto.
L'anima, perché sola è riamante
sola è degna d'amor, degna d'amante.

(Guarini 172–74)

(The true
And liuely loue is of the soule:
All other subjects want what loue requires,
Therefore they not deserue these amorous desires.
The soule because it only loues againe,
Is only worthie of this louing paine.)

(Dymock sig. G2)

Guarini's lovers unknowingly fall spiritually in love through a shared physical kiss (an exchange of breath was equated to an exchange of souls) during a game of Blind Man's Buff in act 3: "Soule knit to soule by th' earthly knot of loue" (Dymock sig. G2v). Eros begins the process of union; Anteros completes it.

The two contrasting loves, earthly Eros and spiritual Anteros, originated in Plato's *Phaedrus* and *Symposium,* then reappeared during the Renaissance in Ficino's *De amore* and in Alciati's Emblems 110 and 111.[28] I will discuss this tradition later in detail. Meanwhile, since Anteros is defined as the love of virtue by Alciati, Guarini's lines, and especially Dymock's translation of *Il pastor fido,* reflect the Italian jurisconsult's Emblem 111 on Anteros overcoming the flames of Eros with the flames of spiritual love:[29]

> Ma chi sa poi come a virtù l'amante
> si desti e come soglia
> farsi al suo foco ogni sfrenata voglia
> subito spenta, pallido e tremante,
> dirà: 'Spirto immortale, hai tu ne l'alma
> il tuo sola e santissimo ricetto'.
> Raro mostro e mirabile, d'umano
> e di divino aspetto;
> di veder cieco e di saver insano;
> di senso e d'intelletto,
> di ragion e desio confuso affetto!
> e tale, hai tu l'impero
> de la terra e del ciel ch'a te soggiace.

(Guarini 244–46)

> (But who feeles after how a louer is
> Wak'ned to Vertue, and how all those flames
> Do tremble out at sight of honest shames,
> (Unbrid'led blust'ring lust is brought down to rest)
> Will call thee Spright of high immortall blisse,
> Hauing thy holy receptacle in the Soule.
> Rare miracle of humane and divine aspectes,
> (That blind) dost see, and Wisedom (mad) corrects,
> Of sence and vnderstanding intellects,
> Of reason and desire confus'd affects.)

(Dymock sig. K2)

Once human lovers understand that what they really love in one another is not the body but the immortal soul, which reflects divinity, they become "true lovers" and can begin to understand that higher spiritual love that transforms their separate suffering into mutual bliss.

Tasso dramatizes the essential contrast between Eros and Anteros in his *Aminta* through the lust of the satyr for Sylvia's nakedness and the shy adoration of the nymph's beauty by Aminta. After Aminta saves Sylvia from the satyr and unbinds her hair from the tree, Sylvia echoes Christ's warning, "Noli me tangere," to Mary Magdalene in the garden after his

Crucifixion and burial. She tells Aminta, "See that thou touch me not, I am Diana's" (Hunt 176). Despairing then of ever being loved by Sylvia, Aminta threatens suicide, but his friend Daphne counsels hope:

> Viui misero, viui
> Ne la miseria tua: e questo flato
> Sopporta solper diuenir felice
> Quando che sia, sia premio de la speme,
> Se viuendo, e sperando, ti mantien
> Quel che vedesti ne la bella ignuda.

(Tasso 276)

> (Live, live, unhappy one, in spite of wretchedness:
> Endure thy state, to be at last made happy.
> If thou dost live and hope, thy hope's reward
> Will be what thou hast seen in that bare beauty.)

(Hunt 179)

All this echoes Diotima's speech to Socrates in Plato's *Symposium* about the effects on the lover who has gazed on beauty bare and his need to see through that which "makes it [beauty] visible"[30] to its underlying truth. Aminta is unable to achieve this vision, however, until after his leap from the cliff to join Sylvia in death (or so he believes) and after suffering the painful wounds that finally arouse Sylvia's pity and her love.

In *Cymbeline,* Shakespeare first embodies the two Cupids or types of love in the characters of Cloten and Posthumus, then displays them again in the two halves of Posthumus's life, before and after his conversion. In addition, Eros and Anteros are referred to iconographically in the play when Iachimo describes the andirons in Imogen's fireplace as "two winking Cupids / Of silver, each on one foot standing, nicely / Depending on their brands" (2.4.89–91), imagery that I shall discuss in detail later. Both Cupids warm the bath of chaste Diana, a scene pictured above on the plaster chimneypiece. Shakespeare, like Tasso, later implies that to be converted from a worshipper of Eros to a follower of Anteros, one must die to the sensory world, as does Imogen after taking the Queen's "doctored" medicine, and as does the shackled Posthumus when he falls asleep and experiences a celestial vision. In Christian terms, the old Adam must first die so that the new or redeemed Adam may be born.

Once the characters in tragicomedy have overcome their worship of Eros and have transferred their allegiance to Anteros, Divine Providence begins to act on their behalf. This strange miracle is commented on by observers withn the play. For example, the wise hermit Elpino reminds us in *Aminta* that,

> Veramente la legge, con che Amore,
> Il suo imperio gouerna eternamente,

Non è dura, ne oblique, e l'opre sue
Piene di prouidenza, e di misterio,
Altri a torto condanna, o con quant' arte,
E per che ignote strade egli conduce
L'huom ad esser beato, e fra le gioie
Del suo amoroso Paradiso il pone,
Quando ei piu crede al fondo esser de' mali.

(Tasso 293)

(Truly the law, with which imperial Love
Governs eternally, is not a harsh
Nor crooked law; and wrongly are his works
Condemned, being full of a deep providence.
Oh with what art and through what unknown paths
Conducts he man to happiness and when
His servant thinks himself plunged down to the depths
Of evil; lifts him with a sparkling hand,
And places him in his amorous paradise.)

(Hunt 190)

Guarini gives similar lines to the Chorus in *Il pastor fido:*

Ma chi sa? Forse quella,
che pare inevitabile sciagura,
sarà lieta ventura.
Oh quanto poco umana mente sale,
ché non s'affisa al sol vista mortale!

(Guarini 115)

But Dymock has old Montano make the above comment in the 1602 translation of the Italian play:

Eternall heavenly powers,
How diuerse are your high vntroden waies
By which your fauours do on vs descend?
From those same crook't deceitfull pathes whereby
Our thoughts would faine mount vp into the sky?

(Dymock sig. Q)

In *Cymbeline,* the god Jupiter himself delivers similar theological truths to the ghosts of Posthumus' family:

Be not with mortal accidents opprest,
   No care of yours it is, you know 'tis ours.
Whom best I love I cross; to make my gift,
   The more delay'd, delighted.

(5.4.99–102)

Thus the central theological message dramatized in all three tragicomedies is very directly stated to the audience: that the suffering and sacrifices of love lead eventually to spiritual joy. Of course this love must be of a higher order than mere physical desire and sexual pleasure. Furthermore, we have in the above statements on Providence, or Divine Love in action, a clear direction toward a common understanding of the authors' thematic intentions in Renaissance tragicomedies, despite the usual critical resistance to intentionalism in the arts.

6. Social Equalizing

A sixth characteristic of Renaissance tragicomedy is the social equalizing mentioned by Tasso's Amor. All the characters in *Aminta*—except perhaps the satyr—represent known figures of the D'Este court at Ferrara, but all are merely shepherds in the play. Social equalizing also occurs among the characters in *Il pastor fido,* a play in which the high priest is as willing to sacrifice his own son as to sacrifice the child of another. In *Cymbeline,* both the king and his stepson Cloten are portrayed as fools, while the Wild Men in the Welsh mountains show themselves to be more pious, more courageous, and wiser than anyone at court. Indeed this tragicomedy ends with an actual demonstration of the brotherhood of man when Cymbeline accepts Posthumus into the royal family, calls Belarius his brother, makes peace with Rome, and agrees to resume the customary payment of tribute, even though the English have actually won the war and need make no further payments to the Roman Empire.

In *Cymbeline,* moreover, Shakespeare makes the telling point that the usual social distinctions in life are at odds with the unavoidable fact of death. In act 4, scene 2, the dialogue emphasizes the similarity of our bodily remains:

> *Arv.* Are we not brothers?
> *Imo.*   So man and man should be;
>   But clay and clay differs in dignity,
>   Whose dust is both alike.

                                                    (4.2.3–5)

The difference between clay and dust is obviously paradoxical, thus a poetic criticism of a society that reflects neither nature nor divine proclamation: "Dust thou art, and unto dust shalt thou return" (Gen. 3:19).

7. A Cave Setting

In addition, all three tragicomedies use a cave setting to symbolize both womb and tomb, and this is a seventh characteristic of the genre. A prison

(*The Winter's Tale*) or a ship (*Pericles*) may substitute for the cave as a Platonic symbol of the body or the tomb of the rational soul from which it may be reborn. Specifically the cave is a mysterious place of transformations. Indeed such "underground chambers" were typical of early mystery religions, according to Mircea Eliade, who points out that, "Retiring into a hiding place or descending into an under-ground chamber is ritually and symbolically equivalent to a *katabasis, a decensus ad inferos* undertaken as a means of initiation. Such descents are documented in the more or less legendary biographies of Pythagoras."[31] A retreat into a cave may also be understood as a return to the womb of Mother Earth to be remade or reformed:

> The initiation myths and rites of *regressus ad uterum* reveal the following fact: the "return to origin" prepares a new birth, but the new birth is not a repetition of the first, physical birth. There is properly speaking a mystical rebirth, spiritual in nature—in other words, access to a new mode of existence (involving sexual maturity, participation in the sacred and in culture; in short, becoming "open" to the Spirit). The basic idea is that, to attain to a higher mode of existence gestation and birth must be repeated; but they are repeated ritually, symbolically. In other words, we here have acts oriented toward the values of Spirit, not behavior from the realm of psycho-physiological activity.[32]

Either way, a renewed and spiritually reformed human being is the result.

Tasso's Aminta and Sylvia, for example, are finally joined together in Elpino's cave from which they will eventually emerge transformed into mature lovers, or so we assume. Sylvia exchanges her virginity and her pride in chastity for compassionate love in the cave, thus renewing Aminta's life. Guarini's Amarilli and Mirtillo are imprisoned together by the Satyr in a cave, although the poet is silent about what actually happens during this period of darkness for the lovers. However, once they emerge to face the trial of Amarilli for adultery, we discover that Mirtillo, who originally entered the cave to spy on his adored Amarilli and to seek vengeance for her supposed infidelity, is now ready to die in his beloved's place as a sacrifice to Diana, goddess of chastity. In *Cymbeline,* Imogen enters the cave of Belarius as a disguised princess invited to dinner, but she emerges as the willing servant of Wild Men. The equalization process begun in the cave goes so far in Shakespeare's play that later Imogen is even able to recognize and grieve for the lineaments of her beloved Posthumus as they are reflected in the dismembered corpse of the once hated and feared satyr of the court whom she knows as Cloten. Although she believes the corpse to be that of Posthumus, the sight of Cloten's maimed remains (or his mortality) arouses her deepest pity and love and undoubtedly helps her to forgive Posthumus's murderous intents toward her own person by the end of the tragicomedy.

Perhaps the most important and seminal literary use of the cave was that of Plato in *The Republic*.[33] To be imprisoned in the cave is to be imprisoned in the body and thus in the deceptive world of the senses or of opinion, according to Socrates. There are two ways of escape for a living person: through dreams and through the use of reason, both of which provide supersensory knowledge to the prisoner. Shakespeare is particularly careful to suggest the Platonic symbolism of his cave imagery in *Cymbeline,* as we shall later see.

8. Apollonian and Dionysian Rituals

At this point, it seems clear that tragicomedy is all that Richard Cody has claimed too narrowly for the "pastoral" form alone in his provocative study *The Landscape of the Mind,* a book that was itself inspired by Edgar Wind's *Pagan Mysteries in the Renaissance*.[34] As I have previously suggested, tragicomedy, whether pastoral or primitive in emphasis, is fundamentally an esoteric genre that reenacts and yet conceals the central mystery of Platonic theology and its most sacred rite, the laceration of the body for the purification of the soul. This ritual is the eighth characteristic of the genre. If the play ended at this point of human sacrifice, it would be called a tragedy. Cody describes the underlying ritual in such dramas as "the enactment of a myth of Apollo and Bacchus reconciled, such as the death of Orpheus or the flaying of Marsyas" (1969, 3). His perceptive choice of myths actually suggests the fundamental difference between a pastoral or lyrical tragicomedy, such as *Aminta* or *Il pastor fido,* and a primitivist or satirical tragicomedy such as *Cymbeline*. The myth of Apollonian Orpheus, shepherd poet and musician, is at first pastoral. His Dionysian death at the hands of Maenads does indeed reflect "the poet's inner life" (1969, 3), as Cody suggests, since an inspired poet is perpetually torn between reason (measure) and passion (feeling) in the composition of his art. Moreover, as a lyric poet determined to experience intellectual beauty through his senses and even to remain conscious during his descent to the underworld, Orpheus is forced at the last moment to relinquish the beautiful body of his beloved Eurydice to death and decay. According to Pico de la Mirandola, the Platonic example of Orpheus in the *Symposium* explains why Ideal Beauty is so difficult to grasp. Orpheus, "desiring to go and see his beloved Eurydice, . . . did not want to go there through death but softened and refined by his music, sought a way of going there alive, and for this reason, says Plato, he could not reach the true Eurydice, but beheld only a shadow or spectre." From then on he had to be satisfied with poetic images or recollections—mere shadows of beauty and truth—in his art. In contrast, argued Pico, "Alcestis achieved the perfection of love because she longed to go to the beloved through death; and dying through love, she was by the grace of the gods revived" (quoted in Wind 1968, 157).

This tragic loss in the Orpheus story of the sensible in exchange for the intellectual leads at first to emotional despair and frustration. The poet discovers that he can recreate neither sensible nor spiritual reality directly in his art, although he can stir his listeners or readers, through his shared recollections of beauty, to strive toward an understanding of intellectual Beauty, Goodness, Truth, and Justice. Finally, this frustration may lead the poet to madness and dismemberment as a human sacrifice himself—a sacrifice acceptable to both Apollo and Dionysos, whose grisly fate of dismemberment Orpheus shared. Since the death of Orpheus is—despite Pico—a love death, happiness will surely follow, as the tragicomic genre always reminds us. Indeed, Ovid reports in Book XI of his *Metamorphoses* that Orpheus and Eurydice were at last joyfully reunited in the underworld after the poet's ritual death and dismemberment.[35]

The myth of Marsyas, on the other hand, concerns the discovery that the body is actually the tomb of the soul, that it is no more than the form or container of meaning and must be transcended.[36] Marsyas's mortality is revealed when Apollo flays the skin from the body of the satyr who had rashly competed with divinity in a musical contest and won. " 'Help,' Marsyas clamoured. 'Why are you stripping me from myself?' "[37] Apollo's unspoken answer was, of course, "So that you may know yourself as mortal and understand the differences between the music of Nature and divine music." Thus the satyr is forced to suffer and to weep until he understands his limitations and is then transformed into "the clearest river in Phrygia" (Ovid 145). To explain the religious point of the Marsyas story, Edgar Wind tells us that,

> Marsyas was a follower of Bacchus, and his flute was the Bacchic instrument for arousing the dark and uncontrollable passions that conflict with the purity of Apollo's lyre. The musical contest between Apollo and Marsyas was therefore concerned with the relative powers of Dionysian darkness and Apollonian clarity; and if the contest ended with the flaying of Marsyas, it was because flaying was itself a Dionysian rite, a tragic ordeal of purification by which the ugliness of the outward man was thrown off and the beauty of his inward self revealed. (1968, 172–73).

Such a process of purification is prime subject matter for the Renaissance tragicomedy.

Cody tells us that in *Aminta,* Tasso achieves the desired reconciliation of Apollo and Dionysos when Sylvia, who has not been eaten after all by wolves in the forest, revives the apparently dead Aminta by her wild kisses:

Tecum habita.

EMBLEMA XXVII.

Apollo flays the piper Marsyas, *pictura* of Nicholas Reusner's Emblem 27, bk. 3, *Emblemata* (Frankfort, 1581), 138. Reprinted by permission of the Folger Shakespeare Library (PN 6349 R4 1581 Cage).

Ma come Siluia il riconobbe, e vide
Le belle guancie tenere d'Aminta
Iscolorite in sì leggiadri modi,
Che Viola non è, che impallidisca
Si dolcemente, e lui languir sì fatto,
Che parea gia ne gli vltimi sospiri
Essalar l'alma, in guisa di Baccante,
Gridando, e percotendosi il bel petto,
Lasciò cadersi in su'l giacente corpo,
E giunse viso a viso, e bocca a bocca.

(Tasso 296)

(but when Sylvia recognized
Amyntas, and beheld his beautiful cheeks
So lovelily discolored that no violet

Could pale more sweetly, it so smote her
That she seemed ready to breathe out her soul.
And then like a wild Bacchante, crying out
And smiting her fair bosom, she fell down
Right on the prostrate body, face to face,
And mouth to mouth.)

(Hunt 192)

These lines, Cody argues, "imply all that Renaissance pastoralism means: an off-stage rite of nature by which Aminta's love is consummated; a 'maimed' rite of the Platonic theology by which a tragic union in death is controverted and the life of the soul in the natural world is celebrated; an Orphic initiation at the hands of a Bacchante by which the shepherd's voice is purified; and a rite of art by which these others become a play scene of Elpino (G.-B. Pigna) telling the Chorus (Ferrara) how the court-poet (Tasso) deserves his patronage" (1969, 74). Aminta's willingness to suffer death and dismemberment for love is all that the gods require in order to transform death into life and separation into union. The same idea is stated as a paradox in Matthew 16:25: "Whosoever will save his life shall lose it: and whosoever will lose his life for my sake shall find it."

A similar offstage rite of nature is celebrated early in *Il pastor fido* when the nymph and her faithful shepherd are imprisoned or buried alive in the cave by the jealous Satyr. But the final act of the play celebrates an even more profound ritual than that of sexual union. Echoing the biblical story of Abraham and Isaac, old Montano prepares to sacrifice his once lost but newly found son Mirtillo (the first Silvio) in order to fulfill his priestly duties to the divine law of Diana. However, the blind Tirenio, priest of Apollo, reminds Montano just in time of the ancient oracle that once promised happiness to Arcadia when "two of heauens issue [Hercules Jupiter and Pan, or heaven and earth] love vnite, / And for the auncient fault of that false wight, / A faithfull shepheards pitie make amends" (Dymock sig. P4). At this point Montano happily remembers that Mirtillo's name was originally Silvio before the flood swept the infant away. Since Amarilli had really been promised to the first Silvio, the natural love between nymph and shepherd was divinely ordained from the beginning. Guarini's tragicomedy ends therefore with the recognition of human blindness and with forgiveness all around, followed by the lovers' joyful matrimonial ceremonies. But even then, on the brink of marital union with his beloved, Mirtillo wonders if he is only experiencing a dream:

Questi mi paion sogni,
a dirti il vero; e mi par d'ora in ora
che'l sonno mi si rompa
e che tu mi t'involi, anima mia.
Vorrei pur ch'altra prova

mi fesse omai sentire
che'l mio dolce vegghiar non e dormire.

(Guarini 408–10)

(This seemes a dreame, and still I am afraid
My sleep should breake, and thou my soule shouldst flye away.
In better proofe my sences would I steepe,
That this sweet sight is not a dreaming sleepe.)

(Dymock sig. Q4ᵛ)

The marriage must be consummated in the physical world for Mirtillo to trust his happy good fortune. Such observations have much in common with Bottom's dream in *A Midsummer Night's Dream*, with Posthumus's celestial vision in *Cymbeline*, and with well-known speeches by Caliban and Prospero in *The Tempest*. They will certainly remind us of that remarkable seventeenth-century tragicomedy *La vida es sueño* by Calderón de la Barca, which like *Cymbeline* emphasizes primitivism rather than pastoralism.[38]

Guarini's happy ending is also made possible by a popular ritual of the hunt—the triumphant display of the quarry's head onstage. Silvio, the younger, a hunter of beasts and a worshipper of chaste Diana, has killed the winter boar, which symbolizes both the fear of death and sexual lust in opposition to life and gentle love. "Behold his head, that seemes to breath out death" (Dymock sig. M), shouts the Chorus of Huntsmen and Shepherds, as they bring in the bloody trophy impaled on a stick. Silvio has now made the pastures safe to plow and to sow by killing the fearsome animal and dismembering it. A successful hunt is also clearly analogous to a character's achievement of self-control.

Like his Italian predecessors, Shakespeare celebrates the sacred rites of Apollo and Dionysos, to say nothing of Orpheus, in all his late tragicomedies. We find the Dionysian myth of Alcestis rescued from death by a drunken Hercules carefully embedded in *The Winter's Tale,* and a Dionysian ritual of drunkenness and revolution, both controlled just in time by Prospero, in *The Tempest.* Although he neither explains nor proves the point, Northrop Frye states that "Orpheus is the hero of all four romances" by Shakespeare.[39] Following Frye's lead, Peggy Ann Knapp makes a convincing case for the similarities between the popular medieval romance of *Sir Orfeo* and *Pericles* in "The Orphic Vision of *Pericles,*" while David Armitage effectively argues the presence of the myth of Orpheus's dismemberment in all Shakespeare's late "romances," as he, like Frye, prefers to call these plays.[40]

In *Cymbeline,* the Ovidian myth of the flaying of Marsyas is first represented through Shakespeare's imagery of removed garments, as it is in *King Lear* as well. When Imogen reads Posthumus's letter to Pisanio accusing her of adultery, she says, "Poor I am stale, a garment out of fashion, / And, for I am richer than to hang by th' walls, / I must be ripp'd:—to pieces with me!" (3.4.52–54). Such a ripping to pieces does not physically occur, although we assume that it does occur psychologically. After Pisanio calms her down, he insists that Imogen exchange her feminine dress for the masculine clothing of a page and continue the search for her husband. By becoming her "other" or male self through this change of outer appearances, Imogen escapes the slander directed at her "woman's part" and learns to humble her royal pride. Posthumus likewise removes his courtly garments and outer protective armor when he receives from Pisanio the bloody cloth proclaiming Imogen's supposed death. In keeping with the equalizing propensity of tragicomedy, he dresses as a humble British peasant: "To shame the guise o' th' world, I will begin, / The fashion less without, and more within" (5.1.32–33). Iachimo calls him in this disguise, "A very drudge of Nature's" (5.2.4), thus identifying Posthumus at this point with Marsyas and the natural world of Pan.

Shakespeare, always the virtuoso, includes the death of Orpheus (a sacrifice to Dionysos) as well as the flaying of Marsyas (a sacrifice to Apollo) in this complex tragicomedy of primitivism. Ironically his Orpheus is Cloten, the satyr in a prince's clothing who is beheaded by Guiderius, the true prince in a satyr's hairy garments. It is the fool Cloten who invokes Apollo through his hired musicians in the lovely *aubade* sung to awaken Imogen to his lust:

> Hark, hark, the lark at heaven's gate sings,
>   And Phoebus gins arise,
> His steeds to water at those springs
>   On chalic'd flowers that lies;
> And winking Mary-buds begin to ope their golden eyes;
> With every thing that pretty is, my lady sweet arise:
>   Arise, arise!

                                                          (2.3.19–29)

It is Cloten who echoes the "Odi et amo" of Catullus, the Roman love poet so often inspired by Apollo: "I love and hate her: for she's fair and royal" (3.5.71). It is Cloten who is advised by a courtier to change his shirt since, "the violence of action hath made you reek as a sacrifice" (1.3.1–2). It is Cloten whose severed head is thrown into the creek that will carry it out to the sea, just as the musician Orpheus's head, now singing prophecies, floated down a river and over to Lesbos after his dismemberment by the Maenads. And it is the beastly Cloten whose bloody trunk is at last embraced by Beauty—as Bottom was embraced by Titania—and who is thus ritually accepted as a sacrifice to Eros and to Dionysos. Since Love, as well as Dionysos, was a death god for antiquity, as Wind reports (1968,

152–70), Cloten must first die physically to earn this embrace, after which the play as a whole passes into the prophetic mode of Orphism. John Warden states that for the philosopher Ficino, Orpheus was both "the lover and prophet of love,"[41] a notion that becomes part of the Shakespearean vision as well. Thus, of the three tragicomedies we have been discussing, *Cymbeline* is perhaps the most direct in its theatrical reenactment of those occult pagan rites of poetry as the art of metaphor that transforms nature into truth and as a divine art that can only be practiced under the auspices of both Apollo and Dionysos.

Yet we must remember that these are indeed "maimed rites." In tragicomedy, heroes and heroines may be wounded, but they never die. Through closeness to death, they are initiated into maturity and spiritual insight. In the words of Lucius in Book 11 of *The Golden Ass,*

> I approached nere vnto Hell, euen to the gates of Proserpina, & after that I was rauished throughout all the Elementes, I returned to my proper place. Aboute midnight I sawe the Sunne shine, I saw likewise the Goddes celestial, and Goddes infernall, before whome I presented myselfe and woorshipped them.[42]

Such liminal experiences are sufficient to reform the inner world of a human being.

9. The Art of Dramatic Poetry

Finally, the ninth characteristic of Renaissance tragicomedy is a deep concern with the art of dramatic poetry itself. As Kirsch reminds us,

> a basic impulse of coterie drama was to make the dramatist's art a subject of his art. In some instances this artistic narcissism led to structures that are significantly similar to Shakespeare's: Malevole's control of the action in *The Malcontent,* for example, is very close to Prospero's role in *The Tempest;* at one point, Malevole, like Prospero, is even explicitly associated with a Providential beneficence. Shakespeare's exploitation of artistic self-consciousness in the last plays is particularly rich, drawing upon the central Renaissance paradox of nature and art and dramatizing, in Northrop Frye's words, "the sense of nature as comprising not merely an order but a power, at once supernatural and connatural, . . . and controlled either by benevolent human magic or by a divine will."[43]

The three tragicomedies we are examining here seem especially concerned with the problems for the artist of transforming sense into intelligence or images into Platonic Ideas. As I see it, there are three common means for transforming perceptions from the world of the senses into ideas: (1) religious rituals such as the Eucharist, (2) the operations of the imagination, which result in works of art, music, and poetry, and (3) the action of love as *caritas,* which leads us from outer nature to inner divinity, from time to eternity. In each case passion and reason must work together for a true metamorphosis to occur—this is to say that we must both feel intensely and understand correctly the meaning of what we feel through an imaginative inner reconciliation of Apollo and Dionysos.

Tasso's tragicomedy implies that the poet must love beauty so completely and hopelessly that he is willing to die for it, just as Orpheus finally accepted a sacrificial death in order to "know" beauty intellectually and spiritually, that is, in order to have metaphorical intercourse with true Beauty. As Orpheus could only possess the real Eurydice in another world, so Aminta can only possess all of Sylvia by momentarily dying for love to this world of shadows. Thus for Tasso, love alone can "enable sense to know the intelligence and provide us with the "sense" or meaning of experience. Guarini agrees that love as Anteros is that

Raro mostro e mirabile, d'umano
e di divino aspetto;
di veder cieco e di saver insano;
di senso e d'intelletto,
di ragion e desio confuso affetto!

(Guarini 246)

(Rare miracle of humane and divine aspectes,
(That blind) dost see, and Wisedom (mad) corrects,
Of sence and vnderstanding intellects,
Of reason and desire confus'd affects.)

(Dymock sig. K2)

Indeed human love can provide us with what Wordsworth later called "intimations of immortality," but only—according to the Renaissance—if we combine desire with reason and remember that reason as the logical intuition of true relationships operates beyond the five senses.

Since the satyr Marsyas had to suffer physically and emotionally for his arrogance toward reason or the god Apollo, there is also much talk of both "sense" and "feeling" in *Cymbeline*—a play that celebrates the ritual of Marsyas as much as it celebrates the death of Orpheus. Shakespeare often puns on the word "sense" to include both Apollo and Dionysos. For example, Posthumus places Imogen's diamond ring on his finger with the words, "Remain, remain thou here, / While sense can keep it on" (1.2.48– 50), although he is soon to wager away the ring through a failure of basic common sense. Imogen attempts to calm the rage of her father by telling him, "I am senseless of your wrath; a touch more rare / Subdues all pangs, all fears" (1.2.66–67). At this point she can feel only love and grief for the banishment of her new husband. The Queen orders Cloten to pursue Imogen and to be "senseless" or unhearing toward the refusal of the princess to permit his courtship. Cloten, however, understands the word to mean "without reason" and responds huffily, "Senseless? not so" (2.3.53). But he also demands sensory experience, which appears to be all he really understands. Later Imogen loses all her five senses in a counterfeit sleep of death symbolizing her complete descent into the dark Dionysian world of unconsciousness that is as much a part of mortality as is reason. Posthumus undergoes a similar sleep of atonement that ends with a celestial vision. The eyes of his mind at last awaken when the eyes of his body are in darkness, but the result is at first one of confusion between the world of the senses and the world of the intellect:

> 'Tis still a dream: or else such stuff as madmen
> Tongue and brain not: either both, or nothing,
> Or senseless speaking, or a speaking such
> As sense cannot untie.

(5.4.146–49)

Finally, when Cymbeline learns of the wickedness of his queen, he stubbornly defends the truth of his senses, which told him that she was beautiful, that her flattering words were pleasant, and that even his "heart thought her like her seeming" (5.5.65). He also knows that Imogen has suffered as a result of his pathetic inability to distinguish between appearance and reality: "O my daughter, / That it was folly in me, thou mayst say, / And prove it in thy feeling. Heaven mend all!" (5.5.66–68). Here the Dionysian mode of feeling or suffering the truth, instead of the Apollonian mode of reasoning it through, reveals the truth at last.

Keeping in mind the above nine specific characteristics shared by *Aminta, Il pastor fido,* and *Cymbeline* in dramatic practice, we should now examine the general theoretical definition of tragicomedy by Guarini as a blend between tragedy and comedy. The tragicomic writer, he says,

> takes from tragedy its great persons but not its great action, its verisimilar plot but not its true one, its movement of the feelings but not its disturbance of them, its pleasure but not its sadness, its danger but not its death; from comedy it takes laughter that is not excessive, modest amusement, feigned difficulty, happy reversal, and above all the comic order.[44]

But why does tragicomedy borrow such elements from opposing genres? Cody insists that these dramas (at least the pastorals) are really initiation rites (1969, 60), which are always serious but cannot end in real death and which must offer the world a reborn and changed initiate. I am certain that the same is true of primitivist tragicomedies. All require a grave and paradoxical conflict in the plot, such as the desire to know in conflict with injunctions not to profane that which is sacred, the desire to love in conflict with the ideal of chastity, natural law in conflict with divine law, etc., or such religious paradoxes as the need to die physically in order to achieve eternal life for the spirit. Various philosophies and religions offer happy solutions for all these conflicts to an initiate who is willing to prepare himself from within for a psychological and spiritual meta-morphosis to a new and mature approach to reality, but Renaissance tragicomedy offers a combination of Neoplatonism, Orphism, and Christianity in particular to its coterie audience.

In *Cymbeline,* for example, the jealous and possessive attitude of Posthumus, Cloten, and even Cymbeline toward Imogen as a reflection of Ideal Beauty must cease, or they become incapable of recognizing her when she dons a disguise or changes her form. Similarly, Imogen, as a human character rather than a desired abstraction, must see her heroic husband as an ordinary man like any other, as a man involved in a tedious life and capable of making serious errors in judgment. Renaissance tragicomic lovers must ultimately accept their beloveds as they are—imperfect—and the same holds true for fathers and daughters. The painful process of letting the ideal imaginary "other" die and of accepting the flawed human "other" with compassion, love, and a sense of humor is an important adolescent initiation rite leading to maturity, a rite present also in Shakespeare's comedies, according to Edward Berry.[45] Generically speaking, imagined or real lapses from the ideal can cause tragedy and the dramatic celebration of a sacrificial death. An unnatural distortion of ideals applied to a real world often generates comedy. In tragicomedy, on the other hand, the imaginative celebration of a communal blood ritual of death and resurrection as a spiritual initiation rite (a rite beyond the adolescent initiation to sexuality and tribal identity) finally reconciles the reality of material needs and sexual desire (Eros) to the intellectual ideals of chastity and the spiritual love of God (Anteros). This ritual may include a reconciliation of Venus to Diana and of Dionysos to Apollo. The result is concord, a tempered scale of values or a harmony between opposites, which brings delight to the audience and which appears to be the final goal of the tragicomic form.[46]

Notes

1. E. D. Hirsch, Jr., *Validity in Interpretation* (New Haven and London: Yale University Press, 1967), 68–126.
2. Ernst Gombrich, *Symbolic Images: Studies in the Art of the Renaissance* (London: Phaidon, 1972), 5.
3. Quoted by J. M. Nosworthy in his Introduction to the Arden edition of *Cymbeline* (London: Methuen & Company Ltd., 1955), xl.
4. Arthur C. Kirsch, "*Cymbeline* and Coterie Dramaturgy," *English Literary History* 34 (1967): 294.

5. Kirsch, *Shakespeare and the Experience of Love* (Cambridge: Cambridge University Press, 1981), 172–73.

6. See, for example, Northrop Frye, *A Natural Perspective: The Development of Shakespearean Comedy and Romance* (New York: Columbia University Press, 1965); Barbara A. Mowat, *The Dramaturgy of Shakespeare's Romances* (Athens: University of Georgia Press, 1976); Howard Felperin, *Shakespearean Romance* (Princeton, N.J.: Princeton University Press, 1972); and Douglas L. Peterson, *Time, Tide, and Tempest: A Study of Shakespeare's Romances* (San Marino, Calif.: The Huntington Library, 1973). Some studies insisting on the term "tragicomedy" for the new form include Marvin T. Herrick, *Tragicomedy: Its Origin and Development in Italy, France, and England* (Urbana: University of Illinois Press, 1955), and Frank Humphrey Ristine, *English Tragicomedy: Its Origin and History* (New York: Columbia University Press, 1910).

7. Caesarea Abartis, *The Tragicomic Construction of "Cymbeline" and "The Winter's Tale"* (Salzburg: Institut für Englische Sprache und Literatur Universität Salzburg, 1977), 18.

8. See Joan Hartwig, *Shakespeare's Tragicomic Vision* (Baton Rouge: Louisiana State University Press, 1972), 3–33, and 61–103. Hartwig summarizes tragicomedy as follows: "The pattern of Shakespeare's tragicomic action, in the simplest terms, is to dislocate settled perceptions through adversity and then to liberate perception through unexpected prosperity. The expanded perceptions of each character reveal a world that is no longer confined by his own limitations. He has confronted a world constituted upon 'nothing,' and from this 'nothing' meaning grows. The reduction is a necessary prelude, as it is in the tragedies, to the realization that correspondences do exist between appearance and reality and between divine and human action, and that the characters may confidently rely upon them" (32–33).

9. See Giambattista Guarini, *The Compendium of Tragicomic Poetry,* in *Literary Criticism from Plato to Dryden,* ed. Allan H. Gilbert (New York: American Book Company, 1940), 523; and Joseph Loewenstein, "Guarini and the Presence of Genre," in *Renaissance Tragicomedy: Explorations in Genre and Politics,* ed. Nancy Klein Maguire (New York: AMS Press, 1987), 33–35.

10. See Gail Kern Paster, " 'To Starve with Feeding': The City in Coriolanus," *Shakespeare Studies* 11 (1978): 124 and 142; and Barbara Bono, *Literary Transvaluation: From Vergilian Epic to Shakespearean Tragicomedy* (Berkeley: University of California Press, 1984), 4.

11. See Mimi Still Dixon, "Tragicomic Recognitions: Medieval Miracles and Shakespearean Romance," in *Renaissance Tragicomedy,* 56–79.

12. On Shakespearean tragicomedy, the morality plays, and Christian homilies, see Robert Grams Hunter, *Shakespeare and the Comedy of Forgiveness* (New York: Columbia University Press, 1965).

13. Richard Cody, *The Landscape of the Mind: Pastoralism and Platonic Theory in Tasso's "Aminta" and Shakespeare's Early Comedies* (Oxford: The Clarendon Press, 1969), 29. See also "Poliziano's *Orfeo,"* trans. Elizabeth Bassett Welles, *La Fusta* 4 (Spring-Fall 1979): 100–20. For various interpretations of the myth of Orpheus, see Charles Segal, *Orpheus: The Myth of the Poet* (Baltimore, Md.: Johns Hopkins University Press, 1989); John Warden, ed., *Orpheus: The Metamorphoses of a Myth* (Toronto: University of Toronto Press, 1982); and C. M. Bowra, "Orpheus and Eurydice," *The Classical Quarterly* n.s. 2 (1952): 113–26.

14. Cody, *Landscape,* 33.

15. See Louise George Clubb, "The making of the pastoral play: Italian experiments between 1573 and 1590," in *Petrarch to Pirandello,* ed. Julius A. Molinaro

(Toronto: University of Toronto Press, 1973), 46–72. For further generic comments on tragicomedy, see Clubb, *Italian Drama in Shakespeare's Time* (New Haven and London: Yale University Press, 1989), 153–87.

16. Margery Corbett and R. W. Lightbown, *The Comely Frontispiece: The Emblematic Title-page in England, 1550–1660* (London: Routledge and Kegan Paul, 1979), 147. For another reading of the Jonson title-page, see Eugene M. Waith, *The Pattern of Tragicomedy in Beaumont and Fletcher* (New Haven: Yale University Press, 1952), 45–47. Further references to Waith's important study will be noted parenthetically in my text.

17. For discussions of the Wild Man *topos,* see Peggy Muñoz Simonds, "The Iconography of Primitivism in *Cymbeline,*" *Renaissance Drama* 16 (1985): 95–120; G. M. Pinciss, "The Savage Man in Spenser, Shakespeare, and Renaissance English Drama," *The Elizabethan Theatre* 8, ed. George R. Hibbard (Port Credit, Ont.: P. D. Meany, 1982), 69–89; Timothy Husband, *The Wild Man: Medieval Myth and Symbolism* (New York: The Metropolitan Museum of Art, 1980); Richard Bernheimer, *Wild Men in the Middle Ages: A Study in Art, Sentiment, and Demonology* (Cambridge, Mass.: Harvard University Press, 1952); and Eugene Waith "Satyr and Shepherd," in *Pattern of Tragicomedy,* 43–85.

18. See Simonds, "The Iconography of Primitivism," 97.

19. See Katherine Basford, *The Green Man* (Ipswich: D. S. Brewer Ltd., 1978).

20. For the Italian text of Tasso's *Aminta,* I have used the Folger Shakespeare Library's early London edition (STC 12414), which is bound together with Giambattista Guarini's *Il pastor fido.* See Torquato Tasso, *Aminta: Fávola Boschereccia* (London: Giovanni Volfeo, 1591). The English translation of *Aminta* (*Amyntas*) is by Leigh Hunt and can be found in *The Genius of the Italian Theater,* ed. Eric Bentley (New York: Mentor Books, 1964). It will be cited in my text as Hunt.

21. Battista Guarini, *Il pastor fido,* ed. J. H. Whitfield (Austin: University of Texas Press, 1976). The Italian lines will be cited in my text as Guarini.

22. See J. P. Brockbank, "History and Historionics in *Cymbeline,*" *Shakespeare Survey* 11 (1958): 42–49; Robin Moffet, "*Cymbeline* and the Nativity," *Shakespeare Quarterly* 13 (1962): 207–18; Homer D. Swander, "*Cymbeline:* Religious Ideas and Dramatic Design," *Pacific Coast Studies in Shakespeare,* ed. Waldo McNeir and Thelma N. Greenfield (Eugene: University of Oregon Books, 1966), 248–62; and Howard Felperin, *Shakespearean Romance,* 181.

23. See R. E. S., " 'Landscape with Sylvia and Satyrs'—Domenichino," in *The Age of Correggio and the Carracci: Emilian Painting of the Sixteenth and Seventeenth Centuries* (Washington, D.C.: National Gallery of Art, 1986), 436–37.

24. All English translations from *Il pastor fido* will be from John Dymock, trans., *Il pastor fido: or the Faithful Shepherd* (London: Simon Waterson, 1602) and will be cited in my text as Dymock.

25. See "Introduction" to Guarini, *Il pastor fido,* 32–33.

26. James J. Yoch, Jr., "The Renaissance Dramatization of Temperance: The Italian Revival of Tragicomedy and *The Faithful Shepherdess,*" in *Renaissance Tragicomedy,* 126; cited hereafter parenthetically. In this excellent discussion of the genre, Yoch argues that "Renaissance tragicomedies illustrated for their audiences right rule of the self, and, by implication, of the body politic" (116).

27. See John Speed, *The History of Great Britaine* (London: William Hall and John Beale, 1611), 124.

28. See Ficino, *Ficino's Commentary on Plato's "Symposium",* trans. Sears R. Jayne (Columbia, Mo.: University of Missouri Press, 1944) 203–4; and Andrea Alciati, *Emblemata cum commentariis* (Padua, 1621), 457 and 461.

29. Emblem 111 has been translated by Virginia W. Callahan as follows:

Nemesis has painted a winged Eros,
   hostile to a winged Eros,
taming bow with bow, and fires with fire,
in order that he might suffer
   what he does to others.
But this boy, formerly
brandishing his arrows fearlessly,
   is wretchedly weeping.
Three times he spits into the depths of
   his bosom: a wondrous thing,
fire is consumed by fire, Eros
   hates the passion of Eros.

See Peter M. Daly, Virginia W. Callahan, and Simon Cuttler, eds., *Index Embelmaticus: Andreas Alciatus,* 2 vols. (Toronto: University of Toronto Press, 1985), 1: Emblem III.

30. *Symposium,* trans. Michael Joyce, in *Plato: The Collected Dialogues,* ed. Edith Hamilton and Huntington Cairns (1963; reprint New York: Pantheon Books, 1966), 563.

31. Mircea Eliade, *Myths, Rites, Symbols,* ed. Wendell C. Beane and William G. Doty (New York: Harper Colophon Books, 1975), 1, 182.

32. Ibid., 175–76.

33. *The Republic,* trans. Paul Shorey, in *Plato: The Collected Dialogues,* ed. Edith Hamilton and Huntington Cairns, 747–50.

34. See Wind, *Pagan Mysteries in the Renaissance,* 2nd ed., rev. and enl. (New York: W. W. Norton & Co., 1968). Further references to this work will be noted parenthetically in my text.

35. Ovid, *Metamorphoses,* trans. Mary M. Innes (New York: Penguin Books, 1955), 247.

36. See Ovid, 144–45, and Sydney Freedberg, "Titian and Marsyas," *FMR* 1 (1984): 51–67.

37. Ovid, 145.

38. For a Marxist discussion of *La vida es sueño* as tragicomedy, see Walter Cohen, "The Politics of Golden Age Spanish Tragicomedy," *Renaissance Tragicomedy,* ed. Maguire, 155–176. For a Renaissance and thus much more convincing and useful analysis of the tragicomedy, see Frederick A. De Armas, *The Return of Astraea: An Astral-Imperial Myth in Calderón* (Lexington, Ky.: The University Press of Kentucky, 1986), 88–138.

39. Frye, *A Natural Perspective,* 147.

40. See Peggy Ann Knapp, "The Orphic Vision of Pericles," *Texas Studies in Literature and Language* 15 (1973–74): 615–26; and David Armitage, "The Dismemberment of Orpheus: Mythic Elements in Shakespeare's Romances," *Shakespeare Survey* 39 (1986): 123–33.

41. Warden, "Orpheus and Ficino," in *Orpheus,* 101.

42. See Lucius Apuleius, *The XI Bookes of the "Golden Asse" conteigning the Metamorphosie of Lucius Apuleius,* trans. William Adlington (London: William How, 1571), 120.

43. Kirsch, "Coterie Dramaturgy," 303.

44. Guarini, *Compendium,* in *Literary Criticism from Plato to Dryden,* ed. Allan H. Gilbert, 511.45.

45. See Edward Berry, *Shakespeare's Comic Rites* (Cambridge: Cambridge University Press, 1984), 16–49.

46. James J. Yoch, Jr., has identified this concord as Plato's idealization of "temperance . . . [which] extends to the whole [state], and runs through all the notes of the scale, and produces a harmony of the weaker and the stronger and the middleclass (4.432)." See "The Renaissance Dramatization of Temperance," 115–16. For a similar interpretation of Tasso's *Aminta,* see Yoch, "The Limits of Sensuality: Pastoral Wildernesses, Tasso's *Aminta* and the Gardens of Ferrara," *Forum Italicum* (Spring–Fall 1982): 60–81.

2
Myths, Explicit and Implicit, in *Cymbeline*

> There is but one god and one goddess, but many are their
> powers and names: Jupiter, Sol, Apollo, Moses, Christus, Luna,
> Ceres, Proserpina, Tellus, Maria. But have a care in speaking
> these things. They should be hidden in silence as are the Eleusi-
> nian mysteries; sacred things must needs be wrapped in fable
> and enigma.
>
> —Mutianus Rufus

According to G. Wilson Knight, "*Cymbeline* . . . probably exceeds any other Shakespearean play in its fecundity of classical, and especially mythological reference."[1] Indeed the tragicomedy does give us that impression, although Ann Thompson has counted only about thirty-five mythological references in *Cymbeline,* some fifteen fewer than she found in *Titus Andronicus.*[2] We sense not only a deep concern with classical mythology in the play but also the tantalizing presence of a strangely familiar mythic substructure that, if we could identify it, might help us to better understand this tragicomedy. But, puzzled by the wealth of explicit textual allusions to classical mythology, especially to Ovid's *Meta-morphoses,* most critics have thus far been content to point out the peculiar confluence of old tales masking—or, in my view, *echoing*—the event of most significance during the reign of Cymbeline in England, namely, the Nativity.[3] Barbara Mowat argues that such an abundance of mythological allusions in all the late plays indicates that Shakespeare had that "special 'ear' " for myth which C. Kerenyi says one *must* have if myth is to work upon one fully:

> i.e., that Shakespeare heard in mythologems musical ground-themes inviting
> variations, inviting new inventions; that he perceived the pictorial quality of
> myth—saw in mythologems that outpouring of images which are at the same
> time an unfolding, a making of story, a making of meaning; that he found in the
> tales of Ovid and of the Bible stories that take us into the primordial.[4]

Before examining the problem of the mythological content of *Cymbeline* in greater detail, it would be useful first to recall how the Renaissance in general chose to understand the pagan myths that its artists employed so abundantly and how the import of these ancient stories was related to the Christian era.

As Charles Trinkaus has pointed out, the Italian humanists, who first resurrected the ancient world as an important forerunner of their own, tended as a group to wed their love for classical poetry to their Christian beliefs by interpreting the classics as allegories, or as "the symbolic vehicle in which the truth was concealed."[5] This practice, Trinkaus tells us, "is exactly a mode of interpretation which discovers the general concealed in the specific; it is a conversion of the literal poetic image into a moral, or a natural-philosophical, or a theological truth, which is a statement in general terms" (1970, vol. 2, 688). Coluccio Salutati, for example, believed that the pagan myths should be understood as analogies to (1) the life of man, (2) the relationship between god and man, and (3) the interrelationship between the various attributes of God, Himself. The third kind of interpretation arises from Salutati's attempt to explain polytheism, in that he wishes to suggest that the Greeks spoke of many gods only out of the artistic need to personify the multiple qualities of divinity and to dramatize the manner in which these qualities or attributes interrelate (Trinkaus 1970, vol. 2, 697–704). All of this seems perfectly natural. Indeed many people still interpret the ancient myths allegorically, particularly modern Freudians and Jungians, and I think we would be justified in suspecting that Shakespeare, like his contemporary Francis Bacon in *The Wisdom of the Ancients,* may well have done the same—but far more subtly, to be sure.

The extent to which Renaissance humanists read classical myths in terms of Christian allegory can be exemplified by Giovanni Caldiera's amazing explanation of the Judgment of Paris in his *Concordantia,* a work completed between 1447 and 1455. Caldiera suggests that the story reported a true judgment between the merits of power (Juno), wisdom (Pallas), and charity (Venus) made by St. Paul in the guise of a Trojan prince:

> But because one ought rightly to be preferred, therefore Mercury, since he is human intellect, by a resounding pipe, which is the language of wisdom, carried a dubious sentence for the dignity of the goddesses and therefore conducted them to Paris, which is to the Apostle Paul, so that he might judge which is more beautiful, who since he saw them nude and without any veil gave the judgement in favour of charity, and since he had placed her ahead, awarded her the golden apple, because the greatest of all is charity. (quoted in Trinkaus 1970, vol. 2, 709)

Edgar Wind explains this incredible Renaissance love for the transference of pagan myths into Christian types as being "sanctioned by a theory of concordance which discovered a sacred mystery in pagan beauty, conceiving it to be a poetic medium through which the divine splendour had been transmitted: 'As Dionysius says, the divine ray cannot reach us unless it is covered with poetic veils.' "[6] And very soon, the veiling of truth or meaning by the judicious use of classical allusions, so that only initiates could understand, became the accepted practice for artists and poets throughout Europe.

In this chapter, I shall discuss only the most important classical myths in *Cymbeline* and explore some of the meanings—psychological, political, and metaphysical—they may have had for Shakespeare and his audience. I shall begin with the explicit mythological references in the play to Ovid's *Metamorphoses,* or those references that are associated with Iachimo's intrusion into Imogen's bedchamber, including the Rape of Lucrece and the myth of Tereus and Philomela, followed by allusions in *Cymbeline* to Ovid's tale of the death of Orpheus. Then I shall discuss the Neoplatonic myth of Cupid and Psyche that, I believe, provides Shakespeare with the implicit substructure of Imogen's feminine quest for her absent lord and informs the play as a whole.

Politics, Morality, and Poetic Ritual

Act 2, scene 1, of *Cymbeline* ends with a prayer by a courtier standing outside the palace for the welfare of his besieged princess:

> The heavens hold firm
> The walls of thy dear honour, keep unshak'd
> That temple, thy fair mind, that thou mayst stand,
> T' enjoy thy banished lord and this great land!

(2.1.61–64)

The very next scene, which takes place not only inside the palace but actually inside Imogen's bedchamber, reveals a defenseless princess lying in her bed and the trunk containing Iachimo already inside her chamber walls. The hidden presence of a vicious slanderer warns us that this is a theologically fallen world, a world divided between the clarity of day (reason and wisdom) and the influences, often evil, of night (the passions and ignorance). Iachimo's later description of the room itself also suggests at first a sacred temple dedicated to the Great Goddess of antiquity in all her aspects. She is depicted as Isis in the Cleopatra tapestry on the wall, as Diana on the plaster bas-relief decorating the chimneypiece, and, finally, as a "recumbent Venus" or a sleeping Ariadne by the partially nude Imogen on her bed in the center of the chamber. The Elizabethan, Richard Linche, translates Vincenzo Cartari's observations on the classical Great Goddess into sixteenth-century English as follows: "Some that haue written of these naturall causes, haue affirmed, that Venus, Iuno, Luna, & Proserpina haue ben al one, retaining only different names and titles, in that many effects and issues proceeding from them, haue ben diuers and seuerall."[7] Such an all-encompassing goddess represents Nature or the feminine principle in the universe, a principle that Shakespeare demonstrates in *Cymbeline* to be highly vulnerable to male slander, misunderstanding, and possessiveness.

For political purposes, Renaissance poets characteristically used pagan goddesses as conventional icons of those female royal personages who serve as the earthly representatives of divinity, and it is in this sense, no doubt, that the Second Lord has previously apostrophized the heroine as "Thou divine Imogen" (2.1.56). However, the audience tends to feel, as do several characters in the play, that Shakespeare means Imogen as a dramatic character to be more than just a member of the royal family and heir-apparent to the throne, particularly when she addresses her lady-in-waiting as "my woman Helen" (2.2.1). The mythological Helen was generally understood to be a mortal embodiment of the abstractions Beauty and Love, as well as an earthly servant or priestess of Venus. She is the mortal shadow of divine Venus. Certainly Iachimo regards Imogen as divinity incarnate after he emerges from his trunk, approaches her bed, and peers down at her revealed beauty: "Cytherea, / How bravely thou becom'st thy bed! fresh lily! / And whiter than the sheets!" (2.2.14–16). For him she is Venus, goddess of love, and chaste Diana at one and the same time; she is that part of the created world which is infused with the sacred. Ficino explains this Neoplatonic concept in an interesting analogy between creation and a work of art:

> All the parts of the world, because they are the works of a single creative artist, and, as components of the same construct, are all alike in their essence and manner of existence, are bound together each with each by a sort of mutual affection, so that love can properly be called the perpetual knot or link of the universe.[8]

Mortality can thus reflect the world of the immortals, which is bound to Nature by love. In this sense, the bedchamber scene in *Cymbeline* tends to remain in the viewer's imagination as an evocative feminine theophany that balances symmetrically with the far noisier descent of the masculine deity Jupiter in act 5, scene 4.

But however much divinity is present in the room, false Iachimo is also there to remind us that the temple of Imogen's fair mind has already been penetrated by untruth through her naive acceptance of Iachimo's previous flattering words in the Petrarchan mode about her lord, the exiled Posthumus, as true: "He sits 'mongst men like a descended god" (1.7.169). In her lack of wisdom about her new spouse, she is a fallen human being exactly like the rest of humanity and no more a divinity than is Posthumus; nevertheless, her essential goodness and chastity do seem to reflect or echo the higher world of ideals throughout the play.

Iachimo's proximity to the chaste sleeping princess reminds him immediately of the mythological rape of Lucrece by the Roman despot Tarquin with whom he identifies: "Our Tarquin thus / did softly press the rushes, ere he waken'd the chastity he wounded" (2.2.12–14). The reference would have had an immediate political as well as a sexual meaning for the more sophisticated members of Shakespeare's audience, since Tarquin's tyrannical behavior toward the beautiful wife of a Roman nobleman ultimately resulted in her suicide and in his own expulsion from Rome. The rape and suicide of Lucrece represent a human sacrifice that preceded the establishment of the Roman Republic, and it was obviously a metaphor, even in antiquity, for the rape of Rome herself by the early kings. The story thus becomes, among other things, an *exemplum* of improper behavior by monarchs toward their subjects and a warning of impending revolution, the probable political result of such behavior.

In one of the most interesting discussions of the Lucrece story and the moral dilemmas it poses for Christians through the suicide of the heroine, Ian Donaldson reminds us of Brutus's rousing call to vengeance at the end of Shakespeare's poem *The Rape of Lucrece:*[9]

"Why, Collatine, is woe the cure for woe?
Do wounds help wounds, or grief help grievous deeds?
Is it revenge to give thyself a blow
For his foul act by whom thy fair wife bleeds?
Such childish humour from weak minds proceeds;
    Thy wretched wife mistook the matter so,
    To slay herself that should have slain her foe."[10]

(1821–27)

Although Donaldson believes that Shakespeare himself was more interested in the wounds of conscience that Tarquin took away with him from the scene of the rape than he was in the political outcome demanded by Brutus,[11] the fact remains that the tyrant's fall from power as a result of the rape stands as an integral part of the myth. Donaldson also remarks on Botticelli's highly politicized painting of *The Tragedy of Lucretia* (c. 1499), which contrasts Lucretia's suicide with the biblical story of Judith and Holofernes and compares Brutus's call to vengeance with David's dismemberment of Goliath.[12] There can be little doubt, therefore, that Iachimo's allusion to Tarquin in *Cymbeline* would have aroused strong unconscious as well as conscious political responses in a Renaissance audience beginning to long for change during the early seventeenth century.

In addition, Shakespeare's poetic version of the Tarquin and Lucrece story exemplifies the moral dangers of individual male pride. Rolf Soellner

states, in an interesting analysis of the poem, that here, "Marital possession proves to be something of a disagreeable concept: it furnishes the
reasons for Lucrece's becoming Tarquin's prey—pride in possessing
Lucrece makes Collatine boast of his wife's beauty rather than, as the
narrator says, keep his 'rich jewel' from Tarquin's thievish ears (33–35).
Because of envy at seeing 'so rich a thing' in the hands of an inferior,
Tarquin sets out for Collatium."[13] The wager story in *Cymbeline,* as many
have noted, echoes this same pattern, while suggesting a similar moral
admonition against boasting of one's possessions before those who might
become jealous. Indeed there is a long standing tradition that a lover
should always remain silent about the object of his affections, if he is a
true lover rather than just an animal in the throes of lust and sexual
possessiveness.

To take one example, a Neoplatonic emblem in Otto van Veen's
Amorum Emblemata, or Emblemes of Love (1608) specifically warns
lovers against the kind of indiscreet speaking about the beloved which
both Collatine and Posthumus foolishly practice. The *inscriptio* of the
emblem states that "The mouth is the discouerer of the mynd." The

**Anteros chastizes Eros in Otto van Veen's *Emblemes of Loue* (Antwerp, 1608), 69.
Reprinted by permission of the Folger Shakespeare Library (STC 24627a.5 copy 1).**

pictura depicts Anteros beating Eros for his inability to keep his own counsel through pride of possession while the *subscriptio* reads,

> There where the smarte is felt the hand is lightly
> layd,
> But what the harte contaynes that doth the mouth discouer,
> Much for to speake of loue doth manifest the louer,
> By often speech of loue loue often is betrayd.[14]

Van Veen's cautionary verse on the surface is merely a commonplace of the period, although one that Posthumus would have done well to heed in *Cymbeline*. However, it is at the same time a reference—to be recognized by the *cognoscenti*—to a higher form of love with which the lover can only commune through silence. As Shakespeare himself wrote in his earlier poem on Lucrece, "Beauty itself doth of itself persuade / The eyes of men without an orator; / What needeth then apology be made / To set forth that which is so singular?" (29–32). Posthumus learns this only at the end of *Cymbeline* when bound and condemned to die in the morning, he says, "O Imogen, / I'll speak to thee in silence" (5.4.28–29), after which he falls asleep and experiences a miraculous dream vision of divinity.

In an important discussion of Protestant poetics during the Renaissance period, Barbara Lewalski quotes J. A. Mazzeo's explanation of this kind of Platonic intellectual progress "through words to the realities themselves, from the temporal realities to the eternal realities, from talk to silence, and from discourse to vision," although she concludes that in lyric poetry the English Protestants were more apt to eschew silence for biblical allusion and imitation.[15] This is certainly true in Shakespeare's Sonnet 154, the last in the sequence, as I have shown elsewhere,[16] but Shakespeare as playwright finds silence a more powerful technique than biblical allusion to suggest spiritual insight and communion onstage, as we can see in both *Cymbeline* and *Measure for Measure*. Mazzeo points out that St. Augustine learned to read silently from St. Ambrose at a time when everyone else read aloud. He learned

> that St. Ambrose's 'good reason' for silence was nothing else than listening to the instruction of the inner teacher. A philosophical theology of silence was present in both Platonism and Christianity, and the latter began to develop it quite early. Its roots can be found in Pauline texts such as Romans 6.25–26 'the revelation of the mystery which was kept secret since the world began' and Hebrews 3.11–18 and 4.1–11 where St. Paul describes the inability of the Israelites to rest in Canaan and the superior rest available to the believer, of which God's rest after the creation is a type. . . . Such conceptions were developed by Ignatius Martyr to include the notion that revelation continued in silence and that the Incarnation was a descent from silence into 'speech' or *logos*.[17]

Thus Posthumus's silent communication with the Imogen he believes to be dead finally allows him access to his inner teacher, to divine will, and to Jupiter's prophecy for the future.

Be that as it may, Iachimo's allusion to the mythic history of Tarquin and Lucrece in *Cymbeline* aso introduces the familiar folk theme of "the violated lady," a motif that is almost immediately reiterated when the intruder notices Imogen's discarded book, evidently a copy of Ovid's *Metamorphoses,* that great poem of change written by a poet exiled from Augustan's Rome. "She hath been reading late," he observes, "The tale of Tereus, here the leaf's turn'd down / Where Philomel gave up" (2.2.44–46). He thus invites us at this point to envision Imogen as the beautiful virgin Philomela, who was raped by her brother-in-law before her transformation into the poetic bird of sorrow, the nightingale. After Tereus cut out her tongue when she threatened to reveal his crime, he imprisoned her in the middle of a dark forest. However, the horrid mutilation of Philomela was depicted in a 1582 illustrated edition of Ovid as taking place in a bed-chamber much like Imogen's, and the same subject was rather surprisingly used as well for a late sixteenth-century embroidered bed valance that remains extant.[18] The narrator of Shakespeare's *The Rape of Lucrece* also compares that violated heroine to "lamenting Philomele" (1079) after her long monologue on Night.

If we return to the myth as it is told in Book VI of the *Metamorphoses,* we find that it forms part of a group of stories on the subject of mortals who challenged the gods, were then summarily punished for their audacity, and learned through suffering what it means to be mortal. Several of these challengers were artists, including the weaver Arachne and the piper Marsyas, rivals of Minerva and Apollo respectively, who were quickly taught that their talent and skill did not endow them with divinity. Nevertheless, if art cannot be used to overcome the gods, it can be employed justifiably to challenge political power in society and without exciting divine jealousy. The ravished and verbally silenced Philomela turns, therefore, to the art of weaving a narrative tapestry to inform her sister Procne of her tragedy and her whereabouts. Ovid next tells us that a servant hired to guard Philomela carries the tapestry, without knowing what secrets it contains, to the palace of Tereus and hands it to Philomela's sister Procne. Together the sisters then exact a terrible vengeance upon Tereus. This story suggests that art can in fact be an effective political weapon against tyrants if its implicit meaning is unclear to the literal-minded, which seems to include most of the world. And, thanks to Ovid, the rapist Tereus later became an easily recognized personification of tyranny and political injustice, as did Tarquin, for sophisticated Roman and Renaissance readers. Like so many other elements in Shakespeare's

Tereo sforza la cognata
Filomena.   8 o

Mena Tereo infedele alla conforte
Sua Progne la bramata sua forella.
S'accende pel cammin di lei si forte,
Che di torle l'honor pensa & fauella.
Effequisce il penfier, le voglie torte,
Conducendo l'afflitta in parte, ch'ella,
Doppo il forzato honor, la perfa lingua,
Non sà che far, se non ch'il reo l'eslingua.

Tereus cuts out Philomela's tongue after violating her in Ovid's *Del Metamorphoseo Abbreviato* (Lyon, 1559), 92. Reprinted by courtesy of the Warburg Institute.

play, the myth of Philomela could thus suggest the presence in *Cymbeline* of a veiled political criticism not only of the player king, overtly called a tyrant by his daughter, but also of the real King James I, who might be tempted to rape his recently acquired English kingdom.

On the other hand, no overt political revolution occurs in *Cymbeline* since the monarch is saved from Roman captivity by the politically exiled Posthumus, Belarius, and the Wild Boys. Instead there is radical change within the characters themselves—change of heart and spirit, change of sexual attitudes, even change in the metaphorical relationship between monarch and subject from that of a husband lording it over his wife to that of loving Christian brotherhood, as we shall later see.

The changes begin in individuals soon after the sacrificial death of Cloten and the apparent or symbolic death of Imogen in act 4. In rapid succession we see Posthumus, who still believes Imogen guilty of adultery, charitably forgive her "For wrying but a little" (5.1.5); we see him vanquish and disarm Iachimo, without killing him, on the battlefield during a seldom remarked on theatrical dumbshow (5.2); and ultimately we hear him forgive Iachimo for slander once he learns the truth about Imogen's chastity. This in turn inspires Cymbeline—despite the deep seriousness of the crimes—to forgive Belarius for kidnapping the royal princes, Guiderius for murdering Prince Cloten, Posthumus for marrying Imogen, and the Romans for invading England to demand their tribute: "Pardon's the word to all" (5.5.422). Although such an ideal ending to a play may make us laugh in unbelief and will surely make us smile, at the same time we are forcefully reminded through the joyful comic finale in *Cymbeline* of those same wondrous ideals existing within our own minds and of the possibilities of a change for the better in our own lives and times, should we actually try to live up to such ideals ourselves.

If there is an implied political message in the play, in my view it is quite simply the old saw that peace can exist in the world if tyrants would only learn that the function of a king, and that of a husband, is the practice of "equity" or mercy toward those for whom they are responsible. Vengeance belongs to divinity alone. In the human sphere, it always provokes further vengeance. However, the implied threat of a more radical change in politics through revolution remains as a warning to those husbands and kings who do not reform themselves before attempting to enforce retributive justice on those subject to their authority.

A third myth from Ovid, which is often discussed in connection with *Cymbeline,* is that of the dismemberment of Orpheus, a type of sacrificial action I have previously shown to be necessary to the tragicomic genre. In the play, Guiderius, after severing Cloten's head from his trunk, displays the gory trophy and casually remarks,

> I'll throw't into the creek
> Behind our rock, and let it to the sea,
> And tell the fishes he's the queen's son, Cloten.

                                                    (4.2.151–53)

Ovid informs readers of his *Metamorphoses* (Bk. XI) that the head of
Orpheus was tossed into a river by the Maenads and that it finally floated
over the sea to Lesbos, murmuring all the while. Some versions of the
story insist that this murmuring was a form of prophesying, since severed
heads were believed in antiquity to be oracular. Therefore, the metamorphosis in this story is not that of Orpheus himself into a bird or animal
but a transformation of his poetic art. In symbolic terms, once the mind of
Orpheus is completely separated from his material body, his sensory
perceptions, and the natural world he so loved, he exists only in the
intellectual or spiritual world, and his song can then become prophetic of
truth. As we know, prophecy was considered to be the height of ecstatic
poetry in Renaissance aesthetics as it is the revealed word of God entirely
inspired by divinity and is uttered in the service of divine love alone.[19] It is
the artistic revelation of Truth to which all poets aspire but few can ever
reach and then only in a state of "frenzy," since one must first die to
nature—or lose rational consciousness—in order to prophesy.

In *Cymbeline,* however, Posthumus, rather than the dismembered
Cloten, becomes the prophet when he falls asleep and dreams of a descent
by Jupiter, who leaves behind a tablet prophesying happy events in the
future (and incidentally proving that his descent was real). This tablet will
be misinterpreted later by the Roman Soothsayer, who has no way of
knowing that what he understands to be a Roman symbol, the eagle, will
soon be transformed into a symbol of Christ and His Church, or that the
future James I will think of himself as the new Augustus Caesar in England
during the early seventeenth century.

The Orphic prophet in *Cymbeline* can be the living Posthumus rather
than the dead Cloten because he and Cloten are mirror images of one
another; in fact, they resemble one another so closely in a physical sense
after Cloten dons Posthumus's courtly suit that Imogen identifies his
headless corpse as that of her husband. In an attempt to explain this
grotesque dramatic moment, Joan Hartwig has argued that Cloten par-
odies Posthumus throughout much of the play:

> Cloten, the true fool, makes Posthumus' deficiencies as a romantic hero even
> more apparent when he dons Posthumus' clothes and parodies Posthumus'
> violent speech with a diatribe of his own (IV.i). Yet by his very violence, which
> is more gratuitous than Posthumus' bitter reaction to Iachimo's lies, Cloten
> takes some of the censure away from Posthumus. In fact, Cloten repeatedly
> "protects" Posthumus' characterization as he absorbs criticism through his
> excessive and parodic actions.[20]

LYRA ET CAPVT ORPHEI. II.   271

After the dismemberment of Orpheus, the Maenads toss his lyre and head into the river. In the background, Apollo kills the python swimming toward the head, which Apollo then establishes as an oracle in Lesbos. From Ovid's *Metamorphoses* (Antwerp: Christopher Plantin, 1591), 271. Reprinted by permission of the Folger Shakespeare Library (PA 6519 M2 1591 Cage).

The two young men look much alike, love the same woman, and behave like jealous louts in their treatment of her. But one will be converted to a new way of seeing, to an attitude of repentance and forgiveness, and the other will die, thwarted in his vicious attempt to rape Imogen and to kill his rival Posthumus. Hartwig defines such parody as "an imitation that both delimits and heightens by contrast," and she further explains that in *Cymbeline,* "What started out as parody ends as identification. When we accept the identification, as Imogen has, it is possible for Posthumus to be reborn out of the visibly present corpse of his counter-person."[21] Inspired Orphic prophecy then illuminates the entire last act of the play, once Cloten-Orpheus has lost his head to the fishes and Posthumus has reformed his manner of thinking and his speech. From an early commitment to the hyperbole of Petrarchan love poetry characteristic of wanton Eros, Posthumus, after his dream vision, converts his speech to the language of religion and prophecy more suitable to Anteros or the love of virtue, except for one moment of notably hyperbolic grief and guilt when he discovers that Imogen was innocent of Iachimo's slanderous accusations (5.5.210–27). In this case, however, he directs the violence against himself as a "most credulous fool" (210) until Imogen attempts to comfort him. At this point, he rashly knocks her down, still thinking she is Lucius's interfering page. Shakespeare seems to suggest by such behavior on the part of Posthumus that violence is and always will be an integral part of fallen human nature, which is why the Redeemer must soon be born.

Gazing on Beauty Bare: Shakespeare's Reconstruction of the Myth of Cupid and Psyche

Although most of Shakespeare's allusions to myth in *Cymbeline* derive from Ovid's *Metamorphoses,* the dramatist was equally familiar with another mythological collection from the classical world with exactly the same title: the second century A.D. *Metamorphoses* by Lucius Apuleius. This Latin romance was translated into English as *The Golden Ass* by William Adlington in 1566 and had an enormous influence on English letters. I believe that the feminine quest myth of Cupid and Psyche, which is the central story of this collection of old tales presented in romance form, provides Shakespeare with the deep structure of the Imogen plot in *Cymbeline* and gives to the play its often remarked upon fairy-tale quality. The presence of this myth also causes significant transformations from a mercantile to a courtly setting and from terrible punishment to forgiveness of the villain in the dramatist's use of his direct source, the popular wager story found in Boccaccio's *Decameron* and in *Frederyke of Jennen.*

No one can doubt Shakespeare's lifelong interest in Apuleius, a Platonist and a superb storyteller. The English playwright used *The Golden Ass* as a source for *A Midsummer Night's Dream,* as Sister M. Generosa and James A. S. McPeek have both demonstrated, and he very probably used it as a source for his portrayal of Cleopatra as Isis in *Antony and Cleopatra,* according to Michael Lloyd.[22] Of course in *Cymbeline* there is a memorable tapestry of Cleopatra reclining in state on her barge, a tapestry that hangs in Imogen's bedchamber to remind us of Isis, the ruling goddess of *The Golden Ass.* Furthermore, both H. Reich and D. T. Starnes have correctly pointed out striking similarities between the poisoning stepmother and the doctor who substitutes a sleeping potion for the poison in Book X of Apuleius and the characters of the Queen and

Cornelius in *Cymbeline*.[23] But no one, to my knowledge, has yet suggested the Cupid and Psyche myth, the central tale of *The Golden Ass,* as a possible paradigm for the Platonic theme of "gazing on beauty bare"— with resulting spiritual transformations—in Shakespeare's complex tragi-comedy.

Aside from spiritual change, the play is primarily concerned with marriage—both human marriage and the marriage between heaven and earth, which is symbolized by the descent of Jupiter, and the Cupid and Psyche myth was frequently depicted on Renaissance *cassoni* or marriage chests as a visual allusion to exactly the same equation between profane and sacred love, to human marriage as reflecting the marriage between Christ and His Church. The myth was, in addition, an exceedingly popular English theatrical subject according to Stephen Gosson, who complained in his antitheater tract of 1579 that *The Golden Ass* had been "thoroughly ransacked to furnish the play houses of London."[24] One such play, which went so far as to include Apuleius as a character, was Thomas Heywood's *Love's Mistress, or The Queen's Masque.* This dramatic retelling of the Cupid and Psyche story has been described by Jackson Cope as "a serpentine maze of plots which coalesce as a single action in which eye and ear are made the instruments to help us realize that poetry is a ritual of resurrection and rebirth."[25]

Briefly summarized, Apuleius's myth of Cupid and Psyche—told by a drunken old woman in a cave—describes a sacrificial marriage of death that is eventually transformed into a divine marriage with an immortal offspring. The princess Psyche is so beautiful that men begin to worship her as the new Venus instead of visiting the temple of Venus herself. The goddess jealously orders her son Eros or Cupid to make Psyche "fall in loue with the moste miserablest creature liuinge, the most poore, the most crooked, and the most vile, that there may be none founde in all the worlde of like wretchednesse."[26] At this point in his career, however, Cupid is still a disorderly god of pure lust and exactly such a vile creature. Apuleius says of Venus's winged son that he is

> rashe inoughe, and hardie, who by his euil manners, contemminge all publique iustice and lawe, armed with fire & arrowes, running up and downe in the nightes from house to house, and corrupting the lawfull marriages of euerie person, doth nothing but that which is euill. (40–41)

This wanton Cupid is immediately attracted by Psyche's external mortal beauty and has Zephyrus carry her off to an enchanted palace where she lives as a prisoner. Here she is espoused in the dark by the love god, who forbids her ever to see him. For a while she exists happily in this dark and unknowing state of sensual pleasure.

But when her two envious sisters are permitted by Cupid to visit her, they deliberately tempt Psyche to see "the serpent" she has married and to cut off his head while he sleeps. In a primal act of disobedience to the god, Psyche takes a razor and a lamp to her bedroom and with the latter illuminates the beautiful nude body of the sleeping Cupid. She falls instantly and desperately in love with Love. Her feelings completely transformed, she guiltily tries to kill herself instead of her husband, but the razor—of its own volition—leaps from her hand. And, when a drop of burning oil from the lamp falls on Cupid's shoulder, he suddenly awakens and the knower is known.

Furious at Psyche's disobedience and suffering from the searing pain of his wound, or the pain of reciprocal love, Cupid flies away to his mother. Psyche follows him, only to be scourged by the servants of Venus. She then performs four labors for the vengeful goddess in an attempt to regain her beloved. Her final labor involves a journey to the underworld to procure a casket containing the secret of beauty from Proserpina. But, curious as usual, Psyche cannot resist opening the casket before delivering it to Venus. It contains, "onely an infernall and deadly sleepe, which immediately inuaded all her members as-sone as the boxe was vncouered, in such sort that she fell downe on ye ground, and lay there as a sleeping corpes" (Apuleius, 60). At last fully aware of his own deep love for Psyche, Cupid awakens his sleeping beauty with the prick of a love arrow. He next flies up to Olympus to beg Jupiter for help against his mother's jealousy. The father of the gods, convinced that Cupid needs to reform and settle down as a married man, benevolently resolves all the family problems and restores peace and order to the world that Cupid has previously disrupted by lust and discord. Venus is persuaded to transform herself from the wicked mother-in-law into the "Good Mother" and to accept Psyche as her now immortalized daughter-in-law; a marriage feast is held in Olympus; and in due time a child called "pleasure" or "joy" is born of the union between Divine Love and Psyche, or the human soul.

This popular tale has been variously interpreted by Christian readers. For example, in the fifth century A.D., the mythographer Fulgentius saw it as a Christian allegory of free will and of the fall of man.[27] In the fourteenth century, Boccaccio, who retells the myth in his *Genealogy of the Gods,* interprets it for the early Renaissance as an Aristotelian and erudite allegory of salvation. Luisa Vertova summarizes Boccaccio's reading as follows:

> For him Psyche (the Soul) is the fifteenth daughter of Apollo (the Sun, Light of the World, God 'qui mundi vera lux est deus') and of Endelechia (the perfect age, the ripeness of time, which engenders the rational soul). Psyche's elder sisters correspond to the lower powers of the soul, the vegetative that is given at birth, and the sensitive, that is bestowed in childhood. Psyche is the youngest

In ædibus Farnesianis.

46

**Psyche punished. From a print of a Roman statue from Giovanni Battista de'
Cavalieri, *Antiquarum Statuarum Urbis Romae* (Rome 1585), 46. Reprinted by permission of the Folger Shakespeare Library (NB 1380 C2 1585 Cage).**

Psiche ibidem

43

Psyche returns from Hades with Proserpina's beauty secret. From a print of a statue in Renaissance Rome by Giovanni Battista de' Cavalieri, *Antiquarum Statuarum Urbis Romae* (Rome, 1585), 43. Reprinted by permission of the Folger Shakespeare Library (NB 1380 CS 1585 Cage).

because rational power is the last to develop, and her loss of Cupid, Divine Love, is the consequence of her following the wicked counsel of her elder sisters, that is of sensuality. Repentant, she brings about their ruin by a return to rationality; and finally, 'purged of conceit and disobedience' she again obtains the blessing of Divine Love. Wedded eternally to him, she lives in glory.[28]

Later Florentine humanists understood the myth more correctly as a Platonic allegory of the Soul's journey toward a union with Desire (Eros), which in turn leads to a union with God, the final goal of human life.[29] However, as previously noted, Edgar Wind reminds us that, "The Renaissance identified [Eros] with Death itself, in its painful no less than its joyous aspect as shown so clearly on the Roman sarcophagi which represent the agonies inflicted on Psyche by Eros as a prelude to their final embrace" (1968, 160). Shakespeare's Jupiter says something similar in *Cymbeline:* "Whom best I love I cross" (5.4.101).

Apuleius, himself, on the other hand, suggests over and over again in the stories of *The Golden Ass* that death is only an appearance. The romance contains an extraordinary number of resurrections, intimating thereby that we must look beyond death for ultimate truth. Indeed we may assume that Apuleius's own intellectual source for the Cupid and Psyche myth, aside from folk tales, *The Greek Anthology,* and classical funerary art, was Diotima's last speech to Socrates in Plato's *Symposium:*

> But if it were given to man to gaze on beauty's very self—unsullied, unalloyed, and freed from the mortal taint that haunts the frailer loveliness of flesh and blood—if, I say, it were given to man to see the heavenly beauty face to face, would you call *his,* she asked me, an unenviable life, whose eyes had been opened to the vision, and who had gazed upon it in true contemplation until it had become his own forever?
>
> And remember, she said, that it is only when he discerns beauty itself through what makes it visible that a man will be quickened with the true and not the seeming virtue—for it is virtue's self that quickens him, not virtue's semblance. And when he has brought forth and reared this perfect virtue, he shall be called the friend of god, and if ever it is given to man to put on immortality, it shall be given to him.[30]

According to Plato, gazing on beauty bare is only fruitful for those who are willing to perform virtuous labors and to die like Socrates for the truth that lies behind the facade of visible beauty. In *Cymbeline,* a play much concerned with appearance versus reality, the voyeur Iachimo is deeply affected by Imogen's naked beauty, but he does not at first either comprehend or attempt to imitate her virtue, that inner quality of a person reflecting true beauty. I shall return to this point later, since a Christian poet may be expected to add a new dimension to the crucial pagan scene of gazing on beauty bare.

A modern psychoanalytic interpretation of the tale of Cupid and Psyche in the mode of Carl Jung is that of Erich Neumann, who sees the story as an initiation myth concerned with the maturing of both the human female and the feminine soul of man. Neumann observes that in order to become an adult woman—or allegorically a soul worthy of immortality—the gentle but overly curious Psyche must move from easy feminine despair at every setback to recognition of the innate masculine strength and courage within herself. She must also gain direct knowledge of the opposing male principle outside herself. And she must be willing to sacrifice herself to it as a bride in order to rule emotionally over the male principle in the end as wife.[31]

> After becoming conscious of her masculine components and realizing them, and having become whole through development of her masculine aspect, Psyche was in a position to confront the totality of the Great Mother in her twofold aspect as Aphrodite-Persephone. The end of this confrontation was the paradoxical victory-defeat of Psyche's failure with which she regained not only an Eros transformed into a man, but also her contact with her own central feminine self. (Neumann 1956, 136)

Thus, in contemporary psychological terms, Psyche achieves bliss through completing her rite of passage from unknowing passivity to knowing actor, from being served and adored by Cupid and his invisible servants to serving Amor and actively adoring his divinity. Love can then espouse Psyche as an equal. This journey to self-realization, Neumann explains,

> leads through suffering and death, sacrifice and annihilation to renewal, rebirth, and immortality. But such transformation is possible only when what is to be transformed enters wholly into the feminine principle; that is to say, dies in returning to the Mother Vessel, whether this be earth, water, underworld, urn, coffin, cave, mountain, ship, or magic cauldron . . . in every case renewal is possible only through the death of the old personality.[32]

Neumann's sensitive modern analysis, as well as earlier Christian and humanist interpretations of the myth, can help us to comprehend today what Shakespeare himself was attempting through his own meticulous reconstruction of the Cupid and Psyche story within *Cymbeline*.

Apuleius provided the Renaissance with the basic pattern of union, loss, search, and reunion typical of the soul's ascent to self-realization or divinity. The pattern, as I see it, includes the following nine elements, all of which are also present in Shakespeare's *Cymbeline:*

1. A base marriage, which involves danger for the bride, is celebrated.
2. One of the partners soon doubts the other's love.
3. Someone (the bride or a representative of the groom) partially gains

forbidden knowledge through entering a dark and sacred chamber with a light and illicitly gazing at naked beauty.
4. Such profanation results in the separation of bride and groom.
5. The bride makes a journey of atonement in search of her spouse.
6. She undergoes an initiation through labors and through a descent to the underworld or to a cave.
7. She opens a casket or jar containing the ultimate mystery, death, and falls into a deathlike sleep from which she later awakens.
8. The husband asks Jupiter for help or for the divine grace necessary to immortalize a mortal soul.
9. Bride and groom are happily reunited, and family peace is restored.

Shakespeare transforms and thus partially conceals the myth of Cupid and Psyche through the techniques of fragmentation and inversion, much as a composer varies a musical theme. However, despite the dramatist's obvious variations, the nine basic elements of the feminine quest pattern are clearly maintained in the Imogen plot of *Cymbeline*. This practice in literature is what Northrop Frye terms myth "displacement."[33]

Many details in *Cymbeline* echo the Cupid and Psyche tale in *The Golden Ass*. First, like Psyche, Imogen is a feminine soul figure, who is later termed "my soul" by Posthumus. Second, as Psyche's beauty rivaled that of Venus, Imogen is called "Cytherea" by Iachimo, and her beauty is considered "divine" by the courtiers. Moreover, Posthumus unwisely boasts of her beauty at a drinking party in Rome. Fearing that the princess has aroused the jealousy of the Great Goddess in the form of Juno, Posthumus's servant Pisanio advises Imogen to "forget / Your laboursome and dainty trimes, wherein / You made great Juno angry" (3.4.165–67). Like Psyche, Imogen becomes an "unknowing" but willing prisoner of an adored but still unworthy husband. Before he leaves England, Posthumus places a gold bracelet on her arm with the words, "For my sake wear this, / It is a manacle of love, I'll place it / Upon this fairest prisoner" (1.2.53–54). Separated from her husband, Psyche frequently gives in to despair and attempts to commit suicide on several occasions. In a like manner, Imogen admits to Cymbeline that without Posthumus she is "Past hope and in despair, that way past grace" (1.2.68). She also begs Pisanio to kill her after she learns of Posthumus's betrayal. Just as Venus in the role of a cruel mother-in-law hopes the four labors will destroy Psyche, Imogen's wicked stepmother hopes that the princess will eventually succumb to despair and die: "Haply, despair hath seiz'd her" (3.5.61). Just to make sure, the Queen prepares poison for Imogen, claiming it is medicine. In *The Golden Ass* Venus sends Psyche to fetch Proserpina's beauty secret from Hades, knowing full well that Psyche's native curiosity will cause her to open the casket and fall prey to the sleep of death.

In order to gain the courage to see the true form of her husband against his wishes, Psyche transforms herself psychologically into a man. When she enters the bedroom with a razor and a lamp, Apuleius tells us that "by her audacitie she chaunged her kinde [gender]" (sig. Pᵛ). When Imogen plans her journey to Wales in *Cymbeline,* Pisanio actually advises her to metamorphose her sex:

> You must forget to be a woman: change
> Command into obedience: fear, and niceness
> (The handmaids of all women, or, more truly,
> Woman it pretty self) into a waggish courage,
> Ready in gibes, quick-answer'd, saucy, and
> As quarrelsome as the weasel.
>
> (3.4.156–61)

In the case of Imogen, Shakespeare employs the popular stage convention of disguising a woman as a man to literalize the metaphor of sex change and to emphasize visually one of his fundamental themes: the possibility of change or metamorphosis.

Imogen then sets off in quest of her husband, who at this point resembles possessive Eros but is definitely not as godlike as she had previously believed, in an interesting inversion of the myth. Another inversion occurs when Posthumus, believing his wife to be an adulteress, orders Pisanio to murder her whereas it is Psyche who plans to kill Cupid in *The Golden Ass.* But, just as Psyche discovers the weariness of ordinary human life within nature after Venus orders her to separate innumerable seeds into orderly piles (symbolizing the intellectual process of classification or the use of reason rather than passion), Imogen must travel alone through wild mountains to gain news of Posthumus. During this ordeal she says plaintively, "I see man's life is a tedious one" (3.6.1). Although she is once more nearly overcome with despair during her journey, she—like Psyche—learns that the meaning of life is to serve others, first by cooking for Belarius and the savage boys in their cave, and later by becoming a page for the Roman general Lucius, her country's enemy.

In *The Golden Ass* Psyche is advised by a divinely inspired reed, at the onset of her second labor, not to drown herself in despair and not to go in quest of the golden fleece until evening:

> Psyches I pray thee not to trouble or pollute my water by the deathe of thee, and yet beware that thou goe not towardes the terrible sheepe of this coaste, untill suche time as the heate of the Sunne be paste; for when the Sunne is in his force, then seeme they most dreadfull, and furious, with their sharpe hornes, their stony forheades, & their gaping throtes wherewith they arme them selues to the destruction of mankinde: but untill they haue refreshed them selues in the riuer, thou mayst hide thy selfe here by me vnder this great plane tree. (57ᵛ–58)

This passage has clear echoes in the dirge sung by Guiderius and Arviragus after the apparent death of Imogen in 4, 2, of *Cymbeline,* "Fear no more the heat of the sun," with its curious reminder that, "To thee the reed is as the oak," which is to say "oracular." The emblematist Otto van Veen also quotes Apuleius on the heat of the sun, which he sees as analogous to intemperate love. Under the motto "First pleasant & afterward painful," van Veen's verse states that,

> Eu'n as the Sun yeilds ioy when it beginnes to rise,
> And at noontyde doth scortche in greatnesse of his heat,
> So loue appeering first, yeilds pleasure passing great,
> But burning in his rage, there payn for pleasure lyes.

(222–23)

The jealous rage of both Posthumus and Cloten in *Cymbeline* does indeed change the pleasure of love into pain for Imogen.

Apuleius then tells us that Psyche must climb a rocky mountain to fetch a bottle of water from the River Styx. She achieves this through the aid of Jupiter's eagle, a bird that also appears in *Cymbeline*. Imogen, on her way to the port of Milford Haven, climbs up to the rocky cave of Belarius in the Welsh mountains. There she spends the night in the cave, which is similar to a descent to the underworld or a return to the earth's womb-tomb, much as Psyche's final labor is to enter into Hades and fetch back to Venus a box of beauty secrets from Proserpina, queen of the underworld. Like Psyche, Imogen carries with her a casket of an underworld queen's medicine, for it seems quite possible that Shakespeare's wicked Queen is meant to be a death figure, or what Neumann calls the archetypal "Terrible Mother," throughout the play. Later succumbing to heart-sickness and despair, Imogen emerges from the cave and opens the little casket. She falls into a deathlike sleep after taking the Queen's medicine, which fortunately has been previously rendered harmless by the physician Cornelius, one who knows that the Queen makes only poisons. At this point, both Imogen and Psyche appear to others "as a sleeping corpes" (Apuleius 1571, 60). Although Psyche is revived by a harmless prick from Cupid's arrow, Imogen later awakens naturally when the drug wears off, only to discover the headless body of Cloten lying by her side.

The corpse of Cloten, Shakespeare's figuration of wanton Eros and of Orpheus, is a stage emblem of the inevitability of death in the natural world. "Stripped of all that is private and individual, the corpse is not simply a dead character, but a warning to others to learn certain truths from his death; the corpse is an emblem that instructs."[34] However, Imogen naively believes the corpse to be Posthumus since it is dressed in her husband's clothes, and she falls beside or upon it and embraces the very lustful beast she most loathes. But in a sense, the body is also that of the jealous Posthumus who has interpreted love as possession and who, like Cloten, has wanted to kill Imogen. Apuleius tells us that Psyche, on the way to cut off Cupid's head, "sometime she hateth the beast, sometime she loveth her husband" (sig. Pᵛ). She then discovers that the beast is in reality a fair youth. Similarly, Imogen at last discovers that the limbs of the beast Cloten are actually as beautiful as those of Posthumus. It was the inner man who was beastly. Thus, both heroines learn that human love is at the same time beastly and beautiful, profane and sacred. In addition, both heroines gain direct knowledge of that final mystery, death, before they are reborn and granted the bliss of fully realized love and marriage.

Despite these obvious similarities between the stories, Shakespeare wished the myth of Cupid and Psyche to remain implicit, carefully buried in mosaic fragments beneath the rich surface texture of *Cymbeline*, as the inner Neoplatonic idea of his tragicomedy. Since this message must be hidden from ordinary sight as the soul is hidden within the body, Shakespeare not only inverted certain elements of the story, as I have already suggested, but he also fragmented the personality of Cupid among the characters in the play. For example, Imogen plays both major roles on occasion—that of Psyche and that of Amor. She does not see the love god but is herself seen asleep by Iachimo. In *The Golden Ass* Psyche leans over the beautiful body of Cupid, "at whose sight the very lampe, encreased his lighte for ioye" (sig. Pii). Peering down at Imogen's naked beauty, Iachimo states in *Cymbeline* that "the flame i' th' taper / Bows toward her, and would under-peep her lids, / To see th' enclosed lights" (2.2.19–20). Here a vice figure gains intimations of immortality. Similarly, Belarius, on first seeing Imogen in her masculine disguise, exclaims, "Behold divineness / No elder than a boy!" (3.7.16–17). This speech unmistakably equates Imogen with Amor, the pagan god of love, who is first seen disguised as a page in Virgil's *Aeneid* when Venus "decided to make Cupid assume the form and features of the charming Ascanius, and go in place of him; he should give Dido the presents, and as he did so enflame her with a distraction of love, and entwine the fire of it about her very bones."[35]

The ambivalent character of Apuleius's Cupid is further fragmented between Cloten and Posthumus. As Venus in *The Golden Ass* wants Psyche to marry the vilest creature in the world, the Queen in *Cymbeline* wishes Imogen to marry her loutish son Cloten, who is called an "ass" several times in the play. Cupid arranges for invisible musicians to serenade Psyche;[36] Cloten, too, serenades the object of his sexual desire and tries to "penetrate" her by means of hired musicians whom Imogen never sees. But, according to Plato's *Phaedrus* and *Symposium,* lust must be spiritualized if the soul is to ascend ultimately from profane to divine love. Cupid is punished by his mother for his disorderly sexual behavior, and

Cloten, when he pursues Imogen to rape her, is killed by Guiderius. Interest then shifts in *Cymbeline* to Posthumus, who is as deeply wounded by Iachimo's slander as is Cupid by Psyche's disobedience. When Posthumus believes Imogen to be dead, he finally realizes the depth of his love for her and undergoes a religious conversion or a spiritual metamorphosis: "So I'll die / For thee, O Imogen, even for whom my life / Is, every breath a death" (5.1.25–27). In *Cymbeline* the would-be rapist Cloten plays the role of wanton Cupid along with his double Posthumus, while the converted Posthumus later plays the role of Amor, once he believes his lady to be dead and learns the true meaning of reciprocal love. The two young men resemble the two aspects—profane lust and divine love—of Cupid, who is first called Cupido by Apuleius but later wins the name Amor in the romance.

The point in both *The Golden Ass* and *Cymbeline* is that an "ass" like Apuleius's Lucius or Shakespeare's Cloten-Posthumus can finally grow up, undergo a painful initiation, change his mode of thinking, and become a new person worthy of beauty and of true love. However, this requires a spiritual conversion. As James Tatum states,

> *The Golden Ass* confronts us with a conversion that is apparently only one final instance of metamorphosis. The logic of this connection is easy to see. "Metamorphosis" is literally a change of form, "conversion" a change of soul. In *The Golden Ass* the first phenomenon leads inexorably to the second—from a narrative that has been the exclusive concern of the literary scholar to one that the historian of religion has marked as his own. But in this novel no sharp distinction need be drawn between metamorphosis and conversion; indeed, the text of *The Golden Ass* does not require us to separate the two. In Book 11 metamorphosis simply serves as a metaphor for spiritual change.[37]

Much the same can be said for *Cymbeline* and the sudden conversion of Posthumus after seeing the bloody cloth sent him by Pisanio as proof of Imogen's death.

It is particularly significant that the god Jupiter performs the role of *deus ex machina* in both works. The god promises Amor and Posthumus ultimate marital bliss with the ladies they have chosen to love. Psyche is immortalized; Imogen is restored to the royal court of Cymbeline, who then makes peace with Rome. Cymbeline's kingdom is now ready for a demonstration of that divine love for the world signified by the birth of Christ in Bethlehem. As the soothsayer Philarmonus says, "The fingers of the powers above do tune / The harmony of this peace" (5.5.467–68), lines that seem to echo Adlington's translation of the same harmonious moment in *The Golden Ass*. At the marriage banquet of Cupid and Psyche,

> the Muses sange with sweete harmony, Apollo tuned pleasauntly to the Harpe, fair Venus daunced finely: Satirus and Paniscus plaide on their pipes: and thus

Psyches was married to Cupide, and after she was deliuered of a childe, whom
we call Pleasure. (61)

In theological terms, as the doctrine of the Incarnation infuses earth or the
body with divinity for the Christian era, so the fertility music of the pipes
of Pan and Satyrus are permitted on this sacred occasion in the classical
world to mingle with the divine music of Apollo's finely tuned strings.
Marriage is simultaneously sacred and profane. The result is *Concordia
mundi* and the reconciliation of Apollo with Dionysos and Pan during the
marriage ceremony on Olympus.

Nevertheless, I believe that the key scene for all of this in both Apuleius
and Shakespeare is not the reunion of the lovers but an earlier one—the
moment of gazing on beauty bare, a scene that also occurs in most
versions of Shakespeare's most obvious plot source, the wager story. In
Cymbeline, as in *The Decameron* and in *Frederyke of Jennen,* it is the
villain rather than the heroine who gazes on naked beauty. The important
factor in Apuleius's version of the scene is Psyche's transformation. She is
diverted from murdering her mysterious bridegroom and is metamorphosed by the sight of Cupid's divine beauty into a person capable of
self-criticism and of self-annihilating love. In contrast, the villain in Boccaccio's ninth novel of the second day and his counterpart in *Frederyke of
Jennen* are in no way changed by the sight of the nude wife they spy on,
any more than Shakespeare's devilish Iago is moved in *Othello* by the sight
of the half-nude but chaste Desdemona strangled on her marriage bed. His
evil objective achieved, Iago simply vows never to speak again—in a
devilish inversion of Platonic or Augustinian silence.

In *Cymbeline,* on the other hand, Shakespeare's villain Iachimo is
slowly but surely transformed by the sight of Imogen, whose beauty at
first arouses him to carnal desire in true Neoplatonic fashion: "How
bravely thou becom'st thy bed! fresh lily! / And whiter than the sheets!
That I might touch!" (2.2.15–16). The forbidden sight makes him at once
aware of the evil in his own behavior, always the first step toward contrition
and change: "I lodge in fear; / Though this a heavenly angel, hell is here"
(2.2.49–50). Although Iachimo still continues in his hellish plot to win
Imogen's diamond ring from Posthumus, he is later overcome with ease—
in a symbolic hand-to-hand combat, a dumbshow of the battle of good
versus evil—by a converted Posthumus, who is now dressed as a humble
peasant (5.2). As Posthumus has previously done, Iachimo at last confesses his faults to the audience:

> The heaviness and guilt within my bosom
> Takes off my manhood: I have belied a lady,
> The princess of this country; and the air on't
> Revengingly enfeebles me.
>
> (5.2.1–4)

In act 5, scene 5, Iachimo publicly admits he has lied about Imogen's virtue, when he tells Cymbeline,

> well may you, sir,
> Remember me at court, where I was taught
> Of your chaste daughter the wide difference
> 'Twixt amorous and villanous.

(5.5.192–95)

Beauty has finally led to truth in this tragicomedy. Iachimo then begs Posthumus to forgive his treachery, as he has previously spared the villain's life on the battlefield: "But now my heavy conscience sinks my knee, / As then your force did" (5.5.414–15). We can be sure that the pricks of conscience aroused by Beauty are something new for Iachimo and distinguish him notably from the earlier Iago.

In distinct contrast to all previous versions of the wager story, Shakespeare's *Cymbeline* ends with the hero's forgiveness of Iachimo, which then inspires the king to pardon everyone else. This difference is enormous. It separates *Cymbeline* from the commercial cynicism of the wager story and firmly moves it from chronological time into the realm of sacred history, hence into the metaphysical world of its hidden substructure, the myth of Cupid and Psyche. Other versions of the wager story conclude with horrendous punishments for the villain. In *The Decameron,* for example, the peeping Tom is "bounded to the stake and anointed with honey . . . devoured, of the flies and wasps and gadflies . . . even to the bones, which latter, waxed white and hanging by the sinews, being left unremoved, long bore witness of his villainy to all who saw them."[38] In *Frederyke of Jennen,* the slanderer's head is cut off and placed on a stake, while the body is laid over a wheel. In *Cymbeline,* however, Posthumus firmly practices true Christian charity toward the villain, even though the audience really does not wish to see Iachimo pardoned and may even doubt that Iachimo is truly repentant.

Shakespeare's point seems to be that charity as mercy is indeed emotionally difficult to practice in the real world, the vengeful world of terrestrial Venus. To forgive their enemies, foolish mortals all need help from a benevolent Jupiter, who symbolizes the necessary divine grace both in Shakespeare's play and in Apuleius's philosophical myth told in a cave by a mysterious old woman. Drunk though she may be, this old woman resembles Plato's Diotima in her profound understanding of Beauty, Goodness, Truth, and Justice, and their relationship to Love, or the desire for all the above. Likewise, Shakespeare's play demonstrates how Imogen's beauty and goodness lead to truth at last and inspire the practice of equity (mercy or the very heart of Justice) by those in power.

Carl Schlam observes that the myth of Cupid and Psyche "is placed by Apuleius at the center of the *Metamorphoses,* a work in which multiplicity and shifts in perspective are essential to the author's thought and technique. His announced subject is change. His final vision is of a divine stability which pervades and transcends the shifting fortunes and appearances of human experience."[39] I think we could say much the same for Shakespeare's *Cymbeline*. Through his eclectic interweaving of the wager story, a moral "thriller" that also originated in the classical world, with the later exquisite Neoplatonic myth of Cupid and Psyche, Shakespeare reconstructs both stories to work together within the new and complex genre of Renaissance tragicomedy in order to dramatize the effects of gazing on beauty bare. The result has considerable cultural resonance.

Notes

1. See Knight, *The Crown of Life* (Oxford: Clarendon Press, 1947), 183.

2. See Thompson, "Philomel in 'Titus Andronicus' and 'Cymbeline'," *Shakespeare Survey* 31 (1978): 29, n.2.

3. See Marjorie Garber, "Shakespeare and the Languages of Myth," *Mosaic* 10 (1977): 105–15; and Joan Carr, "*Cymbeline* and the Validity of Myth," *Studies in Philology* 75 (1978): 316–30.

4. See Mowat, "Lavinia's Message: Shakespeare and Myth," *Renaissance Papers* (1981): 67. Mowat explains that she is "using 'mythologem' here in the sense suggested by C. Kerenyi. Kerenyi says that the content of mythology is 'a body of material contained in tales about gods and god-like beings, heroic battles and journeys to the Underworld—mythologem is the best Greek word for them—tales already well known but not amenable to further re-shaping,' " 58, n.5. See "Prolegomena," *Essays on a Science of Mythology* by C. G. Jung and C. Kerenyi, trans. R. F. C. Hull (Princeton, N.J.: Princeton University Press, 1969), 2.

5. See Charles Trinkaus, *In Our Image and Likeness: Humanity and Divinity in Italian Humanist Thought,* 2 vols. (London: Constable & Co., Ltd., 1970), vol. 2, 689; hereafter cited parenthetically.

6. See Wind, *Pagan Mysteries in the Renaissance: An Exploration of Philosophical and Mystical Sources of Iconography in Renaissance Art,* 2d ed., rev. and enl. (New York and London: W. W. Norton & Co., 1968), 25; hereafter cited parenthetically.

7. See Richard Linche, "Venus," *The Fountaine of Ancient Fiction* (London: Adam Islip, 1599), sign. C c ij^v.

8. Quoted by John Warden, "Orpheus and Ficino," in *Orpheus: The Metamorphoses of a Myth,* ed. John Warden (Toronto: University of Toronto Press, 1982), 102.

9. Ian Donaldson, *The Rapes of Lucretia: A Myth and its Transformations* (Oxford: Clarendon Press, 1982), 53–54.

10. See *The Rape of Lucrece* in *The Riverside Shakespeare*.

11. Donaldson, 52.

12. Ibid., figure 10.

13. See Soellner, "Shakespeare's *Lucrece* and the Garnier-Pembroke Connection," *Shakespeare Studies* 15 (1982): 12.

14. Otto van Veen, *Amorvm Emblemata or Emblemes of Loue* (Antwerp, 1608), 68–69; hereafter cited parenthetically. The English verses in this emblem book

were written by Richard Verstegen, according to Samuel C. Chew, "Richard Verstegan and the *Amorvm Emblemata* of Otho van Veen," *The Huntington Library Quarterly* 8 (1944–45): 192–99.

15. Quoted in Barbara Lewalski, *Protestant Poetics and the Seventeenth Century Religious Lyric* (Princeton, N.J.: Princeton University Press, 1979), 6.

16. See my "Eros and Anteros in Shakespeare's Sonnets 153 and 154: An Iconographical Study," *Spenser Studies* 7 (1987): 261–86 and 311–22.

17. J. A. Mazzeo, *Renaissance and Seventeenth-Century Studies* (New York: Columbia University Press, 1964), 22.

18. For the bed valances, see Plate 34 in Preston Remington, *English Domestic Needlework* (New York: The Metropolitan Museum of Art, 1945). According to Yvonne Hackenbroch, "The story of Philomela from Ovid's *Metamorphoses* was curiously appropriate to needlework, with Philomela considered as a patron of this art. The choice of that story may have been suggested by George Gascoigne's free rendering in English, *The complaynt of Phylomene,* published 1576, followed a generation later by Sir Philip Sidney's sonnet 'The Nightingale'." See *English and other Needlework: Tapestries and Textiles in the Irwin Untermyer Collection* (London: Thames and Hudson, 1960), xviii.

19. For Orpheus as prophet, see Warden, 101.

20. See Hartwig, *Shakespeare's Tragicomic Vision* (Baton Rouge: Louisiana State University Press, 1972), 70.

21. See Hartwig, *Shakespeare's Analogical Scene: Parody as Structural Syntax* (Lincoln and London: University of Nebraska Press, 1983), 192 and 175.

22. See Sister M. Generosa, "Apuleius and *A Midsummer Night's Dream:* Analogue or Source, Which?" *Studies in Philology* 42 (1945): 198–204; James A. S. McPeek, "The Psyche Myth and *A Midsummer Night's Dream,*" *Shakespeare Quarterly* 23 (1972): 69–79; and Deborah Baker Wyrick, "The Ass Motif in *The Comedy of Errors* and *A Midsummer Night's Dream,*" *Shakespeare Quarterly* 33 (1982): 433–48. See also Michael Lloyd, "Cleopatra and Isis," *Shakespeare Quarterly* 12 (1959): 88–94; and J. M. Tobin, *Shakespeare's Favorite Novel: A Study of "The Golden Asse" As Prime Source* (Lanham, Md.: University Press of America, 1984).

23. See Herman Reich, "Zur Quelle des 'Cymbeline'," *Shakespeare Jahrbuch* 41 (1905): 177–81; and Dewitt T. Starnes, "Shakespeare and Apuleius," *PMLA* 60 (1945): 1021–50.

24. Reprinted by John P. Collier, *The History of English Dramatic Poetry in the Time of Shakespeare* (London, 1831), 329.

25. See Cope, *The Theater and the Dream: From Metaphor to Form in Renaissance Drama* (Baltimore and London: The Johns Hopkins University Press, 1973), 174. See also Cope's extended discussion of Heywood's play, 173–96, and Thomas Heywood, *Love's Mistress,* or *The Queen's Masque,* ed. Raymond C. Shady (Salzburg: Institut für Englische Sprache und Literatur, 1977).

26. Lucius Apuleius, *The XI Bookes of the "Golden Ass" conteિginge the Metamorphosie of Lucius Apuleius,* trans. William Adlington (London: William How, for Abraham Veale, 1571), 41; hereafter cited parenthetically.

27. See *Fulgentius the Mythographer,* trans. Leslie George Whitbread (Columbus: Ohio State University Press, 1971), 88–90.

28. See Luisa Vertova, "Cupid and Psyche in Renaissance Painting Before Raphael," *Journal of the Warburg and Courtauld Institutes* 42 (1979): 106.

29. Ibid., 115.

30. Plato, *Symposium* 211e and 212a, trans. Michael Joyce, in *The Collected*

Dialogues of Plato, ed. Edith Hamilton and Huntington Cairns (1963; rpt. New York: Pantheon Books, 1966), 563.

31. See Neumann, *Amor and Psyche: The Psychic Development of the Feminine,* trans. Ralph Mannheim (New York: Pantheon Books, 1956), 108–10.

32. See Neumann, *The Great Mother,* 2d. ed., trans. Ralph Mannheim (Princeton, N.J.: Princeton University Press, 1963), 291–92.

33. See Frye, *Anatomy of Criticism: Four Essays* (Princeton, N.J.: Princeton University Press, 1957), 136.

34. See Daly, *Literature in the Light of the Emblem* (Toronto: University of Toronto Press, 1979), 147.

35. Virgil, *The Aeneid,* trans. W. F. Jackson Knight (Baltimore: Penguin Books, 1956), 47.

36. I suspect that the invisible musicians in *The Golden Ass* are a source for the similar unseen musicians in Shakespeare's *The Tempest.*

37. Tatum, *Apuleius and "The Golden Ass": Eleven Books of Metamorphoses* (Ithaca and London: Cornell University Press, 1979), 29.

38. Giovanni Boccaccio, *The Decameron,* trans. John Payne (New York: The Modern Library, n.d.), 191.

39. See Schlam, *Cupid and Psyche: Apuleius and the Monuments* (University Park, Penn.: The American Philological Association, 1976), 3.

3

The Iconography of Imogen's Bedchamber

And the true order of going, or being led by another, to the things of love, is to begin from the beauties of earth and mount upwards for the sake of that other beauty, using these steps only, and from one going on to two, and from two to all fair forms to fair practices, and from fair practices to fair notions he arrives at the notion of absolute beauty, and at last knows what the essence of beauty is.

—*Symposium* 211

After illicitly entering the bedchamber of England's princess in act 2, scene 2, of *Cymbeline,* Iachimo notes down various particulars of the room and of the sleeping form of Imogen as proof he has been there. When he later repeats these details to Posthumus (2.4) in an effort to persuade Imogen's bridegroom of her infidelity, we discover that the decorations of the chamber are predominantly inspired by classical myths known to have had profound religious and philosophical meanings to the educated members of a Renaissance audience. As Jean Seznec points out, "in the light of Neoplatonism, the humanists discovered in mythology something other and much greater than a concealed morality; they discovered religious teaching—the Christian doctrine itself."[1] The results in art, however, require a roundabout investigation of the Renaissance meanings of pagan deities and heroic adventures in order to decipher the inner Christian and Neoplatonic significance of the myth or myths referred to by the artist.

Iachimo's formal ekphrasis or description of Imogen's bedchamber in 2.2 invites our careful reconsideration of what we have probably seen already in the stage setting but may not as yet have understood.[2] The problem is that his description is highly allusive and suggestive rather than specific or directly allegorical, which makes analysis difficult. In 2.2 he also apostrophizes the beauty of the sleeping Imogen, whose body itself then becomes part of the significance of the bedchamber in conjunction with its decorations. However, in both cases Iachimo merely reports on the room and the woman but does not interpret what he has seen, relying on the latent erotic content of the decorations themselves and on the

95

memory of Imogen's female beauty to inflame and corrupt the imagination of a jealous Posthumus. In the parlance of modern advertising, this technique of slandering Imogen through circumstantial erotic evidence is known as selling the package instead of the product.

In this chapter I shall investigate the meaning and/or meanings of the major decorative images in the bedchamber as the dramatist expected his audience to understand them in contrast to the incorrect surface readings of wanton eroticism implied by Iachimo and accepted by Posthumus. I shall argue here that the bedchamber was actually designed to represent a Renaissance Temple of the Graces and therefore is a suitable resting place for Beauty, or the third Grace, in the form of Princess Imogen. As art historians have abundantly demonstrated, such elaborate iconographic programs for both state and private rooms were very common during this historical period in Europe and England. I shall also demonstrate that the Cleopatra tapestry on one wall of the room represents the goddesses Venus and Isis who preside over natural generation and who symbolize the Neoplatonic notion of "the Many in the One"; that the fireplace with its bas-relief of Diana bathing above the mantel and the two Cupid andirons below is a visual oxymoron of chaste passion, a reconciliation of opposites that can be achieved in marriage; that the beautiful woman asleep in her bed—while Iachimo notes down all the surrounding particulars—is symbolic of that celestial Platonic Beauty (analogous to Truth, Goodness, and Justice), which cannot be ultimately understood through the senses but only through the intellect; and finally that the ceiling of "fretted cherubins" arching overhead is a visual allusion to the unheard harmony of the universe and of the approaching Nativity of Christ.

The critical assumption that lies behind this iconographic interpretation of Imogen's bedchamber is our understanding that the Pythagorean cosmos still envisioned during the sixteenth century by Neoplatonists (and so beautifully reflected in this and other Shakespearean plays) was what S. K. Heninger describes as "a network of correspondent forms."[3] Since the meaningful and harmonious interrelationship between the things in this world, between the visible Images of them and the invisible Ideas they reflect, was taken for granted by Renaissance artists and spectators alike, Shakespeare could employ the techniques of suggestion and allusion, rather than elaborate allegory, to communicate the iconographical significance of Imogen's bedchamber to an alert Jacobean audience.

Cleopatra on Her Barge

Iachimo begins his description of the room to Posthumus and the other gentlemen at Philario's Roman banquet as follows:

                        First, her bedchamber,
(Where I confess I slept not, but profess
Had that was well worth watching) it was hang'd
With tapestry of silk and silver, the story
Proud Cleopatra, when she met her Roman,
And Cydnus swell'd above the banks, or for
The press of boats, or pride. A piece of work
So bravely done, so rich, that it did strive
In workmanship and value; which I wonder'd
Could be so rarely and exactly wrought,
Since the true life on't was—

                                                            (2.4.66–76)

This tapestry, whose realism so impresses the intruder, would have been comparatively rare at the time *Cymbeline* was written since the subject matter was only just coming into vogue among weavers. W. G. Thomson records that the Widow Geubles, one of the most famous tapestry weavers in Brussels, may have introduced the subject of Antony and Cleopatra, which enjoyed great popularity during the later seventeenth century: "In 1607, eight panels representing the *History of Cleopatra* left her looms, the price being 4147 livres."[4] When an inventory was made of the British royal furnishings in 1695 after the death of Mary, Queen of William III, it revealed "5 peeces of hangings of *Cleopatra* 9 foote" in the Standing Wardrobe at St. James Palace, "Eight peeces of Good Tapestry of the Story of Cleopatra Lined with Canvas" in the Hampton Court Wardrobe, and "9 peeces of Cleopatra" in the Windsor Wardrobe.[5] Shakespeare, as a member of the King's Men, may well have seen an early example of one or more of these pieces at the court of James I.

    In fact, such a costly tapestry might even have been borrowed by the acting company to serve as a symbolic backcloth for the bedroom scene in *Cymbeline,* whether performed at Blackfriars or the Globe. During the reign of Queen Elizabeth, such borrowing had apparently been common practice for the production of masques during the Christmas Revels at the Inns of Court. For example, Marie Axton reports that for the Revels of 1566/67, in hopes of persuading Queen Elizabeth to marry,

> George Gascoigne also translated Lodovico Dolce's version of the *Thebiad* and set this contention between Eteocles and Polynices for the throne of Oedipus within his own framework. The Templars had asked for a similar contemporary application of the Theban conflict in their 1561 revels when Desire, the natural mate for Lady Beauty, stood beside a tapestry depicting the miseries brought to Thebes by Oedipus' unnatural marriage.[6]

An Oedipus tapestry had evidently been borrowed by the Templars from a fellow Templar or a friend for their 1561 masque in order to accentuate through iconographic symbolism their political message to the Queen.

The Cleopatra tapestry in Imogen's bedchamber evokes memories of what was vividly described by Enobarbus in Shakespeare's *Antony and Cleopatra* (c.1606–1607) and was well known to readers of Plutarch's *Lives:*

> The barge she sat in, like a burnish'd throne,
> Burnt on the water. The poop was beaten gold,
> Purple the sails, and so perfumed that
> The winds were love-sick with them; the oars were silver,
> Which to the tune of flutes kept stroke, and made
> The water which they beat to follow faster,
> As amorous of their strokes. For her own person,
> It beggar'd all description: she did lie
> In her pavilion—cloth of gold, of tissue—
> O'er-picturing that Venus where we see
> The fancy outwork nature. On each side her
> Stood pretty dimpled boys, like smiling Cupids,
> With divers-color'd fans, whose wind did seem
> To [glow] the delicate cheeks which they did cool,
> And what they undid did.

(2.2.191–205)

We should notice the implied comparison here between Cleopatra and the *Venus genetrix* of Lucretius's *De rerum natura,* possibly via Spenser's *Fairie Queene,* as Barbara J. Bono has argued.[7] Bono further calls our attention to the fact that "Earth, water, air, and fire all amorously follow Cleopatra" (1984, 172) in this sensuous description of a mortal playing the role of a goddess. Reclining in state on her barge, Cleopatra becomes here a symbol of Nature and of the primeval emergence from water of Venus herself, whose beauty is also Imogen's.

At the end of Shakespeare's *Antony and Cleopatra,* the Egyptian queen consciously assumes as well the role of the goddess Isis, ruling deity of Apuleius's *The Golden Ass.* But the rising of Isis from the sea to save Lucius from his animal existence in *The Golden Ass* is clearly prefigured by Cleopatra's earlier journey down the Nile in 40 B.C. to her waiting Dionysos, Mark Antony, at Tarsos. According to William S. Heckscher, in her Nile triumph Cleopatra carefully imitated Apelles's still extant painting of the *Anadyomene* or the Birth of Venus, and "combined on this occasion the theme of the emerging goddess [Aphrodite Anadyomene] with that of the regal *Adventus.*"[8] When Isis emerges from the sea in *The Golden Ass,* she, too, identifies herself with Venus and with all other aspects of the Great Goddess.

> I am she that is the natural mother of all thinges, mistris and gouernesse of all the Elementes . . . my diuinitie is adored throughout all the worlde, in divers manners, in variable customes, and in many names for the Phrigiens call mee

the mother of the Goddes: the Athenians, Minerue: the Cipriens, Venus: the Candians, Diana: the Scicilians, Proserpina: the Eleusians, Ceres: some Iuno, other Bellona, other Hecate: and principally the Ethiopians, whiche dwell in the Orient, and the Egiptians whiche are excellente in all kinde of aunciente doctrine, and by theyr proper Ceremonies accustome to worshippe me doo call me Queene Isis.[9]

It is this same all-encompassing goddess who arranges for the religious initiation through the traditional four elements of earth, air, fire, and water for Lucius in *The Golden Ass* to prepare him to serve justice, who woos Mark Antony to imperial love from his military service to the Roman empire, and who seems to be currently arranging, along with Jupiter, certain spiritual initiations for the young spouses, Imogen and Posthumus, in *Cymbeline* in order to prepare them for the new era soon to begin in sacred history.

Referring to the earlier play *Antony and Cleopatra,* Michael Lloyd has demonstrated that Shakespeare must have been familiar not only with Plutarch's *Lives* but also with the same author's *De Iside et Osiride,* which provides a philosophical analysis of the ancient mystery cult of Isis and compares this cult to Greek beliefs.

Plutarch's account of Isis and Osiris was published in Philemon Holland's translation of the *Moralia* in 1603, and a reading of Holland's text encourages the view that Shakespeare had read it, and was echoing it in parts of [*Antony and Cleopatra*]. The first set of close verbal echoes clusters round the concept of motion. In the cult of Isis, motion has a metaphysical significance which may underlie the soothsayer's profession that he sees the future in his "motion" (II, iii, 14). For the Egyptians, we read in Holland, "have by reprochfull names noted such things as impeach hinder and staye the course of natural things, binding them so, as they cannot go forward" (p. 1311). Isis is, on the contrary, the goddess "of intelligence and motion together", and her name means "a motion animate and wise."[10]

Motion, of course, is life itself, suggesting growth and change, and, as I have previously suggested, a change in mental perspective, or inner reform, is a principal theme of Shakespeare's *Cymbeline*. Plutarch also observes that "Isis is the feminine part of nature, apt to receive all generation, upon which occasion called she is by *Plato,* the nurse and *Pandeches,* that is to say, capable of all."[11] Above all, however, Isis loves the Good and always follows it.

Mythology tells us that in her wanderings, Isis searches for the dismembered body of her divine brother and husband Osiris in order to reassemble it. Plutarch understands this activity as a kind of philosophical search and synthesis inherent to Nature:

there is imprinted in her naturally, a love of the first and principall essence, which is nothing else but the soveraigne good, and it she desireth, seeketh, and pursueth after. Contrariwise, she flieth and repelleth from her, any part and portion that proceedeth from ill. (Plutarch, *Isis* 1309)

These wanderings of Isis in search of her husband or what she believes to be the Good, and her repelling of evil will be imitated in *Cymbeline* by Imogen, who repels the lust of Cloten with vigor and who, like Isis, does indeed eventually find a dismembered body and grieves for its lost head, even though the corpse does not in fact belong to her beloved Posthumus but to his double, Cloten. In any case, a headless corpse symbolically represents the body alone—bereft of both intellect and the soul, or of man's higher nature.

Plutarch further comments on Egyptian beliefs about Isis: "and so they name the Moone, Mother of the World; saying, that she is a double nature, male and female" (1304). Imogen fulfills this hermaphroditic aspect of Cleopatra–Isis in the play when she disguises herself as a boy to begin her wanderings through Wales. According to Edmund Spenser in *The Faerie Queene,* the same double nature belongs to terrestrial Venus, who is veiled by her priests to hide her androgynous sexuality:

> But for, they say, she hath both kinds in one,
> Both male and female, both vnder one name:
> She syre and mother is her selfe alone,
> Begets and eke conceiues, ne needeth other none.[12]

(4.10.41)

The goddess—Isis or Venus—symbolizes, therefore, the central Neoplatonic idea of "the Many in the One," an image of mystical reunification after dismemberment that is essential to the Orphic ritual hidden within all true Renaissance tragicomedies.

Venus herself is Nature resurrected from the genitals of Uranus, which his son castrated and threw into the sea. As Edgar Wind observes, the mythic dismemberment of Uranus

> is of one type with the dismemberment of Osiris, Attis, Dionysus, all of which signify the same mystery to the neo-Orphic theologians: for whenever the supreme One descends to the Many, this act of creation is imagined as a sacrificial agony, as if the One were cut to pieces and scattered. Creation is conceived in this way as a cosmogonic death, by which the concentrated power of one deity is offered up and dispersed: but the descent and diffusion of the divine power are followed by its resurrection, when the Many are 'recollected' into the One.[13]

In respect to *Cymbeline,* I would suggest that the tapestry in Imogen's bedchamber representing Cleopatra–Isis–Venus riding in triumph on the waters of the Nile is symbolic of just that resurrection within nature of a dismembered god, a rebirth in the form of *Aphrodite Anadyomene* after the sacrificial death of Uranus, Dionysus, Osiris, or Christ. In this sense, it prefigures the death and resurrection of Imogen herself in act 4.

The Christian significance of the Antony and Cleopatra story is of course well known. Shakespeare has Octavius Caesar prophesy in *Antony and Cleopatra* that "The time of universal peace is near" (4.6.4). As Frank Kermode explains, "This was 'the Augustan peace' during which Christ was born and the pagan Empire—which Virgil called the Empire without end—was established as a divine preparation for the Christian Empire; Octavius, himself a pagan and demanding no veneration, unknowingly prepared a way for the true City, and his struggles affected not merely the state but all human society, the *orbis terrae* of Augustine, the World."[14] The peace established between Cymbeline and the Roman Empire at the end of Shakespeare's tragicomedy has exactly the same significance.

The Bath of Chaste Diana

After noticing the tapestry of the Great Goddess as Cleopatra–Venus–Isis and emphasizing her mythological association with water, Iachimo then turns his attention to the opposing element of fire and to the decoration of the fireplace in Imogen's bedchamber. He has observed its unusual iconography with great care.

> The chimney
> Is south the chamber, and the chimney-piece,
> Chaste Dian, bathing: never saw I figures
> So likely to report themselves; the cutter
> Was as another Nature, dumb; outwent her,
> Motion and breath left out.
>
> (2.4.80–85)

Such work was not actually carved in marble at this time in England but was molded in plaster like the stunning chimneypiece at Haddon Hall, Derbyshire, of Orpheus taming nature. And, for obvious reasons, the image of virginal Diana was in fact very rarely employed to decorate Renaissance chimneypieces. Diana and her fountain are antithetical to fire and heat, elements of passion that are more appropriately symbolized by Venus, Mars, Vulcan, or Cupid.

There is, however, one notable exception to this rule in Renaissance art, namely, Correggio's "Diana Descending in Her Chariot" painted on the chimneypiece in a room of Abbess Gioanna da Piacenza's apartment within the Benedictine Convent of San Paolo in Parma, although Shakespeare would not have known this particular work. Erwin Panofsky has described the inner room as "the sanctum of the Abbess."[15] Its frescoes were painted by Correggio in 1518–1519, and it could only be entered by first passing through what is now called the "Araldi Room" because of its ceiling decorations by Alessandro Araldi. The fireplace in the "Araldi Room," according to Panofsky, "bears the inscription TRANSIVIMVS PER IGNEM ET AQVAM ET EDVXISTI NOS IN REFRIGERIVM. MDXIIII ('We went through Fire and through Water, but Thou Broughtest Us out into the Place of Refreshment')," a quotation from Psalm 66 (65) that combines the contrary elements of fire and water with the promise of ultimate refreshment or renewal (1961, 7). In contrast, the motto on the mantel of the Correggio Room (beneath the painted Diana descending) is a strident warning to intruders: "IGNEM GLADIO NE FODIAS ('Thou Shalt Not poke a Fire with a Sword')" (Panofsky 1961, 13). Although a nun and thus committed to chastity or Diana, Gioanna da Piacenza was also a passionate defender of the rights of her order to receive visitors at San Paolo despite a papal command of *clausura,* and it is thus her own fiery personality that makes appropriate the association of the descending goddess Diana with the element of fire in Correggio's chimney decoration. The equally chaste Imogen's passionate defense in *Cymbeline* of her marriage to Posthumus against the wishes of her royal father suggests that England's princess combines the warring elements of fire and water within one personality in a similar way.

I mention the Camera di San Paolo here not as a possible source for the decorative details of Imogen's bedchamber but rather to illustrate the high level of sophisticated thought and symbolism that often went into the designing of Renaissance chambers for the wealthy. This included private rooms, such as closets, studies, and bedchambers, to be used only by the owners. Such rooms often morally instructed their occupants because Renaissance art was expected to have intellectual meaning for the viewer as well as to beautify his or her surroundings. At that time we find no complex Romantic theories about communicating with the unconscious mind through aesthetic means alone; art was expected to speak directly, although sometimes ambiguously, to human reason.

Diana is, of course, an appropriate iconographic figure to symbolize both an abbess and a chaste wife such as Shakespeare's Imogen. Indeed Panofsky characterizes the goddess as "a divinity priest-like and virginal, yet motherly in relation to her nymphs and to animals that seek her protection, prepared to be charitable where charitableness is due, but equally prepared to punish foes and detractors" (1961, 46). But since Diana is a huntress, as well as a protector of chastity, she can be exceedingly dangerous to those who oppose her in any way, as the enemies of Abbess Gioanna da Piacenza discovered in Renaissance Parma and the enemies of that most famous royal Diana, Queen Elizabeth, often learned to their sorrow in sixteenth-century England. Richard Linche tells us in his English version of Cartari's *Imagini* that

> Among the Poets Diana is called the goddess of hunting, and imperiall gouerness of pleasant groves, shrub-bearing hils, and christal-faced fountaines: giuen vnto her as some hold, for that in the heauens she neuer keepeth any direct course, but wanders and stragles from that true and perfect circuit which the sunne alwaies obserueth, as likewise hunters in the chase and pursuit of their game leaue the most accustomed and trodden paths, posting through vncouth thickets and way-lesse passage: and they depicture her in the habit of a young nimph, with her bow ready bent in her hand, a quiuer of arrowes hanging at one side of her, and to the other is fast tied a most swiftfooted greyhound, with a coller about his necke set and inchased with many rich stones of infinite value, and after her follow a troope of siluan virgines and light-paced huntresses.[16]

For such reasons Diana was chosen as the patroness of the royal gardens at Nonsuch, a palace built by Henry VIII to serve as a hunting lodge.

The real focus at Nonsuch, however, was on the specific myth of Diana and Actaeon. Ian Dunlop states that there was a famous grove of Diana in the center of the Nonsuch gardens: "In the middle of the grove was a fountain, and in the midst of the fountain a group of statuary portrayed, 'with great art and lifelike execution', the story of Actaeon turned into a stag as he was sprinkled by the goddess."[17] Although the scene may have been intended simply as a practical warning to courtiers to beware of seeing the goddess naked, that is, to beware of stumbling upon the secrets of royalty, a more philosophical meaning is now known to have been attached to the statuary as well through inscriptions on the gateway and walls of a "small vaulted temple" in the vicinity. According to Bruce R. Smith, the verse of Diana reads as follows:

> There is need of intelligence lest a beastly nature in human form
> Parrhasius should paint and Praxiteles carve.
> Actaeon, yours is a stag's heart: why should there not be horns?
> With insight I complain that your heart is that of a beast.[18]

In a more pragmatic vein, Sir Francis Bacon wrote the following interpretation of the Actaeon myth:

> For they who are not intimate with a prince, yet against his will have a knowledge of his secrets, inevitably incur his displeasure: and therefore, being aware that they are singled out, and all opportunities watched against them, they lead the life of a stag, full of fears and suspicions. It likewise frequently happens, that their servants and domestics accuse them, and plot their overthrow, in order to procure favour with the prince: for whenever the king manifests his displeasure, the person it falls upon must expect his servants to betray him, and worry him down, as Acteon was worried by his own dogs.[19]

Leonard Barkan reminds us, in an extended modern discussion of various medieval and Renaissance interpretations of the myth of Diana and Actaeon, that Ben Jonson employed the image in the above Baconian sense as a political warning in *Cynthia's Revels*. In this case, Actaeon was a symbol of the impetuous Earl of Essex, "who dared to burst in upon the Queen in her chamber."[20]

Aside from its political associations with Queen Elizabeth, the Diana and Actaeon story was also widely used to represent the defense of chastity in Renaissance decoration all over Europe. It was a popular subject on painted marriage *cassoni* in Italy, on English embroidered cushions and bed hangings, and even on the painted walls of British country houses. There is an extant wall painting of Diana and Actaeon in Seafield House, Cullen, for example, and Herbert Cescinsky prints two photographs of a wall painting on plaster of the same subject in a now demolished sixteenth-century house at Stodmarsh, Kent.[21] Among Renaissance oil paintings on the theme are those of Lucas Cranach the Elder, who used the Ovidian story to moralize against the folly of hunting as a sport, of Veronese (now in the Philadelphia Museum of Art), and of Titian

Actaeon turned into a stag by the goddess Diana in Ovid, *Metamorphoses* (Leipzig, 1582), bk. 3, 125. Reprinted by permission of the Warburg Institute.

(in the National Gallery of Scotland). The last painting depicts an Actaeon quite as surprised as the goddess and her nymphs by the sudden encounter, thus suggesting an unexpected moment of mystical vision on the part of the hunter.

Indeed the bath of Diana was commonly understood to represent a sacred mystery, a sight forbidden to the uninitiated. Barkan points out that late medieval interpretations of the Actaeon myth in the *Ovide Moralisé* revived "an ancient divine interpretation of the story that will reappear as Renaissance Platonism, i.e., that the hero enters upon visionary experience and as a result must perish" (1980, "Diana" 329). A major source of this Platonic interpretation of the myth was, as many commentators have observed, the ekphrasis in Apuleius's *Metamorphoses,* when Lucius is warned against his attempts to gain forbidden knowledge of the secrets of witchcraft and magic by seeing a statue of Diana and her hounds in the courtyard of the house belonging to a friend of his mother:

> On the contrary parte [opposite a statue of Victory], ye image of ye goddesse Diana was wrought in white marble, which was a meruelous sight to see, for she seemed as though the winde did blowe up her garmentes, and that she did encounter with them that came into the house: on eche side of her, were Dogges made of stone, that seemed to menace with their firie eies, theyr pricked eares, their bended nosethrilles, and their grinning teeth, in such sorte that you would haue thought they had bayed and barked. . . . Behinde the backe of the Goddesse was carued a stone in manner of a cauerne, enuironed with mosse, hearbes, leaues, sprigges, greene braunches, and bowes, growyng in and aboute the same, in so much that within the stone it glistened and shone meruelously, vnder the brimme of the stone hanged appels and grapes carued finely, wherein arte (enuinge nature) showed his great cunnyng . . . moreouer amongst the braunches of the stone appeared the image of Acteon: And how that Diana (which was carued within the same stone standyng in the water because he did see her naked) did tourne him into a Harte, and so he was torne and slayne of his owne houndes. (12ᵛ–13)

Like Shakespeare's Iachimo, Lucius in *The Golden Ass* is not deterred from profaning the sacred by this lifelike warning in art. He insists not only on seeing beauty bare by spying on Pamphile but also on attempting a magical transformation himself, despite a further warning by his mother's friend Byrrhena that Pamphile is capable of reducing "the whole worlde agayne to the olde chaos" (13ᵛ), that is, to undo creation. Lucius is then appropriately metamorphosed into an ass.

Iachimo, who plays the Actaeon role in *Cymbeline,* also ignores the warning against further intrusion suggested by the bas-relief of Diana bathing, but in contrast to Lucius, Iachimo becomes outwardly neither a stag nor an ass when he gazes directly on the partially nude body of the sleeping Imogen. As I have previously suggested, moreover, his understanding of the vast difference between good and evil is expanded by the

sight and his desires are aroused by Imogen's beauty. Much as Duke
Orsino complains in *Twelfth Night* that he is pursued by the hounds of
desire after his first glimpse of Olivia, Iachimo refrains only with great
difficulty from touching and thus awakening the sleeping princess: "How
bravely thou becom'st thy bed! fresh lily! / And whiter than the sheets!
That I might touch! / But kiss, one kiss!" (2.2.15–17). His later repentance
for his defamation of Imogen suggests that other changes also begin to
occur within his heart once he has enjoyed the forbidden vision of a warm,
living "Cytherea" beyond the sculptured warning of Actaeon's fate on the
chimneypiece of "Chaste Diana, bathing." As Abraham Fraunce reminds
his readers, "a wiseman ought to refraine his eyes, from beholding sensible and corporall bewty, figured by Diana: least, as Actaeon was deuoured
of his owne doggs, so he be distracted and torne in pieces with his owne
affections, and perturbations."[22]

The transformation of Actaeon into a stag occurs in most illustrations of
the myth—including Elizabeth Shrewsbury's beautiful embroidered long
cushion at Hardwick Hall—when the goddess or one of her nymphs
splashes water on the intruder. The event is similar to the transformational
purpose of Christian baptism. One early seventeenth-century Christian
reading of the myth suggests that the vision of such a sacred mystery can
sometimes cause tears of repentance and thus precipitate a spiritual
change in the voyeur. For example, Shakespeare's contemporary, John
Davies of Hereford, passionately invites the reader of his poem *The Holy
Roode* (1609) to envision with him the terrible death of Christ on the
Cross. As we subsequently imagine the scene in bloody detail, Davies
exhorts us as follows:

> Now thinke, O thinke, thou seest those hounds of hell,
> (That yelp out blasphemies about their pray)
> With vngraue gate, to runne doe him compell,
> And with tumultuous noyse him lead away:
>   Ah see how He that staid the Sunnes swift course,
>   Through thicke and thin doth (stallesse) run perforce.[23]

The reader is then imagined by the poet as metamorphosed into a stag like
Actaeon, a stag pursued by the longing for divine love and thirsting for
water:

> *Christ,* to thy longing-loue, is as the Riuer
> Vnto the chased Hart, which still he seekes;
> And as Men thirstie, mind but moysture euer,
> So loue doth thinke on nought, but what it likes:
>   If That Bee not, It seekes no more to Bee,
>   But Beeing, It would Be That, bond or free.

(sig. H4)

Davies thus encourages the visionary penetration of sacred mysteries, rather than warning against them, in hopes that humanity will then be moved to penitential tears and undergo a "sea change" or a spiritual conversion. This is exactly what happens to Posthumus in *Cymbeline* when he sees the bloody cloth symbolizing Imogen's death at the hands of Pisanio (a false symbol in this case), and he longs for his own death to atone for hers. Davies describes his poem, which has an engraving of the myth of Diana and Actaeon on its title page, as a "Speaking-picture." The illustration represents the transformational intent of the book itself on the reader.[24]

Although Shakespeare clearly did not write *Cymbeline* as a work of religious propaganda for the secular stage, he may have taken a Christian interpretation of the Actaeon myth like that of John Davies very much for granted and employed it unconsciously in this numinous tragicomedy. And if many scholars have seen Iachimo as an Actaeon figure, it should be noted as well that the audience also shares in the villain's profane act of voyeurism in *Cymbeline*. When we listen to Iachimo's description of Imogen's naked beauty, we too become Actaeon and are equally subject to transformation by the experience of the play as a whole. As Davies intimates in *The Holy Roode*, poetic art—like the water from Diana's sacred fountain—has the power to change those who penetrate its mysteries.

Thus the image of "Chaste Dian, bathing" as a decoration on the fireplace in *Cymbeline* may be interpreted on various levels. First, we may understand it as a symbol of Imogen's true chastity in conjunction with her defiant love for Posthumus—by analogy with the similar Diana fireplace in Correggio's Camera di San Paolo in Parma. The decoration may be interpreted, secondly, as a protective emblem warning intruders against an attempt to gain knowledge of royal secrets, or as an exhortation for humans to use their intelligence against temptation. Finally, the image may be read as a warning against the dangerous transformational powers of sacred mysteries and visions, while acting simultaneously as a provocative Neoplatonic invitation to experience such a transformation through its bold depiction of nude female beauty. Iachimo understands the symbolism of chastity but ignores the warnings and thus becomes subject to transformation and to punishment by death. At the very least, he can expect to be pursued by the hounds of his own desires, a psychological state that Shakespeare does not choose to develop in his treatment of this particular character. However, Iachimo does at least set out on the path of reformation when he publicly confesses in the last scene of the play to having borne false witness against the heiress to England's throne and asks to be forgiven. By listening to Iachimo's ekphrasis, Posthumus and even the audience are given the same warnings and are reminded of the ideal chastity embodied by Diana in her bath.

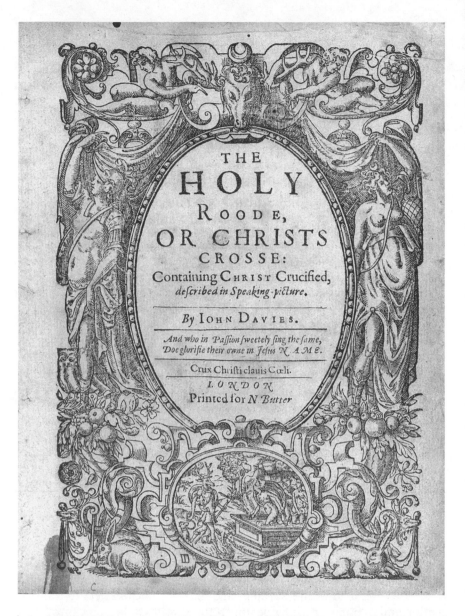

Actaeon turned into a stag on the title page of *The Holy Roode* by John Davies of Hereford (London, 1609) to imply that we must profane sacred mysteries by seeing them. Reprinted by permission of the Folger Shakespeare Library (STC 6330).

Eros and Anteros in the Fireplace

Iachimo notes that in addition to "Chaste Dian, bathing," Imogen's fireplace is further adorned with symbolic fire-dogs. "Her andirons," he says,

> were two winking Cupids
> Of silver, each on one foot standing, nicely
> Depending on their brands.

(2.4.88–91)

Once again Shakespeare describes a very early example of what only later became popular in English decoration. According to Ralph Edwards, most such chimney furniture designed for royalty during the Elizabethan and Jacobean periods was made of cast iron with hammered bronze or gilt brass ornamentation above. Not until after the Restoration did "silver enriched andirons become the fashion" in England.[25] Fortunately there still remains today at Knole Park in Kent a famous pair of beaten silver andirons (dating from about 1670) that are surmounted by naked boys or Cupids. Such work had actually attracted considerable attention by the end of the sixteenth century in Venice through the Cupid fire-dogs sculpted in bronze by the Florentine artist Nicoló Roccatagliata.[26] This fine craftsman based much of his work on designs from various editions of the *Emblemata* by Andrea Alciati, who was also one of the inspirations, or so I will argue here, of Imogen's silver andirons in *Cymbeline*.

The information in the ekphrasis we need to keep in mind is that there are two Cupids, thus implying the *topos* of Eros and Anteros, and that the Cupids with their torches are located within the fireplace, thus appearing to warm Diana's bath on the chimneypiece above with the flames of their torches.

The implied association between Cupid and the bath of Diana in Iachimo's description is at least as ancient as *The Greek Anthology*, in which we find a poem on the subject by Marianus Scholasticus. James Hutton translates the epigram as follows:

> Beneath these plane trees, detained by gentle slumber, Love slept, having put his torch in care of the Nymphs; but the Nymphs said one to another: 'Why wait? Would that together with this we could quench the fire in the hearts of men.' But the torch set fire even to the water, and with hot water thenceforth the Love-Nymphs fill the bath.[27]

This poem inspired Shakespeare's Sonnets 153 and 154, one of which describes the ill effects of profane love on the bather, while the other hints at a cure for "men diseased" and an eternity of love for those who commit themselves to a bath warmed by the torch of divine love: "Loues fire

Anteros and Eros decorate a famous pair of silver andirons at Knole Park, Kent. Photograph by Mancktelow Photography.

heates water, water cooles not loue."[28] Ronald Jaeger has shown that Sonnet 154 echoes the biblical Song of Songs.[29] Thus one bath with its sleeping Cupid infects the lover, and the other warmed by the fire of its "little Loue-God" offers salvation. This second bath may also be a reference to baptism, according to Thomas P. Roche, Jr., who writes: "The cleansing water of the spirit, as symbolized by baptism, releases man from the endless cycle of his fallen nature, leading him to death, but that cycle is broken by the new fire brought to human desire through the incarnation."[30]

Since there are two opposing Cupids in the Sonnets, we should not overlook the presence of two Cupids in Imogen's fireplace, a common doubling in the Renaissance. The first is very likely meant to symbolize physical desire or lust in the form of Eros, who is a possessive and jealous love god, as we have seen in *The Golden Ass;* while the second Cupid represents the Neoplatonic idea of Anteros, the love of virtue in opposition to sexual love. This is certainly true of the Knole Cupids, one of whom holds a bellows with which to inflame passion and displays the intoxicating grapes of Dionysos. The other more mature Cupid holds a shovel with which to bank the fires of physical passion and carries the laurel leaves of Apollo in his other hand. But the Eros and Anteros *topos* may be even further complicated. In the painting called "Venus Bandaging the Eyes of Cupid" by Titian, for example, there are also two Cupids, one of whom is blindfolded by Venus at the request of two aggressive Dianas or Amazons, while his winged brother Eros or "voluptuous pleasure," peers sardonically over the shoulder of his mother Venus. The painting illustrates, according to Edgar Wind, the point that "intellectual love is not an end in itself but must find its fruition in passion *(voluptas)*" (1968, 78–80). This Renaissance notion of love fulfilled is commensurate with the Christian doctrines of the Incarnation as an act of divine love for the world and of Christ's Passion, which together result in human redemption.

The presence of two Cupids in Imogen's fireplace further suggests the classical and Renaissance myth of an ongoing war between Eros and Anteros found in Alciati's *Emblemata*. This myth, which is referred to by a number of English poets, including Edmund Spenser, Sir Philip Sidney, and Ben Jonson, first appears as poem 251 in *The Greek Anthology:*

> Who fashioned a winged Love and set him opposite winged Love? Nemesis, taking vengeance on the boy with the bow, that he may suffer what he did; and he, the bold boy never daunted before, is crying as he tastes the bitter arrows, and thrice he spits in the deep folds of his bosom! Oh, most marvellous! One shall burn with fire, Love has touched Love to the quick.[31]

Alciati's Emblem III offers a Neo-Latin version of this verse under the *inscriptio* "Αντέρως, Amor Virtutis, alium Cupidinem superans" ("Anteros, the love of virtue overcoming the other Cupid"). The *subscriptio* reads as follows:

> Aligervm, aligeroque inimicum, pinxit Amori,
>   Arcu arcum, atque ignes igne domans Nemesis.
> Vt quae alijs fecit, patiatur: at hic puer olim
>   Intrepidus gestans tela, miser lacrymat.
> Ter spuit inque finus imos: res mira, crematur
>   Igne ignis, furias odit Amoris amor.

> (Nemesis has painted a winged Eros hostile to
>   winged Eros,
> taming bow with bow, and fires with fire,
> In order that he may suffer what he does to others.
>   But this boy, formerly
> brandishing his arrows fearlessly, is wretchedly weeping.
> Three times he spits into the depths of his bosom:
>   a wondrous thing,
> fire is consumed by fire, Eros hates the passion of Eros.[32]

The illustrations of the emblem in all editions of Alciati depict a winged and often garlanded Anteros binding a smaller winged Eros to a tree or pillar, while a blazing fire consumes the bow and arrows of sensual love. Such an emblem might very well inspire the decorations for a fireplace. The fire surrounding the andirons would actually suggest the generative passion of Eros and the chaste passion of Anteros, while the image as a whole would serve to remind the beholder of the superior virtues of spiritual love.

The ancient *topos* of chastising physical Eros in revenge for the agonies he has caused mankind[33] forms the subtext of this emblem, and, I believe, the subtext as well of the fireplace and its two Cupid andirons in *Cymbeline,* a play that dramatizes the suffering through experience of both the lovers, Imogen and Posthumus, before they are happily rejoined in marital bliss. At one point, Posthumus, who has been too hot in his jealous behavior toward Imogen, is bound like physical Eros and threatened with execution by British gaolers (5.4) before he is ultimately forgiven and reunited with his bride and with his king. "Most welcome bondage," he says, "for thou art a way, / I think to liberty" (5.4.3–4). By "liberty" he means death, but since he has by now transferred his allegiance from Eros to Anteros, Posthumus is offered life instead. On the other hand, lustful Cloten as Eros is executed by the Wild Boy, Guiderius, before he can carry out his plan to rape Imogen.

Alciati explains his second Cupid, or Anteros, most clearly in Emblem 110 under the *inscriptio,* "Αντέρως, id est, Amor virtutis" ("Anteros, that is, love of virtue"). The *subscriptio* begins with a question:

Ἀντέρως, Amor virtutis alium Cupidinem superans.

EMBLEMA CX.

Anteros chastizing Eros in Andrea Alciati, *Emblemata*, p. 386 of the 1581 edition.
Reprinted by permission of the Folger Shakespeare Library (PN 6349 A8 1581 Cage).

> Dic vbi sunt incurui arcus? vbi tela Cupido?
>   Mollia queis iuvenum figere corda soles.
> Fax vbi tristis? vbi pennae? tres vnde corollas
>   Fert manus? vnde aliam tempora cincta gerunt?

> (Tell me, where are your curved bows?
>   where your arrows, Cupid,
> With which you are wont to pierce the soft hearts of
>   youths?
> Where your gloomy torch? where your wings?
> Whence the three garlands in your hand?
> Whence the fourth wreathing your brow?)

Cupid makes the following answer:

> Haud mihi vulgari est hospes cum Cypride quicquam,
>   Vlla voluptatis nos neque form tulit.
> Sed puris hominum succendo mentibus ignes
>   Disciplinae, animos astraque ad alta traho,
> Quatuor eque ipsa texo virtute corollas:
>   Quarum, quae Sophiae est, tempora prima tegit.

> (I have no ties of friendship with the common Venus, nor
>   did any form of pleasure bear me.
> Rather I kindle in the pure minds of men the fires of
> learning, and I draw their spirits to the stars on high.
> And I weave out of virtue itself the four garlands.
> The foremost of these, that of Wisdom, covers my brow.)

The subject of this emblem appears to be the "four cardinal virtues"—justice, wisdom, fortitude, and temperance—that are discussed by Plato in *The Republic* as all that is necessary for citizens of the ideal state (4.427ff). Anteros symbolizes for Alciati the love of such virtues in contrast to sexual love, which includes the dangerous passions of lust and jealousy. Emblem 110 derives from another epigram by Marianus Scholasticus entitled "On Love garlanded" in *The Greek Anthology*.[3]

The philosophical sources of the Eros and Anteros *topos* for Alciati are the two "loves," both representative of desire, mentioned in the *Phaedrus* and the *Symposium* of Plato and in Marsilio Ficino's *Commentary on the Symposium* published in 1475 and later widely read in England. According to Ficino,

> Both kinds of love seek the beautiful. Certainly the love which rules and governs the body tries to feed its charge with foods as tasty, delicious, and beautiful as possible, and to procreate handsome offspring by a beautiful woman. Similarly, the love which pertains to the soul tries to imbue it with the most elegant and pleasing learning, and to spread knowledge like its own by writing in an elegant and beautiful style, and to reproduce it, by teaching, in some very beautiful soul

ibidem

Roman statue of Venus with her two sons Eros and Anteros. From a print by
Giovanni Battista de' Cavalieri, *Antiquarum Statuarum Urbis Romae* (Rome, 1585),
51. Reprinted by permission of the Folger Shakespeare Library (NB 1380 C2 1585
Cage).

that is to say, which is pure, intelligent, and excellent. Certainly we cannot see the soul itself. And for this reason we cannot see its beauty. But we can see the body, which is the shadow and image of the soul. And so, judging by its image, we assume that in a beautiful body there is a beautiful soul.[35]

By Shakespeare's time, however, the idea that a beautiful body always contained a beautiful soul was no longer accepted, as we can see by his characterization of the beautiful but evil Queen in *Cymbeline*. Erasmus, a Platonist himself, had taught the later Renaissance to be suspicious of outer forms: that the quality of the mind is more important than a person's outward appearance, and, in the *Enchiridion*, that the spirit always takes precedence over the letter of legal and of sacred texts.[36] The Protestant reformers, although often literalists in biblical interpretation, agreed with the Erasmian criticism of form without content and shifted their religious emphasis from external rituals of worship to an inner attentiveness to individual conscience, or to the God within. Shakespeare and his audience believed, therefore, that true beauty always remains invisible to the human eye, although it can be comprehended through the intellect and the heart, and through noting the good actions of individuals in the world.

Later sixteenth-century emblematists tend to accentuate the Platonic origins of the two Cupids even further than did Alciati. Achille Bocchi, for example, is particularly clear about the philosophical meaning of his emblems. His Symbol 20 is based on Alciati's Emblem 111. Here Anteros holds both torches, one pointing upward and the other aimed as a weapon at a fleeing and blindfolded Eros, who has dropped his bow and arrows on the ground. Once again profane Cupid's own fire is used against him. The motto of the emblem is "Platonico Cvpidini" ("To Platonic Cupid"), and the verse informs us as follows:

> Vulgi profani indocta cohors tuam
>   Nil percipit, diuine Amor inclytam
>   Virtutem, & illam flammulam, unde
>   Certa hominum, atque Deum est uoluptas.
> Mens namque uerum capta oculis bonum
>   Dum nescit usquam cernere, fallitur,
>   Semperque uitans expetenda
>   Insequitur sua damna praeceps.
> At cognitum immortale decus tuum
>   Mortalibus si esset miseris, uti
>   Dis est beatis, qui soluti
>   Carcere corporeo, & tenebris
> Viuo fruuntur lumine, rectius
>   Exempta saeuis nostra doloribus
>   Vita haec iter, securiusque,
>   Quòd minimè assequitur, teneret.
> Tunc omnium pulcherrima denuò

Forma illa rerum, secula & aurea
Prorsus redirent, denique omnes
Ambrosia fruemur alma.
O aure uotis si facili adnuas
Olim uocatus, sancte puer, meis.
En uror, uror, toto ab illis
Corde tuis facibus peruri.

(The untutored crowd of the vulgar understands nothing about your renowned power, divine Amor, nor about that little flame from which come the sure delights of men and of gods.—For the mind, when captivated by the eyes, not knowing how to recognize the true good anywhere, fails, and always avoiding what is truly desirable, rushes headlong toward its own destruction.—But if your immortal beauty were known to miserable mortals, as it is to the blessed gods who are free from the prison of the flesh and the shadows, and enjoy the living light, then, exempt from cruel sorrows, this life of ours would more directly and safely follow the path that it attains too little. Then the most beautiful Forms of all things, and the Golden Age, would return anew. At last all of us would enjoy the nourishing ambrosia.—O holy child, if your ear is favorable, once called upon, hear my prayers. See how I burn, I burn, and with all my heart I pray to be consumed by your flames.)[37]

The lost innocence of the Golden Age so yearned for in Renaissance tragicomedies can only return, Bocchi implies, when men learn to see through that which makes beauty visible, as Diotima had instructed Socrates in Plato's *Symposium*.

In *Cymbeline*, the foolish Cloten's lust to possess Imogen's body proceeds from his eyes or from Eros, and he "rushes headlong toward [his] destruction" in his attempt to ravish her. His punishment is the actual loss of his head, which has "no brains," according to Guiderius, and for this reason he was intellectually unable to recognize Imogen's inner virtue. Posthumus's murderous jealousy, aroused by Iachimo, sends the hero on a similar path of peril until, through his repentance and conversion, he changes his fundamental understanding of the nature of love and of the character of his beloved Imogen. He finally describes her in act 5 as "The temple of Virtue" (5.5.220–21) and even as the embodiment in the world of Virtue itself, which means that to love Imogen is indeed to love Virtue. But we know too much about her tendency to despair and her absurd adoration of Posthumus, both of which indicate a lack of temperance and wisdom, to believe that she is in fact a personification of virtue, although we would certainly agree that she is sexually virtuous.

In any case, Posthumus has matured sufficiently at last to recognize virtue as the inner truth of the bride he believes to be lost forever and to love this virtue wisely and even more than his own life. He has achieved the Platonic level where, "Beholding beauty with the eye of the mind, he will be enabled to bring forth, not images of beauty, but realities (for he has

Anteros chastizing Eros, Symbol XX, from Achille Bocchi's *Symbolicarum quaestionum . . . libri quinque* (Bologna, 1555), LX. Reprinted by permission of the Folger Shakespeare Library (PN 6349 B57 1555 Cage).

hold not of an image but of a reality), and bringing forth and nourishing true virtue to become the friend of God and be immortal, if mortal man may" (Plato, *Symposium* 212). He has also learned that true justice is based on forgiveness or charity rather than on social notions of honor and revenge.

To summarize this *topos*, Spenser perhaps most clearly states the difference between Eros and Anteros in the first verse of Book III, canto iii, in *The Faerie Queene*. Here the narrator introduces the theme of "Love" and immediately defines it as follows:

Not that same which doth base affections move
In brutish mindes, and filthy lust inflame,
But that sweete fit that doth true beautie love,
And choseth vertue for his dearest Dame,
Whence spring all noble deedes and never dying fame.

In *Cymbeline,* Shakespeare first embodies the two Cupids of Imogen's andirons, or the two Platonic types of love, as part of the characters of Cloten and Posthumus (in whom Eros is also at first predominant); then he illustrates them once more in the two contrasting halves of Posthumus's life, before and after his spiritual conversion. Posthumus's movement from one type of love to the other is reminiscent of the changes between wanton Cupid and the mature Amor who marries Psyche in Apuleius's myth of Cupid and Psyche. Moreover, the references in the bedchamber scene to the rape myths of Philomela and Lucrece are obviously associated with the activities of an uncontrolled Eros, as embodied in the play by Cloten who is killed. Fortunately for the spouses, Anteros becomes the ruling god of lovers in *Cymbeline*.

Imogen's fireplace by itself, therefore, is a visual oxymoron of chaste passion, a functional yet decorative icon representing the familiar Renaissance effort to reconcile or harmonize contrary elements, in this case fire and water. The attempt begins by accentuating their differences as passion versus chastity, but then, according to the Neoplatonic humanists, through Anteros, or a chaste passion for virtue, the desired *discordia concordans* can finally be achieved.

The Sleeping Ariadne

Between the provocative Cleopatra tapestry and "chaste Dian, bathing" on the chimneypiece is a bed, no doubt partially curtained by embroidered hangings. This is the bed on which Imogen lies asleep. The audience would probably have imagined her in the classical artistic pose of sleep with one arm curved over her head and at least one bare breast visible to the

intruder, who pulls aside the bed curtain like a satyr revealing the mysteries of the natural world. We only hear Iachimo's praise of Imogen's beauty
rather than seeing her since the role of the princess was played by a boy
actor:

Cytherea,
How bravely thou becom'st thy bed! fresh lily!
And whiter than the sheets! That I might touch!
But kiss, one kiss! Rubies unparagon'd,
How dearly they do't: 'tis her breathing that
Perfumes the chamber thus: the flame o' the taper
Bows toward her, and would under-peep her lids,
To see th' enclosed lights, now canopied
Under these windows, white and azure lac'd
With blue of heaven's own tinct.

(2.2.14–23)

Since the image of a beautiful sleeping woman was a popular iconographic
figure of Nature during the Renaissance, a Jacobean audience would
automatically imagine her sleeping in a pose like that of the famous
Hellenistic sculpture of a sleeping goddess resembling either Venus-
Cleopatra or Ariadne. This marble was rediscovered in the early sixteenth
century and was first erroneously identified as the dying Cleopatra because of the snake bracelet on her arm, although the piece is now understood to represent the pagan goddess Ariadne on Naxos. It was one of the
most widely known works of art displayed in the Cortile Belvedere of the
Vatican at the time.

There are two epigrams on this *topos* of the sleeping Ariadne in "The
Planudean Appendix" to *The Greek Anthology*. Poem 146 exhorts the
reader to respect the repose of the sleeping woman: "Strangers, touch not
this stone Ariadne, lest she leap up seeking Theseus." But Poem 145,
which also praises the lifelike art of the piece, reminds us that the sleeper
is beloved by a divinity: "No mortal was thy sculptor, but he carved thee
even as thy lover Bacchus saw thee reclining on the rock."[38] Drawings and
prints of the Cleopatra–Ariadne statue and of other famous pieces in the
Belvedere statue court in Rome circulated throughout Europe, so that,
according to Smith,

By the time Shakespeare was beginning his career, two complete sets of engravings of ancient marbles and bronzes had made the Apollo Belvedere, the
Farnese Hercules, the mounted Marcus Aurelius, the dead Cleopatra, and other
Roman statues the imaginative property of all Europeans. Antoine Lafrery's
series of engravings *Speculum Romanae Magnificentiae,* begun in the 1540s and
completed in the 1580s, included several plates of antique sculpture among its
views of Roman ruins. An anthology of more than fifty prints devoted to
classical statues was published at Rome by Giovanni Battista de'Cavalieri in the

Nymphae cuiusdam dormientis simulacrum e marmore mira arte factum, in uiridario
Vaticano Romæ quidam, propter adiectum serpentem Cleopatrae imaginem putant.

6

Statue of Ariadne, thought to be Cleopatra dying, over a grotto guarded by satyric
hermes in the Belvedere Gardens of the Vatican. From a print in Giovanni Battista
de' Cavalieri, *Antiquarum Statuarum Urbis Romae* (Rome, 1585), 6. Reprinted by
permission of the Folger Shakespeare Library (NB 1380 C2 1585 Cage).

early 1560s: Successive editions of his *Antiquarum Statuarum Urbis Romae* added more and more engravings to bring the complete set to two hundred plates in 1594.[39]

The pose of the Ariadne statue is also very like the pose of the sleeping nude being uncovered by a satyr and two satyrini on the Fountain of Venus woodcut from Francesco Colonna's *Hypnerotomachia Poliphili* (1527). The fountain illustrates a female mystery revealed by profane satyrs, who are deliberately violating the privacy of a goddess and gazing upon her beauty while she sleeps, as has been pointed out by Millard Meiss and others.[40]

Colonna's mysterious little book was translated into English in 1592 by R. D. (Robert Dallington) as *The Strife of Love in a Dreame,* dedicated to the Earle of Essex, and published in memory of the virtues of the slain knight Sir Philip Sidney. In it Colonna describes the sleeping nymph as "Lying vpon her right side with that subiected arme retract, and her open palme vnder her faire cheeke, wherevpon she rested her head."[41] But the lady is threatened in her sleep:

> At hir feet stood a satire in prurient lust vppon his gotishe feet, his mouth and his nose ioyning together like a gote with a beard growinge on either sides of his chin, with two peakes and shorte in the middeste like Goates hayre, and in like manner about his flankes and his eares, grewe hayre, with a visage adulterated betwixt a mans and a Goates, in so rare a sort as if the excellent woorkman in his caruinge had had presented vnto him by nature the Idea and shape of a *Satire*.[42]

The scene is very similar to what the audience sees onstage in *Cymbeline* when Iachimo pulls back the bed hangings and peers down at the sleeping princess, although the sleeping beauty must herself remain mostly invisible in this case.

Fortunately for Imogen's chastity, Iachimo only wants to steal her bracelet at this point and actually fears to awaken her:

O sleep, thou ape of death, lie dull upon her,
And be her sense but as a monument.
Thus in a chapel lying. Come off, come off.

(2.2.31–33)

This comparison of the sleeping woman to a funerary sculpture is apt for the Vatican sleeping Ariadne about to be awakened by Dionysus could very well have been carved originally for just such a purpose, despite its later association with a grotto in the Belvedere gardens. Indeed Michelangelo's sepulchral figure of Night in the Florentine Medici Chapel, whose pose is similar to that of the Cleopatra-Ariadne statue, is made to speak the following words by the artist:

ΠΑΝΤΩΝ ΤΟΚΑΔΙ

The Venus fountain as illustrated in the French edition of Francesco Colonna's
Hypnerotomachia, 2, 23. Reprinted by permission of the Folger Shakespeare Library
(PQ 1410 C6 Cage).

I prize my sleep and more by being stone
As long as hurt and shamefulness endure
I call it lucky not to see or hear
So do not waken me, keep your voice down.[43]

Moreover, the figure of Ariadne sleeping was a not uncommon figure of promised resurrection on Roman marble sarcophagi. The message of comfort is obviously that one who sleeps will eventually be reawakened by divine love.

Abandoned by Theseus on Naxos, Ariadne was originally a Cretan moon deity, a goddess of birth and death and an antecedent of Artemis and Aphrodite, who knew the secret of the underworld labyrinth and how to return from it.[44] For this reason, no doubt, she is chosen as his bride by divine Dionysos, a year god subject to dismemberment during the harvest season. Each spring, Ariadne restores the god to life by holding one of his legs on her lap, as we know from a scene on the huge bronze krater from Grave *Beta* at Derveni.[45] In *Cymbeline,* an abandoned Imogen plays a role similar to that of Ariadne during her sojourn in the mountains. When she emerges from Belarius's cave, she appears to die after taking the Queen's drug and is given funeral obsequies by the three Wild Men. Later she reawakens to the sight of a dismembered man, whom she believes to be her husband, and she embraces the corpse with passionate grief. Posthumus of course reappears alive in the last act to her relief and joy.

Renaissance artists, especially the Venetians, did numerous paintings of sleeping women like Ariadne, who—without their knowledge—are being looked at by voyeurs. A major literary source of the sleeping woman *topos* for Italians was Boccaccio's tale in the *Decameron* of Cimone, an idiot who falls in love with a sleeping beauty and becomes a superb student of the arts, music, and letters in an effort to win her (Meiss 1976, 225). Cimone's latent abilities are awakened by Efigenia's revealed beauty. But although the subject may have been philosophically that of gazing on beauty bare, the erotic effect of such paintings of sleeping beauties on the beholder was probably more in the mode of Eros than of Anteros, and deliberately so. As Meiss puts it,

> The sleeper is always unaware of spectators, and the *vacatio* serves along with important aspects of Renaissance style to maintain a distance between the pictorial and the real world. Sleep is a means of idealization, especially valuable in the new and emotionally charged sphere of the erotic. (1976, 225)

Aside from pleasing male patrons with the opportunity to gaze undisturbed at a beautiful female body painted on canvas,

> The Venetian painters . . . found the image of the sleeping woman so expressive of their conceptions of love, of life, and of the power of natural generation that in

a couple of decades, with remarkable expertise and consistency, they and their colleagues in Mantua revived all relevant ancient myths. They drew from ancient texts as well as from surviving ancient monuments, even illustrating aspects of stories, such as that of Amymone, that were rarely if ever illustrated in antiquity. (Meiss 1976, 225–26)

Some of this fascination with sleep as a prelude to natural and artistic generation evidently made its way north and found a new literary life in *A Midsummer Night's Dream* and in the late tragicomedies of William Shakespeare.

The Platonic irony behind the image of a sleeping woman is that during sleep her mind and soul are absent or withdrawn, *vacatio,* so that the male voyeur contemplates nothing but a desirable body or externality, nature's painted or sculpted image of the female, a mere shadow of beauty. He sees art without life instead of reality or spirit, and what he falls in love with is ephemeral. The spectator standing before the picture of a voyeur gazing at a sleeping woman sees even less—a shadow of a shadow. Consequently, when Leonard Barkan states in *The Gods Made Flesh* that in his view "A symbolic rape is a reading"[46] of a physical text or, in this case, of the exposed body of Imogen, he then observes that in *Cymbeline,*

> a picture is all Iachimo gets. Voyeurism as a type of rape turns out, despite its immorality, to be peculiarly ineffectual. Iachimo has penetrated Imogen's room but not her body. The limits of his success are parodied by the immediately following scene in which Cloten, who has not even succeeded in getting into her room, stands outside attempting ineptly to *penetrate* (he uses the word three times) with music—once again Shakespeare contrasting the various artistic media. For Iachimo's part, his relation to rape is precisely that of images to reality. (1986, 250)

The reason for the failure of both Cloten and Iachimo to "penetrate" is quite simply that Imogen is not there to know the men attempting to know her. Since she is asleep, she does not perceive external stimuli through her senses. According to Ficino, during the state of sleep "the rational soul collects itself in some way and is occupied not in feeling corporeal qualities, nor in ruling and moving the members of its body, nor in transacting external affairs. . . . The more the exterior act is set aside, the more the interior intensifies."[47] Imogen has escaped to the interior realm of reason and imagination. The Platonists would add, of course, that "knowing" the body itself would not ultimately satisfy anyway, since one must *see through* that which makes Beauty visible to the Truth, Goodness, Beauty, and Justice of transcendent Reality.

Imogen's image as a beautiful woman asleep is a haunting recollection in *Cymbeline* of Shakespeare's earlier sleeping goddess Titania, as becomes clear when Iachimo evokes the chariot of night: "Swift, swift, you dragons of the night" (2.2.48), an echo of *A Midsummer Night's Dream* (3.2.379). Shakespeare found Titania's name in the Latin version of Ovid's story of Actaeon. In fact Ovid uses the name Titania for both Diana and Circe, two transformational moon goddesses who supply metaphors to poets and phantasms to lunatics.

While Imogen sleeps, however, Iachimo–Actaeon steals the bracelet Posthumus has given her as an external token of her physical bondage to him through marriage; now it will serve to prove the loss of her honor. But, since an intimate description of her body will even more effectively convince Posthumus that Iachimo has been her lover, the villain observes: "On her left breast / A mole cinque-spotted: like the crimson drops / I' th' bottom of a cowslip" (2.2.38–40). This detail also remains no more than an external image of reality, and as Barkan observes, Posthumus's acceptance of such evidence is much like Imogen herself identifying the body of Cloten as Posthumus merely on the basis of the clothes it wears (Barkan 1986, 250). On the other hand, the number five is associated with matrimony[48] and with the crimson wounds of Christ as well, as Shakespeare's audience knew.

The sleeping Imogen and the presence of a Cleopatra tapestry in the room are subtle reminders of the death of Cleopatra and of the Cleopatra-Ariadne sculpture in the Vatican that supposedly celebrated that event. Since Christianity was primarily concerned with the redemption rather than with the worship of nature as symbolized by Cleopatra, Venus, and Isis, I shall digress here for a moment to a later cultural phenomenon. Cleopatra as the mortal embodiment of Venus and Isis was reborn during the Middle Ages in the form of a courtesan who became a Christian female saint. This exotic personage—before her conversion—liked to celebrate colorful pomps like that of Cleopatra on her barge, wafting perfume behind her wherever she went, and driving men mad with desire to possess her beauty, no matter what the cost. She was later baptized and became a Diana figure or St. Pelagia. According to William Heckscher,

St. Pelagia (Margarita, Marina) of Antioch in Syria, who died in Jerusalem (Oct. 6(8), was a fifth century saint of the Eastern Church. She was also recognized in the West. Originally Pelagia (whose name was one of the chief-epithets of Aphrodite-Venus), had been in the service of *luxuria;* she was widely known as a dancer and *mima* and also as a *meretrix*. (1985, 134)

Her legend began in "the second quarter of the fifth century after her triumphant procession through the city had been witnessed by Bishop Nonnus of Heliopolis (d.458 A.D.)." Nonnus later had a dream vision of Pelagia's baptism in a *concha* or maritime shell, a baptism that imitated the birth of Aphrodite from a *concha*.

On this occasion elements Christian and pagan interpenetrated one another in a miraculous fashion. Plunged into an enforced bath in the *concha,* Pelagia, who thus far had assumed the appearance of the black dove of Aphrodite, was transformed into the white dove representing the heaven-aspiring Christian soul. (Heckscher 1985, 146)

Heckscher further explains that the concha is an ancient symbol of the womb and a common attribute of Aphrodite herself. "Venus' shell, serving as both matrix and vehicle of the new-born divinity, may well be related to the vast group of messianic hiding-receptacles which frequently offer to the youthful god or redeemer a means of maritime conveyance" (1985, 144–45). It then became a popular form of the early Christian baptismal font and was associated with the Virgin Mary during the Renaissance. For example, the concha appears on the Virgin's reading stand in Leonardo's "Annunciation," thus identifying her immediately as the new Heavenly Venus and as the shell from which Christ, the pearl, will emerge.

After St. Pelagia's conversion by Bishop Nonnus, she became a penitent who lived in a cave at the foot of Golgotha. Curiously enough, the cave was a site identified by the early church fathers Eusebius and Ambrosius as a *Venarium* since Venus had been the original patroness of Golgotha and its dead. Here Pelagia "changed her sex, turning from Pelagia to Pelagios, the way Aphrodite would change into Aphroditos" (Heckscher 1985, 146), and at this point she became St. Pelagius (1985, 155), just as Imogen will soon become Fidele in *Cymbeline.* The type of scallop shell from which Venus was born and Pelagia was reborn was often used later as the form of the basin below the sleeping nymphs (modeled after the Vatican statue of Cleopatra–Ariadne) in the watery grottoes of Renaissance gardens, where they served as a reminder to the viewers of cyclical rebirth within nature. More significantly for this study, St. Pelagia herself, as Aphrodite reborn and purified, was obviously very important to William Shakespeare, who had just recently dramatized her personal story as the character Marina in his first tragicomedy *Pericles* (c.1608–1609). Indeed, the sleeping form of Imogen and the surrounding images of Cleopatra on the river Cydnus and of Diana in her bath, apparently reflect Shakespeare's earlier dramatization of Marina's rebirth from the sea and her defense against any suspicion of unchastity, despite her sojourn in an Antioch brothel.

Although Imogen's bedchamber as a whole in *Cymbeline* seems to have been decorated as a Temple of the Great Goddess, the addition of the sleeping figure of Imogen is ultimately the focal point of all the surrounding art works. A chaste married woman, on one level she resembles the spouse of the Song of Songs who longs for her absent lord, while on another level she is also the human soul who awaits the fiery embrace of the God of Love. She is called Diana by Cloten; yet she is also termed "Cytherea" or Venus by Iachimo as he gazes down on her revealed external beauty, which combines the Petrarchan contraries of red and white, fire and water, all attributes of *Venus genetrix*. The imagery of the Cleopatra tapestry and the imagery of the Diana fireplace with its two Cupids appear to merge in the beautiful figure of Imogen herself as a chaste but passionate wife. She reflects, I believe, that ideal Platonic Beauty thought to mediate between *Castitas* and *Amor,* a theme entering Renaissance iconography in 1486 by way of Virgil's *Aeneid* (1.315) when Venus, disguised as a chaste nymph of Diana, welcomes the Trojans to Carthage (Wind 1968, 73–75).

This classical image of Venus-Virgo as a statement that "Beauty is Love combined with chastity" (Wind 1968, 73–75) could be applied during the Renaissance rather indiscriminately to sweethearts, wives, mistresses, and even to virgin queens such as Elizabeth of England:

> In [Venus–Virgo] the Renaissance Platonists thought they had found a fine poetical confirmation for their doctrine of the unity of Chastity and Love. While it is doubtful whether Virgil intended the image to convey any mystery of that kind, they expanded it into a semi-chaste, semi-voluptuous cult of Venus, in which her double nature could be refined to the highest points of either reverence or frivolity or both. A popular ornament on Florentine marriage *cassoni,* the emblem acquired a new courtly twist in France and England, where its potentialities were developed more fully than in Italy itself. (Wind 1968, 77)

Wind's examples of the French and English uses of the Venus–Virgo theme include the Clouet portrait of Diane de Poitiers, where the "mythological 'bath of Diana' is transformed into a *toilete de Venus*" (1968, 77), and the engraving by Crispin van de Passe of one of Isaac Oliver's portraits of Queen Elizabeth. As Wind indicates, the engraved version of the portrait bears an inscription obviously inspired by the above-mentioned passage from Virgil (1:315): *"Virginis os habitumque geris, divina virago."* Spenser makes similar allusions to Elizabeth as Virgil's Venus–Virgo in his *Shepheardes Calendar, Aprill* and in *Faerie Queene* IV (Wind 1968, 78, n.87). Hence, it seems very possible that the union of Chastity and Love through the Beauty of the sleeping Imogen—amplified by the surrounding and complementary images of Cleopatra as Venus/Isis and of Diana bathing—in Shakespeare's *Cymbeline* could also be read politically as a delicate compliment to another Elizabeth, the soon to be married Princess of England.

On the other hand, Iachimo sees none of these subtle allusions or philosophical echoes. He simply describes what he sees from a sensory point of view, which is all Posthumus is capable of understanding at this point since he has not yet achieved an Erasmian distrust of outer appearances. The spirit within the works of art and the soul within the sleeping Imogen are still as opaque to Posthumus's erotic sensibilities as they are to those of his double Cloten. Only the actual sight of sacrificial blood stains provided by Pisanio, or an encounter with death, will finally shock him into a new level of spiritual awareness.

The Fretted Ceiling of Cherubim

Once we add the sleeping woman and all her mytho-religious associations to our mental picture of the bedchamber, I think the overall iconography of the Great Goddess changes somewhat in meaning. The bedchamber now becomes a Temple of the Three Graces—Beauty, Chastity, and Love—deriving from Imogen as Beauty, Diana as Chastity, and Cleopatra–Venus as Love. The Eros and Anteros andirons suggest a choice in the type of desire one feels toward these entities. In a recent essay on Milton, Stella Revard has explained the significance of the Graces and their important role as patrons of poetry:

> For the ancients poetry was essential to the well-ordered society, and the Graces as patrons of poetry also function to preserve social order. In fact, their ordering of festival or dance symbolizes the infusing of grace and well-being to promote good government on earth. Their very name in Greek, Χάριτες, signifies the favor or grace (χάρις) that they grant to mortals, a grace that Renaissance mythographers believe signifies the ultimate grace or mercy of God toward human beings (Comes 274–75). Renaissance mythographers interpret the dance of the Graces—in which they link hands and form a circle, the one Grace turned away, the other two facing—as an emblem for the giving, receiving, and returning of benefits. Through this visual symbol, they say, God teaches us that as he gives good gifts to us through his heavenly grace, we should return favor to our fellow human beings and live with them in peace, felicity, and commonality.[49]

These points should remind us of the artistic purposes of early Italian tragicomedies. The emphasis on temperance and the ordered poetry of tragicomedy will help "to promote good government on earth," and the emphasis of the genre on forgiveness as the ultimate grace of God (which we must return to our fellow humans) exactly reflects the Renaissance meaning of the Graces. As the architect of their temple through his poetry, Shakespeare partakes of the power of the Graces and makes them visible to us in this extraordinary scene in the bedchamber at a moment when they are very nearly violated by an intruding satyr dressed as a courtier.

Not surprisingly, the word "temple" is used six times in *Cymbeline,* twice in reference to Imogen herself. In act 2, scene 2, the Second Lord prays for the beleaguered princess as follows: "The heavens hold firm /

The walls of thy dear honour, keep unshak'd / That temple, thy fair mind, that thou mayst stand, / T'enjoy thy banish'd lord and this great land!" (2.1.61–64). Unlike Iachimo and Posthumus, the Second Lord understands that Imogen's true beauty lies within. Moreover, as I have noted earlier, Posthumus finally describes his bride as "The temple of Virtue" (5.5.220–21), once again emphasizing inner rather than outer beauty.

Torquato Tasso explains the importance of the temple as an analogue of beauty in Renaissance aesthetics in his brief dialogue "Il Minturno overo de la bellezza" ("Minturno, or On Beauty"). Here Antonio Minturno, basing his remarks on Plotinus (*Enneads* I.6.7), discusses the beauty of the eternal soul:

> if it could be defined, it would have a limit, but perhaps it is impossible to describe or circumscribe the beauty of the soul in place, time, matter, or in words, and to seek more than this is perhaps too daring and presumptuous, or a sign of too audacious a faith, as with those who go beyond the curtain in a temple and enter the *sancta sanctorum*.[50]

According to Minturno, most of us see only the decorations that surround the *sancta sanctorum,* "the columns and the beams of cedar and scented cypress, the arches, the vault, the capitals and the statues that support them, and call beautiful whatever we see, or rather what seems beautiful to us and flatters our senses." But for those who understand the mystery within, "there is nothing that resembles beauty so much as a temple" (1982, 237). When Iachimo enters the *sancta sanctorum* of Imogen's bedchamber, for example, he perceives only sensory superficialities of sight, smell, and touch that have nothing to do with faith or virtue, the qualities of Imogen's soul for which Posthumus actually yearns. Iachimo fails to see that this place is a Temple for the Three Graces—Love, Beauty, and Chastity—although he does sense that Imogen is in some way "a heavenly angel" and that he himself is a profaning representative from "hell" (2.2.50).

Since for Christians the union of the three Graces was only truly achieved when Jesus Christ was born, it is very significant that Imogen's bedchamber also boasts an elaborate cosmic ceiling with musical implications conveyed through a pun on the word "fretted." This term refers both to a type of Renaissance interior decoration in plaster and to the construction of musical instruments with strings, such as lutes and viols. Iachimo blandly informs Posthumus that, "the roof o' th' chamber / With golden cherubins is fretted" (2.4.87–88). According to the *OED,* "cherubins" is a form of the word cherubim, but it also manages to suggest in this context the pagan cherubs *(amorini)* commonly associated with Venus as well as winged "cherubim," biblical guardians of the Tree of Life (Gen. 3.24). Another evocative biblical use of the word "cherubim" occurs in Psalm 18.10, which describes the thunderous descent of Jehovah to David in terms almost exactly paralleling the descent of Jupiter on an eagle to Posthumus in act 5, scene 4, of *Cymbeline:* "He rode upon the cherubim and did fly." This image of Jehovah seated on winged cherubim is repeated in Psalm 99.1.

Shakespeare's Lorenzo makes a fuller statement of the Pythagorean and cosmic idea of Imogen's musical ceiling in the garden scene of *The Merchant of Venice:*

> Soft stillness and the night
> Become the touches of sweet harmony.
> Sit, Jessica. Look how the floor of heaven
> Is thick inlaid with patens of bright gold.
> There's not the smallest orb which thou behold'st
> But in his motion like an angel sings,
> Still quiring to the young-ey'd cherubins;
> Such harmony is in immortal souls,
> But whilst this muddy vesture of decay
> Doth grossly close it in, we cannot hear it.

(5.1.56–65)

This is the harmony of an ordered universe; it is reflected in our souls, and it ties us together with everything else in God's creation, according to Renaissance Platonism.

To express this integration of all things, ceilings of the Elizabethan period were often "fretted" in fact with interlaced designs of raised plaster. Geoffrey Beard describes an elaborate ceiling of this type at Sizergh Castle, Westmorland, as follows: "The room is dated about 1575 and the design of the frieze and ceiling is based on the repetition of a demi-figure of a winged cherub and shallow ribs in a geometric pattern interspersed with goats and stags, heraldic shields, and intertwined acorns."[51] Of course we must also recall that the purpose of actual frets on the fingerboards of stringed instruments is to help the musicians play in tune, that is, to achieve concord in earthly performance.

Although Iachimo's description of the "fretted" ceiling conflates the visual image of winged cherubim with a verbal evocation of heavenly harmonies, such harmonies will only resonate in human ears on a winter's night during Cymbeline's reign, when the God of Love at last finds a local habitation in Bethlehem and "a multitude of the heavenly host" sings His praises to the waiting shepherds. And at this point, speaking generically, the primitivism in *Cymbeline* will give way at last to pastoralism.

I am convinced, therefore, that the stage setting and Iachimo's ekphrasis of Imogen and her decorated bedchamber ought to be understood as essential elements of the tragicomedy rather than as mere erotic ornamentation. They tell us a great deal about the symbolic meaning of Imogen herself within the play, her mythic associations with life, death, and rebirth, and why we feel so deeply horrified at Posthumus's betrayal of what he should hold most dear—Virtue and Grace, to say nothing of Nature, or the classical "woman's part" of creation. In dramatic terms, these visual details foreshadow (1) much of the action to come in respect to changes in gender, costume, and moral perspective; (2) the happy ending of the tragicomedy which is achieved through Christian forgiveness and Jupiter's Grace; (3) the universal political peace established in the last scene by Cymbeline; and (4) the impending but never directly articulated Nativity of Christ. Above all, a careful reading of the iconography of Imogen's bedchamber helps us as modern playgoers to wend our way through the "curiously wrought" philosophical labyrinths and the decorative interweaving of motifs that characterize the achievement of the best in Renaissance art. Unfortunately, such complications by the time of Samuel Johnson and the Age of Reason began to seem impossibly "overwrought," and critics no longer wished to make the effort to understand them.

Notes

1. Jean Seznec, *The Survival of the Pagan Gods: The Mythological Tradition and Its Place in Renaissance Humanism and Art,* trans. Barbara F. Sessions (New York: Pantheon Books Inc., 1953), 98.

2. I cannot agree with the commonly held notion that Shakespeare and his company would have been content with a bare stage, especially for productions at Blackfriars, which attracted a coterie audience accustomed to elaborate court masques. The bedroom as described by Iachimo would have been very simple to reproduce on a stage by means of a borrowed tapestry or a painted cloth, a painted wooden chimneypiece, and a movable bed with hangings.

3. S. K. Heninger, Jr., *The Cosmographical Glass: Renaissance Diagrams of the Universe* (San Marino, Calif.: The Huntington Library, 1977), 8. The Aristotelians saw the cosmos, in contrast, as "a continuum of matter."

4. See W. G. Thomson, *A History of Tapestry, from the Earliest Times to the Present Day,* 3d ed., rev. by F. P. and E. S. Thomson (London: EP Publishing Ltd., 1973), 376.

5. Ibid., 366–68.

6. Marie Axton, *The Queen's Two Bodies: Drama and the Elizabethan Succession* (London: Royal Historical Society, 1977), 54.

7. See Bono, *Literary Transvaluation: From Vergilian Epic to Shakespearean Tragicomedy* (Berkeley: University of California Press, 1984), 173–79; hereafter cited parenthetically.

8. William S. Heckscher, "The *Anadyomene* in the Medieval Tradition," in *Art and Literature: Studies in Relationship,* ed. Egon Verheyen (Durham, N.C.: Duke University Press, 1985), 138–39; hereafter cited parenthetically.

9. See Apuleius, *The XI Bookes of the "Golden Ass" conteininge the Meta-*

morphosie of Lucius Apuleius, trans. William Adlington (London: William How, for Abraham Veale, 1571), 113–113ᵛ; hereafter cited parenthetically.

10. Michael Lloyd, "Cleopatra as Isis," *Shakespeare Survey* 12 (1959): 91.

11. See Plutarch, *The Philosophie, commonlie called, The Morals Written by the learned Philosopher Plutarch,* trans. Philemon Holland (London: Arnold Hatfield, 1603), 1309; hereafter cited parenthetically.

12. Spenser, *The Faerie Queene,* ed. Thomas P. Roche, Jr., with the assistance of C. Patrick O'Donnell, Jr. (1978; reprint New Haven: Yale University Press, 1981).

13. See Wind, *Pagan Mysteries in the Renaissance,* rev. and enl. ed. (New York: W. W. Norton & Co., Inc., 1968), 133; hereafter cited parenthetically.

14. *The Riverside Shakespeare,* 1344.

15. See Panofsky, *The Iconography of Correggio's Camera Di San Paolo* (London: The Warburg Institute, 1961), 6; hereafter cited parenthetically.

16. Richard Linche, *The Fountaine of Ancient Fiction* (London: Adam Islip, 1599), sigs. Hᵛ–Hiii.

17. See Dunlop, *Palaces and Progresses of Elizabeth I* (London: Jonathan Cape, 1962), 109.

18. See Smith, "Landscape with Figures: The Three Realms of Queen Elizabeth's Country-house Revels," *Renaissance Drama* 8 (1977): 83.

19. Francis Bacon, *Fables of the Ancients,* ed. Dr. Shaw (London: J. Cundee, 1803), 90.

20. See Barkan, "Diana and Actaeon: The Myth as Synthesis," *English Literary Renaissance* 10 (1980): 333.

21. Herbert Cescinsky, *English Furniture from Gothic to Sheraton,* 2d ed. (Garden City, N.Y.: Garden City Publishing Company, Inc., 1937), 59.

22. Abraham Fraunce, *The Third part of the Countesse of Pembroke's Iuychurch: Entitled Amintas Dale* (London: Thomas Woodcocke, 1592), 43.

23. John Davies of Hereford, *The Holy Roode, or Christs Crosse: Containing Christ Crucified, described in speaking-picture* (London: John Windet for Nathaniel Butter, 1609), sig. B; hereafter cited parenthetically.

24. See Margery Corbett and R. W. Lightbown, *The Comely Frontispiece: The Emblematic Title-page in England 1550–1660* (London: Routledge & Kegan Paul, 1979), 6. The authors inform us that once title pages were made as line engravings on copper plates, they were carefully designed for a particular book and became "an elaborate allegorical and emblematic visual introduction to the book."

25. Ralph Edwards, *The Dictionary of English Furniture,* rev. ed., 2 vols. (London: Country Life Ltd., 1954), vol. 2, 55. See also L. A. Shuffrey, *The English Fireplace* (London: B. T. Batsford, 1912), 146–47.

26. See Leo Planiscig, *Venezianische bildhauer der renaissance* (Vienna: A. Schroll & Co., 1921), 597–617. I am grateful to Mary D. Garrard for calling this work to my attention.

27. James Hutton, "Analogues of Shakespeare's Sonnets 153 and 154: Contributions to the History of a Theme," in *Essays on Renaissance Poetry,* ed. Rita Guerlac (Ithaca, N.Y.: Cornell University Press, 1980), 150.

28. For a fuller discussion of the topos in the Sonnets, see my essay, "Eros and Anteros in Shakespeare's Sonnets 153 and 154: An Iconographical Study," *Spenser Studies* 7 (1987): 261–85 and 311–23.

29. Ronald Jaeger, "A Biblical Allusion in Shakespeare's Sonnet 154," *Notes and Queries,* n.s. 19 (1972): 125.

30. Thomas P. Roche, Jr., "How Petrarchan Is Shakespeare?" in *Shakespeare's*

Art from a Comparative Perspective, ed. Wendall M. Aycock (Lubbock: Texas Tech Press, 1981), 161.

31. Trans. W. R. Paton, *The Greek Anthology,* 5 vols. Loeb Classical Library (Cambridge, Mass.: Harvard University Press, 1958), vol. 5, 309, number 251. Spitting into one's bosom was, in antiquity, a way of asking pardon of the gods for excessive presumption. See Pliny 28.7 and Erasmus, *Adages* (257E) 1.7.94. I am indebted to Virginia W. Callahan for providing this information.

32. See Peter M. Daly, Virginia W. Callahan, and Simon Cuttler, eds., *Andreas Alciatus: Index Emblematicus,* 2 vols. (Toronto: University of Toronto Press, 1985), 1: Emblem 116. All English translations of Alciati's emblems come from this volume, which lacks page numbers.

33. See *The Greek Anthology,* vol. 5, 275–77, for epigrams on this *topos.*

34. Ibid., 277. For surveys of most of what is known about the Eros and Anteros topos, see Robert V. Merrill, "Eros and Anteros," *Speculum* 19 (1944): 265–84; Guy de Tervarent, *Attributs et symboles dans l'art profane 1450–1600* (Geneva: Libraire E. Droz, 1958), col. 20; and de Tervarent, "Eros and Anteros: Or Reciprocal Love in Ancient and Renaissance Art," *Journal of the Warburg and Courtauld Institutes* 28 (1965): 205–08.

35. See Marsilio Ficino, *Commentary on Plato's "Symposium" on Love,* trans. Sears Jayne (Dallas, Texas: Spring Publications, Inc., 1985), 131–32.

36. Desiderius Erasmus, *Enchiridion,* trans. and ed. Raymond Himelick (Bloomington: Indiana University Press, 1963), 53.

37. Achille Bocchi, *Symbolicarum . . . Libri Quinque* (Bologna, 1555), Bk. 1, 41. Translation by Roger T. Simonds.

38. *The Greek Anthology,* vol. 5, 245.

39. Smith, "Sermons in Stones: Shakespeare and Renaissance Sculpture," *Shakespeare Studies* 17 (1985): 3–5. According to William Heckscher, "Prints travelled fast and their enormous range of influence cannot easily be exaggerated." See "Shakespeare and the Visual Arts" in *Art and Literature: Studies in Relationship,* ed. Egon Verhayen (Durham, NC: Duke University Press, 1985), p. 410. See also Samuel C. Chew, *The Pilgrimage of Life* (New Haven: Yale University Press, 1962), 263. Here Chew quotes a diatribe by Henry Peacham in *The Gentleman's Exercise* (ed. 1612), 9, against the current sale of lascivious art in London:

> What lewde art is there showne in many prints and peeces that are daily brought over out of Italy, Flanders, and other places, which are oftener enquired after in the shops then any other, little use is there in most of the wax pictures of Curtizans in Rome and Venice being drawne naked, and sold up and down as Libidinis Fomenta, surely I cannot but commend art in them, as many times there is excellent good, but verily do hate their wicked makers and abhominable ends.

40. See Millard Meiss, "Sleep in Venice: Ancient Myths and Renaissance Proclivities," *The Painter's Choice: Problems in the Interpretation of Renaissance Art* (New York: Harper and Row, 1976), 215; hereafter cited parenthetically.

41. Francesco Colonna, *Hypnerotomachia. The Strife of Loue in a Dreame* (1592; reprint, New York & London: Garland Publishing, Inc., 1976), sig. K2.

42. Ibid., sig. K2ᵛ.

43. See Elisabeth B. MacDougall, "The Sleeping Nymph: Origins of a Humanist Fountain Type," *Art Bulletin* 57 (1975): 357. MacDougall also points out that the humanists in Rome associated the ancient statue of Ariadne–Cleopatra with an epigram then believed to be ancient: "Huis nympha loci, sacri custodia fontis / Dormio dum blandae sentior murmur aquae. / Parce meum quisquis tangis cava

marmora somnum / Rumpere: sive bibas, sive lavere taces" (357). This verse was later translated by Alexander Pope as follows: "Nymph of the Grot, these sacred springs I keep / And to the Murmur of these Waters sleep; / Ah, spare my slumbers, gently tread the cave! / And drink in Silence or in silence lave!" (365). I am grateful to Mary D. Garrard for calling my attention to this and related essays on the sleeping nymph *topos,* including her own brilliant study of "The Dying Cleopatra" by Artemisia Gentileschi in *Artemisia Gentileschi: The Image of the Female Hero in Italian Baroque Art* (Princeton, N.J.: Princeton University Press, 1989), 244–77.

44. See Robert Graves, *The Greek Myths,* 2 vols. (Baltimore, Md.: Penguin Books, 1955), 1, 347, n.5.

45. See *The Search for Alexander: An Exhibition* (New York: Little, Brown and Company, 1980), plate 20.

46. See Leonard Barkan, *The Gods Made Flesh: Metamorphosis & the Pursuit of Paganism* (New Haven and London: Yale University Press, 1986), 249; hereafter cited parenthetically.

47. Marsilio Ficino, *Theologica platonica,* trans. Abigail Young (forthcoming).

48. See Alistair Fowler, *Triumphal Forms: Structural Patterns in Elizabethan Poetry* (Cambridge: Cambridge University Press, 1970), 148–51.

49. Stella P. Revard, " 'L'Allegro' and 'Il Penseroso': Classical Tradition and Renaissance Mythography," *PMLA* 101 (1986): 341.

50. See *Tasso's Dialogues: A Selection,* trans. Carnes Lord and Dain A. Trafton (Berkeley: University of California Press, 1982), 237.

51. Geoffrey Beard, *Decorative Plasterwork in Great Britain* (London: Phaidon, 1975), 27.

4

The Iconography of Primitivism in *Cymbeline*

We gather daily what we need
For that day and don't have to hoard
For all these gifts we thank the Lord
If death should come or one fall ill
We know that this is just God's will
Which always sets things for the best
And so our minds remain at rest
As we await within our border
That great change in the civil order
When all the world will see the light
And everyman live true, upright,
In equal, unconniving good
It's then we'll gladly leave the wood
And rejoin mankind in tears
Of joy.

—Hans Sachs, *Lament of the Wild Forest
Folk over the Perfidious World,*
trans. Fred A. Childs

In contrast to the courtly Italianate iconography of Imogen's bedchamber, act 3 introduces the equally rich but very different iconography of primitivism and hunting to the tragicomedy. Unfortunately, however, most contemporary critics insist that *Cymbeline* is a pastoral play, mistaking a primitive setting in the Welsh mountains for an ideal pastoral world, complete with sheep and shepherds naively ready for fleecing by a character like Autolycus.[1] Although Shakespeare does indeed employ pastoralism in a number of his plays, both sheep and shepherds are notably lacking in *Cymbeline,* to the despair of the heroine herself. As I have noted earlier in this study, Imogen wishes for the innocence and familiarity of a pastoral world when she laments in act 1, "Would I were / A neat-herd's daughter, and my Leonatus / Our neighbour-shepherd's son!" (1.2.79–81). However, the dramatist chooses to present her with a cave and three self-proclaimed savages, or Wild Men, in opposition to the corrupt and superficially civilized world of the king and his elegant courtiers. Violence and death are everyday aspects of this wilderness life, as Imogen soon discovers, despite the natural courtesy and courage she also finds in Wales.

Although William Empson believed that *any* alternative world was "pastoral,"[2] there is actually a sharp dichotomy between Wild Men and shepherds in iconography. Of course these figures may appear together in tragicomedy, as in fact they do in Guarini's *Il pastor fido,* which opposes a lustful satyr to a princely shepherd, and in Shakespeare's *The Winter's Tale,* which introduces a brief fertility dance by satyrs into a shepherds' springtime festival. But in *Cymbeline* there are no shepherds, only hunters, and here the alternative world to the court is distinctly primitive. As the word "pastoral" itself indicates, pastoral characters are shepherds and shepherdesses, while pastoral art by definition concerns the lives of those who domesticate and protect animals from the savage aspects of nature. In sharp contrast, "primitivism" denotes the actions of savages or hairy (sometimes leafy) Wild Folk who live what would usually be considered a subhuman, beastly existence in the wilderness, without any of the arts of civilization, sometimes without even the gift of human speech. Imogen, in *Cymbeline,* later cuts up roots for the Wild Boys in the shape of letters and makes alphabet soup in hopes of teaching them to read and write.

The shepherds of the pastoral convention, on the other hand, are often poets, musicians, and true lovers, while Wild Men were originally depicted in the Middle Ages as fierce, lustful rapists. Shepherds protect their flocks from foxes and wolves; the Wild Man is a hunter of savage beasts and is often described in terms of the predacious animals he hunts. Predatory himself and often a cannibal, he is a natural enemy to the inhabitants of the domesticated pastoral world. Since Shakespeare's innocent pastoral characters tend to be clowns, their simplicity makes them easy dupes for the trickery of those who enter their Edenic haunts. Shakespeare's Wild Men, in contrast, derive from the tougher, more radical tradition of postlapsarian primitivism that depicts a moral and physical descent from the human state to that of the brute.[3] Most Christians believed during the Renaissance that Wild Men originated right after the Fall as described in Genesis 3:21: "Unto Adam also and to his wife did the Lord God make coats of skins, and clothed them."

But the figure is notably ambivalent in meaning. The Wild Man may, like Caliban, represent man's lower nature, which must be controlled, or, during the late Middle Ages and the Renaissance, he may represent what Timothy Husband describes as "a free and enlightened creature living in complete harmony with nature," who is no longer "a symbol of all that man should eschew but, on the contrary . . . [a] symbol of all that man should strive to achieve."[4] In the latter role, he becomes a conventional and thus a safe way to satirize the rigid social hierarchy of the Jacobean age, even when he goes so far as to lop off the empty head of an ungentle

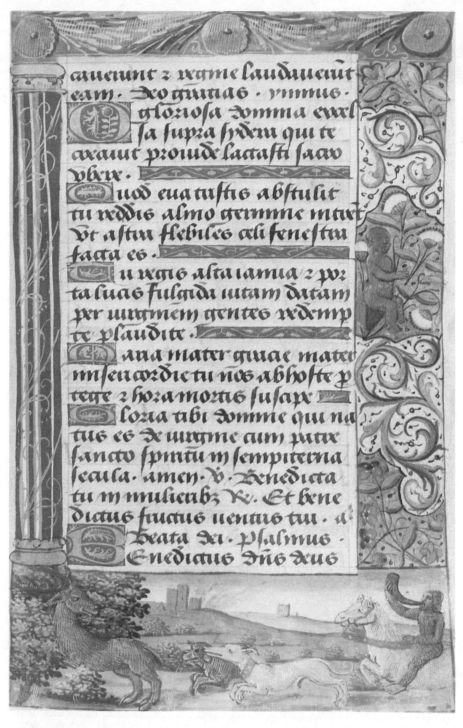

A Wild Man and his hounds hunting a deer. From the border of an illuminated Book of Hours (c.1500). Jean de Montlucon shop, Bourges, France (Ms. 436, folio 25). Reprinted by courtesy of the Beinecke Library, Yale University.

Wild Men judge and execute a courtly hunter. Detail from an illuminated Book of Hours (c.1500), Jean de Montlucon shop, Bourges, France (Ms. 436, folio 76). Reprinted by permission of the Beinecke Library, Yale University.

prince in *Cymbeline*. Yet judging and executing erring courtiers was also quite within the accepted tradition of the Wild Man, as a manuscript illustration from a Book of Hours (c.1500) clearly indicates.

In this chapter I shall discuss the significance of this carefully selected iconography of cultural primitivism and relate it to the basic reformation themes of the play and to the Jacobean court it both flatters and satirizes. I will show here that the iconography of primitivism serves three major functions in *Cymbeline*. It ironically portrays the savage life as virtuous and instructive in contrast to life in a depraved court; it focuses our attention on Shakespeare's use of the literary convention of the hunt, which permeates much of the play's action; and, finally, it endows the newly reformed court of Britain with fecundity, strength, and justice, through its human representatives, the Wild Men.

Noble Wild Men and Savage Courtiers

The first function of Shakespeare's iconography of primitivism in *Cymbeline* is to portray the wild life as virtuous and instructive in contrast to life in a corrupt court. Twenty years before the first scene opens, a malicious courtier had slandered Belarius to the king, who had promptly exiled his formerly trusted advisor. As the type of educated Wild Man unjustly thrust out of civilization and into the wilderness, Belarius at first seems to derive topically from the biblical figure of Ishmael: "and he will be a wild man, his hand will be against every man, and every man's hand against him" (Gen. 16:12). Desiring immediate revenge for his dishonor, Belarius kidnapped the infant sons of Cymbeline and took them with him into a desolate exile in the Welsh mountains, where we first meet all three of them in act 3, scene 3, living in a cave.

They are simple worshippers of the goddess Natura and of the sun, Platonic symbol of the Good. By now their only clothes are those they have fashioned themselves from the skins of animals they hunt for food. Belarius is later described as having a long white beard, and the boys must be equally shaggy in appearance, since Arviragus complains of their state in terms clearly identifying them as ignorant and savage Wild Men: "We have seen nothing: / We are beastly: subtle as the fox for prey, / Like warlike as the wolf for what we eat" (3.2.39–41). According to Hayden White, "In most accounts of the Wild Man in the Middle Ages, he is as strong as Hercules, fast as the wind, cunning as the wolf, and devious as the fox."[5]

Cymbeline's other kidnapped son, Guiderius, calls their cave dwelling "A cell of ignorance" (3.3.33), which further suggests the traditional medieval image of Wild Folk cut off from civilization, unable to read or write. However, Belarius, who knows "the art o' th' court," sees their lives as pious rather than bestial: "This rock, and these demesnes, have been my world, / Where I have liv'd at honest freedom, paid / More pious debts to heaven than in all / The fore-end of my time" (3.3.70–73). He has consciously tried to raise the boys to a life of courtesy within nature.

Husband tells us that early medieval myths of the Wild Man describe him as a hairy hunter who often lives in a cave located on a desolate mountain or deep within the forest. His behavior tends to be brutish and violent, "not only against wild animals but also against his own kind."[6] Shakespeare's Guiderius displays just this natural aggressiveness in a prompt and ferocious way when he beheads the king's foolish stepson Cloten in 4, 2. In telling contrast to the hairy Guiderius, Cloten is decked out in elegant court garments he has stolen from Posthumus, yet he arrogantly calls the honest Wild Man a "thief" and "villain base" (4.2.75 and 80), clear evidence of the dramatist's implicit social satire. Guiderius, in turn, considers Cloten of no more value than a tailor's mannequin and coolly chops off his head, to the horror of the former courtier Belarius. The contrast in this scene between the two younger men represents an important symbolic inversion of the Wild Man *topos,* since in *Cymbeline* the savage is indeed a true prince, and Cloten is a crude courtly impostor who has obtained his social position at the top of the hierarchy only through his mother's marriage to the king. As Derek Traversi notes, Cloten is "a court parody of the truly 'natural' man, enslaved to his base passions."[7]

His opposites, the Wild Boys—despite their innate and still uncontrolled violence—are natural young noblemen, well-born but bred in the wilderness and innocent in their own lives of all courtly artifice. They may therefore have a partly Celtic origin in the myth of Perceval of Wales, who was called *"le valet sauvage"* by Chrétien de Troyes. As Richard Bernheimer indicates, "the very fact that a man was brought up in the woods may confer upon him a certain incorruptible quality which alone enables him to resist temptations to which others succumb, and thus to attain aims inaccessible to them."[8] In act 3, scene 7, of *Cymbeline,* when the wandering Princess Imogen, disguised as a page, unexpectedly meets her shaggy and still unrecognized brothers in the mountains, she wishes they were indeed her father's lost sons:

> Great men
> That had a court no bigger than this cave,
> That did attend themselves, and had the virtue
> Which their own conscience seal'd them, laying by
> That nothing-gift of differing multitudes,
> Could not out-peer these twain.

(3.7.54–59)

They, in turn, instantly love her and accept her as a "brother," although they instinctively doubt her masculinity. Cloten, on the other hand, desires to rape her, as the Wild Man Caliban longs to ravish Miranda in *The Tempest.*

Unlike these natural young noblemen, Belarius himself is a Wild Man of a more sophisticated Renaissance variety, an exile from contemporary civilization. When he emerges from his cave in 3.3, he may well have reminded Shakespeare's audience of Emblem 37 in Andrea Alciati's widely read *Emblemata.* The *inscriptio* or motto of this emblem, "Omnia mea mecum porto" ("I carry everything I own with me"), derives from an Erasmian adage, "Sapiens sua secum bona fert" ("The wise man carries his goods with him").[9] It refers to that which we carry within us, such as learning and virtue. The adage is an allusion to Bias, one of the Seven Sages of the classical world, who left all his material goods behind him after a fire. The *pictura* in the 1551 edition of Alciati depicts a Wild Man dressed in skins that have been stitched together. In the background are a cave, trees, and the Scythian Sea, suggesting a reference to the *De Germania* of Tacitus and his ironic descriptions of the barbarians of the north as virtuous in contrast to the Romans of his own time. The *subscriptio* of the emblem reads:

Hunnus inops, Scythicique miserrimus accola Ponti,
  Ustus perpetuo livida membra gelu:
Qui Cereris non novit opes, nec dona Lyaei,
  Et pretiosa tamen stragula semper habet.
Nam murinae illum perstringunt undique pelles:
  Lumina sola patent, caetera opertus agit.
Sic furem haud metuit, sic ventos temnit et imbres;
  Tutus apudque viros, tutus apudque Deos.

(The poor Hun, the most miserable dweller near the Scythian Sea, constantly has his limbs pinched livid with cold. He knows not the wealth of Ceres, nor the gifts of Bacchus, nevertheless, he always has precious clothing. For skins of martens envelope him on all sides: only his eyes are visible, every other part is covered. Thus he fears no thief, thus he disdains the winds and rain-storms. He is safe among men, and safe among the gods.)

Some editions of the *Emblemata* show the "poor Hun" as naked, a not uncommon variant of the Wild Man *topos*.

Shakespeare's Belarius appears to be a Wild Man of this virtuous Erasmian type so wistfully celebrated by Alciati. He is a soldier-scholar, who carries his learning and virtue with him into the wilderness to escape the multiple evils of life at court. He assures Arviragus and Guiderius, who complain of their savage existence, that, "this life / Is nobler than attending for a check: / Richer than doing nothing for a robe, / Prouder than rustling in unpaid-for silk: / Such gain the cap of him that makes him fine, / Yet keeps his book uncross'd: no life to ours" (3.3.21–26). One may object, of course, that Belarius is also a kidnapper. In this respect, Husband informs us that the mythical Wild Man did characteristically abduct children, "but often only to fulfill parental instincts."[11] In fact, Belarius has considerably better parental instincts than does Cymbeline, who is described by his daughter Imogen as behaving like the tyrannous north wind that "Shakes all our buds from growing" (1.4.37).

The audience witnesses in 3.3 of *Cymbeline*, on the other hand, an excellent model of the proper education of princes when the Wild Man Belarius, by pointing out examples in nature, trains his royal pupils against moral abuses arising from the unnatural hierarchy of the Renaissance social order. Even the mouth of their humble cave provides a lesson in natural piety: "Stoop boys: this gate / Instructs you how t'adore the heavens; and bows you / To a morning's holy office. The gates of monarchs / Are arch'd so high that giants may get through / And keep their impious turbans on, without / Good morrow to the sun. Hail, thou fair heaven!" (3.3.2–7). These Wild Men are indeed comfortably "safe among the gods," as Alciati had put it. The antithesis to such pious humility can be seen at Cymbeline's court, where "You do not meet a man but frowns; our bloods / No more obey the heavens than our courtiers / Still seem as does the king's" (1.1.1–3).

A naked Wild Man, from Emblem 37, Andrea Alciati, *Emblemata*, 1581 edition, 168. Reprinted by permission of the Folger Shakespeare Library (PN 6349 A8 1581).

Defending the wild life in the kind of speech termed an *argumentum emblematicum* by Albrecht Schöne,[12] Belarius also informs the princes that in the wilderness, "often, to our comfort, shall we find / The sharded beetle in a safer hold / Than is the full-wing'd eagle" (3.3.20–21). As H. W. Crundell noted in 1935, this peculiar image originated with Aesop, was later elaborated upon by Erasmus, and then was used by John Lyly in both *Euphues and Endimion* before reappearing in Shakespeare's *Cymbeline*.[13] However, Shakespeare and the educated members of his audience would undoubtedly have known as well Alciati's epigram of the eagle and the beetle in Emblem 169 of his *Emblemata*. Since Alciati's *inscriptio* reads "A Minimis quoque timendum" ("Even the smallest is to be feared"), the reference in *Cymbeline* may be understood as a warning by Belarius to the princes not to abuse their own future dependents as he himself has been abused by the tyrant Cymbeline. By extension, a gentle warning is also being sent by the playwright to his own patron, James I, who owned a copy of Alciati and could not possibly be offended by what had become a Renaissance commonplace taught to schoolboys.[14]

The *subscriptio* of Alciati's emblem tells us that,

> Bella gerit Scarabaeus, et hostem provocat ultrò,
>   Robore et inferior, consilio superat.
> Nam plumis Aquilae clam se neque cognitus abdit,
>   Hostilem ut nidum summa per astra petat.
> Quaque confodiens, prohibet spem crescere prolis:
>   Hocque modo illatum dedecus ultus abit.

> (The beetle is waging war and of its own accord provokes its enemy: and, though weaker in strength, it conquers through strategy. For without being discovered, it hides itself in the eagle's feathers, in order to seek out the enemy nest through the lofty stars; and piercing the eggs it prevents the hope of offspring from growing. Having avenged in this way the shame inflicted on it, it departs.)

Alciati's emblem sums up the situation in Shakespeare's play very well indeed, although we have no reason to consider it a direct source. In the tragicomedy, Cymbeline has unwisely dishonored Belarius, who in turn has stolen the king's male offspring from the palace (or nest) in order to keep them from becoming tyrants like their father and to avenge his own wounded honor. On the other hand, Belarius—unlike the beetle—does not prevent the boys from growing; instead he educates them in what he understands to be the universal laws of nature.

The *pictura* of this emblem in the 1534 Wechel edition of Alciati shows an angry eagle at the left, his tongue extended, looking up at the beetle in a tree. In the 1551 edition, seven eaglets can be seen falling out of the tree, thus indicating the extent of damage to the eagle's posterity that a single discontented beetle can wreak. The source of the emblem was Erasmus's adage "Scarabeus aquilam quaerit" ("The beetle seeks the eagle"). Although Erasmus retells an Aesopian fable in his commentary on the adage, he adds the detail that the beetle actually pushed the eggs out of the eagle's nest. The meaning of the fable, he explains, is that no enemy is to be despised no matter how unimportant.[15] Later, in *The Education of a Christian Prince,* the Dutch humanist states that in making use of such fables as the eagle and the beetle, "the teacher should . . . point out its meaning: not even the most powerful prince can afford to provoke or overlook even the humblest enemy. Often those who can inflict no harm by physical strength can do much by the machinations of their minds."[16]

Belarius as teacher cannot, of course, fully explain his emblematic

The eagle and the beetle from Andrea Alciati, *Emblemata* (Paris: Wechel, 1534), 68. Reprinted by permission of the Folger Shakespeare Library (PN 6349 A8).

argument in *Cymbeline* at this point, but he does remind the boys that "it is place which lessens and sets off" (3.3.13), and he suggests that certain responsibilities go with high position. At once Guiderius unconsciously associates himself and his brother with the eagle rather than with the lowly beetle: "Out of your proof you speak: we poor unfledg'd, / Have never wing'd from view o' th' nest; nor know not / What air's from home" (27–29). The irony of this regal association with the eagle by the Wild Boy would have been immediately apparent to the educated members of Shakespeare's audience. Belarius himself later proclaims, " 'Tis wonder /

That an invisible instinct should frame them / To royalty unlearn'd, honour untaught, / Civility not seen from other, valour / That *wildly* grows in them, but yields a crop / As if it had been sow'd" (4.2.176–81; emphasis mine).

Life in the wilderness does indeed bring out the native virtue of the kidnapped princes, as Belarius has hoped it would. He comments on this result in a prayer to Natura:

> O thou goddess,
> Thou divine Nature; thou thyself thou blazon'st
> In these two princely boys: they are as gentle
> As zephyrs blowing below the violet,
> Not wagging his sweet head; and yet, as rough,
> (Their royal blood enchaf'd) as the rud'st wind
> That by the top doth take the mountain pine
> And make him stoop to th' vale.
>
> (4.2.169–76)

Once more there is a parallel between Belarius's nature imagery and the emblem tradition. Geffrey Whitney's "Nimium rebus ne fide secundis" (Be not too confident in prosperity) in *A Choice of Emblemes* (1586) has the following *subscriptio:*

> The loftie Pine, that on the mountaine growes,
> And spreades her armes, with braunches freshe, & greene,
> The raginge windes, on sodaine ouerthrowes,
> And makes her stoope, that longe a farre was seene;
> So they, that truste to muche in fortunes smiles,
> Thoughe worlde do laughe, and wealthe doe moste abounde,
> When leste they thinke, are often snar'de with wyles,
> And from alofte, doo hedlonge fall to grounde:
>   Then put no truste, in anie worldlie thinges,
>   For frowninge fate, throwes downe the mightie kinges.[17]

In *Cymbeline* Belarius compares the Wild Boys to the rude wind that makes the pine "stoop to the vale" right after Guiderius has described how he cut off the head of an excessively arrogant Cloten. Thus Cloten is the proud pine that does "hedlonge fall to grounde" when the true heir to Cymbeline's kingdom meets him like the raging wind of fate.

The Motif of the Hunt in *Cymbeline*

Our recognition of the primitive mode with the presence of Wild Men in *Cymbeline* leads us directly to what may be the principal metaphor of the tragicomedy: the hunt of love. Shakespeare's savage hunters Belarius, Arviragus, and Guiderius "do" literally for survival what Posthumus,

Imogen, Cloten, and even Iachimo do metaphorically throughout the play. In fact, the entire middle section of the play is devoted to hunts of various kinds—including a war hunt—in the mountains of Wales, and in this focus the play once again resembles Guarini's *Il pastor fido,* which contains what Bernard Harris calls a "great central episode of the boar-hunt."[18] As we analyze the play in terms of the chase, we should keep in mind that hunting was the favorite sport of Shakespeare's royal patron.

Marcelle Thiébaux identifies the significance of the literary *topos* of the hunt as follows:

> Metaphorically and symbolically . . . the chase becomes an imperative Journey by which a mortal is transported to a condition charged with experience: a preternatural region where he may be tested or placed under an enchantment; a transcendent universe; or the menacing reaches of the self. The act of the chase may reflect not only the compulsion arising from within his own nature to undergo change, but also an external force that imposes this necessity on him: that is, the god. For we are frequently aware of some power outside the hunter himself, with which his own will is made to coincide, both of these, driving, luring, compelling him.[19]

In Shakespeare's tragicomedy, the deity is very close indeed, and, not surprisingly, he finally appears to the hero and to the audience in a dream vision. As many students of *Cymbeline* have pointed out, the doctrine of the Incarnation must in some way inform the play as a whole, since the Nativity of Christ was the only "historical" event of real importance to occur during the reign of Cymbeline. And, if the Nativity is in fact the hidden center of the play, then a morally fallen world must be properly prepared for such an event. The wilderness, which represents iconographically that fallen world, is an obvious setting for both physical and metaphysical hunts during a period of such preparation primarily because the Wild Men who inhabit the wilderness are instantly recognizable symbols of postlapsarian humanity.

Thiébaux tells us that four distinct types of metaphorical hunts occur in literature, although they frequently change and even dissolve into one another: "The sacred chase, the mortal chase, the instructive chase, and the amatory chase" (1974, 58). The quarry of a sacred chase lures the hero to a direct confrontation with a god (or a goddess, in the case of Actaeon), and may cause his conversion and/or his death. In the mortal chase, the hunter is led by the quarry as psychopomp from the world of the living to the world of the dead. In the instructive chase, the protagonist undergoes an initiation of some sort, during which he passes "from a condition of ignorance to one of knowledge or self-knowledge" (1974, 58). Finally, in the amatory chase the hunter is lured by the quarry into the nets of a passionate love. All of these forms of hunting occur in *Cymbeline,* with the peculiar twist that in every instance the character thinks he is on one kind of chase, only to discover in the end that he has been on an entirely different type of hunt. In all cases, the quarry is love: love of God, love of knowledge, love of beauty, love of a spouse, or ordinary lust for the unattainable.

To begin with a literal chase, the three Wild Men in *Cymbeline* must of course hunt for their food, but Belarius insists that they do this in the courtly form of a ritualized sport, thus bringing the chivalric rules of the chase and all of its attendant metaphorical meanings into the play. In 3.3, Belarius exhorts the Wild Boys to the chase with the shout, "Now for our mountain sport, up to yond hill!" (10). Arviragus, however, yearns for military pursuits instead and complains that "Our valour is to chase what flies" (3.3.42). He would much rather face a worthy foe in battle than kill a deer for supper, although hunting was actually considered an ideal way to train the best fighting men (Thiébaux 1974, 49). Belarius cuts off the boys' discontent with a reminder of the ritual nature of their hunt and with a satirical comment on the sinister aspects of a refined life at court:

> But up to th' mountains!
> This is not hunter's language; he that strikes
> The venison first shall be the lord o' th' feast,
> To him the other two shall minister,
> And we will fear no poison, which attends
> To place of greater state. I'll meet you in the valleys.
>
> (3.3.73–78)

The whooping music of horn and hounds then becomes an integral part of the theatrical performance, prompting occasional interpretations by Belarius, who remains on stage: "Hark, the game is rous'd!" (98) and, finally, "The game is up" (107).

This literal chase—to the astonishment of the hunters—ends as a sacred chase. While the Wild Men pursue a stag, the true quarry takes shelter in their deserted cave. At last the hunters return home carrying their deer, prompting Belarius to announce ceremoniously, "You, Polydore, have prov'd best woodman, and / Are master of the feast: Cadwal and I / Will play the cook and servant: 'tis our match" (3.7.1–3). But the weary Guiderius replies, "There is cold meat i' th' cave, we'll browse on that" (11). With his use of the word "browse," Guiderius transforms the successful hunters themselves into three deer, who are then captured or captivated by their mysterious intruder. Imogen, disguised as the page Fidele, suddenly emerges from the cave to face them, causing the startled Belarius to exclaim, "Behold divineness / No elder than a boy" (16–17). The line is an obvious allusion to Amor or Cupid. Such an unexpected confrontation with the "divine" beauty of Imogen–Fidele has an instant civilizing effect on the hunters, who piously invite her to share their humble meal.

Of course I do not mean to imply here that Imogen is a type or personification of Christ; rather I believe that she is a soul figure on her own painful quest for love in the wild mountains of Wales, and—in this most Neoplatonic of plays—her beauty and goodness seem to reflect for many of the characters something of the sacred quality of the Love-God soon to be born. For example, when Arviragus first looks at Imogen, he understands at once the essence of Christ's ethical teaching: "He is a man, I'll love him as my brother" (3.7.44). Further echoes of the Christian myth occur when Imogen–Fidele sickens, apparently dies after taking the Queen's medicine, and is later resurrected. She has previously called herself "Th' elected deer" (3.4.111), which can refer to Christ as the quarry of man's desire but is more often a symbol of the human soul pursued by God.[20]

As for the wild hunters, they see Imogen as a winged creature untimely brought to earth. "The bird is dead," mourns Arviragus (4.2.197). Then, after a brief funeral ceremony for both Imogen and the beastly Cloten, who has been judged unworthy of the new era to come and executed by Guiderius, the three Wild Men go off on another type of hunt. This patriotic war hunt takes place on the battlefield, where they chase after the invaders of their native land and at last reveal their true princely mettle to the courtly world.

In contrast to the earlier sacred chase of the Wild Men, the courtier Cloten embarks on a *chasse d'amour,* which soon becomes a mortal chase. Lusting to "penetrate" Imogen, as the hunter penetrates the stag with his arrow or lance, Cloten first unsuccessfully attempts to gain access to her bedchamber through bribery: " 'Tis gold / Which buys admittance (oft it doth) yea, and makes / Diana's rangers false themselves, yield up / Their deer to th' stand o' th' stealer" (2.3.66–69). When Imogen runs away from the court, the frustrated poacher says, "I will pursue her / Even to Augustus' throne" (3.5.101–2).

Soon afterward the vicious hunter from court meets Guiderius in the mountains, where he becomes the Wild Boy's prey in a mortal hunt. As Thiébaux points out,

> The encounter with the quarry or the struggle to which the quarry had conducted the hero may result in the dissolution of his former or human identity, perhaps the loss of his life. The hunter himself becomes the hunt's object; he, not the quarry, is sacrificed. Failing to survive the crisis to which the hunt has brought him, he is annihilated in the act. (1974, 57)

Guiderius lops off the arrogant Cloten's head with his victim's own sword, only to find the head ludicrously empty. Thiébaux informs us that in

Wild Man and knight in a trial by combat. Detail from a border in a Book of Hours (c.1500), Montlucon shop, Bourges, France (Ms. 436, folio 52 verso). Reprinted by courtesy of the Beinecke Library, Yale University.

literature, "Details of the quarry's dismemberment may correspond to the hero's conquest of [a] former self, which he is now enabled to cast from him" (1974, 57). Although, in this case, the casting away of the empty head is performed by the Wild Boy, the dismemberment of Cloten does clearly resemble the "breaking up" of a deer after the hunt, since cutting off the quarry's head was part of the established ritual. Indeed *Turbervile's Booke of Hunting* (1576) informs us that after the prince slits open the animal's belly, "we vse to cut off the Deares heades. And that is commonly done also by the chiefe personage. For they take delight to cut off his heade with their woodknyues, skaynes, or swordes, to trye their edge, and the goodnesse or strength of their arme."[21] The brains were then usually given to the hounds as a reward, but of course Cloten had none to spare.

Iachimo, the other poacher in the play, also sets off in pursuit of "ladies' flesh," although he is really on a hunt for the riches he hopes to gain by seducing Imogen and winning his wager with Posthumus. Once again the hunter becomes the hunted. After scheming his way through flattery into Imogen's bedchamber, Iachimo ignores the warning iconography of Diana bathing depicted on a bas-relief over her fireplace. He continues to the bed, where he boldly gazes down on beauty bare. As I have mentioned earlier, the sight of the sleeping princess makes him acutely aware of his own evil and of its untimate results for his soul: "I lodge in fear; / Though this a heavenly angel, hell is here" (2.2.49–50). Many commentators on *Cymbeline* have pointed out Iachimo's likeness in this scene to the voyeuristic hunter Actaeon, but there are also Platonic suggestions here of the moral effect of beauty on the beholder. Although Iachimo is not at once punished as is Actaeon, or even deflected from his wicked plot, he is indeed subtly changed by the experience. At the end of the play, he admits to Cymbeline that "I was taught / Of your chaste daughter the wide difference / 'Twixt amorous and villainous" (5.5.193–95), a lesson in feeling he had not expected to learn.

Imogen herself sets out for the wilderness at first on an amatory hunt for her banished husband. Then Pisanio makes her aware that she is also the quarry for another hunter when he shows her the letter from Posthumus ordering her murder for adultery. Her first reaction is despair: "Prithee, dispatch," she cries out to Pisanio. "The lamb entreats the butcher. Where's thy knife?" (3.4.97–98). At this moment, she closely resembles the medieval iconographic figure of "the driven soul" as a "harried stag" (Thiébaux 1974, 44) pursued by the vices of wrath and jealousy (Posthumus), envy and greed (Iachimo), and vanity and lust (Cloten). She turns at bay to face Pisanio, who then refuses to obey his master's written order to kill her. "Why has thou gone so far," she asks, in the language of the hunt, "To be unbent when thou hast ta'en thy stand, / th' elected deer before thee?" (3.4.109–11). Convinced of her innocence, Pisanio suggests that she disguise herself as the boy Fidele and continue alone on her love hunt for Posthumus in Wales. Agreeing to persist in her flight from the court and in her hunt for Posthumus, Imogen is now like the fleeing wounded deer of Emblem 47 by Hadrianus Junius, which has an inserted Italian motto from Petrarch: "De dvolimi strvggo, et di fvggir mi stanco" or "I am consumed with anguish, and I exhaust myself with flight."

Junius's Latin verse reads as follows:

Wild Men as hunters quarter a deer they have just killed. From the illuminated border in a Book of Hours (c.1500), Jean de Montlucon shop, Bourges, France (Ms. 436, folio 14). Reprinted by courtesy of the Beinecke Library, Yale University.

Quid, Cerue, Cressa fixus arundine
Laxas habenas praecipiti fugae?
Haec sors amantis, quem fuga concitat:
Mentem intus exest vulnus atrox nimis.

(Why, Stag, pierced by the Cretan arrow,
do you give free rein to headlong flight?
This is the lover's luck, whom flight stirs up:
So grievous a wound drives him out of his mind.)[22]

At this point, Imogen's amatory hunt is transformed into an instructive chase, during which she is initiated into some of the mysteries of love. First she learns to understand the powers of her own beauty for either good or evil. When they encounter her beauty in masculine disguise, the Wild Men immediately vow to befriend her, offering all they have; but Cloten literally loses his head over her, since he desires not to serve beauty but to possess it selfishly. She learns, in addition, to love deeply—to love not only Posthumus, despite his now obvious imperfections, but all suffering mortality as well, no matter what their social rank or their degree of sinfulness. The princess in disguise soon discovers that "man's life is a tedious one" (3.6.1), and that she, although born to royalty, can enjoy serving as a cook for humble but good savages: "Gods, what lies I have heard! / Our courtiers say all's savage but at court; / Experience, O, thou disprov'st report" (4.2.32–34). Then she observes in a similar vein that empires "breed monsters" while "sweet fish" are found in small rivers (35–36), another instance of hunting imagery and a Christian allusion as well. The comment is also a satirical reminder to the audience of the dangers inherent in King James's ambitious dreams of founding a new Augustan empire in Britain. Most significantly, however, in mistaking the dead Cloten for her beloved Posthumus, she learns that all men are essentially alike and are equally to be pitied in the end, and that—to borrow the words of John Donne—"Any man's death diminishes me, because I am involved in mankind" (Meditation 7).

When Imogen awakens in 4.2 from her counterfeit death caused by a drug taken as medicine for love-sickness, she confronts not only real death lying beside her but also the first victim of her own beauty, a headless Cloten. Love is a positive force for good, but at the same time it is mortally dangerous. Thinking that she has at last found her husband, the grief-stricken Imogen daubs her face with the dead man's blood. Although the scene may indeed be grotesque, as many critics have complained, it is also entirely appropriate to the primitive world of this play. By smearing her face with her quarry's blood, Imogen performs a familiar hunter's initiation ritual called "blooding." According to tradition, the hunter of wild beasts is ritually daubed after his first kill with the blood of his victim, thereby acquiring its spirit as well as a heightened awareness of the close

Hinc dolor;inde fuga,grauis.

DE DVOL/MI STRVGGO, ET
DI FVGGIR MI STANCO

Quid, Cerue, Creſſa fixus arundine
Laxas habenas præcipiti fugæ?
Hæc ſors amantis,quem fuga concitat:
Mentem intus exeſt vulnus atrox nimis.

D 3 Prin-

Emblem 47 from the *Emblemata* of Hadrianus Junius (Antwerp: Christopher Plantin, 1565) depicts the wounded deer as a figure of the anguished human soul, fleeing from its pursuer. Reprinted by permission of the Folger Shakespeare Library (PN 6349 J8 1595 copy 1, p. 53).

interrelationship between the hunter and the hunted. For example, in Shakespeare's "Venus and Adonis," when the divine huntress Venus sees her slain "deer" Adonis, she "stains her face with his congealed blood" (line 1122). William Faulkner describes a similar rite of "blooding" in his stories "The Bear" and "The Old People."

The irony in *Cymbeline* is that the dead man is not Posthumus at all but the would-be rapist Cloten. Nevertheless, Imogen's heartbreak over the bleeding corpse of her hated pursuer is, when properly performed, an extremely moving dramatic experience for the audience. Her embrace of the corpse appears to symbolize on a metaphysical level the soul's incredible fusion with the gross body. It is a visual stage emblem of the shocking love union between beauty and the beast that lies at the heart of all human existence and that also lies behind the mystery of the divine incarnation so soon to take place.

In contrast to Imogen, her husband Posthumus deliberately sets out right from the beginning on an instructive chase when he consents to the unholy wager with Iachimo. He initiates a metaphoric hunt for forbidden knowledge about the nature of love. Instead of having faith in his bride's sworn love for him, he wants public proof of it, which is analogous theologically to demanding proof from God that he is to be saved. According to St. Paul in Ephesians 5, the union of matrimony is directly comparable to the redemptive union of Christ with his congregation; both are mysteries and both must be taken on faith. Therefore, when the profane hunter Posthumus impiously seeks to penetrate the sacred mystery of Imogen's love, he is permitted only false knowledge of infidelity and a bloody scrap of cloth to indicate falsely his quarry's death. Like Cloten, Posthumus has understood love only as a simple matter of sexual possession rather than as a holy lure to ultimate self-sacrifice.

Although Posthumus's subsequent conversion at the sight of the bloody token sent by Pisanio is often criticized as too sudden and unconvincing, it is in fact another venerable convention in the literature of the hunt and is certainly not intended by the dramatist to be analyzed in terms of realism. In *Cymbeline* the shock of seeing a death symbol—the blood-soaked veil that separates life from death—enlarges the hero's capacity to love uncritically in imitation of a forgiving Christ, and once again the hunter becomes the hunted. As Arthur C. Kirsch has said of the hunter Silvio, who accidentally wounds his loving pursuer Dorinda in *Il pastor fido,* "Her suffering by his hand transforms him, and the arrow he has loosed upon her leaves its shaft in his heart. He is the happy prey of his own hunt."[23] But Posthumus's repentance does not immediately bring him happiness. Instead it drives him to begin a new chase, this time a mortal hunt, which—after his capture by the British—transmogrifies into another unexpected sacred chase. It is significant that Posthumus's deliberate quest for a death of atonement leads him directly in *Cymbeline* to a vision of divinity.

First, however, the forces of evil must be overcome. Searching the battlefield for his own death in penitential exchange for the presumed death of Imogen, Posthumus easily defeats the evil Iachimo in a dumb show, after which he helps the three Wild Men turn back the invading forces of Rome. He tells others of the latter event in hunting language, since battles were also considered a form of the chase (Thiébaux 1974, 49–50). The Wild Boys, Posthumus reports, stopped the British retreat with the cry, " 'Our Britain's harts die flying, not our men: / To darkness fleet souls that fly backwards; stand, / Or we are Romans, and will give you that / Like beasts which you shun beastly' " (5.3.24–27). Accordingly, the British ceased running and began, Posthumus says, "to grin like lions / Upon the pikes o' th' hunters" (37–38). The enemy then flew from the fury of the Wild Boys like "Chickens, the way which they stoop'd eagles" (42). However, Posthumus himself is unable to find his own quarry—that "ugly monster" death (5.3.70)—on the battlefield.

Still grimly determined to complete a mortal hunt, he resumes his Roman armor in order to attract British revenge against an invader: "Fight I will no more, / But yield me to the veriest hind that shall / Once touch my shoulder" (5.3.76–78). In another of Shakespeare's imaginative reversals of the chase, the hunter Posthumus consciously agrees to become the quarry of the hind.[24] But once again the hero fails to find death, even after he is captured by the British. Instead, like Imogen, he only sleeps. His ensuing dream vision, reuniting him with his deceased family and with his divine Creator, spectacularly encompasses three different worlds at once: his own, the underworld, and the heavens. Thus Posthumus's hunt, unconsciously a *sacred* chase from the very beginning, ends with an astounding theophany and with an unmistakably Christian answer to his instructive chase for forbidden knowledge of love and salvation. According to Jupiter, "Whom best I love I cross; to make my gift, / The more delay'd, delighted" (5.4.101–2). This pronouncement suggests that the true quarries of God's love hunt are those who share with Christ the agonies of the cruel capture and crucifixion of the "elected deer" on Calvary, the consummation of the sacred chase.

Before man's quarry can be born in Bethlehem, however, the major characters in *Cymbeline* must complete their hunts for love in the wilderness and help bring a momentary peace to the world. According to the motto of an emblem by Otto van Veen, "The chasing goeth before the taking." The verse states, in words much like those of Shakespeare's Jupiter, that,

A M O R V M.

The sacred chase of divine love from Otto van Veen's *Emblems of Loue* **(Antwerp, 1608), 131. Reprinted by permission of the Folger Shakespeare Library (STC 24627a.5 copy 1).**

> Before the deer bee caught it first must hunted bee,
> The Ladie eke pursu'd before shee bee obtaynd,
> Payn makes the greater woorth of ought thats thereby
>   gayned,
> For nothing easily got wee do esteemed see.[25]

The idea, says the emblematist, derives from Pindar. Van Veen's *pictura* illustrates the divine hunt of love in which Cupid and his hounds of desire eagerly pursue a deer in flight, the latter a symbol of an anguished human soul, as I have previously noted.

Wild Men as Positive Heraldic Figures

Finally, the great denouement scene (5.5) of *Cymbeline* begins with an heraldic tableau that makes striking use of the Wild Man *topos* and helps bring the tragicomedy to a happy close. After winning his war against the

Romans, thanks to Belarius and the two Wild Boys, Cymbeline places the Wild Men next to him onstage with the words, "Stand by my side, you whom the gods have made / Preservers of my throne" (1–2). Husband tells us that Wild Men began appearing in heraldry as supporters of family shields at the end of the fourteenth century and became increasingly popular figures in this role as time went on.[26] For example, the coat of arms of the earls and dukes of Atholl (now Murrays but descended from the Stewart family or the royal house of Scotland) is an excellent example of the two characteristic uses of the Wild Man in heraldry. First, he appears as an *emblem* within the coat of arms. Husband suggests that through this use of the figure, "The two hundred or more European families who incorporated the wild man in their coats-of-arms may . . . have wished to . . . display their hardiness, strength and fecundity."[27] Second, the Wild Man appears as a supporter of the shield. According to Bernheimer, "The purpose of stationing the wild man as a retainer outside the shield rather than (as) an emblem within it was probably a talismanic one . . . the wild man could surely be trusted to protect and defend the escutcheon" (1952, 177–78). Thus, by surrounding himself with the Wild Men who have almost singlehandedly saved both the king and Britain from the invading Romans, Cymbeline draws to himself their savage strength, their fertility, and their loyalty. Furthermore, Shakespeare has here literalized the king's heraldic metaphor "Preservers of my throne," since the two Wild Boys are actually Cymbeline's true sons and will indeed transmit his royal succession to the future of Britain. Despite the previous criticism of the British court we have noted in passing and the implied warnings to the monarch of dangerous corruption in his palace, Shakespeare is careful to end his tragicomedy on a note of Jacobean affirmation. As Frances Yates has suggested, a reference to James I, who also had two sons and a daughter, may well be intended in the play.[28]

In fact, the possibilities are very high that Shakespeare was indeed ironically flattering the court in the heraldic moments of act 5, as about one fourth of all Scottish noble families employed Wild Men in their coats of arms. There are seventeen such devices illustrated in the plates accompanying Wood's *The Peerage of Scotland,* and many of the families were closely associated with the life of King James.[29] Among these, Walter Stewart, Lord Blantyre, had a coat of arms supported by both a lion and a Wild Man. He "was bred up along with King James VI of Scotland under George Buchanan," and he later became a commissioner for the treaty of union with England (Wood 1813, vol. 1, 213). Edward Bruce, Earl of Elgin and Kincardine, with two savages supporting his shield, was sent in 1600 to England by James "to congratulate Queen Elizabeth on her suppression of the Essex rebellion" (Wood 1813, vol. 1, 514). On the accession of James to the English throne, he accompanied his sovereign south where he became a privy-counselor and master of the rolls for life. Perhaps the most exotic of the Scottish peers, with two Wild Men as supporters of his shield, was Sir Robert Gordon of Lochinvar, Viscount of Kenmure, who was something of a Wild Man himself. After Sir Robert had earned a notorious Celtic reputation by plundering his neighbors' cattle, burning their houses, and even taking them prisoner on occasion, James VI sent out a force to arrest him. But "he deforced his Majesty's officers, making the principal eat the warrant." His father and friends managed to obtain a pardon for him, after which he became one of the king's gentlemen of the bedchamber. Later, at a royal tournament, "Sir Robert Gordon was one of the three successful champions to whom prizes were delivered by Princess Elizabeth" (Wood 1813, vol. 2, 26–27).

Indeed, any of these noble families could have felt themselves honored by Shakespeare in the heraldic tableau of 5.5 in *Cymbeline,* and perhaps the dramatist hoped they would *all* see themselves celebrated as preservers of the king's throne. However, I believe the most likely specific candidate for the honor was Alexander, seventh Lord Livingston, who was created the Earl of Linlithgow by King James "at the baptism of Prince Charles on December 25, 1600" (Wood 1813, vol. 2, 127). Lord Livingston was also one of the commissioners appointed by Parliament to negotiate the union between England and Scotland.

We know of course that the three rustics who defended a narrow lane against invading Danes in the legendary past of Scotland were ancestors of the Hay family, so that the parallel heroism of Belarius, Guiderius, and Arviragus dramatized in *Cymbeline* seems to be an obvious compliment to Lord John Hay, a courtly favorite of the king, as Glynne Wickham has argued.[30] The iconographical problem here is that there are absolutely no Wild Men in the Hay coat of arms. Nevertheless, it seems that Alexander Livingston, Earl of Linlithgow, was married to Lady Helenor Hay, daughter of the 7th Earl of Errol. Through this union, a female member of the Hay family did acquire a new coat of arms with one Wild Man as emblem above the shield and with *two* Wild Men as supporters, thus giving us the necessary *three* Wild Men seen in the play. Moreover, one of the charters granting the Livingstons more land in Scotland and dated 13 March 1600, "makes honourable mention of the great care and fidelity bestowed by the Lord Livingston and his lady in the education of the King's children, and the expence incurred in maintaining them and their servants" (Wood 1813, vol. 2, 127).

This fact appears to throw some light on Belarius's saucy demand in 5.5 that the king "pay me for the nursing of thy sons" (323). He then delivers the Wild Boys to their father with the glowing praise,

Here are your sons again, and I must lose
Two of the sweet'st companions in the world.

Linlithgow coat of arms with three Wild Men as depicted in Wood's *Scottish Peerage*, pl. xi. Reprinted by permission of the Folger Shakespeare Library (CS 468 D74 1813 v.2).

The benediction of these covering heavens
Fall on their heads like dew, for they are worthy
To inlay heaven with stars.

(349–53)

In actuality, the Livingstons primarily had the care of Princess Elizabeth, and we are told "they discharged that trust so much to the satisfaction of King James VI [of Scotland], that, when they delivered her safe at Windsor, in 1603, they obtained an act of approbation from the King and council" (Wood 1813, vol. 2, 127). In *Cymbeline,* Imogen is restored to her father at the same time that he recovers his lost sons.

The venerable figure of the wild soldier Belarius as a true defender of Britain in this final heraldic tableau of the play has a contemporary iconographic counterpart as well. The image of a Wild Man labeled "A Britaine" dominates the emblematic title page by Jodocus Hondius for John Speed's *The History of Great Britaine* (1611).[31] The ancient savage towers over the other four soldiers representative of Britain's military ancestry: a Roman, a Saxon, a Dane, and a Norman. Here again James is reminded of the native worth of his people, who—if they are welcomed at

The title page for John Speed's *The History of Great Britaine* (London, 1611) by Jodocus Hondius depicts the original British warrior as a Wild Man. Reprinted by permission of the Folger Shakespeare Library (STC 23045 copy 1).

court—can help to preserve the throne and maintain peace in the land. Although the Wild Man in cultural history was originally a lawless figure like Caliban, by Shakespeare's time he was also a positive heraldic figure who could be trusted to maintain law and order. Indeed two of them were used in 1610 as part of the pageant offered by the city of Chester to honor Prince Henry. The actors leading the St. George Procession were "disguised, called Greene-men, their habit Embroydred and Stich'd on with Iuie-leaues with blacke-side, hauing hanging to their shoulders, a huge blacke shaggie hayre, Sauage-like, with Iuie Garlands vpon their heads, bearing Herculian Clubbes in their hands."[32] Instead of behaving in a primitive and lustful manner, these Wild Men essentially performed the role of St. George in pantomime. They fought against evil by engaging in battle with "an artificial Dragon, very liuely to behold," who pursued "the Sauages entring their Denne, casting Fire from his mouth, which afterwards was slaine, to the great pleasure of the spectators, bleeding, fainting, and staggering, as though he endured a feeling paine, euen at the last gaspe, and farewell."[33]

In religious iconography, the Wild Man also faces the dragon as a symbol of the natural strength and fortitude available to defeat evil. To take one example, he performs this function in a spandrel on the porch entrance of St. Michael's in Peasenhall, Suffolk. Or we can see him poised as a guardian pinnacle, in conjunction with a crowned lion representing the monarchy, on the battlements of the north porch of St. Mary's in Mendlesham, Suffolk.

But we must also recall that the Wild Man, however strong and fertile, still remained for theology a symbol of fallen humanity. According to

Two Wild Men battle a dragon in a Book of Hours (Bourges: Montlucon shop, c.1500), folio 90. Reprinted by courtesy of the Beinecke Library, Yale University (Ms. 436).

Detail of a Wild Man over the porch door of St. Michael's Church, Peasenhall, Suffolk, England. A dragon is carved in the opposite spandrel. Photograph by Peggy Muñoz Simonds.

The Wild Man as a guardian pinnacle on the North Porch, St. Mary's Church, Mendlesham, Suffolk, England. Photograph by Peggy Muñoz Simonds.

A pensive green man as a roof boss from Norwich Cathedral. Photograph by Peggy Muñoz Simonds.

Bernheimer, since the Wild Man was not created wild by God but fell from grace and descended into brutishness as the result of his own actions, "the state of wildness was not usually regarded as irrevocable, but as amenable to change through acculturation" (1952, 8). Thus we find that the Wild Man and his vegetable counterpart the Green Man were also permitted inside English churches from the very earliest times. The great cathedrals of Ely, Exeter, and Norwich, for example, are extraordinarily rich in Green man iconography, with roof bosses in the gates and cloisters at Norwich serving as sorrowful reminders of still unredeemed nature, even within the church itself, and of the sad truth that "All greenness comes to withering."[34] Therefore, *inside* many churches, the Wild Man and the uncrowned lion seem to represent that aspect of fallen nature that must be overcome and controlled by the word of God, especially when they appear together on the stems of Baptismal fonts. Above them, on the exterior of the basin, the four Evangelists and their symbols are generally carved as representations of the saving power of the Gospels.

For this reason, the Wild Men in *Cymbeline* must—for their own salvation, as well as for that of the kingdom—be removed from the cave of

Wild Man (one of two) on the stem of the baptismal font in St. Peter's Church, Sibton, Suffolk, England. Photograph by Peggy Muñoz Simonds.

Wild Man and lion on the stem of the baptismal font with Evangelists and their symbols carved on the basin: St. Peter's Church, Sibton, Suffolk, England. Photograph Peggy Muñoz Simonds.

ignorance (called a "prison" by Guiderius, in what appears to be a Platonic allusion to the prison of the body or nature) and be reintegrated with a now purified court and with its formal religious celebrations. Their redemption is indeed essential to the redemption of Cymbeline's entire kingdom. In Shakespeare's dramatic context, the Wild Boys may actually symbolize the true defenders of the reformed church in Jacobean Britain, since they almost singlehandedly drive off the "Roman" invaders of the island kingdom, rescue the captured ruler, and are finally revealed as the rightful heirs to the English throne.

Thus Shakespeare's primitive and hairy Wild Men—Belarius, Guiderius, and Arviragus—ultimately serve three functions in *Cymbeline*. First, their wholesome (if violent) lives within nature are an implicit negative criticism of the dangerous excesses of a luxurious life at court. Second, their ritual vocation of hunting both underlies and informs the major strands of action within the play. And, third, they are positive heraldic supporters of both a reformed Church and a reformed state. Hence—by extension—they are supporters of the dual functions of James I, sovereign of what he hoped would eventually become the United Kingdom of Great Britain.

Notes

1. See, for example, Michael Taylor, "The Pastoral Reckoning in 'Cymbeline'," *Shakespeare Survey* 36 (1983): 97–106; and G. M. Pinciss, "The Savage Man in Spenser, Shakespeare, and Renaissance English Drama," in *The Elizabethan Theatre* 8, ed. George R. Hibbard (Port Credit, Ont.: P. D. Meany, 1982), 69–89. Space does not permit me to discuss Spenser's use of the Wild Man *topos* in *The Faerie Queene*.

2. William Empson, *Some Versions of the Pastoral* (London: Chatto & Windus, 1950).

3. See Arthur O. Lovejoy and George Boas, *Primitivism and Related Ideas in Antiquity* (1935: reprint New York: Octagon Books, 1973), 7–11.

4. Timothy Husband, *The Wild Man: Medieval Myth and Symbolism* (New York: The Metropolitan Museum of Art, 1980), 13.

5. Hayden White, "The Forms of Wildness: Archaeology of an Idea," in *The Wild Man Within: An Image in Western Thought from the Renaissance to Romanticism,* ed. Edward Dudley and Maximilian E. Novak (London: Harry M. Snyder & Co., 1972), 21.

6. Husband, p. 3.

7. Derek Traversi, *Shakespeare: The Last Phase* (Stanford: Stanford University Press, 1955), 49.

8. Richard Bernheimer, *Wild Men in the Middle Ages: A Study in Art, Sentiment, and Demonology* (Cambridge: Harvard University Press, 1952), 19; hereafter cited parenthetically.

9. See Margaret Mann Phillips, *The 'Adages' of Erasmus: A Study with Translations* (Cambridge: Cambridge University Press, 1964), 134.

10. Peter M. Daly, Virginia W. Callahan, and Simon Cuttler, eds., *Andreas Alciatus: Index Emblematicus,* 2 vols. (Toronto: University of Toronto Press, 1979), vol. 1: Emblem 37. All further translations of Alciati are taken from this work.

11. Husband, 3.

12. See Peter M. Daly, *Literature in the Light of the Emblem* (Toronto: University of Toronto Press, 1979), 140.

13. H. W. Crundell, "Shakespeare, Lyly, and Aesop," *Notes and Queries* 168 (1935): 312.

14. See T. W. Baldwin, *William Shakespeare's Small Latine & lesse Greeke,* 2 vols. (Urbana: University of Illinois Press, 1944), vol. 1, 535.

15. Phillips, 262. For another emblem of the eagle and the beetle, based either on Alciati or directly on Erasmus, see Giles Corrozet, *Hecatomgraphie* (Paris: Denys Ianot, 1543), sig. H iiiᵛ.

16. See Desiderius Erasmus, *The Education of a Christian Prince,* trans. Lester K. Born (New York: Columbia University Press, 1936), 147.

17. Geffrey Whitney, *A Choice of Emblemes* (Leiden: Christopher Plantin, 1586), 147.

18. Bernard Harris, "'What's past is prologue': 'Cymbeline' and 'Henry VIII,'" in *Later Shakespeare,* Stratford Upon-Avon Studies 8 (London: Edward Arnold Ltd., 1966), 212. Harris briefly mentions the presence of hunting imagery in *Cymbeline* as well.

19. Marcelle Thiébaux, *The Stag of Love: The Chase in Medieval Literature* (Ithaca and London: Cornell University Press, 1974), 57–58; hereafter cited parenthetically.

20. See Michael J. B. Allen, "The Chase: The Development of a Renaissance Theme," *Comparative Literature* 20 (1968): 306–7.

21. See George Turbervile, *Turbervile's Booke of Hunting* (1576; reprint, Oxford: Clarendon Press, 1908), 134.

22. Hadrianus Junius, *Emblemata* (Antwerp: Christopher Plantin, 1565), 53. Translation by Roger T. Simonds. Engravings by Geeraard Jansen van Kampen and Arnaud Nicolai after designs by Geoffrey Ballain and Pieter Huys.

23. Arthur C. Kirsch, *Jacobean Dramatic Perspectives* (Charlottesville: The University Press of Virginia, 1972), 12. For another accidental wounding in tragicomic form, see the title page illustration for Beaumont and Fletcher's *Philaster.*

24. The word "hind" in this context is usually understood to mean a simple countryman, but since it occurs within a large cluster of hunting terms, it must refer here to a female red deer, or perhaps to both significations at once.

25. Otto van Veen, *Amorum Emblemata or Emblemes of Loue* (Antwerp, 1608), 130–31.

26. Husband, 186.

27. Ibid., 185.

28. See Frances Yates, "Cymbeline," in *Shakespeare's Last Plays: A New Approach* (London: Routledge and Kegan Paul, 1975), 41–61.

29. See John Philip Wood, *The Peerage of Scotland,* 2 vols. (Edinburgh: George Ramsay and Co., 1813); hereafter referred to parenthetically.

30. Glynne Wickham, "Riddle and Emblem: A Study in the Dramatic Structure of *Cymbeline,*" in *English Renaissance Studies: Presented to Dame Helen Gardner on her 70th Birthday* (Oxford: Clarendon Press, 1980), 112–13.

31. John Speed, *The History of Great Britaine* (London: William Hall and John Beale, 1611), title page.

32. Quoted by Robert Hillis Goldsmith, "The Wild Man on the English Stage," *Modern Language Review* 53 (1958), 485.

33. Ibid.

34. See Katherine Basford, *The Green Man* (Ipswich: D. S. Brewer Ltd., 1978), 19.

5

Anti-Courtier Imagery in *Cymbeline*

> If thou be a governor, or hast over other sovereignty, know
> thyself, that is to say, know that thou art verily a man compact of
> soul and body, and in that other men are equal unto thee. . . .
> The dignity or authority wherein thou differest from other is (as
> it were) but a weighty or heavy cloak, freshly glittering in the
> eyes of them that be purblind, where unto thee it is painful, if
> thou wear him in his right fashion, and as it shall best become
> thee. And from thee it may be shortly taken of him that did put it
> on thee, if thou use it negligently. . . . Therefore whiles thou
> wearest it, know Thyself.
>
> —Thomas Elyot, *The Governor*

As if Shakespeare's suggestion that Wild Men are superior to the king and
his court in sensitivity, virility, and courage were not satire enough in
Cymbeline, the dialogue itself contains numerous conventional attacks on
the courtier and the humiliating quality of his life at court as a pretender to
power and as a sycophant to royalty. Such anticourtier *topoi* originated in
the classical world, where they were particularly prevalent in Rome after
the establishment of the empire. The parasite is the stock character of the
courtier in Roman comedy, for example, while in poetry Horace and
Juvenal provided satirical models for the later Neo-Latin poets to imitate.
Among Greek writers, the attacks on courtiers by Plutarch and Lucian
were especially influential throughout Renaissance Europe. According to
Pauline M. Smith, "Plutarch's contribution to this [anticourtier] trend lies
in his treatise on flatterers, *Quomodo Adulator ab Amico Internoscatur. It
was among those works of the *Moralia* which were translated into Latin
by Erasmus, and it has the distinction of being the first of Plutarch's works
to be published in a French translation" in 1520.[1] Although Philemon
Holland did not produce an English translation of the *Moralia* until 1603,
both Erasmus and Sir Thomas More did translate Lucian's satires into
Latin during the early sixteenth century. William Shakespeare's interest in
the anticourtier satires of Lucian and Plutarch, both of whom wrote a

Timon, is clearly evidenced by the English playwright's own rather bitter version of *The Life of Timon of Athens* for the theater.

During the Middle Ages there had been a native British attack on courtiers in the work of John of Salisbury, whose *Policraticus*

> was written with the intention of correcting abuses in the ranks of the ruling classes which undermined the moral foundations, and therefore threatened the welfare of, the body politic. The writer's fundamental proposition is that man's estrangement from virtue and from reason is the result of his contact with court society. The activities, arts and preoccupations of this society, hunting, gambling, music-making, jesting, astrology and the practice of the occult arts, flattery and power-seeking, are in his view illustrative of its decadence. Written by the foremost representative of humanistic thought before Petrarch, the *Policraticus* enjoyed a wide diffusion in Europe throughout the Middle Ages. (Smith 1966, 47–48)

The most influential anticourtier works of the Renaissance itself were undoubtedly the *Encomium Moriae* by Erasmus and Thomas More's *Utopia,* both of which were widely read in England and elsewhere.

Soon equally popular among Neo-Latin readers were the emblems of Andrea Alciati, which contain a number of anticourtier *topoi.* Variations of some of these emblems reappear in Shakespeare's satirical tragicomedy *Cymbeline,* although they may have come from other sources to the English theater rather than directly from Alciati. In any case, such emblems help us to identify the specific *topos* and to discover any new elements introduced by Shakespeare. In this chapter I shall discuss *topoi* concerning (1) the courtier shackled by his own golden chain, (2) the caged bird, (3) the ravished tree, (4) the tailor's model with an empty head, and (5) the false perspectives of the princely mountain.

The Courtier Shackled by His Own Golden Chain

Cymbeline actually begins with an attack on the court by a disaffected courtier, who complains that here "you do not meet a man but frowns: our bloods / No more obey the heavens than our courtiers / Still seem as does the king's" (1.1.1–3). No one at court feels free to express his real thoughts about the natural virtue of Posthumus, the ignobility of Cloten, and the correctness of Imogen's choice of a husband. The Wild Men, in contrast, are free to say what they wish about anybody and are unaffected by desires for the wealth a king may bestow upon his flatterers. Just as they feel no fear of the king's changes in mood, they are equally free of debt for court clothes and all the fancy trappings that announce the courtier's high status to the world. Belarius explains this to his adopted sons in an anticourtier speech on accounting that I have previously quoted in the chapter on primitivism:

> this life
> Is nobler than attending for a check:
> Richer than doing nothing for a robe [or badge],
> Prouder than rustling in unpaid-for silk:
> Such gain the cap of him that makes him fine,
> Yet keeps his book uncross'd: no life to ours.

(3.3.21–26)

The young Guiderius is not convinced, however, by the virtues of a quiet life in a cave, which he refers to as equally confining—"A cell of ignorance" and "a prison" to youthful ambition (3.3.33–34).

Aside from the traditional contrast here between the values of the active life and the contemplative life, Shakespeare is also drawing on the familiar *topos* of the courtier shackled by his golden chain. Andrea Alciati's Emblem 87, "In aulicos" ("On courtiers"), states in the *subscriptio* that "Vana Palatinos quos educat aula clientes, / Dicitur auratis nectere compedibus." ("The vainglorious court is said to bind with golden fetters those retainers it trains as chamberlains.").[2] The *pictura* shows a courtier wearing a heavy golden chain but sitting with his feet in stocks.[3] During the Renaissance, the golden fetters confining successful courtiers were metaphorically understood to be the gold chains from which hang those golden badges of office that bind them to the prince. But in Thomas More's ironic *Utopia,* the Anemolian ambassadors are considered to be no better than slaves by the natives because they arrive wearing golden chains like those used by the Utopians as symbols of disgrace and slavery.[4] Julius S. Held discusses the same problem in his study of *Rembrandt's Aristotle,* a painting in which the philosopher wears a magnificent gold chain.

> The ancient custom of giving a special reward in the form of a golden chain was revived in the Renaissance and widely practiced in the 17th century. Being an object of considerable material value and of noble connotations, the chain admirably fulfilled two functions: that of a very real financial reward, and of a rather spectacular demonstration of recognition in high quarters. Yet there are signs that it was soon recognized as something else: chains, after all, are symbols both of eminence and servitude.[5]

One of the earliest classical sources of this "golden fetters" trope is Theophrastus, who scolded Aristotle for remaining at the court of Philip of Macedonia as the young Alexander's rather well-paid tutor. Diogenes later cynically remarked that Aristippus in golden chains at a royal court could not fly away even if he wanted to. It is this classical tradition to which

Alciati's emblem on the "golden fetters" *topos* depicts a courtier wearing a golden chain but fettered by stocks in the palace courtyard: Andrea Alciati, *Emblemata* (Paris: Wechel, 1534), sig. H. iii. Reprinted by permission of the Folger Shakespeare Library (PN 6349 A8 1534b Cage).

Erasmus refers in his adage "Aureae compedes" or "Golden fetters" [II.III.XXV (531A)].

Belarius's speech to the Wild Boys is, however, more directly reminiscent of the emblem "Aureae compedes" ("Golden fetters") in Geffrey Whitney's *A Choice of Emblemes* (1586), an English adaptation of Alciati's Latin *Emblemata,* than it is reminiscent of Alciati's version of the *topos*. Whitney adds to his personal variation of the theme a proverb of Dionysius Longinus stating that, "Bondage is the prison of the mind." According to his verse,

It better is (wee say) a cotage poore to houlde,
Then for to lye in prison stronge, with fetters made of goulde.
Which shewes, that bondage is the prison of the mind:
And libertie the happie life, that is to man assign'de,
And thoughe that some preferre their bondage, for their gaines:
And richely are adorn'd in silkes, and preste with massie chaines.
Yet many others liue, that are accompted wise:
Who libertie doe chiefly choose, thoughe clad in gounes of frise.
. . . .
And, if I should be ask'd, which life doth please mee beste:
I like the goulden libertie, let goulden bondage reste.[6]

Whitney's woodcut of the courtier wearing a golden chain while fettered by stocks is the same as the woodcut in the Plantin edition of Alciati.

This venerable tradition of the "golden fetters" has important implications, I believe, for one of the few textual problems in *Cymbeline*. Belarius's line, which the Arden edition transcribes as "Richer than doing nothing for a robe" (3.3.23), has been the subject of considerable debate. J. M. Nosworthy informs us that the word "robe" has been read as "bauble" by Rowe, "brabe" or badge of honor by Johnson, "brave" by Singer, and as either "badge" or "robe" by Bullock, while Nosworthy himself prefers "robe."[7] The Folio used the word "babe." The emblem tradition so familiar to Shakespeare and his audience appears to suggest, however, that "badge" may well be the correct modern reading. Belarius is thus referring to the token of slavery that usually hung from what Whitney calls the courtier's "massie" chain of gold.

The Caged Bird

As we have noted above, the Wild Boys are not convinced by Belarius's insistence that a natural life is better than a courtly life. When he calls their humble cave "A prison" (3.3.34), Guiderius equates their natural life with the shadowy existence of the prisoners dependent on their senses alone for knowledge in Plato's cave analogy. Arviragus agrees, but then he admits, "our cage / We make a quire, as doth the prison'd bird, / And sing our bondage freely" (3.3.42–44). Neither the Arden nor the Riverside edition of *Cymbeline* glosses these lines, but do we really understand them?

A major courtier *topos,* with a number of interesting variations, during the Renaissance was based on precisely this image of a caged bird—usually a nightingale—which either sings or does not sing in captivity. A classical source of the trope is Aesop's fable of "The Nightingale and the Bat" in which the bat asks the caged nightingale why she no longer sings in the daytime. Because that is how she was captured in the first place, the nightingale replies. The bat then sarcastically reminds her that—since she is already confined in a cage—she is now in no further danger of discovery. The moral of the fable is that "A wrong reason for the doing of a thing is worse than no reason at all."[8] In contrast to Aesop, Aelian assumes that the love of liberty is an essential part of the nightingale's nature. He writes that,

> It seems that the Nightingale passionately loves its freedom, and for that reason when a mature bird is caught and confined in a cage, it refrains from song and takes vengeance on the bird catcher for its enslavement by silence. Conse-

quently men who have had this experience let them go when they are older and do their best to catch the young.[9]

This is undoubtedly a major source for the Renaissance of the popular equation between the nightingale, bondage, and silence.

The bird in the cage motif, John F. Moffit informs us, eventually came to "refer . . . to a personal loss of freedom, in the general sense of deprivation of choice or opportunity in economic, political or religious life-activities."[10] This meaning was probably originated by Anicias Manlius Severinus Boethius (480–524 A.D.) in his *De consolatione philosophiae*, Book III, Poem II, lines 17–26:

> If the bird who garrulously sings from the high branches is captured only to be put in a cage, men may entertain themselves giving her honeyed drink and copious food. But if from her narrow prison she should espy the shady woods she loves so well, she will trample upon that food with fouled feet. In her sorrow she only craves the woods; with dulcet tones she sings sadly to her forest.
> (quoted in Moffit 1983, 143)

In this version, the bird appears to symbolize the soul imprisoned in the body and longing to escape despite the pleasures of life. Moffit indicates that the motif was then continued in the work of two famous translators of Boethius's *Consolation of Philosophy*, Jean de Meun and Geoffrey Chaucer. In one of Meun's additions to the *Roman de la Rose* (vss. 13941–66), the trope is used to refer to the desire of all women to escape their bondage to men. Chaucer also employs the image as a metaphor of female faithlessness in love, and in the "Manciple's Tale" of the *Canterbury Tales*, he writes as follows:

> Taak any bryd, and put it in a cage
> And do all thyn entente and thy corage
> To fostre it tenderly with mete and drynke
> Of all deyntees that thou kanst bithynke,
> And keep it al so clenly as thou may,
> Although his cage of gold be never so gay,
> Yet hath this brid, by twenty thousand foold,
> Levere in a forest, that is rude and coold,
> Goon ete wormes and swich wrecchednesse.
> For evere this brid wol doon his bisnesse,
> To escape out of his cage, yif he may,
> His libertee this brid desireth ay.
>
> (quoted in Moffit 1983, 143–44)

Chaucer uses the trope once more in the "Squire's Tale," but this time to refer to male faithlessness in love when the falcon laments her mate's flight.

In contrast, Petrarch sees that one can be a willing prisoner in a love relationship and points this out with the line "Perch'io stesso mi strinsi" in Poem 266, *Signor mio caro:* "Devotion to my lord, love of my lady are the chains where with much labor I am bound, and I myself took them on."[11] Apparently Petrarch is referring here to his patron, Cardinal Giovanni Colonna, and to his poetic muse, Laura. In the early sixteenth century, Erasmus conflates the pro and con love associations of the caged bird with the imprisonment of the soul in the body in his marriage colloquy *Proci et Puellae*. In the dialogue between Maria and her suitor Pamphilus, Maria remarks that marriage is often considered to be a halter or yoke by men afraid of losing their freedom.

> Pam. Now on my fayth they are well worthie an halter that so termeth it. Tell me I praye you is not your soule bounde unto your body.
> Mar. I thinke so.
> Pam. Yea surely even as a bird unto hir cage, and yet if ye shoulde aske him the question, whether he woulde bee loosed or no, I suppose he would saye nay. And why so? bicause he is willinglie and gladie bound thereunto.[12]

As the bird accepts her cage, lovers willingly bind themselves to one another in the state of matrimony.

According to Dora and Erwin Panovsky, Hesiod's tale of Pandora in *Works and Days* underlies the woodcut of Alciati's Emblem 46, "Illicitum non sperandum" ("The unlawful should not be hoped for")—on page 84 of the 1534 Paris edition of the *Emblemata*. The woodcut depicts Hope together with Nemesis and uses the caged bird as a late medieval attribute of Hope. The bird is, on this occasion, a crow, while Hope has both her feet on the cage to keep it closed. Similar woodcuts of Hope and the caged bird appear in the 1551 and 1557 editions as well. As the Panofsky translation of a related Alciati emblem on Hope ("In simulacrum Spei" or Emblem 44) tells us, the crow is the "most faithful of Augurs: when he cannot say, 'All is well,' he says 'All will be well,' " or *Cras, Cras.*[13] With such Renaissance emblems based on classical and medieval traditions, the bird in the cage as a symbol of hope entered the early modern history of the *topos*.

In the next major variation of the bird in the cage, the French emblematist Guillaume de la Perrière combined the Aesop version of the caged nightingale with what appears to be a commentary on Alciati's choice of the bird in the cage as a symbol of hope. Emblem 38 in *Le Théatre des Bons Engins* (1539), translated in 1593 by Thomas Combe as *The Theater of Fine Devices,* employs a woodcut of the caged bird without the figure of Hope to illustrate quite a different motto: "Patience brings the minde to rest, / And helps all troubles to digest." An emblem of consolation for life's vicissitudes, the verse reads as follows:

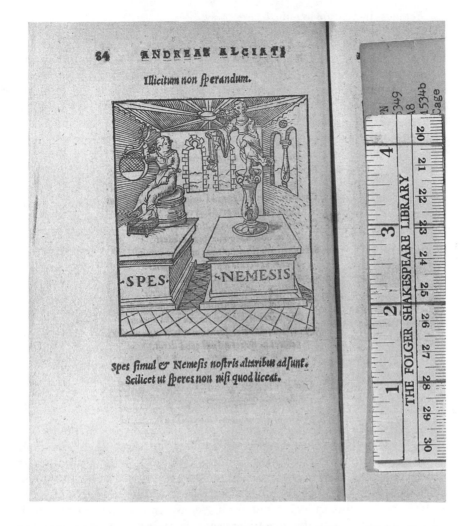

Hope is not only personified as a woman but also symbolized as a bird in the cage underneath her feet in Andrea Alciati's emblem "Illicitum non sperandum," *Emblemata* (Paris: Wechel, 1534), 84. Reprinted by permission of the Folger Shakespeare Library (PN 6349 A8 1534b Cage).

The bird in cage restrained from libertie,
For all her bondage ceasseth not to sing.
But in the midst of all capituitie,
With songs some comfort she her selfe doth bring.
So when as men do stand in ieopardie,
And feele that sorrowes do their senses sting,

> Yet must they striue to put all cares away,
> And make themselves as merry as they may.[14]

Thus, for Perrière, the state of captivity and the fact of human losses and sadness must be endured, even sweetened by beautiful song. This attitude of stoic resignation seems much like Arviragus's comment that, despite our frustrations in the prison of nature, we can still "sing our bondage freely," a privilege usually denied to courtiers. Lear expresses much the same stoic philosophy when he accepts his fall from power and tells Cordelia, "come let's away to prison: / We two alone will sing like birds i' the cage" (5.3.8–9).

The meaning of the caged bird image is once again modified in Emblem 56 of the *Emblemata* (1565) by the Dutch humanist Hadrianus Junius, who spent part of his life in England. For his *inscriptio,* Junius borrows from the rhetorician Dionysius Longinus the same proverb later used by Whitney in his "Aureae compedes" emblem: "Animi scrinium servitus" ("Bondage is the prison of the mind"). The *subscriptio* explains that,

> Luscinia veris nuncia,
> Mutescit inclusa caueae.
> Est seruitus scrinium animi,
> Linguam que vinclo praepedit.
>
> (The nightingale, messenger of spring,
> Falls silent when confined in a cage.
> Slavery is the cage of the spirit,
> And it shackles the tongue with a fetter.)[15]

The succeeding prose commentary by Junius speaks further of intellectual bondage as "a halter on the spirit, which does not allow us to speak out freely and express what we have conceived in our minds, bound in the service of magnates or indeed prohibited by their tyranny, as if muzzled by a bridle; while liberty is the nurse and parent of eloquence." Junius is particularly careful to point out in his commentary that Renaissance princes may even cause history to be rewritten in order to cover their evil acts with words of false glory and virtue. He continues his discussion of censorship as follows:

> That custom of favoring vices, established by use and received into fashion, so corrupted the character of writing by base servitude that nothing could be made healthy in it; the sacrosanct confidence in historical truth utterly perished, and we have nearly equated the infamous Busires with portents from the heavens. Thence was thought out that ingenious punishment and reproach, by which books were ordered to be committed to the flames by a Senatus-consultum to please the Emperors (I shall not say scourges of the Earth); as Seneca records concerning the writings of Labienus or Tacitus concerning [the writings of]

Cremutius Cordus. The emblem is derived from Philostratus' portrait of the sophist Scopelianus who, importuned by the Clazomenians to conduct an exercise at home, replied, "The nightingale is to sing in his cage."

Junius bitterly concludes, "The picture speaks for itself, showing the nightingale enclosed in a cage, but sitting idly and not flying."[16] What is described here is obviously the contemporary humanist who has been foolish enough to go into the service of a prince instead of remaining poor and writing what he pleases.

In 1586 the same woodcut was reprinted in Whitney's *A Choice of Emblemes* and once again with the identical Latin motto by Dionysius Longinus. According to the verse,

According to Hadrianus Junius in his *Emblemata* (Antwerp, 1565), patronage results in intellectual bondage for the humanist-poet. Reprinted by permission of the Folger Shakespeare Library (PN 6349 J8 1565 copy 2 Cage, p. 62).

The Prouerbe saithe, the bounde muste still obey.
And bondage bringes, the freest man in awe:
Who serues must please, and heare what other saye,
And learne to keepe Harpocrates his lawe:
   Then bondage is the Prison of the minde:
   And makes them mute, where wisedome is by kinde.

The Nightingall, that chaunteth all the springe,
Whose warblinge notes, throughout the wooddes are harde,
Being kepte in cage, she ceaseth for to singe,
And mournes, bicause her libertie is barde:
   Oh bondage vile, the worthie mans deface,
   Bee farre from those, that learning doe imbrace.

(1586, 101)

Since Harpocrates was the Egyptian god of silence, the grim warning of Junius that true learning and eloquence depend entirely on freedom of thought and expression is doubly emphasized in the Elizabethan emblem book. We have here what seems to be an impassioned Renaissance plea for academic freedom as the key to new scholarly discoveries.[17]

Whitney includes a second caged bird emblem in his collection, this one a direct attack on the economic distress that causes men to become courtiers. The motto is "Duram telum necessitas" ("Necessity is a hard weapon"). The verse reminds us that,

Necessitie doth vrge, the Popiniaye to prate,
   And birdes, to drawe their bucketts vp, and picke theire
      meate through, grate:
Which warneth them, whoe needes must eyther serue, or pine:
With willing harte, no pains to shunne, and freedome to
      resigne.

(1586, 36)

The reference is to Terence, and the unfortunate life of a parasite is the subject matter of this emblem. He who serves a prince must give up his freedom in order to survive. The woodcut depicts a child and a man observing a caged parrot, which can only echo what his owner says.

During the seventeenth century, most caged bird emblems and poems concerned the love theme and paralleled a fashion for caged birds with openly sexual meanings in Dutch genre paintings.[18] But in 1608, Otto Van Veen more delicately than other artists of the time summed up the "willing bondage" theme in an emblem called "For Freedom Servitude":

   The cap of libertie loue vnder foot doth tread,
And holdeth fast the yoke of thraldom seeming sweet,
the name of beeing free is to no louer meet,
For loue him freely doth to willing bondage lead.[19]

Perhaps the most remarkable of such poems, however, is a song written much later by William Blake:

> How sweet I roam'd from field to field,
> And tasted all the summer's pride,
> Till I the Prince of Love beheld
> Who in the sunny beams did glide!
>
> He show'd me lilies for my hair,
> And blushing roses for my brow;
> He led me through his gardens fair
> Where all his golden pleasures grow.
>
> With sweet May dews my wings were wet,
> And Phoebus fir'd my vocal rage;
> He caught me in his silken net,
> And shut me in his golden cage.
>
> He loves to sit and hear me sing,
> Then laughing, sports and plays with me;
> Then stretches out my golden wing,
> And mocks my loss of liberty.[20]

Although we cannot be certain whether the bird is caged here by Cupid or by Christ, the love imprisonment is complete in either case.

Shakespeare's version of the *topos* in *Cymbeline* appears to be primarily in the spirit of Junius's anticourt theme when Arviragus says, "our cage / we make a quire, as doth the prison'd bird, / And sing our bondage freely" (3.3.42–44). In the context of the discussion contrasting court life with savage life, the Wild Boy may be admitting that one at least has freedom of speech in the wilderness. Or he may be harking back to the Alciati interpretation of the caged bird as an attribute of Hope and predicting that Belarius will eventually take him and his brother to court, where they may be educated to earn fame through deeds of honor. A third possibility is that he may be alluding to Perrière's tradition of "courage in adversity." In any case, Shakespeare means us to consider the line as part of the boy's continuing argument against life in the wilderness as sufficient unto itself.

Albrecht Schöne has indicated that a given emblem is often employed by characters in Renaissance drama with radically different applications, depending on what intellectual point of view is being argued.[21] In answer to Belarius's praise of the simple life in the mountains where the boys' minds—though admittedly untrained—are not fettered to the whims of a prince, Arviragus uses an *argumentum emblematicum* to remind the old man that they are still prisoners in a cage or a cave resembling Plato's "Den of Shadows." He ironically points out that they can only sing in terms of their bondage to the natural world, as do birds. Belarius is apparently amused by the aptness of the argument. "How you speak!" (3.3.44), he chides gently. On the other hand, he and the audience both know that at court bondage is indeed "the prison of the mind" in a very serious sense. In particular, the outside is in opposition to the inside at Cymbeline's court, where the courtiers must hypocritically pretend to dislike Imogen's marriage to Posthumus. No one dares to tell the king that he is wrong to oppose the match and wrong to listen to the wicked advice of his queen and her son, Cloten.

The Ravished Tree

Belarius immediately marshals another emblematic argument in answer to the boys' complaints of imprisonment in nature. As might be expected, he chooses a courtier *topos* pointing out the dangers of court life—the emblem of the ravished tree.

> Cymbeline lov'd me,
> And when a soldier was the theme, my name
> Was not far off; then was I as a tree
> Whose boughs did bend with fruit. But in one night,
> A storm, or robbery (call it what you will)
> Shook down my mellow hangings, nay, my leaves,
> And left me bare to weather.
>
> (3.3.58–64)

The image of the ravished tree was very common in emblem literature and appeared in two main variants.[22] One represents the tree laid bare after a storm, symbolizing the vicissitudes of life in general. The second form illustrates the deliberate robbing of the fruitful tree, usually a nut tree. Virginia W. Callahan has traced the latter *topos* from its classical man-ifestations in Aesop, to an epigram in the *Greek Anthology,* to a Latin poem attributed to Ovid called *The Nux, The Lament of the Nut Tree,* and finally to its rebirth in 1523.[23] In that year, she tells us,

> Erasmus sent as a Christmas gift to John More, the fifteen year old son of Thomas More, a text of *The Nux* (which he considered 'truly Ovidian') together with his commentary on the poem. In the dedicatory epistle to the young man Erasmus makes it clear that the gift is intended not only as an exhortation to virtue and to progress in his studies, but also as a reminder of his responsibility to emulate his distinguished father in repayment of the generosity of his nurture. (1980, 199–200)

The text of *The Nux* and Erasmus's commentaries on it were published by Froben in 1524, with other editions published during the same year in Antwerp, Cologne, and Paris. Since Alciati was an avid reader of and admirer of Erasmus, the plight of the nut tree robbed of its fruit soon entered Renaissance emblem literature with the publication of the Italian jurist's *Emblemata* in 1531.

The *inscriptio* of Alciati's Emblem 193, which depicts boys stealing nuts from a tree, reads "On fertility harmful to itself" ("In foecunditatem sibi ipsi damnosam"). The verse is as follows:

Andrea Alciati's emblem "In fertilitatem sibi ipsi damnosam" depicts the robbing of a nut tree by little boys: *Emblemata* (Paris: Wechel, 1534b), 43. Reprinted by permission of the Folger Shakespeare Library (PN 6349 A8 1534b Cage).

Lvdibrivm pueris lapides iacientibus, hoc me
  in triuio posuit rustica cura nucem:
Que laceris ramis, perstrictoque ardua libro,
  Certatim fundis per latus omne petor.
Quid sterili posset contingere turpius? Eheu
  Infelix, fructus in mea damna fero.

(A plaything for boys hurling stones, here
at the crossroads a peasant's care has placed me,
  a nut-tree:
Towering aloft with shredded
  branches and with bruised bark,
I am eagerly sought by slings from all sides.
What more shameful thing could befall a sterile
  tree? Alas,
unhappy me, I bear fruit to my own detriment.)

Callahan points out that this emblem later returned to England in two variations. First, the woodcut was copied onto a carved oaken panel in an Oxford house built in 1572 but later torn down. This panel, along with twenty-seven other designs from Alciati carved in English oak, is now part of the decoration of the Fellows Common Room at University College, Oxford.

The second form of the emblem appeared in Whitney's *Choice of Emblemes* also under the *inscriptio* "In foecunditatem sibi ipsi damnosam." The verse reads:

The robbing of a nut tree, from a later edition of Andrea Alciati's *Emblemata* as carved by an English craftsman on the paneling of an Oxford house. The panel is now part of the decorations of the Fellows Common Room in University College, Oxford. Photograph by Peggy Muñoz Simonds.

If sence I had, my owne estate to knowe,
  Before all trees, my selfe hath cause to crie,
In euerie hedge, and common ways, I growe,
Where, I am made a praye, to passers by:
  And when, they see my nuttes are ripe, and broune,
  My bowghes are broke, my leaues are beaten doune.

Thus euerie year, when I doe yeelde increase,
My proper fruicte, my ruine doth procure:
If fruictless I, then had I growen in peace,
Oh barrenness, of all most happie, sure
Which wordes with griefe, did Agrippina grone,
And mothers more, whose children made them mone. (174)

Whitney's knowledge of the Erasmus Christmas gift is obvious in his punning reference to "mothers more."

Although both Alciati and Whitney use the *topos* of the nut tree to condemn ungrateful children, thus following Erasmus's admonition to John More, Shakespeare once again introduces an original variation of a familiar figure by employing the ravished tree to describe the plight of an unjustly banished courtier and to illustrate the theme of stolen honor. Belarius tells the young princes in *Cymbeline* that two slanderers had robbed him of the fruits of his good service to the king in just one night. But, before discussing this "robbery," Belarius expands on the courtier *topos* in contrast to the noble life in the wilderness they now enjoy:

             the art o' the court,
As hard to leave as keep: whose top to climb
Is certain falling: or so slipp'ry that
the fear's as bad as falling: the toil o' th' war,
A pain that only seems to seek out danger
I' th' name of fame and honour, which dies i' th' search,
And hath as oft a sland'rous epitaph
As record of fair act.

                                                      (3.3.46–53)

Now, his honor besmirched by calumny, Belarius is—after years of faithful service—indeed like the once fruitful tree, left "bare to weather" after a "robbery" that "shook down [his] mellow hangings."

The Tailor's Model with an Empty Head

Perhaps the most telling criticism of the courtier's life in *Cymbeline* occurs in 4.2, when the queen's son Cloten enters the natural world of Belarius. He is elegantly dressed in courtly garments he has stolen from Posthumus, indeed the very ceremonial garments that Posthumus had worn on his last day at court when he bade farewell to Imogen. Looking like Posthumus, whom he is savagely determined to murder, and loudly threatening to rape Imogen as soon as he finds her, Cloten suddenly comes face to face with the Wild Boy Guiderius on the mountain path.

> *Clo.*   Thou art a robber,
> A law-breaker, a villain: yield thee, thief.
> *Gui.* To who? to thee? What art thou? Have not I
> An Arm as big as thine? a heart as big?
> Thy words I grant are bigger: for I wear not
> My dagger in my mouth. Say what thou art:
> Why should I yield to thee.
> *Clo.*   Thou villain base,
> Knowst me not by my clothes?
> *Gui.*   No, nor thy tailor, rascal,
> Who is thy grandfather: he made those clothes,
> Which (as it seems) make thee.
>
> (4.2.74–83)

Since only the nobility was permitted to wear certain types of clothes in Renaissance England, Guiderius would have easily recognized Cloten's rank if he had not been bred in the wilderness. But the irony in this scene of a man who is wearing stolen clothes accusing another of being a thief is typical of Shakespeare's basic irreverence toward such hierarchical codes and leads directly into what we will discover to be a conventional Renaissance attack on the absurd fashions adopted by courtiers.

After further youthful vaunting, the noble savage and the savage but well-dressed courtier exit fighting hand-to-hand. A few seconds later, Guiderius reenters holding up Cloten's severed head. Once again we may suspect an ironic allusion to the emblem tradition. Arviragus has previously compared his brother and himself to the wolf and the fox: "We are beastly: subtle as the fox for prey, / Like warlike as the wolf for what we eat" (3.3.39–41). The *pictura* of Alciati's Emblem 189 depicts a fox holding a male head, or in some editions a tragic mask, in his paws, much as Guiderius holds the head of Cloten in *Cymbeline*. Guiderius remarks,

> This Cloten was a fool, an empty purse,
> There was no money in't: not Hercules
> Could have knock'd out his brains, for he had none:
> Yet I not doing this, the fool had borne
> My head, as I do his.
>
> (4.2.113–7)

The Satyr in *Il pastor fido* makes a similar remark about Corisca's empty wig.

Andrea Alciati's emblem of "The mind not the form matters" from his *Emblemata* (Paris: Wechel, 1534). Reprinted by permission of the Folger Shakespeare Library (PN 6349 A8 1534b Cage, 52).

Both comic observations most probably derive from Alciati's Emblem 189, the *inscriptio* of which reads "Mentem, non formam, plus pollere" ("The mind, not the form, matters"), in criticism of the elegant courtiers of the times. The verse states,

Ingressa vulpes in Choragi pergulam
Fabre expolitum inuenit humanum caput,
Sic eleganter fabricatum, vt spiritus
Solum de esset, caeteris viuisceret.
Id illa cum sumpsisset in manus, ait:
O quale caput est: sed cerebrum non habet.

(A fox, having entered the work-shop of a stage-manager, came upon a smoothly polished mask of a human head, so elegantly fashioned that although it lacked breath, it appeared to be alive in other respects. When the fox took the mask in its paws, it said: "What a fine head this is! But it has no brains.")

As is true of so many Alciati emblems, the epigram comes from an adage of Erasmus [III.II.XL—(812)], "Caput vacuum cerebro" ("Empty-headed"). Erasmus cites the following Aesop fable as his own source:

> As a fox was rummidging among a great many carv'd figures, there was one very extraordinary piece among the rest. He took it up, and when he had consider'd it a while, well, (says he) what pity 'tis, that so exquisite an outside of a head should not have one grain of sense in't.

The moral of the fable is that " 'Tis not the barber or the taylor that makes the man: and 'tis no new thing to see a fine wrought head without so much as one grain of salt in't."[24]

The same image appears in the fables of Phaedrus (I.7) as "The Fox Before the Tragic Actor's Mask":

> A fox after looking by chance at a tragic actor's mask, remarked: "O what a majestic face is here, but it has no brains!" This is a twit for those to whom Lady Luck has granted rank and renown, but denied them common sense.[25]

The idea is a commonplace critique not only of courtiers but also of Greek and Platonic thought, which saw the ideal man as beautiful both in mind and body. However, Erasmus explains that his own adage meant "beautiful in body, but lacking in *ingenio*" [*Ad* IIIIV.XL—(812E)], thereby expressing sixteenth century doubts about the true relationship between inner and outer selves. External beauty does not necessarily indicate the presence of intelligence or of a beautiful soul within.

It seems very likely that Shakespeare drew upon this venerable classical tradition as the model for his stage image of the Wild Boy holding up the courtier's severed head for the audience to see that it contains no brains at all. By reducing an otherwise bloody scene to a witty commentary on external and internal values, the dramatist provokes laughter instead of horror and somewhat absolves Guiderius from charges of homicide. After all, he has not killed a real person at all—just a mask, or a tailor's mannequin.

After demonstrating Cloten to be the embodiment of rapacious lust and brainless ignorance, Shakespeare then depicts Belarius and the savage princes as the saviors of Britain. In 5.3 Posthumus describes the battle in which, after a complete rout of the Britons by invading Romans, a bearded old man and his sons defend a narrow lane against the entire Roman army and change the course of history:

> Athwart the lane,
> He, with two striplings (lads more like to run
> The country base than to commit such slaughter,
> *With faces fit for masks,* or rather fairer

Than those for preservation cas'd, or shame)
Made good the passage, cried to those that fled,
"Our Britain's harts die flying, not our men"

                                   (5.3.18–24; emphasis mine)

Here Posthumus declares the faces of these wild heroes—the true heirs to the throne of Britain—to be fit for commemorative masks. His speech recalls once more the image of the fox with the empty actor's mask as applied to Cloten, except that in this case the heads are truly noble and fair.

Perspective and the Princely Mountain

In act 3, scene 3, as we have seen, Belarius sends Guiderius and Arviragus up to the top of a nearby mountain to hunt a deer for the evening meal. He also asks them to learn a moral from nature during this exercise, since "To apprehend thus, / Draws us a profit from all things we see" (17–18). The lesson Belarius wants to teach his foster sons on this occasion concerns the problem of optical perspective, a new Renaissance science demonstrating that the vantage point from which we view something will in some way always determine our understanding of and responses to what we see. And seeing truly is a fundamental difficulty in *Cymbeline,* just as it was in the earlier Italian tragicomedies, which comment over and over again on basic human blindness. As Imogen puts it, "Our very eyes / Are sometimes like our judgments, blind" (4.2.348–50). Indeed, Northrop Frye observes of *Cymbeline* that "What strikes one at once about the play is the extraordinary blindness of the characters in it."[26]

In addition, scholars often call our attention to the very clear description of the new art of perspective in Imogen's imaginary visual farewell to Posthumus as his ship dwindles away in the distance and finally disappears.

Imo.   Thou shouldst have made him
        As little as a crow, or less, ere left
        To after-eye him.
Pis.   Madam, so I did.
Imo. I would have broke mine eye-strings, crack'd them, but
        To look upon him, till the diminution
        Of space had pointed him sharp as my needle:
        Nay, followed him, till he had melted from
        The smallness of a gnat, to air: and then
        Have turn'd mine eye, and wept.

                                   (1.4.14–22)

What is apparently not noticed, however, is Imogen's specific reference here to the perspective vanishing point in air or the sky, which became in painting a symbol of another world or of infinity. This type of perspective is usually termed atmospheric perspective. Thus open windows or doors in religious paintings often lead the eye beyond the historically specific scene of the Annunication, the Last Supper, or the like, to a view of the heavens, of eternal time and infinite space. A well-known example is Leonardo's "Last Supper" in which Christ's head is framed by such a window opening to a view of sky and clouds. The total of three windows in that particular fresco refers of course to the mystery of the Trinity. In terms of atmospheric perspective, the mentally envisioned disappearance of her bridegroom into air or infinity is for Imogen an analogue to his death, to his transference into another world where she can greet him only through prayers "At the sixth hour of morn, at noon, at midnight, / . . . for then I am in heaven for him" (1.4.31–33). In a theological sense, Posthumus does in fact eventually die to the old Adam within himself, and the next time Imogen sees him, he will have undergone a spiritual conversion to become a "new man" with a somewhat better chance of making the journey to heaven, despite his sins.

However, Imogen's imaginary vision of Posthumus's apotheosis indicates her current lack of knowledge about him as a man. He is neither godlike nor in a state of grace at this point in the play. Knowledge will come to the hero and heroine only after separation and suffering have altered their perspectives of one another. Imogen must learn to see Posthumus as an imperfect man, while Posthumus must learn to see his wife not just as a proudly possessed royal sex object but as virtuous and even as Fidele, the visual embodiment of faith, which is his only hope for salvation in a Protestant context.

As Ernest Gilman states, "It is not surprising that perspective should have become a cognitive metaphor, its elements providing a set of terms for the act of thought itself—an observer, an object of perception, a point of view, a focal point, a horizon. Although the analogy between seeing and knowing is as old as Plato's *Republic,* and has been a vital mode of thought in both the Greek and the Christian traditions, linear perspective revitalized the analogy by making it more detailed and concrete."[27] However, perspective is more than just a metaphor of cognition and knowledge. For example, the following Sonnet by John Davies of Hereford entitled "The Trinity Illustrated by a Three-square Perspective Glasse" transports us immediately into the realm of theology and of "dark Mystery."

If in a three-square Glasse, as thick, as cleare,
(Being but dark Earth, though made Diaphanall)

Beauties diuine, that rauish Sence, appeare,
Making the Soule with ioy, in Trance to fall,
What then, my soule, shalt thou in Heau'n behold,
In that cleare mirror of the TRINITY?
What? O It were not THAT, could it be told:
For, tis a glorious, yet dark Mistery!
It is THAT which is furthest from description;
Whose beaming-Beauty's more than infinite!
It's *Glorious Monument,* whose *Superscription*
Is *Here lies LIGHT, alone indefinite!*
    Then, O Light, limitlesse, let me (poore me)
    Still liue obscure, so I may still see thee.[28]

Here Davies shows the perspective glass to be no more than a dark analogy to the true light of divinity, which cannot be known by man except through reflection and in contrast to the surrounding darkness on earth. He reminds us of the simple truth that to look like something is not to be something.

Shakespeare also investigates the potentials of vertical as opposed to horizontal perspective in *Cymbeline*. From the viewpoint of a groundling, the Soothsayer reports, "I saw Jove's bird, the Roman eagle, wing'd / From the spongy south to this part of the west, / There vanished in the sunbeams" (4.2.348–50). The bird vanishes via linear perspective into infinity and disappears above into the source of light itself, the sun. The play provides us with the opposite movement as well, the descent from above of the eagle bearing Jupiter down into our visual space. The supreme deity descends from infinity into a finite form that human eyes can see, and he promises to "uplift" the lowly human individual when the time is ripe. Although the scene pretends to be only a dream in the mind of Posthumus, the god actually leaves a real tablet behind as proof of his brief visit to earth. In this case, that which only seems to occur is true—at least in the theater.

On a more mundane level, the poet also examines the vertical social hierarchy by means of perspective. Belarius tells the boys,

Now for our mountains sport, up to yond hill!
Your legs are young: I'll tread these flats. Consider,
When you above perceive me like a crow,
That it is place which lessens and sets off,
And you may then revolve what tales I have told you
Of courts, of princes; of the tricks in war.
This service is not service, so being done,
But being so allow'd.

(3.3.10–17)

Once again we have the person seen from afar diminished to the size of a crow, a symbolic bird we shall consider in a later chapter. At this point, only the crow's relatively small size is significant, and it was a commonly used simile in discussions of perspective. For example, Sir John Davies in *Nosce Teipsum* (1599) observes that "When Men seeme Crowes farre off vpon a Towre, / *Sense* saith, th'are crows, what makes vs think them men?"[29] Although Belarius may seem small to the Wild Boys from their vantage point on the mountain, they know how largely he has influenced their lives. But they do not yet know everything. Belarius then mentions the previously discussed emblem of the eagle and the tiny beetle, which destroys the offspring of the larger creature. The banished courtier thereby hints at the way in which he had earlier kidnapped the boys from the royal nursery in an act of revenge against a tyrant who wrongly deprived him of his lands. His point is that although something may look small to us, it can still be dangerous, a lesson Cymbeline forgot but that the princes must learn.

Ben Jonson used the same perspective *topos* in the 1603 production of his Roman tragedy *Sejanus*. Once he has become counselor to the emperor, Sejanus muses on the differences in his perceptions:

> Reared to this height,
> All my desires seem modest, poor, and slight,
> That did before sound impudent; 'tis place,
> Not blood, discerns the noble and the base.[30]

(5.1.9–12)

Ethics thus appear to become relative to one's place in the social hierarchy, a very disturbing observation indeed. In *Cymbeline* we find the same point made. The king, from his position at the top of the hierarchy, sees the nobleman Posthumus as not a prince and therefore as not sufficiently noble to espouse Princess Imogen. Later he accepts the virtuous actions of Posthumus on the battlefield and in forgiving Iachimo as sufficient proof of true nobility and worthy of his own imitation. Deeds, not social level, ultimately provide the true distinction between "the noble and the base" in Shakespeare's tragicomedy.

Returning to 4.3, the Wild Boys then climb up "yond hill," which we must presume is offstage. However, the mountain has been verbally presented by Belarius to our imaginations where it remains as a thing seen. In an interesting discussion of the use of artificial mountains in masques, pageants, and gardens, James J. Yoch, Jr., has pointed out that in *The Tempest*, "Like the surveying ruler on a princely mount, Prospero often overlooks scenes in the play, and the stage directions once specifically site him 'on the top' (3.3)." From this vantage point he surveys the world below and controls it with his magic, exercising the prerogatives of a king on the top of the social hierarchy. According to Yoch,

The figure of "mervelous mounts of mountayns" had long been available in court as well as civic entertainments: two came before Catherine of Aragon in 1501, and the Stuart masques continued such traditional emblematic staging to assert superiority, as in *The Vision of the Twelve Goddesses.* In his production, Daniel noted the first concern was "the hieroglyphic of empire and dominion, as the ground and matter whereon this glory of state is built." Within a few years there was a rage for mountains that so often rise on the stage of the Banqueting Hall that Plutus complains in 1613: "Rocks? Nothing but rocks in these masquing devices?"[31]

And the rage for princely mounts soon extended from the theater to English gardens. Deriving from Italian models, symbolic artificial mountains were designed for the gardens of both Queen Anne and Prince Henry so that from the top of such hills, royalty could assure itself of dominance by surveying the smaller world below.

In this situation, however, perspective provides a false vision of relationships. When the observer on the mountain top sees others as smaller and less important than himself, he forgets that all men are actually brothers in the sight of God. Because his subjects seem to him small and insignificant from his high vantage point, a king may be tempted to treat them unfairly, as Cymbeline has mistreated Belarius, thus forgetting that optical perspective is an illusion and not reality. Linear perspective was originally invented by Alberti and Brunelleschi to demonstrate mathematically that everything in the universe is related to everything else through geometry. As Samuel Y. Edgerton, Jr., has explained, "linear perspective came about in the early Renaissance, not in order to reveal visual 'truth' in the purely heuristic sense. . . , but rather as a means of— literally—squaring what was seen empirically with the traditional medieval belief that God spreads His grace through the universe according to the laws of geometric optics."[32] For this reason, Belarius reminds the Wild Boys that, since "it is place which lessens and sets off," they must always keep in mind the particular perspective from which they view the world in order not to be fooled by their own eyes, as was their father Cymbeline.

On the other hand, Douglas L. Peterson points out that the mountain itself originally symbolized a place for circumspection and the learning of prudence in worldly affairs. He quotes Thomas Elyot, who wrote that the circumspect "may, as it were on a mountain or place of espial, behold on every side far off, measuring and esteeming everything, and either pursue it, if it be commendable, or abandon it or eschew it, if it be noyful." Elyot adds that circumspection "is not only expedient but also needful to every estate and degree of men, that do continue in the life called active."[33] The attitude of the viewer when he finds himself in a high place is of essential importance, therefore, whether the mountain signifies pride and dominance over others, or whether it signifies prudent circumspection before initiating an action.

Undoubtedly other readers will find more such anticourtier *topoi* in *Cymbeline* and call attention to them, but the four we have examined here should be sufficient to demonstrate that Shakespeare as an artist is not merely reflecting the power of the Jacobean state. Instead the poet criticizes—through the use of easily recognizable tropes—the Renaissance social hierarchy that imprisons the minds of men and women who have been economically forced into serving rulers of limited vision. As one of the "Servants of the King" himself, Shakespeare surely sings his own bondage freely in *Cymbeline*.

In the case of Posthumus, once he has humbled himself by dressing as a common British man of the soil, he is granted a spectacular divine vision in direct contrast to the blindness of Cymbeline. On awakening from his dream of Jupiter, Posthumus then provides us with a final series of anticourtier observations: "Poor wretches, that depend / On greatness' favour, dream as I have done, / Wake, and find nothing" (5.4.127–29). In contrast, Posthumus himself has been promised a happy ending by the deity, and now, as a man of faith armed with a prophetic tablet or a divine text, he moves confidently toward the dénouement of the play, intellectually puzzled, but certain that he and his marriage will both be saved. After all, Jupiter has clearly pronounced that, "He shall be lord of lady Imogen, / And happier much by his affliction made" (5.4.107–8). Posthumus also notes once more the contrast between inner and outer man at court when he apostrophizes the book left him by the descended god:

> A book? O rare one,
> Be not, as is our fangled world, a garment
> Nobler than that it covers. Let thy effects
> So follow, to be most unlike our courtiers,
> As good as promise.
>
> (5.4.133–37)

For the newly reformed gentleman, the outside must correctly reflect the inside, and promises must be kept to the letter, a naive attitude Shakespeare later shows to be unworkable in this "fangled" world where we must learn to recognize the hidden spirit within. Posthumus fails to recognize Imogen disguised as Fidele; indeed, he never does learn to distinguish between seeming and being because of his insistence on a literal interpretation of what he perceives. Perhaps Shakespeare is implying here a mild criticism of the tendency of his fellow Protestants to interpret the Scriptures themselves too literally and thus to miss the poetic subtleties of irony and metaphor that distinguish the Bible as a work of literature and will forever complicate its interpretation.

In this chapter we have seen how Shakespeare cleverly draws upon conventional but variable anticourtier *topoi* to satirize the prevailing social hierarchy of his time. Like most poets in need of patronage, he would obviously prefer to serve a nobility based on virtuous behavior in contrast to an entrenched nobility placed above others by birth or by marriage (as in the case of Cloten). But, like Erasmus, he also appears to have some hope for hereditary princes who have been properly educated by good tutors such as Belarius to respect the moral lessons of nature and of books and to respect the dignity of other human beings, no matter how small and insignificant they may seem to the imperfect human eye.

Significantly, the tragicomedy does not advocate political rebellion against the bumbling tyranny of Cymbeline, despite the early example of Belarius in kidnapping the princes. Rather it seems to advocate the spiritual reform of those in power to act in accordance with the Christian ideals of love and brotherhood, ideals they loudly profess but so seldom follow. Moreover, by couching so much of his social criticism in terms of recognizable emblems in *Cymbeline,* Shakespeare guarantees his own safety within the court of King James. After all, the king and all his nobles have been reading the works of Alciati, Perrière, Junius, and Whitney since boyhood and could hardly see such emblems as a personal attack. The conventional wisdom of the anticourtier *topos* was always general in nature and was employed by court poets as a reminder of corruption at court to the courtly, not as a dangerous rallying cry to the populace for revolution.

Notes

1. Pauline M. Smith, *The Anti-Courtier Trend in Sixteenth Century French Literature* (Geneva: Libraire Droz, 1966), 17–18; hereafter cited parenthetically.

2. See Peter M. Daly, Virginia W. Callahan, and Simon Cuttler, eds., *Andreas Alciatus: Index Emblematicus,* 2 vols. (Toronto: University of Toronto Press, 1985), vol. 1: Emblem 87.

3. A variation of this *topos* is the faithful servant in bondage. In *King Lear,* Shakespeare shows us the roughly dressed Kent placed in stocks for speaking the truth. Either way—as a flatterer or a frankly speaking observer—the courtier is subject to bondage.

4. Sir Thomas More, *Utopia,* ed. Edward Surtz, S.J., and J. H. Hexter (New Haven: Yale University Press, 1965), 153–57. There is a spiritual level to this *topos* as well, specifically in the variation employed by Petrarch in his *Secretum.* Here St. Augustine accuses the poet of being still held down to earth, like a person bound hand and foot in golden chains who gazes at his bonds with delight and fails

to recognize that they are, after all, chains. See *Prose,* ed. G. Martelloti, et al., in *La Letteratura Italiana: Storia e Testi* (Milano: Ricciardi, 1955), 7, 130. I am indebted to Thomas P. Roche, Jr., for this reference.

5. Julius S. Held, *Rembrandt's Aristotle* (Princeton, N.J.: Princeton University Press, 1969), 35.

6. See Geffrey Whitney, *A Choice of Emblemes* (Leyden: Christopher Plantin, 1586), 202; hereafter referred to parenthetically.

7. See the Arden edition of Shakespeare's *Cymbeline,* ed. J. M. Nosworthy, 84 n. 23.

8. Aesop, *Fables of Aesop According to Sir Roger L'Estrange* (New York: Dover Publications, 1967), 5.

9. Aelian. *On The Characteristics of Animals,* trans. A. F. Scholfield, 3 vols., Loeb Classical Library (Cambridge: Harvard University Press, 1958), vol. 1, 201.

10. John F. Moffit, "Paul Klee's *Twittering Machine* and the Emblematic 'Birds-in-Bondage-Vile' Theme," *Studies in Iconography* 9 (1983): 142–43; hereafter referred to parenthetically. See also George Economou, "Chaucer's Use of the Bird in the Cage Image in the *Canterbury Tales,*" *Philological Quarterly* 54 (1975): 679–84.

11. See *Petrarch's Lyric Poems: The 'Rime Sparse' and Other Lyrics,* ed. and trans. Robert M. Durling (Cambridge, Mass.: Harvard University Press, 1976), 434.

12. Desiderius Erasmus, *A Modest Meane to Marriage (Proci et Puellae),* trans. Nicholas Leigh (London: Henrie Denham, 1568), sig. Ci.

13. See Dora and Erwin Panofsky, *Pandora's Box: The Changing Aspects of a Mythical Symbol* (New York: Pantheon Books, 1956), 28–33.

14. See Thomas Combe, *The Theater of Fine Devices* (London: Richard Field, 1614), sig. D.

15. Hadrianus Junius, *Emblemata* (Antwerp: Christopher Plantin, 1565), 62. Translated by Roger T. Simonds.

16. Ibid., 146–47.

17. See my "Freedom of Speech and the Emblem Tradition," *Acta Conventus Neo-Latini Sanctandreani,* ed. I. D. McFarlane (Binghamton, N.Y.: Medieval & Renaissance Texts & Studies, 1986), 605–16.

18. See E. De Jongh, "Erotica in Vogelperspectief," *Simiolus* 3 (1968–69): 22–74.

19. Otto van Veen, *Amorvm Emblemata or Emblemes of Loue* (Antwerp, 1608), 72–73.

20. Blake, "Song," *The Poetical Works of William Blake,* ed. John Sampson (London: Oxford University Press, 1914), 8–9.

21. Schöne's views are summarized in Peter Daly's useful study *Literature in the Light of the Emblem* (Toronto: University of Toronto Press, 1979). See especially 140–42 for the *argumentum emblematicum.*

22. See Arthur Henkel and Albrecht Schöne, *Emblemata* (Stuttgart: J. B. Metzlersche Verlagsbuchandlung, 1967), 149–51, and 179.

23. Virginia W. Callahan, "Ramifications of the Nut Tree Fable," *Acta Conventus Neo-Latini Turonensis,* ed. Jean-Claude Margolin (Paris, 1980), 197–204. Further references will be noted in my text.

24. *Aesopica,* 2 vols., ed. Ben Edwin Perry (Urbana: University of Illinois, 1952), vol. 2, 332.

25. *Babrius and Phaedrus,* ed. Ben Edwin Perry, Loeb Classical Library (Cambridge, Mass.: Harvard University Press, 1965), 201.

26. Northrop Frye, *A Natural Perspective: The Development of Shakespearean Comedy and Romance* (New York: Columbia University Press, 1965), 67.

27. Ernest Gilman, *The Curious Perspective: Literary and Pictorial Wit in the Seventeenth Century* (New Haven and London: Yale University Press, 1978), 29.

28. John Davies of Hereford, *Wittes Pilgrimage,* in Alexander B. Grosart, ed., *The Complete Works of John Davies of Hereford* (d. 1618), 2 vols. (Edinburgh: Edinburgh University Press, 1878), vol. 2, 21.

29. Sir John Davies, *Nosce Teipsum* (London: Richard Field, 1599), 18.

30. See *Sejanus* in *Ben Jonson,* 11 vols., ed. C. H. Herford, Percy and Evelyn Simpson (Oxford: Clarendon Press, 1941), vol. 4, 349–485.

31. See James J. Yoch, Jr., "Subjecting the Landscape in Pageants and Shakespearean Pastorals," in *Pageantry in the Shakespearean Theater,* ed. David M. Bergeron (Athens, Ga.: University of Georgia Press, 1985), 212.

32. See Samuel Y. Edgerton, Jr., *The Renaissance Rediscovery of Linear Perspective* (New York: Basic Books, Inc., 1975), 162.

33. Douglas L. Peterson, "*Cymbeline:* Legendary History and Arcadian Romance," in *Time, Tide, and Tempest; A Study of Shakespeare's Romances* (San Marino, Calif.: The Huntington Library, 1973), 110 and 148, n.2.

6

The Iconography of Birds in *Cymbeline*

> But ask now the beasts, and they shall teach thee; and the fowls
> of the air, and they shall tell thee.
>
> —Job. 12.7

According to G. Wilson Knight, "Bird-life is very significantly used in
Shakespeare," while J. M. Nosworthy remarks in his introduction to the
Arden edition of the tragicomedy that bird imagery absolutely pervades
Cymbeline.[1] In fact, twelve different species are alluded to in the text,
each of which had multiple symbolic meanings for Shakespeare's audience. They include the crow, the eagle, the puttock or kite, the jay, the
raven, the nightingale or Philomel, the lark, the wren, the ruddock (robin),
the cock, the owl, and the phoenix. Their symbolic and moral meanings
seem to correspond at times to the personal, at other times to the political,
and almost always to the spiritual levels of *Cymbeline*. I shall consider in
this chapter only those traditional significations of each bird that seem
relevant to this particular play, since Shakespeare may and often does use
the same bird elsewhere to symbolize a completely different value.

It is well known that the interrelationship of birds, animals, plants, and
minerals with everything else in the universe as originally planned by the
Divine Creator was a widely held Medieval and Renaissance belief. Art
reflects nature, which in turn is the mirror of God. The concept is particularly familiar to students of English literature through the often reproduced emblematic engraving in Robert Fludd's *Utriusque Cosmi
Historia* (1617–19) under the Latin *inscriptio* "Integrae Naturae speculum, Artis que imago" ("The mirror of Nature as a whole, and the image
of Art").[2] The *pictura* of the emblem represents a circular cosmos, above
which the hand of God holds a chain attached to the goddess Natura, who
stands on a world consisting of animal, vegetable, and mineral components, as well as the four elements. Natura herself holds another chain that
is attached to the left wrist of an ape symbolizing Art as the imitator of
Nature. This ape of nature sits below the goddess on a smaller world at the
center of the emblem and measures a tiny circular model of the cosmos

with a pair of compasses. Since any single part of this universe can correspond to any other part symbolically, artists are encouraged to make use of objects and creatures in the realm of nature to symbolize Platonic Ideas, celestial spirits, and even aspects of the Divinity Himself, all of which exist in their purest form outside the natural world.

The Elizabethan clergyman Edward Topsell refers to these correspondences in the dedication of his *Histories of Beasts* to the Dean of Westminster:

> I see no cause why any man should doubt that the knowledge of the beasts, like the knowledge of the other creatures and works of God, is divine, seeing that at the first they were created and brought to man, and all by the Lord Himself. So their life and creation are divine in respect to their maker, and their naming was divine in respect to Adam, for out of the plenty of his own divine wisdom he gave them their names, as it were out of a fountain of prophecy, foreshadowing in one elegant and significant denomination the nature of every kind. When I affirm that the knowledge of beasts is divine, I mean no other than the right and perfect description of their names, figures, and natures. This is in the Creator divine, and therefore such as is the fountain, such are the streams issuing from the same into the minds of men.[3]

Topsell further points out that the Bible makes three uses of beasts: in sacrifices, visions, and "reproof and instruction to man." Since the latter is of particular interest to him, he provides several examples of how the study of animals can teach morality to human beings. "Who is so unnatural and unthankful to his parents," he asks, "but by reading how the young storks and woodpeckers do in their parents' old age feed and nourish them, will not repent, amend his folly, and be more natural?"[4]

For this reason, during the Middle Ages and the Renaissance, birds and animals were widely employed as moral symbols in art, including the decorative arts within the home. A particularly fine example of this practice can be found in the emblematic bed hangings believed to have been embroidered around 1570 by Mary Queen of Scots and Bess of Hardwick while Mary was a prisoner at Chatsworth.[5] The creatures decorating the hangings were first traced from Konrad Gesner's encyclopedic books on birds and animals, then cross stitched with silk thread onto pieces of canvas cut out in the shape of the *crux quadrata,* now called the Greek Cross but also suggestive of the four-part Pythagorean universe. The craftswomen then applied the embroidered pieces of canvas to a background of green velvet, which probably symbolizes the vegetable world where the animals live along with the descendants of Adam and Eve. Some of the embroidered creatures on these large hangings have their names stitched into the pictures, as if this were a book for children. These include "A Pellican," "A Spider," "A Tiger," and "Knotted serpentes." Careful identification of this sort may remind us of Topsell's comment that

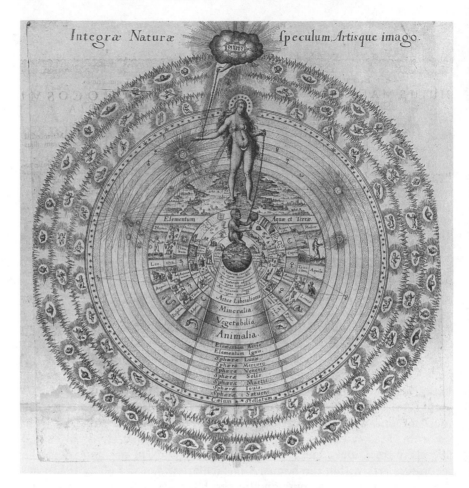

The artist as Nature's ape, from Robert Fludd, *Utriusque Cosmi Historia* (Oppenheim: J. Theodore De Bry, 1617), 1, Pl. 2. Reprinted by permission of the Folger Shakespeare Library (BD 500 F4 1617c Cage).

"their naming was divine in respect to Adam." Other birds, such as the eagle capturing a rabbit with his talons and the blackbird, are not identified.

The hangings also include embroidered moral emblems with mottos, one of which depicts the hand of God with a pruning knife cutting away unfruitful branches from a vine. The motto reads "Virescit vulnere virtus" ("Virtue thrives by a wound"), and it urges—not very subtly—the removal of Queen Elizabeth as an unfruitful branch of the royal family.[6] Above this emblem is Mary's monogram and an embroidered phoenix as a symbolic reference to the captive queen's political hopes.

Shakespeare's *Cymbeline* contains equally resonant images from nature, including birds. In this chapter, I shall point out what seem to be the most appropriate symbolic meanings of the more briefly mentioned birds in the play and then discuss in greater detail Shakespeare's three major avian allusions: the crow, the eagle, and the phoenix. These three birds reemphasize the dominant themes of the tragicomedy—marriage and concord, the fall and redemption of man, and his regeneration after inner reform.

The Choir of Birds Accompanying the Phoenix

Since the phoenix, to which Imogen is compared by Iachimo, is a sun bird primarily symbolizing "self-renewing time," its death and resurrection must be witnessed by a multitude of other birds, which are then present to greet the new phoenix and the new era he initiates. R. Van den Broek tells us that,

> various authors include in the version of the burning the story that the rejuvenated phoenix was accompanied by a huge flock of birds, honoring it as their king. According to Coripus, the birds await the appearance of the new phoenix tensely: the avian choir watches for the sun and the sun bird, and as soon as it appears they loudly acclaim their new king.[7]

Most such birds in *Cymbeline* are referred to only once. Although each of them has some symbolic significance, they seem to be present mainly to form part of the phoenix's choir—in this case, a choir that resonates through verbal references throughout the play.

First, the nightingale is suggested by Imogen's bedtime reading. According to Iachimo, "She hath been reading late, / The tale of Tereus, here the leaf's turn'd down / Where Philomel gave up" (2.2.44–46). The nightingale has always had strong erotic associations, especially with adulterous love, from the first telling of the Tereus myth and later throughout the Middle Ages and the Renaissance. As Beryl Rowland reminds us, Chaucer's Criseyde hears the song of the nightingale before she gives herself to Troilus. It sang "a lay of love, that made her herte fresh and gay." Even to listen to such a song in Boccaccio's *Decameron* is "a humorous euphemism for making love, and the nightingale itself is finally identified with the male sex organ."[8] We have previously seen the caged nightingale employed by both Jean le Meun and Chaucer as a symbol for faithlessness in love, but since Pliny had also reported that the nightingale died at the end of its song, it became associated with sexual orgasm as well. During the English Renaissance, therefore, Barnabe Barnes blithely announces, "I'll sing my Plain Song with the turtle dove / And Prick Song with the nightingale rehearse" (in Rowland 1978, 108).

In contrast, the nightingale also has important spiritual meanings, thus signifying the highest type of love rather than the lowest. According to Rowland, John Lydgate wrote two religious poems on nightingales, one commemorating Christ's Passion through its mournful song and the other crying out for vengeance "on those who do not appreciate Christ's salvation." The first of these poems actually identifies the bird with the human soul and with Christ himself:

> this nyghtingale, that thus freshly can
> Both wake and singe, as telleth us scripture,
> Is Crist hym-self ande every cristen-man.

Sometimes in religious lyrics the nightingale symbolizes the Virgin Mary, or even the soul waiting in anguish throughout the night for the savior's coming (Rowland 1978, 109).

Particularly important for our tragicomedy, however, is the ancient Greek association between the nightingale and the poet, an association that reaches its modern culmination in the poetry of Shelley and Keats. Indeed, Pausanius reports that "the nightingale that rests on the tomb of Orpheus sings more sweetly and louder than any others" (*Description of Greece* IX, XXX, 6). The metaphorical relationship of the bird to Orpheus lamenting in song the death of Eurydice and to the lament of nature for the death of Orpheus himself makes the evocation of Philomela almost a necessity in an Orphic play like *Cymbeline,* which actually dramatizes a death and resurrection. But in the medieval bestiaries the bird always transcends such grief through the linguistic suggestions of her name: "The Nightingale bird, LUCINA takes this name because she is accustomed to herald the dawn of the new day with her song, as a lamp does *(lucerna).*"[9] Moreover, the nightingale is also a herald of the springtime and of new life within nature, as we have already seen in Emblem 56 by Hadrianus Junius. The bird laments the fact of death, whether sexual or literal, but it also points forward to resurrection in *Cymbeline*.

Since Iachimo mentions that Imogen was reading the story of Philomel before she fell asleep, the first significance of the nightingale is obviously sexual: "here the leaf's turned down / Where Philomel gave up" (2.2.45–46). This observation provides one more lascivious detail for the intruder to use in his slander, if it should become necessary. According to popular belief, such bedtime reading about the nightingale could actually inspire dreams of lust in the sleeping Imogen. On the other hand, the associations of the nightingale with Orpheus and with resurrection from the dead through Christ clearly add to the spiritual implications of *Cymbeline*. The heraldic bird also points toward the dawn of a new era shortly to begin with the birth of Christ, once the Augustan peace is established at the end of the play.

Iachimo appears to ally his own wicked personality with that of the raven. When he crawls back into the trunk to hide himself at the end of the bedchamber scene, he intones the following prayer to Hecate:

> Swift, swift, you dragons of the night, that dawning
> May bare the raven's eye. I lodge in fear;
> Though this a heavenly angel, hell is here.
>
> (2.2.48–50)

Among the multiple symbolic values of this bird, one seems to be particularly appropriate to Iachimo: the raven carries tales, according to Ovid's *Metamorphoses*. Originally associated with Apollo, the garrulous raven informed the sun god that it had seen his beloved Coronis lying with a young man of Thessaly. In a jealous fury, Apollo shot an arrow into breast of Coronis, but then his grief at her loss was so great that the god changed the silvery feathers of the raven to black as a punishment for its needless gossip.[10] For Christians, the fact that the raven did not return to Noah on the ark but remained away to eat carrion clearly associates the bird with evil as early as Genesis. We may also assume that Shakespeare had in mind here that when the raven does open its eye in the morning, it flies out to the battlefield to perform its folkloric function of pecking out the eyes of fallen soldiers, once again associating itself with the demonic forces that at this point are so dear to Iachimo's heart.

Another bird of ill-repute was the colorful blue jay, so brilliant on the outside but corrupt within. After Imogen reads Posthumus's letter to Pisanio accusing her of adultery, she reasons that "Some jay of Italy / (Whose mother was her painting) hath betray'd him" (3.4.50–51), and she means by this that her husband is obviously judging her by the behavior toward him of a prostitute in Italy. The significance of the blue jay is amply explained by Nosworthy in the Arden edition of the play: "The jay here signifies a loose woman, and as Capell pointed out long ago, the Italian word *puta* means both jay and wanton—as Shakespeare and most of his contemporaries were doubtless well aware" (1955, 91).

Cloten is associated with the puttock or kite, one of the most unattractive birds that make up Shakespeare's avian flock in *Cymbeline*. Imogen announces that "I chose an eagle, / And did avoid a puttock" (1.2.70–71). According to Nosworthy, the puttock ranks lower than the eagle in the bird hierarchy (1955, 10). More importantly, it symbolized "greed, cowardice, and deceit" for earlier times (Rowland 1978, 93), all qualities that Cloten reveals. But, despite its many other meanings, in *Cymbeline* the bird particularly suggests rapine, the seizing of others' property, including their women (Rowland 1978, 93–94). Cloten steals Posthumus's clothes, then threatens to kill Posthumus and rape Imogen if he can find them in the mountains. This symbolic meaning of the kite is to be found in

CORON. AB APOLL. TRANSFIXA. XI. 65

The raven gossips to Apollo about seeing Coronis with a Thracian lad, and then, in a fit of jealousy, Apollo shoots his beloved with an arrow. From an abbreviated edition of Ovid's *Metamorphoses* (Antwerp: Christopher Plantin, 1591), 65. The illustration is by Pieter van der Borcht. Reprinted by permission of the Folger Shakespeare Library (PA 6519 M2 1591 Cage).

Valeriano, Alciati, and Geffrey Whitney, whose emblem "Feresimile praecedenti, ex Alciato" paraphrases the Italian emblematist as follows:

> The greedie kyte, so full his gorge had cloy'de,
> He coulde not brooke his late deuoured praie:
> Wherefore with griefe, vnto his damme hee cry'de,
> My bowelles lo, alas doe waste awaie.
>   With that quoth shee, why doste thou make thy mone.
>   This losse thou haste is nothinge of thy owne.
>
> By which is meante, that they who liue by spoile,
> By rapine, thefte, or griping goodes by mighte,
> If that with losse they suffer anie foile,
> They loose but that, wherein they had no righte?
>   Hereof, at firste the prouerbe oulde did growe:
>   *That goodes ill got, awaie as ill will goe.*[11]

Puttocks or kites were also considered to be cowardly birds of prey and unwilling to attack any quarry that was not already half dead of wounds or at least sick. In *Julius Caesar,* Cassius observes that, in company with ravens and carrion crows, "kites / Fly o'er our heads, and downward look on us / As we were sickly prey" (5.1.84–86). Equally descriptive of the rapacious but cowardly Cloten, who is bested in arms with no difficulty by both Posthumus and Guiderius, is Stephen Batman's portrayal of the carrion loving hawk:

> A kite is weake in flight & in strength. . . . And he is a rauishing foule, and hardy among small birds, & a coward & fearefull among great birdes, and dreadeth to lie in waite to take wilde birds, and dreadeth not to lye in waite to take tame birds.[12]

Batman undoubtedly means females when he refers to "tame birds," and the female Imogen is most certainly Cloten's hoped for prey in the tragicomedy.

In 3.7 of *Cymbeline,* Arviragus welcomes Imogen/Fidele to the cave of Belarius with the following words: "The night to th' owl and morn to th' lark less welcome" (66). I doubt if there is any esoteric significance to be found in this not surprising use of familiar nature imagery by the Wild Boy, but the song "Hark, hark, the lark," which Cloten's musicians sing to the sleeping Imogen outside her window or door, is quite another story. Here Cloten enacts the role of Orpheus singing a hymn in praise of his patron god Apollo and attempting to awaken his sleeping beloved from death through an *aubade*:

> Hark, hark, the lark at heaven's gate sings,
> 　　And Phoebus 'gins arise,
> His steeds to water at those springs
> 　　On chalic'd flowers that lies;
> And winking Mary-buds begin to ope their golden eyes
> With everything that pretty is, my lady sweet arise:
> 　　Arise, arise!

$$(2.3.19\text{–}25)$$

Unfortunately, Cloten's real intentions appear to be entirely sexual, in keeping with his other role as wanton Eros: "Come on, tune: if you can penetrate her with your fingering, so: we'll try with tongue too" (2.3.13–14). On the other hand, the punning line contains a truth about Orpheus: he both played a lyre with his fingers, as did Apollo, and gave tongue to inspired verbal poetry. Through the dual arts of music and poetry, he was indeed able to penetrate the underworld and was very nearly successful in resurrecting his lost Eurydice from the dead and restoring her beauty to the light of the sun. Cloten's music appears to be unheard, however, by Imogen, who continues immersed in sleep, that "ape of death."

As for the lark, its song was believed by the Church Fathers to be a natural hymn of praise to the Creator. Countless poets, including Shakespeare and Milton, mention this religious association, as does the more scientific ornithologist Ulisse Aldrovandi.[13] Since the lark heralded the dawn, it was a popular poetic *topos* for indicating "time and transitions" (Rowland 1978, 99). Perhaps Imogen does not hear Cloten's impassioned *aubade* because she is not yet ready to awaken to a new life of disillusionment about the perfections of her beloved and of confidence in her own powers to perform faithfully the labors of love as the page Fidele, despite this disillusionment and the initial despair it causes. In any event, she will soon learn that Posthumus is no more divine at this time of his life than is Cloten, who seeks without success to penetrate her ears with hired but divine music.

Curiously enough, Cloten is associated not only with the lark but also with that other herald of dawn and of the nativity of Christ, the cock—in terms, however, that accentuate his native foolishness. The Second Lord says in an aside, "You are cock and capon too, and you crow, cock, with your comb on" (2.1.22–23). Aside from the sexual implications of this line, such a coxcomb or Erasmian fool will soon become the bloody sacrificial victim to love necessary to save *Cymbeline* from becoming a tragedy. On the other hand, Aldrovandi reports that the rooster "is a bird extremely given to lust, who follows womanly ways and is a greater lover of pleasures than he is of God, whence it is said in Isaiah: 'Lo, the Lord will cause you to be transported just as a rooster is transported.' "[14]

Arviragus's evocation of the robin as "the ruddock" during the funeral ceremonies for Imogen/Fidele is purely folkloric:

> With fairest flowers
> Whilst summer lasts, and I live here, Fidele,
> I'll sweeten thy sad grave: thou shalt not lack
> The flower that's like thy face, pale primrose, nor
> The asur'd harebell, like thy veins: no, nor
> The leaf of eglantine, whom not to slander,
> Out-sweet'ned not thy breath: the ruddock would
> *With charitable bill* (O bill, sore shaming
> Those rich-left heirs, that let their fathers lie
> Without a monument!) bring thee all this;
> Yea, and furr'd moss besides. When flowers are none,
> To winter-ground thy corse—
>
> (4.2.218–29; my emphasis)

The bird symbolizes charity because "According to a Breton legend, the robin stained its breast with Christ's blood while attempting to pluck a thorn from His crown. By the late fifteenth century its charity was devoted to the dead" (Rowland 1978, 149–50). Hence the robin, often helped by the wren, was commonly believed to strew graves with flowers and moss. Equally folkloric is Imogen's mention of the wren shortly after she awakens from her deathlike sleep: "but if there be / Yet left in heaven as small a drop of pity / As the wren's eye, fear'd gods, a part of it!" (4.2.303– 5). The wren's small size and its close association with the robin's charity are tearfully evoked here by one just resurrected from the dead.

The Crow as a Symbol of Marriage and of Political Consensus

Apart from several references to carrion crows by Cloten, in *Cymbeline* the crow is primarily associated with the characters Belarius and Posthumus, who are banished from England by the king. In both cases the bird is mentioned in the context of visual perspective as part of a metaphor stating that a person seen in the distance may look as small as a crow. The first appearance of this metaphor occurs in 1.4 when Pisanio describes the departure of Posthumus from Britain in a ship. Imogen protests, "Thou should'st have made him / As little as a crow, or less, ere left / To after-eye him" (14–16). The second appearance of the crow metaphor occurs in 3.3 when Belarius sends the Wild Boys up the mountain to hunt for deer: "Consider / when you above perceive me like a crow, / That it is place which lessens and sets off" (11–13). Perhaps the bird's size was all that really interested Shakespeare; however, he might then have chosen any other bird, the even smaller sparrow, for example, or the larger eagle, a bird also identified with Posthumus and a common symbol of vision. But he did not, which suggests that the crow may have had meanings beyond that of perspective, although its relative smallness in contrast to the princely eagle is certainly important within the context of the play, as we have seen.

Nosworthy tells us that "Belarius, who is wise, is 'like a crow' " (lxxiii). Yet wisdom is not generally associated with crows, particularly in Renaissance emblem books, although Topsell does admit that it is often considered a bird with "witte and subtilitie."[15] In fact, the raven is a more likely symbol of intelligence. For example, in Joachim Camerarius's *Symbolarum et Emblematum,* we find that the raven rather than the crow is famous for its ability to gain knowledge from its natural surroundings. The *inscriptio* of Emblem 79 in Book III is "Ingenio experiar" ("I shall know by instinct"). The *pictura* displays a raven perched on top of an amphora it has cleverly filled with stones in order to raise the water level high enough for it to have a drink, while the *subscriptio* reads,

Mira est ingenii vis & solertia corvis,
Natura ut doceat quam sit ubique potens.

(Wonderful is the force and ingenuity of the raven's instincts; For nature teaches him what is everywhere efficacious.)[16]

However, in *Cymbeline* it is the clever villain Iachimo—not Belarius—who is associated with the raven, and he uses his subtle instincts for evil purposes.

Medieval symbolic meanings of the crow might be more appropriate for the cave-dwelling Belarius. As E. P. Evans reminds us, Ambrosius chose

The raven displays its intelligence in this emblem by Joachim Camerarius, *Symbola et Emblemata*, 2nd ed. (Nuremberg: Voegelinianis, 1605), 79. Reprinted by permission of the Folger Shakespeare Library (PN 6349 C13 1605 Cage).

the crow "as the type and pattern of hospitality" in his *Hexahemeron,*[17] and Belarius is the epitomy of the hospitable host to Imogen in 3.6 of *Cymbeline*. A faithful widower, he lives happily in the mountains of Wales, piously communing with nature and the gods and teaching natural law to the young princes, Arviragus and Guiderius. According to Evans,

> Both the crow and the turtle-dove are typical [in medieval church architecture] of Christian constancy and devotion. If either of these birds loses its mate, it never takes another. As our Lord went with only three disciples to the Mount of Olives, where He was transfigured before them and heard an approving voice from heaven, so His followers should withdraw from the world and devote themselves to religious meditation.[18]

Perhaps Belarius is suggesting to the Wild Boys that they look down upon him from the mountaintop as such an example of constancy to marriage, to the contemplative life, and to God.

Even more in keeping with the characters of Belarius and Posthumus, however, is the ancient tradition of the crow's bravery against such royal birds as hawks and eagles, since both of these men actively defy the king's tyranny in *Cymbeline*. Topsell tells us that crows "dare meddle with Eagles, who beinge longe prouoked by their importunities teareth them in piecces: ffor this cause also they adventure vpon Falcons, although to their oune detriment. Yet Aristotle writeth that many tymes by watchinge advauntages they harme both Eagles and Haukes" (*The Fowles* 1972, 226). Shakespeare actually refers to this tradition of crow rebellion in *Coriolanus* when his aristocratic hero complains that "the rabble . . . will in time / Break ope the locks a' th' Senate, and bring in / The crows to peck the eagles" (3.1.136–39). In *Cymbeline,* although Posthumus is not of royal blood, he marries the king's daughter and then is exiled at once from Britain. He returns later as part of the invading Roman force. Belarius, after being falsely accused of treason by a courtier, is also exiled, but he takes immediate revenge on the king (like an angry crow) by kidnapping the infant princes and carrying them off with him to Wales.

The crow is most famous for its faithfulness or constancy, according to Topsell, since "They choose their mates and contynue constant vnto them, without chainge, both while they lyve, and after they be dead" (*The Fowles* 1972, 222). I believe this is the symbolic meaning of the crow that Shakespeare wishes to evoke most strongly in *Cymbeline*. Belarius is faithful to his dead wife Euryphile and ultimately to his king, whom he later helps save from the Romans. Posthumus, on the other hand, has to learn through painful experience this quality of faithfulness in love during his separation from his bride, although Imogen yearns after him most faithfully as her disappearing crow husband in 1.4.

In fact the crow's association with matrimony is clearly established by the Graeco-Roman writer Aelian in a passage translated into Latin during the Renaissance by Poliziano (*Miscell.* 67):

> Crows are exceedingly faithful to each other and when they enter into partnership they love one another intensely, and you would never see these creatures indulging freely in promiscuous intercourse. . . . if one dies the other remains in widowhood. . . . men of old actually used to sing at weddings "The Crow" after the bridal song by way of pledging those who came together for the begetting of children to be of one mind.[19]

This same tradition was christianized for the Middle Ages by the anonymous author of the *Physiologus,* source book for countless medieval bestiaries.

> Jeremiah bore witness saying, "You sat like a little crow who has been abandoned" [cf. Jer. 3:2]. Physiologus stated that the little crow belongs to but one husband and, if he dies, she will not become another's nor will she be joined with another female's husband.
>
> And thus, therefore, the synagogue of the Jews in the earthly Jerusalem is now an abandoned little crow who killed its heavenly man in not receiving Jesus Christ and for this was abandoned. The Apostle said of those among the Gentiles who believed, "I have decided to present you to Christ as a pure bride to her one husband" [2 Cor. 11:2]. Therefore, we have the divine man in the Word which is in our minds, so that a stranger cannot approach us and we be found in the cave of thieves.[20]

The Pauline analogy implicit here between Christ's faithful espousal of the church and a husband's faithful espousal of his bride continued to be an important element of Renaissance belief.

As a Renaissance writer, Topsell sees an important moral lesson for humanity in the legendary marital harmony of the crow:

> Their concorde in marriage is a symbole vnto man; for the Male and the female doe neuer fall out or part asunder. Gesner saieth that he knewe a friende of his that had obserued one paire or couple to haunt his house for meate tenne yeres together. Therefore Mantuan hath this verse:
>
> > Concors Nyctimene, Cornix cum coniuge Progne
> > As Night Owles lyve in peace together,
> > So Crowes from females sieldome seuer.
>
> > (*The Fowles* 1972, 224)

This faithful aspect of the crow further suggested to the Renaissance emblematist and jurist Andrea Alciati a political correspondence of harmony between a king and his people, as Topsell is careful to note.

Emblem 38 of Alciati's *Emblemata* (1621 ed.) depicts a sarcophagus with an upright scepter on top of it. Facing this symbol of royal power, which arises from past inheritance, are two crows, one on either side.

Three birds in the air fly down toward the scepter. The *pictura* is framed on both sides by fragments of buildings, suggesting an urban setting and the notion of civitas. The *inscriptio* of this emblem, which employs crows to emphasize the role of the subject in upholding the power of any monarchy, is "Concordiae Symbolum" or "symbole of Concorde" (Topsell, *The Fowles* 224). Topsell translates Alciati's Latin *subscriptio* as follows:

> Admired concorde Crowes with themselues doe keepe,
> And neuer doe defile each others faith:
> Hence fowles beare scepters in their concorde deepe,
> Consent makes Lords to stand or fall he saieth.
>   Which once remoued then headlonge discord brings.
>   The fate of people, and the fall of Kings.

(The Fowles 1972, 224)

In other words, Alciati believes that a monarchy can only be maintained when the king is supported by a united people who agree with his policies, which is certainly a major political theme in Shakespeare's *Cymbeline*. The image of *consensus populi* in Emblem 38 is that of the attendant crows supporting the scepter.[21]

Camerarius's version of Alciati's *Concordia* emblem retains the same political meaning and employs a similar woodcut of crows supporting a scepter. In the verse, which argues that political consensus must be wedded to virtue, the emblematist reemphasizes the familiar notion of marital harmony as symbolic of the required harmony between a prince and his people. Camerarius chooses "Concordes vivite" ("Live in peace") as the motto of his crow emblem. His epigram reads,

> Iuncta pudicitiae si sit concordia, sancto
> Conjugio haud quicquam dignius orbis habet.
>
> (If unanimity be joined to virtue,
> The world has hardly anything worthier than holy matrimony.)[22]

The implied correspondences here are that the legendary fidelity of crows to their mates teaches men and women to live harmoniously within the bonds of holy matrimony, which in turn is analogous to a nation united in support of its king—if he is virtuous—and ultimately is analogous to all nations joined in support of the King of Kings, who is the source of all virtue and harmony.

It seems very possible, therefore, that Shakespeare wanted his audience to observe certain aspects of Cymbeline's England through the symbolic perspective of the crow, a bird that reminds us of the ideal of concord so lacking at first in Cymbeline's kingdom. First, in exiling his new son-in-law Posthumus, whom Imogen sees as a faithful crow husband, the king

Two crows supporting a scepter represent political consensus in Andrea Alciati's Emblem 38, *Emblemata* (Antwerp: Christopher Plantin, 1577), 183. Reprinted by permission of the Folger Shakespeare Library (PN 6349 A8 1577 Cage).

provokes discord within the royal family. This discord soon spreads into the marriage of Posthumus and Imogen and into world affairs as well, causing a war between England and Rome that threatens to destroy Cymbeline's kingdom. Second, in exiling his honest advisor Belarius, who compares himself to a crow or a faithful subject to the king, Cymbeline provokes dangerous discord among his own people, a discord that is described in the first lines of the play: "You do not meet a man but frowns: our bloods / No more obey the heavens than our courtiers / Still seem as does the king's" (1.1.1–3). By the end of the tragicomedy, however, husband and wife—neither of whom has been sexually unfaithful—are happily rejoined in matrimony, and the two faithful crows of King Cymbeline, the banished courtiers Posthumus and Belarius, once more support their ruler in war and remain beside him in the joyful peace he ultimately proclaims. The Soothsayer Philarmonus greets this happy state of political concord with the pronouncement that "The fingers of the powers above do tune / The harmony of this peace" (5.5.467–68).

The Hero as a Molting Eagle

Many students of *Cymbeline* have wondered why Posthumus is also compared to an eagle by Imogen, who proudly informs her father, "I chose an eagle, / And did avoid a puttock" (1.2.70–71). The three traditional meanings of the eagle during the Renaissance were keen vision, royalty, and the ability to gaze directly into the sun. When we consider each of these in turn, we soon realize that Posthumus has none of these qualities.

First, the eagle was known as a bird with exceptionally keen vision. According to Rowland,

> In the [iconographic] presentation of the Five Senses, the eagle was the attribute of Sight. Isidore had claimed that even the eagle's name *aquila* derived from *acumine,* the acuteness of its eyes, and as late as 1652 Bernini chose an eagle flying towards the sun as the frontispiece for a scientific work on optics. (1978, 54)

In 1582, Stephen Batman reminded his Elizabethan readers that "ye eagle is called Aquila, and hath that name of sharpnesse of eien, as Isidor sayth."[23] Yet Shakespeare's Posthumus sees very little of the reality underlying appearances throughout most of the play. He is naively willing to believe calumny against his bride; he fails to see through the bloody cloth that serves as a false token of her death; and in the last scene of *Cymbeline,* he still does not recognize Imogen disguised as the page Fidele and roughly knocks her down for interrupting his histrionic expressions of grief.

Second, the eagle was widely considered to be the bird of royalty, and Shakespeare had made previous use of it as a regal symbol in *3 Henry VI:* "Nay, if thou be that princely eagle's bird, / Show thy descent by gazing 'gainst the sun" (3.2.1). Posthumus, however, is not royal by birth, although he assumes royalty through his marriage to Imogen and is then considered "poison" to the blood of the king. Nor does the hero at first display the royal qualities of "fearlessness, intrepidity and magnanimity"[24] usually associated with the eagle, if we judge him by his actions rather than by what others say of him. Indeed, James Siemon correctly observes that "the judgment of Posthumus' worth in I, i, is at odds with much of the play's action."[25] Actors struggling to prepare the role of Posthumus have been especially puzzled by this rather foolish "eagle." Roger Rees of the Royal Shakespeare Company reports, for example, that finally "I realized that poor Posthumus had so much to live up to that he had to take a tumble, sooner or later. Being famous at too early an age is a gift that only the most resilient prodigy can handle. . . . [But then] I started to get a sense of the ridiculous, which leads to fondness and eventual redemption in characters so stiff."[26] However, to be amusing, the eagle must be seen as molting or in some way vulnerable.

Lower on the social scale than Imogen, the hero seems to fear that his wife does not really love him, or surely he would not feel the need to test her chastity. Far from being intrepid, Posthumus cannot endure the public loss of dignity that occurs when Iachimo returns from Britain with circumstantial and false evidence of Imogen's adultery, and he absurdly threatens to kill Iachimo if he should change his story: "If you will swear you have not done't you lie, / And I will kill thee if thou dost deny / Thou'st made me cuckold" (2.4.144–46). Furthermore, Posthumus is anything but magnanimous toward Imogen since he immediately sends instructions for her execution to Pisanio once he is convinced that his wife has betrayed him with another man.

Third, the Renaissance believed that the eagle could gaze directly into the sun. Rudolf Wittkower points out that this peculiar ability of the eagle often had an amorous meaning in that "The beloved is the sun at which the lover alone is allowed to look."[27] However, at Philario's house in Rome, the Frenchman does not seem very impressed by Posthumus as an ideal Neoplatonic lover in competition with the French courtiers: "I have seen him in France; we had very many / There could behold the sun with as firm eyes as he" (1.5.10–11). At least he does admit that Posthumus can gaze directly at the sun in true eagle fashion. Nonetheless, Posthumus soon completely fails the test of his own proclaimed faithfulness in love when he makes a wager on his bride's chastity and thereby permits Iachimo to gaze upon Imogen's naked beauty while she sleeps. Significantly, the men who behave this way in Shakespeare's principal sources for the wager story, *The Decameron* and *Frederyke of Jennen*, are husbands from the merchant class rather than the nobility and are plainly more interested in the money they hope to win from the wager than in the honor of their wives. More importantly, neither of them is ever compared to an eagle.

But there was a widely known myth about the eagle, which Shakespeare and his Renaissance audience knew and which might have allowed the audience to accept Posthumus as legitimately analogous to the eagle, despite his obvious failings. This was an early Christian story of the eagle written down by Physiologus in Greek, possibly as early as the second century A.D., and regularly included, often with further commentaries, in the bestiaries of the Middle Ages. It reappeared as a commonplace in Renaissance emblem books and was again recounted in the mythological sections of early attempts at scientific ornithology, such as the exhaustive 1599 Latin encyclopedia on birds by Aldrovandi. The myth describes three separate events in the life of the eagle, all of which were part of an attempt by Physiologus to explain David's promise in Psalm 103 that "Your youth will be renewed like the eagle's" and to relate the three motifs symbolically to the spiritual fall, reform, and regeneration of humanity. Essentially it is the story of a religious conversion, an event that Shakespeare actually dramatizes in act 5, scene 4 of *Cymbeline*. Moreover, the general pattern of decline into sin, the fall, and the ultimate renewal described in this eagle myth is roughly analogous to the pattern of Posthumus's life in the play. He betrays Imogen through the sin of pride when he boasts of her chastity in Rome; he falls into the temptation of gaining forbidden knowledge about her chastity from Iachimo; and he later renews himself through humble penitance and a symbolic change of clothing, or the molting of his fancy Roman feathers.

The first stage of the myth occurs when the eagle has grown old, which Physiologus means us to understand as a spiritual rather than a physical decline. It takes place as the individual becomes increasingly aware of his sinfulness, when he notices that he is wearing the old clothes of Adam and that "the eyes of [his] heart have grown dim" (Curley 1979, 12). In the second stage of the myth, the bird flies upward and stares directly into the sun, which "burns away his wings and the dimness of his eyes." Physiologus explains this event also in theological terms: "As you fly into the height of the sun of justice [Mal.4:2], who is Christ as the Apostle says, he himself will burn off your old clothing which is the devil's." Third, the eagle falls from the heights. He plunges into a fountain of pure water, understood as another symbol of Christ by Physiologus, and he "bathes himself three times . . . is restored and made new again" (Curley 1979, 13). This part of the eagle myth is a rather literal image of the sacrament of baptism after conversion, although it may also be interpreted as a reference to the cleansing effect of repentant tears.

During the sixteenth and seventeenth centuries, the first motif—that of flying toward the sun—became a symbol of hubris or intellectual arrogance for those thinkers who were influenced by their knowledge of Greek literature and mythology. Eagles may indeed gaze directly into the sun's light, it was admitted, but men cannot do so without going blind. If they attempt to fly too close to the sun, they, like the young Greek hero Icarus, will fall into darkness, as Alciati reminds his readers in Emblem 104, "In Astrologos" ("Against Astrologers").[28] This emblem appears to offer a conservative answer to the more optimistic Catholic humanists of the late fifteenth century who believed that philosophy could discover "the secrets of God" with the help of theology. Pico della Mirandola, for example, had stated boldly in his "Oration on the Dignity of Man" that "through the agency of theological piety and the most holy worship of God, we may like heavenly eagles boldly endure the most brilliant splendor of the meridian sun."[29] Dante had previously used the same image (but substituted a falcon for the eagle) in the *Paradiso* to describe the mystical experience granted him through the intervention of Beatrice:

> When Beatrice, intent upon the sun,
>   Turned leftward, and so stood and gazed before;
>   No eagle e'er so fixed his eyes thereon,
>
> And as the second ray doth evermore
>   Strike from the first and dart back up again,
>   Just as the peregrine will stoop and soar,
>
> So through my eyes her gesture, pouting in
>   On my mind's eye, shaped mine; I stared wide-eyed
>   On the sun's face, beyond the wont of men.[30]

Alciati replies to such optimistic proponents of mystical vision with the pagan example of a falling Icarus, who flew too close to the sun and was punished by death for his audacity.

In 1586 Geffrey Whitney translated "In Astrologos" into English, and once again we see a woodcut of Icarus molting eagle feathers from his wings as he plunges headlong to a watery death. According to Whitney's verse,

> Heare, Icarus with mountinge vp alofte,
>   Came headlonge downe, and fell into the Sea:
> His waxed winges, the sonne did make so softe,
> They melted straighte, and feathers fell awaie:
>   So, whilste he flewe, and of no dowbte did care,
>   He moou'd his armes, but loe, the same were bare.
>
> Let such beware, which past theire reache doe mounte,
> Whoe seeke the thinges, to mortall men deny'de,
> And searche the Heauens, and all the starres accoumpte,
> And tell therebie, what after shall betyde:
>   With blusshinge nowe, theire weaknesse rightlie weye,
>   Least as they clime, they fall to their decaye.

(1586, 28)

The warning is directed both at astrologers who attempt to know the future and at anyone else who desires to gain forbidden knowledge in defiance of religious prohibitions against the magic of Renaissance science.

The Fall of Icarus in Andrea Alciati's *Emblemata* (Antwerp: Christopher Plantin, 1577), 333. The same woodcut was used as well by Whitney. Reprinted by permission of the Folger Shakespeare Library (PN 6349 A8 1577 Cage).

In *Cymbeline,* Posthumus is clearly guilty of hubris, although it is not of the scientific variety. His fault is both psychological and theological since excessive jealousy is to love what doubt is to religious faith. Although he has gained the right to "know" Imogen physically through his participation in the marriage sacrament, a formal ceremony that took place offstage in Jupiter's temple (see 5.4.105–6), he has not thereby acquired the right to test her chastity and thus to know the absolute quality of her love for him. This would be analogous to his testing God's love and demanding to know for certain whether or not he will be saved. As we know, the marital relationship was considered to be like the relationship between God and his Church.

Before Posthumus and Imogen are separated by Cymbeline, they renew their wedding vows on stage through the exchange of jewels—a diamond ring and a gold bracelet—in 1.2. The audience witnesses this act, much as a formal marriage would ordinarily be celebrated "in the sight of God, and in the face of his congregation."[31] We, like Imogen, then expect her husband to have faith in her continued chastity during his absence from Britain, but once in Rome, Posthumus falls from grace when he seeks proof of his bride's virtue (or lack of virtue). He is unwittingly demanding forbidden knowledge of love when he enters into the despicable wager with Iachimo, the tempter, instead of having faith in his beloved. As I have suggested, this is analogous to insisting on absolute proof that God really loves him.

In any case, Shakespeare provides us with considerable evidence that the wager itself should be seen not only in terms of human psychology but in terms of theology as well. First, the wager is made in Rome, where certainty of God's love in the form of papal indulgences could be purchased with gold at the time the play was written. Second, Posthumus speaks of Imogen entirely in the language of religion during the male discussion of female virtue in Philario's house: "I profess myself her / Adorer, not her friend" (1.5.65–66). Yet, as Imogen's Petrarchan worshipper, Posthumus permits Iachimo to approach his wife and to assault her virtue in order to know for certain that she will stand firm, and on Iachimo's triumphant return to Rome, Posthumus allows her name to be sullied in public.

In the fictive world of the play, the hero's folly in making such an unholy wager on his bride's chastity very nearly brings a potentially happy marriage to a tragic end. From a theological point of view, Posthumus is here defying the Protestant belief that one cannot know what is in the mind of God beyond that which is already revealed in the scriptures. Martin Luther insisted that the deity is hidden from man and "in His own nature and majesty is to be left alone; in this regard, we have nothing to do with Him, nor does He wish us to deal with Him. We have to do with Him [only] as clothed and displayed in his Word, by which He presents Himself to us, That is His glory and beauty, in which the Psalmist proclaims Him to be clothed."[32] Hence the extent of divine love, and its forgiving quality, is the ultimate mystery of life and a major aspect of faith for a Protestant audience. On the other hand, intimations of immortality may also penetrate our insubstantial dreams, as Shakespeare so lavishly displays in his theatrical dream visions. And one of the most spectacular of these visions occurs in *Cymbeline* with the descent of Jupiter on the back of the divine eagle, which is also a symbol of Saint John the Evangelist and of the divine word itself for Christians.

Carlo Ginzburg has pointed out that the Christian injunction against the gaining of forbidden knowledge originated historically with a misunderstanding of the Latin translation of St. Paul's admonition against moral pride in the eleventh chapter of his epistle to the Romans. The passage concludes in the Vulgate with the words "noli altum sapere, sed time" ("be not high-minded but fear"), which was understood during the Renaissance to mean "do not think to know high things."[33] The words appeared to be a warning against intellectual curiosity, science, and even scholarship. Thus the motto of an emblem by Johannes Sambucus on the eagle gazing at the sun is "Nimium sapere" ("Knowing too much"). Influenced by Alciati, Sambucus's *pictura* depicts a man and an eagle both staring at the sun, while Icarus with molting wings falls miserably to his death in the background. The *subscriptio* clarifies the meaning of the woodcut as follows:

> Cominvs, aduersum qui spectat lumine Phoebum,
>   Nititur & radiis vincere, caecus abit.
> Vane quid affectas caelestibus addere lucem,
>   Ardentemque oculis sollicitare Deum?
> Sola potest magni hoc ales prestare Tonantis,
>   Haec quoque visum acuit, non superare solet.
> Alta nimis lingue, & donata sorte beatum
>   Te dic, quódque velis esse, fuisse puta.
> Non bene conueniunt Phaêthon tibi regna suprema,
>   Icarus optatis decidit atque polis.

> (Cominus, who looks directly at the light of Phoebus and strives to overcome his rays, goes away blind. What light do you vainly seek to add to the heavens and to disturb the burning God with your eyes? Only the eagle can stand up against the great Thunderer, and this sharpens its vision without getting it into habits of arrogance. You speak with too high-flown a tongue, and what you wish to be given was perhaps the endowment of a saint. The lofty kingdom of Phaethon does not well suit you; Icarus fell down and likewise the best and the strongest.)[34]

This Renaissance emblem, which combines the Christian story of the eagle gazing at the sun with the pagan myth of Icarus falling because he fails to keep the middle way, reflects the hero's situation in *Cymbeline*. A violent man by nature, Posthumus is always strangely blind when he tries to stare directly at the truth of Imogen. Equally human, she in turn is at first incapable of distinguishing between her ideal husband and the real Posthumus and between dream and reality. When she awakens from her sleep of death in 4.2, she comments piously that "Our very eyes / Are sometimes like our judgements, blind" (301–2). The statement is one of many in the play reminding us that the human *mundus intellectualis* is extremely limited by the inadequacies of the five senses.

Flatteringly termed "the best feather of our wing" (1.7.186) by Iachimo in his conversation with Imogen, Posthumus eventually realizes that he had sinned deeply when he ordered Imogen's death. In act 5 he initiates the first stage of Physiologus's myth of the eagle when he admits that he had no right to judge his wife:

> You married ones,
> If each of you should take this course, how many
> Must murder wives much better than themselves
> for wrying but a little? . . . .
> .   .   .   . Gods, if you
> Should have ta'en vengeance on my faults, I never
> Had liv'd to put on this: so had you saved
> The noble Imogen, to repent, and struck
> Me, wretch, more worth your vengeance.

(5.1.2–11)

Understanding at last that judgment belongs to divinity alone, whether Imogen is guilty or not, Posthumus admits the dimness of his eyes or his wrongdoings. In the second stage of the eagle myth, the bird flies upward to the sun or to divine justice. Posthumus does something similar during his formal repentance, when he submits his own erring will to that of the gods: "And make me blest to obey" (5.1.17). As the sun then burns off the old feathers of the eagle, Posthumus strips off his Roman armor and his courtly clothes, or molts like the eagle: "I'll disrobe me / Of these Italian weeds, and suit myself / As doth a Briton peasant" (5.1.22–24) Changing into the simple garments of a humble peasant, Posthumus continues his reformation with the words "To shame the guise o' th' world, I will begin, / The fashion less without, and more within" (5.1.32–33).

The third stage of the eagle myth occurs after the old feathers have been burned off by the sun. "Then at length, taking a header down into the fountain," says the Cambridge *Bestiary,* "he dips himself three times in it, and instantly he is renewed with a great vigour of plumage and splendour of vision" (White 1960, 105). After his descent into poverty and humility and his later formal speech of repentance (5.4.8–23), Posthumus experiences that very night a "splendour of vision" that restores his dead family, the Leonati, to him and actually provides him with what he has desired all along: Jupiter's promise of the restoration of Imogen and of his own eventual salvation. According to Ulisse Aldrovandi, the eagle's feathers symbolized riches and luxury for the Renaissance, which is why the bird's molting must occur periodically.[35] But much earlier, the author of *The Bestiary,* in his adaptation of Physiologus, had exhorted his readers to imitate the eagle's behavior:

The eagle can stare into the sun, but Icarus falls when he gets too close to the sun. From Johannes Sambucus, *Emblemata,* 4th ed. (Antwerp: Christopher Plantin, 1576), 23. Reprinted by permission of the Folger Shakespeare Library (PN 6349 S2 1576 Cage).

> Do the same thing, O Man, you who are clothed in the old garment and have the eyes of your heart growing foggy. Seek for the spiritual fountain of the Lord and lift up your mind's eyes to God—who is the fount of justice—and then your youth will be renewed like the eagle's. (105–7)

The eagle motif of repentance and renewal continues with some variations throughout the Renaissance in emblem books.

The Protestant Reformation added an important new element to the myth—the ideal of a reformed and renewed church. For example, in 1581 Nicolas Reusner, a Saxon emblematist, dedicated an eagle emblem to his friend Joachim Camerarius, whose father had been the biographer of the renowned Protestant reformer Philipp Melanchthon. Under the *inscriptio* "Renouata iuuentus" ("Renewed youth"), Reusner's *pictura* shows an

The eagle flies up into the sun and burns off her feathers or her old clothes in Emblem 14 by Joachim Camerarius, *Symbola et Emblemata*, 2nd ed. (Nuremberg: Voegelinianis, 1605), 14. Reprinted by permission of the Folger Shakespeare Library (PN 6349 C13 1605 Cage).

eagle in full glory after her bath as a striking symbol of the reformed church.

The *subscriptio* reads as follows:

A Lituûm regina potens, & fulminis expers:
    Sola aquila est summi sida ministra Iouis.
Quae si longaeua nimium sit tarda senecta:
    Flumine se liquido terque quaterque lauat:

Renouata iuuentus.

EMBLEMA XXXIIX.

Ad Philippum, Ioach. F. Camerarium
Iurisconsultum.

A Lituúm regina potens, & fulminis expers:
  Sola aquila est summi fida ministra Iouis.
Quæ si longæua nimium sit tarda senecta:
  Flumine se liquido terq, quaterq, lauat:
Subuolat hinc, Solisq, capit de lumine lumen;
  Et renouat pennas, membraq, fessa sibi.
Qui pius est, sacro lustratus fonte salutis:
  Fulmineo nunquam laditur igne Iouis.

Namq,

The eagle renews its youth after plunging into a fountain in Nicholas Reusner's
Emblem 38, *Emblemata* (Frankfort, 1581), 101. Reprinted by permission of the
Folger Shakespeare Library (PN 6349 R4 1581 Cage).

Subuolat hinc, Solisque capit de lumine lumen:
　　Et renouat pennas, membraque fessa sibi.
Qui pius est, sacro lustratus fonte salutis:
　　Fulmineo nunquam laeditur igne Iouis.
Namque fide certa numen coeleste tuetur:
　　Sollicitatque suo lumine lumen heri.
Sol est iustitiae Christus, vitaeque perennis:
　　Quem qui corde videt simplice, saluus erit.

(A powerful queen, but without auguries or thunderbolts,
Only the eagle is the celestial servant of great Jove;
If she is slowed down too much by old age,
　　She bathes herself three or four times in a flowing river,
Flies up thence, takes light from the light of the Sun,
　　And renews her feathers and her tired wings.
He who is upright, cleansed in the sacred fount of salvation,
　　Is never harmed by Jove's fiery thunderbolt.
For by steadfast faith he beholds the divine will;
　　And by his own light he seeks out the light of the Lord.
Christ is the Sun of justice and of everlasting life,
And whoever sees him with a simple heart will be saved.)[36]

Here Reusner's major point is that faith alone is sufficient for salvation. He also suggests that a simple heart and the inner light (or conscience) will enable us to discover God's will without priestly help. Behind all such Protestant emblems on the eagle is not only the myth of Physiologus and David's promise of renewed youth but Isaiah 40:31 as well, a verse promising heaven to the faithful: "But they that wait upon the Lord shall renew their strength; they shall mount up with wings as eagles."

In *Cymbeline* Posthumus finally attains such unquestioning faith when he is captured by the British and believes he will die in the morning. In a formal speech of repentance, he asks, "Is't enough I am sorry? / So children temporal fathers do appease; / Gods are more full of mercy" (5.4.11–13). Offering his own life as a sacrificial atonement for the loss of Imogen's life, Posthumus places his soul fully in the hands of a merciful deity. His immediate reward is a dream vision of the descent of Jove's eagle carrying the god on its back, a god who delivers a verbal promise of happiness to come. To seal this promise of salvation for the faithful, Jupiter leaves behind a tablet that very likely symbolizes the New Testament. When Posthumus awakens, he says, "A book? O rare one, / Be not, as is our fangled world, a garment / Nobler than that it covers" (5.4.133–35). After reading its message, he calls it, "Senseless speaking, or a speaking such / As sense cannot untie" (5.4.148–49), or inspired language that can only be understood by an inspired reader, which is to say, a reader who has been transformed spiritually by conversion to the Protestant faith.

The eagle stands on a rock and shakes off its old feathers (the past) in Joachim Camerarius's Emblem 16, *Symbola et Emblemata*, 2nd ed. (Nuremberg: Voegelinianis, 1605), 16. Reprinted by permission of the Folger Shakespeare Library (PN 6349 C13 1605 Cage).

Emblem 16 in Book III of the *Symbolarum & Emblematum* (1593) by Camerarius examines both individual and church reformation under the suggestive motto, "Vetvstate relicta" ("The past shaken off"). The woodcut illustrates an eagle standing on a rock by the sea and shaking out its old feathers, or molting. The rock is understood to the Christ, a symbol deriving from 1 Cor. 10:4: "And [our fathers] did all drink the same spiritual drink: for they drank of that spiritual Rock that followed them;

and that Rock was Christ." In fact there seems to be an allusion to this
very same biblical passage in *Cymbeline* when Imogen throws her arms
around Posthumus' neck in 5.5 and cries, "Think that you are upon a rock,
and now / Throw me again" (262–63). The verse of the emblem tells us that

> Inveterata tuae jam tandem crimina culpae
> Exue, si rediet laeta juventa tibi.

> (Now at last you must lay aside your deep-rooted faults and vices, if you would
> have joyful youth returned to you.)[37]

Not surprisingly, the emblems of the Lutheran Camerarius were very
popular in England at this time and were widely used as patterns for wall
and ceiling decorations in Protestant great houses. Many of the painted
panels of Lady Drury's study (now in the Branch Museum, Christchurch
Mansion, Ipswich) are typical examples.[38]

In respect to *Cymbeline,* I think that we may understand Posthumus to
believe at first in the older church, which is why he chooses Rome as his
place of exile and why he accompanies the Roman forces (he calls them
"Italian gentry") in their invasion of Britain. When Imogen begs to be
killed by Pisanio in 3.4, she removes Posthumus's false love letter from its
place over her heart:

> The scriptures of the loyal Leonatus,
> All turn'd to heresy? Away, away,
> Corrupters of my faith! you shall no more
> Be stomachers to my heart: thus may poor fools
> Believe false teachers: though those that are betray'd
> Do feel the treason sharply, yet the traitor
> Stands in worse case of woe.

> (3.4.82–88)

The religious terminology in these lines is surely suggestive of more than
just a betrayal of sworn love. Moreover, Posthumus's commitment to an
idolatrous religion ("I profess myself her adorer") would help to explain
Shakespeare's peculiar anachronisms in a play that constantly confuses
Romans and Renaissance Italians. If I am correct in this suspicion, not
only does *Cymbeline* look forward to the birth of Christ, but it also
reminds its audience of the later schism between the worshippers of Christ
and of the presumed moral superiority of the reformed church in England
and Germany over the luxurious Roman church of the south. Although I
do not insist on the accuracy of this reading, I do think it is worth our
consideration, since immediately after Posthumus changes his elegant
clothes for simple ones, he easily vanquishes Iachimo in a dumb show

duel, a curious stage action possibly symbolizing the spiritual preeminence of reformed Protestantism over Roman Catholicism in the minds of Shakespeare and his audience.

Aside from its association with Posthumus, the eagle is also cited in *Cymbeline* as the insignia of Caesar and the Roman army[39] by the Soothsayer:

> the Roman eagle,
> From south to west on wing soaring aloft,
> Lessen'd herself and in the beams o' the sun
> So vanish'd; which foreshadow'd our princely eagle
> Th' imperial.Caesar, should again unite
> His favour with the radiant Cymbeline,
> Which shines here in the west.

(5.5.471–77)

Although The Soothsayer naturally takes the Roman point of view, Shakespeare's audience would probably have understood the lines as a prediction of the diminution of the Roman church in the light of the English Reformation, which renews the youth of Christianity as Posthumus has been renewed by his repentance and his conversion.

The Roman Soothsayer, moreover, misinterprets his own dream in 4.2 of *Cymbeline* because he understands the eagle only as a Roman symbol:

> Last night the very gods show'd me a vision
> (I fast, and pray'd for their intelligence) thus:
> I saw Jove's bird, the Roman eagle, wing'd
> From the spongy south to this part of the west,
> There vanish'd in the sunbeams, which portends
> (Unless my sins abuse my divination)
> Success to th' Roman host.

(4.2.346–51)

But, as we know, the Roman host is soundly defeated by the Britons in *Cymbeline,* thereby reinforcing the new Christian meanings of the eagle, which include: Christian kingship, the Gospel According to St. John, inner moral reform, rebirth into a new life in Christ through baptism, and reformation of the church itself.

Admittedly, however, the allusions to the eagle myth of Physiologus and its Renaissance variations do not seem to have been systematically worked out as an allegory within the play and thus remain no more than allusions. But then, questions of religious doctrine could not legally be discussed in Jocobean theaters, despite the interest of such forbidden questions to audiences of the period. The poet's main recourse in the face of this prohibition was the art of poetic allusion.

"She is alone th' Arabian bird": Imogen as the Phoenix

Closely related to the eagle in iconography is the mysterious phoenix associated with Imogen by Iachimo: "If she be furnish'd with a mind so rare, / She is alone th' Arabian bird: and I have lost the wager" (1.7.16–18). Both birds were believed to have long lives; both were associated with the sun; and both symbolized renewal and resurrection. In addition, both the eagle and the phoenix were associated with the Roman empire and with the later European monarchies that imitated it.

The Romans primarily believed that the phoenix heralded the beginning of a new epoch, which was at the same time a cyclical return to the Golden Age. R. Van den Broek, in his monumental study *The Myth of the Phoenix,* tells us that the

> Emperor Claudius exhibited a so-called phoenix at the Forum during the celebration of the 800th anniversary of Rome. . . . This exhibition, which was taken very seriously by Claudius' contemporaries, was meant to support the idea that the beginning of the new century introduced an entirely new era that would be characterized, under the salutary leadership of the emperor, by the joy of the Golden Age. (1972, 417)

With this same idea in mind, many Roman emperors celebrated their accession to power by issuing coins that pictured on the reverse side a phoenix under a motto such as "Saeculum Aureum." Later European monarchs, since they inherited the throne from a dead relative, were also called by the name of phoenix, especially at the beginning of their reigns. For this reason, scholars who believe that every reference to the phoenix in English poetry always refers to Queen Elizabeth are quite wrong. Henry Petowe, for example, in a poem celebrating the coronation of James I of England, calls the new ruler *England's Caesar* (the poem's title), a second sun "which made Heauens Sunne amaze," and a phoenix that has arisen from the ashes of the old queen and is now "the Phoenix of all Soueraignty."[40]

Glynne Wickham and David Bergeron remind us that phoenix imagery was extensively used by Thomas Dekker in his coronation pageant for King James I performed at the Arch of *Nova Faelix Arabia,* which Dekker designed for the city of London.[41] At the climax of the pageant, a chorister of St. Paul playing the role of Circumspection addressed the new ruler in terms of the five senses:

> Great Monarch of the West, whose glorious Stem,
> Doth now support a triple Diadem,
> Weying more than that of thy grand Gransire *Brute,*
> Thou that maist make a King thy substitute,
> And doest besides the Red-rose and the white,

With the rich flower of *France* thy garland dight,
Wearing aboue Kings now, or those of olde,
A double Crowne of Lawrall and of gold,
O let my voyce passe through thy royall eare,
And whisper thus much, that we figure here,
A new *Arabia,* in whose spiced nest
A *Phoenix* liu'd and died in the Sunnes brest,
Her losse, made Sight, in teares to drowne her eyes,
The Eare grew deafe, Taste like a sick-man lyes,
Finding no relish: euery other Sence,
Forgat his office, worth and excellence,
Whereby the Fount of *Vertue* gan to freeze,
Threatened to be drunke vp by two enemies,
Snakie *Detraction,* and Obliuion,
But at thy glorious presence, both are gone,
Thou being the sacred *Phoenix,* that doest rise,
From th' ashes of the first: Beames from thine eyes
So virtually shining, that they bring,
To *Englands new Arabia,* a new Spring:
For ioy whereof, *Nimphes, Scences, Houres,* and *Fame,*
Eccho loud Hymnes to his imperiall name.[42]

Even the sun imagery of this speech is typical of *Cymbeline,* as Wickham points out. The laurel and gold in the king's crown derive from Petrarch, who describes the phoenix in conjunction with the laurel tree of Apollo, patron god of poetry.[43]

Shakespeare himself points forward to King James in *Henry VIII* with the phoenix imagery of Archbishop Thomas Cranmer's prophetic speech at the baptism of Elizabeth:

Nor shall this peace sleep with her, but as when
The bird of wonder dies, the maiden phoenix,
Her ashes new create another heir
As great in admiration as herself,
So shall she leave her blessedness to one,
(When heaven shall call her from this cloud of darkness)
Who from the sacred ashes of her honor
Shall star-like rise as great in fame as she was,
And so stand fix'd.

(5.4.39–47)

In this spine-tingling oration, the patriotic symbols of earlier Tudor propaganda are passed on to James Stuart through the inspired vision of one who became a martyr of the Protestant Church and could be expected to have true visions of the future.

Ernst H. Kantorowicz in *The King's Two Bodies* provides us with an extended discussion of the legal implications of the phoenix as it relates to royalty. Referring to the "Dignitas" or office of the king, which never dies,

Kantorowicz explains that every monarch is metaphorically considered self-begotten and eternal, arising naturally as he does from the death of the previous monarch in much the same way that the phoenix arises from the ashes of its own corpse.[44] According to Baldus, "The phoenix is a unique and most singular bird in which the whole kind *(genus)* is conserved in the individual."[45] And, since the phoenix also represents a time span or an epoch, it is often used as well to signify an individual reign.

However, King James was not the only phoenix in the royal family. Queen Anne was also compared to the bird in an emblem published in the anonymous collection entitled the *Mirrour of Maiestie* (1618). The motto "Al mondo * unica * eterna" is inscribed within an oval frame surrounding the phoenix, which sits in its fiery nest and holds a leafy branch in its beak. The branch apparently refers to the mythological belief that the phoenix itself picks the fragrant herbs with which it eventually immolates itself, an event illustrated on folio 36 of the Cambridge *Bestiary*. The numerological verse of the emblem may derive from Shakespeare's poem *The Phoenix and the Turtle* (1601), although similar poems had also previously appeared in honor of Elizabeth I in the collection of sonnets entitled *The Phoenix Nest* (1593):

> Here aboue number, doth one *wonder* sit;
> But *One,* yet in her owne, an infinit:
> Being simply rare, no *Second* can she beare,
> Two *Sunnes* were neuer seene stalke in one Spheare.
> From old *Eliza's* Vrne, enricht with fire
> Of glorious wonders, did your worth suspire:
> So must, from your dead life-infusing flame,
> Your *Multiplyed-selfe* rise thence the *Same:*
> She whose faire Memories, by *Thespian* Swaines
> Are sung, on Rheins greene banks, and flowrie plaines.
> Thus Time alternates in its single turnes:
> One *Phoenix* borne, another *Phoenix* burnes.
> Your rare worths (matchlesse Queene) in you alone
> Liue free, vnparalle'd, entirely *One*.[46]

The paradoxes quite dizzy the mind, although the central idea of the emblem is clear. It affirms the cyclical immortality of the English monarchy. As Anne has inherited the unique office of queen from Elizabeth I, so another—one of her multiplied selves or offspring—will eventually inherit from her. Meanwhile *she* is the only female phoenix, as was Elizabeth before her. Obviously, on the political level of meaning, the womb of a king's daughter is the phoenix's nest.

Because this is so, the Princess Elizabeth Stuart could be termed a phoenix as well during the celebrations of her marriage to the Count Palatine. John Donne's *Epithalamion or Marriage Song on the Lady*

Elizabeth and Count Palatine being married on St. Valentine's day commemorates this event. The poet informs the saint of lovers that,

> Till now, Thou warmd'st with multiplying loves
>> Two larkes, two sparrowes, or two Doves.
>> All that is nothing unto this,
> For thou this day couplest two Phoenixes;
>> Thou mak'st a Taper see
> What the sunne never saw; and what the Arke
> (Which was of foules and beasts, the cage and park)
> Did not containe, one bed containes through Thee,
>> Two Phoenixes whose joyned breasts
> Are unto one another mutual nests,
> Where motion kindles such fires, as shall give
> Yong Phoenixes, and yet the old shall live,
> Whose love and courage never shall decline,
> But make the whole year through, thy day, O Valentine.[47]

Since phoenix imagery may be extended to any member of the royal family, both lovers are phoenixes in this poem because both are royal and will become one entity in marriage. Such usage evidently does not violate the uniqueness of the bird, which is most often depicted in emblem literature under the *inscriptio* "Unica semper avis" ("But alwayes one Phenix in the world at once"). For example, Claude Paradin's phoenix emblem in his *Heroical Devises* states in the *subscriptio* that "Like as the Phenix whereof there is but one at any time to be seene, is a rare bird, so all good & precious things are hard to be found."[48]

In addition to its association with royalty, the phoenix myth is essentially the story of the sun's annual waning, death, and renewal as well as the story of great cosmic renewals believed to take place over longer periods of time that usually involve cycles of five hundred or a thousand years. Since plants, animals, man, and even the sun itself can be observed to grow old and weak with Time's flux, it was assumed that the cosmos as a whole suffered the same changes. From the perfection of original creation, everything moves steadily toward decay and death and must therefore be ritually renewed at specified intervals. According to Mircea Eliade,

> It is possible that the mythico-ritual New Year scenario has played such an important role in the history of humanity principally because, by ensuring renewal of the Cosmos, it also offered the hope that the bliss of the "beginnings" could be recovered. . . . The Year has an end, that is to say, it is automatically followed by a new beginning.[49]

The death and resurrection of the phoenix bird is one among many myths of such cyclical renewal, and as such was considered to be an ideal analogue to the story of Christ. Any mention of the phoenix in *Cymbeline*

HEROÏQVES.

Vnica femper auis.

Claude Paradin's phoenix emblem, "Unica semper auis" ("But always one Phenix in the world at once"), from the 1557 French edition of his *Heroicall Devises* (Lyon: Turnes & Gazeau). Reprinted by permission of the Folger Shakespeare Library (PN 6349 P3 1557 Cage, 89). The woodcut is by Bernard Salomon.

is thus one more reminder of the approaching birth of the savior. In *The Winter's Tale,* Shakespeare indicated a similar pattern of chronological regeneration by the metaphor of the hourglass, which Time as chorus turns over in 4.1 to begin the story of Perdita and Florizel. Like the phoenix, the hourglass is self-renewing. When the sands run out, the glass is turned over, and the very same sands begin their fall downward once more.

Apart from the year cycle during which Christ is born, dies, and is reborn, a cycle that parallels the behavior of the sun and the earth's vegetation, Christians believe simultaneously in a linear form of sacred history. There was only one major renewal of the world, and this occurred with the birth of Christ during the historical reign of Augustus Caesar, at which moment the New Dispensation began. Indeed Renaissance paintings of the Nativity often symbolize this sense of death and renewal by displaying the Holy Family with its new baby within an architectural setting of ruined classical buildings representative of both the Old Dispensation and the death of the classical or pagan world.[50] From the Nativity onward, although individual Christians may renew themselves spiritually in Christ, time itself runs forward to its end, when a final catastrophe will occur. As Eliade reminds us,

> The Cosmos that will reappear after the catastrophe will be the same Cosmos that God created at the Beginning of Time, but purified, regenerated, restored to its original glory. This Earthly Paradise will not be destroyed again, will have no end. Time is no longer the circular Time of the Eternal Return; it has become a linear and irreversible Time.[51]

This notion of an unchanging Eternity to be enjoyed or suffered after a final judgment by God is unique to the Judeo-Christian myth. In this vision, after the Day of Judgment, the sands of time will never run out; the hourglass will never have to be turned again.

For Christian writers, therefore, the phoenix symbolizes on a religious plane the unique renewal granted to the world by Christ. In the words of the Cambridge *Bestiary:*

> Our Lord Jesus Christ exhibits the character of this bird, who says: 'I have the power to lay down my life and to take it up again'. If the Phoenix has the power to die and rise again, why, silly man, are you scandalized at the word of God— who is the true Son of God—when he says that he came down from heaven for men and for our salvation, and who filled his wings with the odours of sweetness from the New and the Old Testaments, and who offered himself on the altar of the cross to suffer for us and on the third day rise again? (White 1954, 126)

Shakespeare's *Cymbeline,* as we know, celebrates the time of Christ's birth and the beginning of a new era during the reigns of Augustus Caesar in Rome and of Cymbeline in Britain—the very moment of time's redemption in Christian theology. It is in this historical and theological context that we must consider any allusions to the phoenix in this play, since the appearance of the bird "always indicates an important turn in world history" (Broek 1972, 416).

Because of its association with Christ, the phoenix also came to be a symbol of resurrection. The author of the Cambridge *Bestiary* reminds us that,

This bird without anybody to explain things to it, without even the power of reason, goes through the very facts of the resurrection—and that, in spite of the fact that birds exist for the good of men, not men for birds. Let it be an example to us, therefore, that the author and creator of mere birds did not arrange for his holy ones to be destroyed for ever, but wishes the seed to be renewed by rising again. (White 1954, 127)

Similar lore was repeated over and over again during the Renaissance in such books as *Batman uppon Bartholome,* to take one English example.[52] The sixteenth-century emblematist Camerarius refers to most of the classical sources of the phoenix myth in the extended commentary accompanying his own use of the bird in his *Symbolorum & Emblematum.* The *inscriptio* of Emblem 100 in Camerarius's Book III is "Vita Mihi Mors Est" ("Life to me Death is"), referring to the Christian paradox that by dying the phoenix enters into eternal life. The *subscriptio* reads:

Ex seipsa nascens, ex se reparabilis ales,
    Quae exoriens moritur, quae moriens oritur.

(Giving birth to itself, renewable out of itself,
    This bird dies in arising and arises in dying.)[53]

At this point, the phoenix obviously represents not only the resurrection of the flesh after reformation, which Physiologus had claimed for it much earlier, but now more precisely the immortality of the human soul as well.

Henry Green provides us with an English translation of Nicholas Reusner's Emblem 26 on the phoenix. Under the motto "Unica semper auis," Reusner eulogizes the bird as follows:

On tears of frankincense, and on the juice of balsam lives
    The Phoenix, and bears its cradle, the coffin of its sire.
Always alone is this bird;—itself its own father and son,
    By death alone does it give to itself a new life.
For oft as on earth it has lived the ten ages through,
    Dying at last, in the fire it is born of its own funeral pile.
So to himself and to his, Christ gives life by his death,
    Life to his servants, whom in equal love he joins to himself.
True Man is he, the one true God, arbiter of ages,
    Who illumines with light, with his spirit cherishes all.
Happy, who by holy baptism in Christ is reborn,
    In the sacred stream he takes hold of life,—in the stream he obtains it.
If men report true, death over again forms the Phoenix,
    To this bird both life and death the same funeral pile may prove.
Onward, executioners! of the saints burn ye the sainted bodies;
    For whom ye desire perdition, to them brings the flame new birth.[54]

The burning of heretics by the Inquisition was for Reusner the surest way to give them spiritual immortality through analogy with the death and resurrection of the phoenix. Indeed Roy T. Eriksen has argued persuasively that Shakespeare's poem "The Phoenix and the Turtle" echoes Giordano Bruno's *De gli eroici furori* and commemorates the death by fire in 1601 of Bruno himself, who had written of "Un certo amoroso martire" and had aligned "the smoke issuing from the *furioso's* sacrifice in the phoenix's flames with 'the sacrifice of praise upon an altar enkindled in the heart of these poets'."[55]

In addition, the phoenix was considered to be androgynous, "possibly because it was taken among the Hermetics and Gnostics as a symbol of the highest being or of the Primeval Man, both considered to be bisexual" (Broek 1972, 421). Since it requires no mate, it became a common symbol of chastity. In fact, the rose window in the Cathedral of Notre Dame in Paris depicts Chastity holding the flaming phoenix as her attribute. A sun bird itself, the phoenix also escorts the sun across the sky each day and protects the earth with its wings from the great heat of the sun (Broek 1972, 261–304). Before it dies, the phoenix strews itself and its nest with aromatic herbs because, according to Broek, "The pleasing fragrance of the aromatics was an indication of the life that triumphs over death" (1972, 171). Moreover, the phoenix is a bird associated with peace:

> Lactantius and Claudian stress the fact that peace rules wherever the phoenix is present, not only in its own perfect abode and at the place at which it renews itself, but also among the birds accompanying it during its stay in our world. It is the peace of the Golden Age and of Paradise, which in our reality manifests itself around the phoenix. (Broek 1972, 229)

In England, both Queen Elizabeth and King James were determined to maintain peace during their respective reigns and thus they earned the name of phoenix. And, finally, the phoenix became a paradigm for the human soul, its journey through life to death, and its final resurrection through Christ.

In *Cymbeline,* Imogen is not only likened to the phoenix by Iachimo but she also unknowingly lives out all nine of the major details of the phoenix myth. First, she is a female member of the immediate royal family and therefore may properly be called a phoenix and the nest of phoenixes. Second, she lives during the time of Augustus Caesar and Cymbeline, which means she is part of the new Christian epoch about to begin. Third, when she changes into the clothes of a page, she becomes androgynous like the phoenix. Fourth, Belarius likens her to the love god Eros (who will be transformed into Christ, the God of Love) when he first sees her in the mountains as the page Fidele: "By Jupiter, an angel! or, if not, / An earthly paragon! Behold divineness / No elder than a boy!" (3.7.15–17). Fifth, despite Iachimo's slander, she is the epitome of chastity; sixth, her apparent corpse is strewn with aromatic herbs by her brothers; seventh, although she suffers death, or so it seems, she is resurrected to return to her father and her husband; eighth, her return home signals the renewal of peace between Rome and Britain; and ninth, the pattern of her journey to enlightenment and to a life of service to others is a paradigm of the heroic journey of the human soul, or of Psyche.

In this chapter we have seen that, according to myth, birds of many varieties accompany the phoenix to witness its marvelous transformations from life to death and from death to new life, and that this may help to explain why Shakespeare mentions twelve different avian species in *Cymbeline*. At the moment of the phoenix's immolation, peace was believed to reign within the entire flock, much as the music of Orpheus caused all natural strife to cease. The rebirth of the phoenix from its own ashes heralded the return of the Golden Age and the longed for redemption of nature. Arthur Kirsch describes the significance of all this in *Cymbeline* as follows: "the phoenix, that Arabian bird that died and was reborn in its own ashes, was a traditional symbol of Christ, and Iachimo's allusion to it in describing Imogen is especially compelling because she literally enacts its significance . . . we actually experience the process by which Imogen dies, 'to be more fresh, reviving' (I.v.42)."[56] We do indeed. However, from this moving experience we should not presume Imogen to be Christ since the myth of the phoenix was considered to be equally analogous to the journey of the human soul through life, death, and rebirth.[57]

Yet if Imogen does represent in some way the beauty and the love necessary to redeem that which has fallen from grace, Posthumus imitates the Fall of Man itself through his desire for forbidden knowledge and his violence. Like the eagle, however, he ultimately reforms and rises again to experience a divine vision. He also undergoes a much more radical moral change than does King Lear, for example, who can never quite relinquish his desire for revenge against Goneril and Regan, despite his new concern for "poor naked wretches" (3.4.28). From a stereotypical revenge hero concerned only with honor and the sword, Posthumus emerges—after his baptism of repentant tears—as a new man capable of that most difficult (and perhaps most impossible) of human feats: forgiveness. When the villain Iachimo finally listens to the voice of his own conscience and kneels before Posthumus, the previously deceived hero becomes at last the magnanimous "eagle" Imogen thought she had married in the first place:

> Kneel not to me:
> The power that I have on you, is to spare you:
> The malice towards you, to forgive you. Live
> And deal with others better.

(5.5.418–21)

What we hear are echoes of Christ's words in John 8:7 to the woman accused of adultery ("go and sin no more"), which is a wonderful bit of irony in a play about allegations of adultery by a man who is deliberately bearing false witness against another human being. But, as Posthumus has told himself earlier, none of us is without sin, and therefore, none of us has the right to cast stones at another sinner (or to take revenge on him or her). We also hear in the above lines echoes of the Lord's Prayer itself, which will soon be taught throughout the pagan world: "And forgive us our trespasses, as we forgive them that trespass against us."

Cymbeline ends with the restoration of the wrongly banished crows, who faithfully support the scepter of the king once he again associates himself with virtue. As for Cymbeline, having learned forgiveness from the example of his reformed son-in-law, he offers pardon to everyone, so that Posthumus and Belarius are once more respected noblemen, the princes are rejoined to their royal father, and *consensus populi* is regained by the crown. The resulting concord provides the peace necessary for the beginning of a new era in the sacred history of the world.

Notes

1. G. Wilson Knight, "The Shakespearean Aviary," in *The Shakespearean Tempest*, 3rd. ed. (London: Methuen & Co. Ltd., 1953), 293; and Nosworthy, ed., *Cymbeline*, The Arden Edition (London: Methuen & Co. Ltd., 1955), lxxiii. For an interesting essay on the use of emblems as aids to our understanding of Renaissance bird symbolism, see Peter M. Daly, "Of Macbeth, Martlets and other 'Fowles of Heauen,'" *Mosaic* 12 (Fall 1978): 23–46.

2. Robert Fludd, *Utriusque Cosmi Historia* (Oppenheim: Aere Johan-Theodor De Bry, Typus Hieronymi Galleri, 1617–1619), Pl. 16. The engraving is reproduced in *The Riverside Shakespeare*, Pl. 17.

3. See *Topsell's Histories of Beasts,* ed. Malcom South (Chicago: Nelson-Hall, 1981), 3.

4. Ibid.

5. These beautiful bed hangings, now owned by the Victoria and Albert Museum, are currently on loan to Oxburgh Hall, Norfolk. For further information on them, see Margaret Swain, *The Needlework of Mary Queen of Scots* (New York: Van Nostrand Reinhold Co., 1973), 62–75 and 106–20.

6. Ibid., 75. The phoenix was originally the impresa of Mary's mother, Mary of Lorrain, who used the following motto: "en ma fin git mon commencement" (Swain 106).

7. See Roelof Van den Broek, *The Myth of the Phoenix: According to Classical and Early Christian Traditions* (Leiden: E. J. Brill, 1972), 227; hereafter to be cited parenthetically.

8. See Beryl Rowland, *Birds with Human Souls* (Knoxville: University of Tennessee Press, 1978), 106; hereafter cited parenthetically.

9. See *The Bestiary: A Book of Beasts,* ed. and trans. T. H. White (New York: G. P. Putnam's Sons, 1954), 139; hereafter cited parenthetically.

10. Ovid, *Metamorphoses,* trans. Mary M. Innes (New York: Penguin Books, 1955), bk. 2, 64–67.

11. Geffrey Whitney, *A Choice of Emblemes* (Leiden: Christopher Plantin, 1586), 170; hereafter cited parenthetically.

12. See Stephen Batman, *Batman vppon Bartholome, his Booke De Proprietatibus Rerum* (London: Thomas East, 1582), bk. 12, 186.

13. See Ulisse Aldrovandi, *Ornithologiae hoc est de avibus historiae,* 3 vol. (Bononiae: Franciscum de Francis Senensem, 1599), 2, bk. 18, 831.

14. See Aldrovandi, *Aldrovandi on Chickens: The Ornithology of Ulisse Aldrovandi (1600), Volume II, Book XIV,* trans. L. R. Lind (Norman: University of Oklahoma Press, 1963), 232. Lind points out that there is nothing resembling Aldrovandi's "quotation" from Isaiah in the Bible.

15. See Edward Topsell, *The Fowles of Heauen or History of Birdes,* ed. Thomas P. Harrison and F. David Hoeniger (Austin: The University of Texas Press, 1972), 30; hereafter to be cited parenthetically.

16. Joachim Camerarius, *Symbolarum et Emblematum,* 2d ed. (Nuremberg: Voegelinianis, 1605), bk. 3, 79. English translation by Roger T. Simonds.

17. See E. P. Evans, *Animal Symbolism in Ecclesiastical Architecture* (1896; rpt. Detroit: Gale Research Co., 1969), 55.

18. Ibid., 147.

19. Aelian, *On the Characteristics of Animals,* 3 vols., trans. A. F. Scholfield, Loeb Classical Library (Cambridge, Mass.: Harvard University Press, 1958), vol. 1, 165–67.

20. Michael J. Curley, trans., *Physiologus* (Austin: University of Texas Press, 1979), 54–55.

21. See also Peter Daly on Alciati's "Concordia" emblem in *Emblem Theory* (Nendeln, Liechtenstein: KTO Press, 1979), 82–85, and the same author's "Alciato's 'Emblem Concordiae Symbolum': A Medusa's Mirror for Rulers?" *German Life and Letters* 41 (July 1988): 349–62.

22. Camerarius, bk. 3, 57. Translated by Roger T. Simonds.

23. *Batman vppon Bartholome, his Booke De Proprietatibus Rerum,* bk. 12, 176.

24. See Rudolf Wittkower, "Eagle and Serpent," *Journal of the Warburg Institute* 2 (1938–39), 316, n.3.

25. See James Edward Siemon, "Noble Virtue in *Cymbeline,*" *Shakespeare Survey* 29 (1976): 61.

26. See Roger Rees, "Posthumus in *Cymbeline,*" in *Players of Shakespeare 1: Essays in Shakespearean Performance by Twelve Players with the Royal Shakespeare Company,* ed. Philip Brockbank (1985; rpt. Cambridge: Cambridge University Press, 1988), 146.

27. Wittkower, 316, n.3.

28. See Andrea Alciati, *Emblemata* (Antwerp: Christopher Plantin, 1577), 353.

29. Pico della Mirandola, "Oration on the Dignity of Man," trans. Elizabeth Livermore Forbes, in *The Renaissance Philosophy of Man,* ed. Ernst Cassirer, et al. (Chicago: The University of Chicago Press, 1948), 236–37.

30. Dante, *The Divine Comedy,* "Paradise," trans. Dorothy L. Sayers and Barbara Reynolds (Baltimore: Penguin Books, 1962), Canto I, lines 46–57.

31. See *The Book of Common Prayer 1559,* ed. John E. Booty (Charlottesville: The University Press of Virginia, 1976), 290.

32. Quoted in Paul R. Sellin, "The Hidden God: Reformation Awe in Renaissance English Literature," in *The Darker Vision of the Renaissance,* ed. Robert S. Kinsman (Berkeley: University of California Press, 1974), 154.

33. See Carlo Ginzburg, "High and Low: The Theme of Forbidden Knowledge in the Sixteenth and Seventeenth Centuries," *Past and Present* 73 (November 1976): 28 and 30.

34. Johannes Sambucus, *Emblemata, et Aliqvot,* 4th ed. (Antwerp: Christopher Plantin, 1576), 28. Translated by Roger T. Simonds.

35. Aldrovandi, *Ornithologiae,* vol. 1, bk. 1, 69.

36. Nicholas Reusner, *Emblemata* (Frankfort, 1581), bk. 2, 101–2. Translated by Roger T. Simonds.

37. Camerarius, bk. 3, 16. Translated by Roger T. Simonds.

38. See Norman K. Farmer, Jr., "Lady Drury's Oratory: The Painted Closet from Hawstead Hall," in *Poets and the Visual Arts in Renaissance England* (Austin: University of Texas Press, 1984), 77–105. Although Farmer calls the closet an "oratory," there are no biblical or directly religious pictures among the panels, so that the room is more likely to have been a study. However, secular emblems invariably did contain spiritual messages, many from the classics.

39. See Claude Paradin's emblem on the Roman eagle in *The Heroical Devises of M. Claudius Paradin (1591),* A photoreproduction with an Introduction by John Doebler (Delmar, N.Y.: Scholars' Facsimiles & Reprints, 1984), 250–51. The motto is "Celo imperium iouis extulit ales" ("The Eagle hath lifted vp the gouernment of the Empire to the heauens"). According to the commentary,

> The Egle hath alwayes bene the chiefest ensigne amongst the Romaines, the which euen at this day belongeth to the holy Empire. And this Caius Marius, after that he had attained to the honour of the second Consulship, dedicating an Egle altogither to his legions or armies, according to Plinie his relation, preferred before all other ensignes. And the Egle, because she is formidable and to be feared before all other birds, and as though (as it is commonly said) she is counted for the king of all birds, was chosen for a simbole or ensigne to signifie a people, or nation which hath subdued all other whatsoeuer. But this also is true, that in the Romanes ensignes the Egle was wont to carrie the similitude of lightning, either as a bird dedicated to Iupiter, or as carrying his armes and ensignes formost, or finally because, as Plinie saith, she is neuer touched with lightning.

40. See Henry Petowe, *England's Caesar. His Maiesties Most Royall Coronation* (London: John Windet for Mathew Law, 1603), sigs. Ciii and Cii.

41. See Glynne Wickham, "Riddle and Emblem: A Study in the Dramatic Structure of *Cymbeline,*" in *English Renaissance Studies: Presented to Dame Helen Gardner in honour of her 70th Birthday,* ed. John Carey (Oxford: The Clarendon Press, 1980), 101–2; and David Bergeron, *English Civic Pageantry 1558–1642* (London: Edward Arnold, 1971), 81.

42. Quoted by Wickham, 101–2.

43. See Petrarch's Rima 323.

44. See Ernst H. Kantorowitz, *The King's Two Bodies: A Study in Medieval Political Theology* (Princeton, N.J.: Princeton University Press, 1957), 386–401.

45. Ibid., 389.

46. *The Mirrour of Maiestie: or, The Badges of Honovr,* ed. Henry Green and James Croston (1618; rpt. London: Trübner & Co., 1870), sig. B3.

47. *The Complete Poetry of John Donne.* ed. John T. Shawcross (New York: New York University Press, 1968), 174–75.

48. Paradin, 110.

49. See Mircea Eliade, *Myth and Reality,* trans. Willard R. Trask (New York: Harper & Row, 1963), 50–51. See also Mircea Eliade, *The Myth of the Eternal Return,* trans. Willard R. Trask (New York: Pantheon Books, 1954).

50. See such paintings as "The Adoration of the Magi" by Fra Angelico and Fra

Filippo Lippi (c. 1445) and Sandro Botticelli's "The Adoration of the Magi" (1481–82), both at the National Gallery of Art, Washington, D.C.

51. Eliade, *Myth and Reality,* 64–65.

52. Batman, bk. 12, 183.

53. Camerarius, bk. 3, Emblem 100.

54. Henry Green, *Shakespeare and the Emblem Writers* (London: Trübner & Co., 1870), 386. See also Reusner, Emblem 36, bk. 2, 98.

55. See Roy T. Eriksen, " 'Un certo amoroso mirtire': Shakespeare's 'The Phoenix and the Turtle' and Giordano Bruno's *De gli eroici furori,"* *Spenser Studies* 2 (1981): 210.

56. Arthur C. Kirsch, *Shakespeare and the Experience of Love* (Cambridge: Cambridge University Press, 1981), 150–51.

57. Aside from the bestiaries, an obvious source of knowledge for Shakespeare and his contemporaries about the phoenix as a Christ symbol was the widely read book *The Travels of Sir John Mandeville,* which imparts the following information:

> In Egypt also is a city that is called Eliople [Heliopolis]—which means the city of the sun. In this city is a temple round like the Temple of Jerusalem. The priest of that temple has a book in which is written the birthdate of a bird that is called the Phoenix; and there is only one in all the world. And this bird lives five hundred years, and at the end of the five hundredth year it comes to the temple and burns himself all to powder on the altar. And the priest of the temple, who from his book knew the time of the bird's coming, makes the altar ready and lays on it divers spices and *sulphur uviuum* [virgin sulphur] and twigs of the juniper tree, and other things that burn quickly. And then the bird comes and alights on the altar, and fans with his wings until the things mentioned be alight; and there he burns himself to ashes. On the morrow they find in the ashes as it were a worm; on the second day that worm has turned into a perfectly formed bird; and on the third day it flies away from that place to where it normally lives. And so there is never more than one. This same bird is a symbol of Our Lord Jesus Christ, in as much as there is but one God, who rose on the third day from death to life. . . . This bird is no greater than an eagle in body; he has on his head a crest like a peacock, but it is much greater than a peacock's. His neck is yellow, his back indigo; his wings are red and his tail is barred across with green and yellow and red. And in the sunlight he seems marvellously beautiful, for these are the colours that shine most fairly.

See *The Travels* (1356), trans. C.W.R.D. Moseley (New York: Penguin Books, 1983), 64–65.

7

The Iconography of Vegetation

For there is hope of a tree, if it be cut down, that it will sprout
again, and that the tender branch thereof will not cease.
—Job 14:7

Mats Rydén has counted some twenty plant and fruit references in *Cymbeline,* adding up to sixteen different species.[1] But only a few of these seem to relate significantly to the play's meaning. In this chapter I shall discuss, first, the cedar tree and its lopped branches and second, the elm and the vine as the predominant marriage *topos* in the tragicomedy, with related vegetation references of importance. The major thematic *topoi* in *Cymbeline* concerned with vegetation are reform through pruning, which leads in turn to rebirth or regeneration, and marriage as a union between social equals, thus a metaphor of Christian brotherhood and spiritual renewal through Christ's espousal of His Church.

The Cedar Tree and the Concepts of Sovereignty, Reform, Rebirth

In act 5, scene 4, Jupiter leaves a prophetic tablet behind for Posthumus to read upon his awakening. This oracle includes the promise that "when from a stately cedar shall be lopp'd branches, which, being dead many years, shall after revive, be jointed to the old stock, and freshly grow, then shall Posthumus end his miseries, Britain be fortunate, and flourish in peace and plenty" (140–45). This part of the divine message is easily explained later on by the Roman Soothsayer, who proclaims that

The lofty cedar, royal Cymbeline,
Personates thee: and thy lopp'd branches point
Thy two sons forth: who, by Belarius stol'n,
For many years thought dead, are now reviv'd,
To the majestic cedar join'd; whose issue
Promises Britain peace and plenty.

(5.5.454–59)

241

Three distinct but related thematic *topoi* are actually included in this oracle: the relationship between the cedar and royalty, the notion of reform through judicious pruning, and the theme of the dry tree and the green tree, or the dry tree with green shoots.

It is common knowledge that the mature cedar tree produces an aromatic wood that is widely used for the preservation of both textiles and corpses, but since the tree is also an evergreen and reaches great height, it early became a popular symbol of sovereignty (Ezek. 17:23). For example, as Thomas Cranmer prophesies in biblical terms of James I in Shakespeare's *Henry VIII,* "He shall flourish, / And like a mountain cedar reach his branches / To all the plains about him" (5.4.52–54). This metaphorical association between cedars and kings may have originated with Psalm 104:16, which rejoices that "The trees of the Lord are full of sap; the cedars of Lebanon, which he hath planted," because kings were believed to be divinely appointed just as the cedars were divinely planted. Moreover, the Egyptian vegetation god Osiris was thought in antiquity to be the first human king, and after his death and dismemberment, Isis finally discovered his preserved parts hidden within the trunk of a cedar tree, according to mythology.

As we have previously seen, kings were associated with the phoenix bird as well. According to some versions of the phoenix myth, the self-renewing bird builds its aromatic nest on the top branches of a cedar tree.[2] This belief apparently derives from the notion that since the sacred cedars of Lebanon grew in the East, or the abode of the Phoenix, the bird must have built its nest on the top of a cedar tree. The cedar then became a world tree in Judeo-Christian mythology and a symbol of "the eschatological bliss of Israel."[3] Ezekiel 17:22–23 reports God's promise that

> I will also take of the highest branch of the high cedar, and will set it; I will crop off from the top of his young twigs a tender one, and will plant it upon an high mountain and eminent:
> In the mountain of the height of Israel will I plant it: and it shall bring forth boughs, and bear fruit, and be a goodly cedar: and under it shall dwell all fowl of every wing; in the shadow of the branches thereof shall they dwell.

Later Christian writers decided, therefore, that the phoenix lived not in India or Egypt but in Lebanon, "the earthly reflection of Paradise,"[4] where the finest cedars were thought to grow. Furthermore, since Psalm 92:12 states that the righteous man "shall grow like a cedar in Lebanon," the cedar was obviously God's elected tree on which the phoenix should in fact build its aromatic nest. That Shakespeare and his contemporaries did indeed associate the phoenix with the cedar tree is clear from the elegy composed for Sir Philip Sidney in the Elizabethan collection of poems entitled *The Phoenix' Nest:*

And that which was of wonder most,
The Phoenix left sweet Araby,
And on a Caedar in this coast,
Built vp hir tombe of spicerie,
    As I coniecture by the same,
    Preparde to take hir dying flame.[5]

In the tragicomedy, Imogen is then the phoenix associated with royal
Cymbeline, who is "the sole Arabian tree" or the divinely planted cedar
tree symbolizing God's chosen ruler in Britain.

Pruning and the Notion of Reform and Rebirth

But trees, kings, and kingdoms can become overgrown, overconfident,
and even tyrannical to those living in their shade. At this point, reform
through careful pruning of the tree of state must follow or revolution is
likely to occur. The political importance of such pruning is clearly explained in the famous garden scene of *Richard II,* when the gardener tells
his assistants to

Go thou, and like an executioner
Cut off the heads of [too] fast growing sprays,
That look too lofty in our commonwealth:
All must be even in our government.
You thus employed, I will go root away
The noisome weeds which without profit suck
The soil's fertility from wholesome flowers.

(3.4.34–39)

When one of the men asks why they should bother to trim the garden since
the land as a whole has become overgrown with weeds (or with flatterers
of the king), the gardener replies that Bulingbroke's revolution has violently uprooted them all.

                    O, what pity is it
That he [Richard] had not so trimm'd and dressed his land
As we this garden! [We] at time of year
Do wound the bark, the skin of our fruit-trees,
Lest being over-proud in sap and blood,
With too much riches it confound itself:
Had he done so to great and growing men,
They might have liv'd to bear and he to taste
Their fruits of duty. Superfluous branches
We lop away, that bearing boughs may live;
Had he done so, himself had borne the crown,
Which waste of idle hours hath quite thrown down.

(3.4.55–66)

In *Cymbeline,* the king allows his queen and her son Cloten to become overproud and to dominate his counsel; while, in contrast, he banishes or prunes his good counsellor Belarius and thus never tastes his "fruits of duty." This deliberate inversion of the *topos* by Cymbeline causes a bitter Belarius to compare himself to a ravished tree in 3.3.60–64, as I have previously noted. Cymbeline's son Guiderius must finally act the role of princely executioner and lop off Cloten's head in the same way that a gardener prunes or tops a fast growing tree.

Gerhart B. Ladner points out that "reform" is actually represented as an act of pruning in Cesare Ripa's *Iconologia:*

This abstract concept *[Riforma]* is to be personified by an old woman in a simple, short, and unornamented dress. She is to hold in her right hand a small pruning knife or a pair of clippers and in her left an open book showing the words:

> Pereunt discrimine nullo
> Amissae leges.
>
> (Lucan, *Pharsal.* III, 119 f.)

Ripa himself explains the image as follows: Old age more than any other is germane to reform; through reform good and lawful customs should be brought back to the form which they once had *(si riducano alla lor forma).* The simple dress signifies rejection of all superabundance. Most importantly, just as pruning knife or shears cut away superfluous branches, which sap the strength of trees and prevent them from bearing fruit, so reform removes abuses and transgressions: the virtue of lawful observance, which though lost by evildoers never perishes in itself, is thus reformed and through it good government.[6]

Such ideas help to explain why, after Cymbeline's reform at the end of the tragicomedy, he agrees to pay tribute to the Romans once again ("lawful observance" of custom), even though he has won the war against Rome. Since the resulting peace and universal harmony allow for cosmic change through the Nativity, I shall discuss this problem further in a later section on harmonist theories in politics. Of course Ripa himself is concerned primarily here with the Counter-Reformation in Italy (Ladner, "Vegetative Symbolism," 1961, 303).

The woodcut accompanying Ripa's comments on "Riforma" does indeed depict a barefoot old woman in a simple dress. In her left hand she holds an open book on which the words "Pereunt discrimine nullo amissae leges" ("Superfluous words or customs perish without making any difference") are printed, and in her right hand she wields a pruning knife. However, there are added details: to her right is a dry tree and to her left a green tree in the 1611 edition. These trees undoubtedly allude to Ezekiel 17:24:

DI CESARE RIPA.   435
RIFORMA.

pereunt discrimine rullo   *Anisse leges*

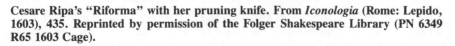

Cesare Ripa's "Riforma" with her pruning knife. From *Iconologia* (Rome: Lepido, 1603), 435. Reprinted by permission of the Folger Shakespeare Library (PN 6349 R65 1603 Cage).

And all the trees of the field shall know that I the Lord have brought down the high tree, have exalted the low tree, have dried up the green tree, and have made the dry tree to flourish.

Thus all personal, political, and ecclesiastical reform is believed to be ultimately the work of God Himself, even though men such as Belarius and Guiderius in *Cymbeline* may be used by the deity as instruments to effect reform. Belarius prunes Cymbeline when he kidnaps the king's two sons (the "lopp'd branches") and brings them up in the mountains as virtuous Wild Men instead of spoiled princes, while Guiderius further prunes the royal cedar when he kills Prince Cloten, Cymbeline's lustful and foolish stepson. But the resulting dry tree of Cymbeline turns green once more with the restoration of his true children at the end of the play.

The vegetation symbolism of "lopp'd branches" echoes once more the theme of the impending birth of Christ through its allusion to the thirteenth-century legend of Seth. When Adam lies on his deathbed, he sends his son Seth to Paradise to ask for the oil of mercy. There Seth encounters the Tree of Knowledge as a dry tree, which has been made that way by Adam's sin, but as he looks, the tree returns to life and a new born child appears among the leaves at the top. This is a vision of Christ, who will ultimately redeem Adam and his descendents from original sin.[7]

In its use of such tree imagery, *Cymbeline* becomes, like all Renaissance tragicomedies, a dramatization of *renaissance* or of rebirth itself. However, according to Ladner,

> J. Trier has shown that the metaphorical meaning of *renasci (rinascita)* is not necessarily "to be reborn," but may be "to grow again," the metaphor being taken from the realm of the horticulturist and forester, from tree life, where the "damage" done by cutting (pruning) results in new growth, in a "Renaissance." One might add that *renasci* is thus closely related to *revirescere* ("to grow green again," "to grow strong, young again," "to reflourish") and to *reviviscere* ("to revive"), both terms frequently used by Cicero, also to *reflorescere* (to blossom again"), found, for instance, in Pliny and in Silius Italicus.[8]

We have already seen similar "vitalistic renewal ideas" (Ladner 1959, *Reform* 21) expressed by Shakespeare through the myths of the eagle (Posthumus) and the phoenix (Imogen). In addition, the renewal of the royal cedar in *Cymbeline* by the return or reflourishing of the "lopp'd branches" Guiderius and Arviragus has an important political significance within the tragicomedy. As Ladner informs us, "In Machiavelli's *History of Florence* the life of nations is seen as a succession of cycles each of which turns from *virtù* (civic and political excellence) through peace and quiet to disorder and ruin whence new order is born" (Ladner, 1959 *Reform* 23). In Shakespeare's play we see Cymbeline's Britain undergo its period of disorder under the influence of the Queen and Cloten, but finally the nation returns to virtue with the rebirth of the three royal children to the king, who then calls himself "A mother to the birth of three" (5.5.370). In the same vein, Imogen's dramatic "revival" from death in Wales is a thematically significant scene in the tragicomedy because it is a visual allusion to the cosmic renewal about to occur during the Augustan peace:

Crispin van de Passe's engraving of the withered branch that blooms, with Christ as the green shoot growing from the Tree of Jesse in the background. From George Wither, *A Collection of Emblemes, Ancient and Modern* **(STC 25900c, 217). Reprinted by permission of the Folger Shakespeare Library.**

"And there shall come forth a rod [a shoot] out of the stem [stock] of Jesse, and a Branch shall grow out of his roots [shall bear fruit]" (Is.11:1).

The *topos* of the withered branch that blooms as symbolic of Christ's death and resurrection and of human hopes for immortality after physical death is the subject of a lengthy personal emblem by George Wither in his 1635 *Collection of Emblemes*. The English inscriptio tells us that "*When* Hopes, *quite frustrate were become,* / *The* Wither'd-branch *did freshly bloome.*" The verse begins by likening the poet himself to a withered branch, one apparently devoid of both hope and worldly esteem, but he does not despair, however, because he has seen twigs abandoned on the path in winter suddenly put out roots in the springtime, establish themselves, and eventually grow into trees. Similarly, he expects to achieve new life himself, even after death:

       For, I, whoe by *Faith's* eyes have seene,
Old *Aaron's* wither'd *Rod* grow fresh and greene;
And also viewed (by the selfe-same *Eyes*)
Him, whom that *Rod,* most rightly typifies,
Fall by a shamefull *Death,* and *rise,* in spight
Of *Death,* and *Shame,* unto the glorioust *height.*
       Ev'n I, beleeve my *Hope* shall bee possest,
       And, therefore, (ev'n in *Death*), in *Hope* I'le rest.[9]

The same image of a withered branch with green shoots at the top is used as a tournament impresa in *Pericles* to express the hero's hope for a change in fortune. In *Cymbeline,* despite the despair of Imogen, Posthumus, and the king himself that all has been lost through folly and malice, regeneration does occur. The lost princes, thought of as two withered branches, revive within the court and are grafted back on to the royal tree, even as Imogen herself becomes a living, fruitful vine to be once again supported by an elm tree, or her husband.

The Elm and the Vine as Marriage *Topos*

Perhaps the most emotionally satisfying stage image in Shakespeare's *Cymbeline* occurs in act 5, scene 5, where it elicits from Posthumus the most lyrical poetry in the entire play: "Hang there like fruit, my soul, / Till the tree die" (5.5.263–64). This is the moment when a joyful Imogen flings her arms about the neck of her long-lost spouse, who at last returns her loving embrace. Although such reunions occur elsewhere in the Shakespeare canon, this one is unusual for the haunting beauty of Posthumus's words, which are often quoted but—to my knowledge—have never been fully explained.

The matrimonial embrace is also visually unusual, since Imogen is still dressed as the boy Fidele. What we see on the stage is the rather shocking spectacle, for the early seventeenth century, of two young men (or at least of a man and a boy) passionately hugging one another, a sight Shakespeare was careful to avoid in his earlier plays. For example, in the finale of *As You Like It,* the disguised Rosalind—although played by a boy—is re-costumed in female clothing before she is led onstage by Hymen to rejoin her father and her bridegroom Orlando. With a similar regard for decorum and the social sensibilities of his audience, Shakespeare does not even allow Viola in *Twelfth Night* to embrace her twin brother Sebastian until she has relinquished her "usurp'd attire" and regained her proper "maiden weeds." We may well ask, therefore, why in *Cymbeline* the playwright suddenly changes his habitual practice to a variation of costuming that must suggest a specific meaning associated with Posthumus's resonant lines.

A related problem I wish to consider here as well is the significance of Arviragus's speech in act 4, scene 2: "Grow patience! / And let the stinking-elder, grief, untwine / His perishing root, with the increasing vine!" (58–60). This, too, is a memorable example of vegetation imagery that needs explanation and that appears to be in some way related to Posthumus's reference to himself as a supporting tree and to his wife as the fruit adorning his branches. Once again, the study of a popular iconographic convention of the Jacobean period and earlier may help us to answer all of these questions, for, as Dieter Mehl has rightly pointed out, an important "form of the emblematic in drama is the insertion of allegorical scenes or tableaux providing a pictorial commentary on the action of the play, thus creating that mutually illuminating combination of word and picture which is central to the emblematic method."[10]

My purpose is to demonstrate not only the presence of a familiar marriage *topos* in *Cymbeline* but also to explore the significance of the several ways in which Shakespeare varies its use and its meanings in respect to matrimony, politics, and Protestant theology.

Most seventeenth-century readers of Greek and Roman poetry, or of Renaissance emblems based on classical sources, would have recognized that Posthumus's affecting words, "Hang there like fruit, my soul, / Till the tree die" derive from the ancient marriage *topos* of the elm and the vine. These plants were wedded in antiquity by farmers for the survival and fecundity of the vine. Such once conventional agricultural lore, however, is no longer generally known to modern theater-goers or readers, who are left to contemplate only the aesthetic quality of a sentence that used to have profound meaning. According to the Arden edition of *Cymbeline,* Tennyson described Posthumus's speech as "among the tenderest lines in Shakespeare," while Carolyn Spurgeon called it, "Ten words which do more than anything else in the play to bring [Posthumus] in weight and value a little nearer to Imogen."[11] Neither commentator recognized the previously familiar image of a fruitful marriage that is embedded both in Posthumus's words and in the sight of Imogen with her arms entwined about her husband's neck. Indeed, since *Cymbeline* is a play intrinsically concerned with marriage—or with the union between man and woman, between nations, and between heaven and earth, the dramatist really ought to provide us with some popular and emphatic image of matrimony in the last act to crystallize this pervasive conjugal concept. Shakespeare's visual and verbal reference to the elm and the vine *topos* does just that.

Peter Demetz's illuminating essay on "The Elm and the Vine: Notes Toward the History of a Marriage Topos" still remains the most important source of information on this image, and I shall make considerable use of it here, as well as offering a few additions and corrections. For example, Demetz is unfortunately in error when he tells us that "the intimate union of marital elm and bridal vine as a poetic image of blissful marriage" derives from the "Greek epithalamium" or *Carmen* 62 by Catullus, who may have learned it from a lost poem by Sappho.[12] I believe that the most probable original source of the *topos* is an extant epigram in the *Greek Anthology* by Antipater of Thessalonica that reads as follows:

> I am a dry plane-tree covered by the vine that climbs over me; and I, who once fed clusters from my own branches, and was no less leafy than this vine, now am clothed in the glory of foliage not my own. Such a mistress let a man cherish who, unlike her kind, knows how to requite him even when he is dead.[13]

Although Antipater's poem suggests that the original Greek agricultural practice was to wed the grapevine to a plane tree rather than to the elm, which was the preferred support in Italy (Demetz 1958, 522–23), the idea of the fruitful female giving new life to the dying male is indeed identical to the image in *Carmen* 62 by Catullus.

As Demetz rightly points out, the first Latin version of the *topos* occurs in Catullus's so-called "Greek epithalamium" when a group of youths argue the case for marriage against a group of maidens, who prefer the preservation of virginity (1958, 521). They employ the following analogy to the cultivation of the grape:

> As an unwedded vine which grows up in a bare field never raises itself aloft, never brings forth a mellow grape, but bending its tender form with downward weight, even now touches the root with topmost shoot; no farmers, no oxen tend it: but if it chance to be joined in marriage to the elm, many farmers, many oxen tend it: so a maiden, whilst she remains untouched, so long is she aging untended; but when in ripe season she is matched in equal wedlock, she is more dear to her husband and less distasteful to her father.[14]

The youths take a one-sided masculine viewpoint when they insist that the elm uplifts and makes the vine fertile, while Ovid, as we shall later see, emphasizes the mutual benefit of the marriage to both parties. Further echoes of this same marital image may be found in such Augustan poets as Horace, Vergil, and Quintilian (Demetz 1958, 523).

The elm and vine *topos* was employed by the early Christians as a "theological type." According to Demetz, "In the centuries before the advent of Christianity, the vine and the grape symbolized fertility, and with fertility an afterlife sustained by vegetative permanence; early Christian art and literature made grape and vine refer to a transcendental and spiritual kind of immortality" (1958, 524). This notion was legitimized by Psalm 128:3 ("Thy wife shall be as a fruitful vine by the sides of thine house") in the Old Testament, and by verse 1 of John 15 in the New Testament: "I am the true vine, and my Father is the husbandman." Therefore, Christ was often pictured as a fruitful vine hanging from the cross, and the recurring image of the vine "wedded" to a tree in early Christian sepulchral art is usually understood as a reference to the mystical marriage of Christ and the Church. The relevance of such traditional Christian symbols to our overall understanding of *Cymbeline* has been amply demonstrated by recent scholarship to which I have referred earlier on the theological subtext of this tragicomedy.

In his brief and illuminating "History," Demetz traces the rediscovery of the classical elm and vine motif in the Renaissance by such humanist writers as Jovannus Pontanus, who used it in his *De Amore Coniugali,* and by the Dutch Neo-Latin writer Joannes Secundus (1958, 526–27), but surprisingly he overlooks the even more obvious and influential example of Desiderius Erasmus, who employed the same marriage topos in his colloquy "Proci et Puellae." This charming courtship dialogue was translated into English in 1568 as *A Modest Meane to Marriage* by N. L., thought to be Nicholas Leigh, and is at least an analogue, if not a direct source, of Shakespeare's dialogue on virginity between Helena and Parolles in *All's Well That Ends Well* (1.1.106–86).[15] Erasmus's young lover in *A Modest Meane to Marriage* attempts to possess his sweetheart by asking "whether it is a better sight for a vine to lye vppon the grounde and rot, or the same to embrace a poale, or an elme, and lode it full with purple grapes."[16] Since the vine must indeed be supported in some way if it is to produce a healthy crop of fruit, by analogy the human husband offers similar support to his bride and becomes in turn the trunk of the family tree.

As Demetz observes, the *topos* later became a familiar symbol of an ideal marriage among the English poets of the Renaissance, including Milton, who has the still innocent Adam and Eve "marry" the elm and the vine in Book 5 of *Paradise Lost:*

> they led the Vine
> To wed her Elm; she spous'd about him twines
> Her marrigable arms, and with her brings
> Her dow'r th' adopted Clusters, to adorn
> His barren leaves.
>
> (11.215–19)

The image also appears in Spenser's *Faerie Queene* 1.1.8 as "the vine propt elme," *in Sidney's Arcadia* (Dicus: Epithalamium, St. 2), and in Shakespeare's *Comedy of Errors,* this time in conjunction with its opposite form—the tree and the parasitical ivy—that symbolizes lust (Demetz 1958, 527–29). Meeting the wrong Antipholus in the streets of

Ephesus, Adriana believes he is her husband and addresses him as follows:

> Come, I will fasten on this sleeve of thine:
> Thou art an elm, my husband, I a vine.
> Whose weakness, married to a stronger state,
> Makes me with thy strength to communicate:
> If aught possess thee from me, it is dross,
> Usurping ivy, brier, or idle moss;
> Who, all for want of pruning, with intrusion
> Infect thy sap, and live on thy confusion.

(5.2.174–81)

The adulterous nature of Titania's embrace of Bottom, a mortal, in *A Midsummer Night's Dream* is indicated by the moon goddess's comparison of herself not with the vine but with "the female ivy [which] so / Enrings the barky fingers of the elm" (4.1.43–44). Obviously, Shakespeare knew the *topos* well, as did Ben Jonson, who made this image the center of a battle between the allegorical figures of Truth and Opinion in his 1606 court masque *Hymenaei, or, the Solemnities of Masque and Barriers at a Marriage* (Demetz 1958, 527).

Jonson's masque is of particular importance because it celebrated the marriage of Sir John Hay, a Scottish favorite of Shakespeare's royal patron James I, with Honora, daughter of the English Lord Denny. As mentioned earlier, Glynne Wickham points out that in *Cymbeline,* Shakespeare also honored the Hay family by retelling the famous story of Hay's ancestors, the old man and the two boys who held a narrow lane against the invading Danes, as narrated in Holinshed's *The Description & History of Scotland*.[17] Furthermore, Jonson's personification of Truth in *Hymenaei* makes a comment similar to Arviragus's later "perishing root"—"increasing vine" contrast in *Cymbeline:*

> For as a lone vine, in a naked field
> Never extols her branches, never bears
> Ripe grapes, but with a headlong heaviness wears
> Her tender body, and her highest sprout
> Is quickly levelled with her *fading root;*
> By whom no husbandman, no youths will dwell;
> But if by fortune, she be married well
> To th' elm her husband, many husbandmen
> And many youths inhabit by her, then.[18]

Jonson's "Fading root" and Arviragus's reference to a "perishing root" (4.2.60) seem very close indeed, unless one agrees with J. M. Nosworthy that Shakespeare used the word "perishing" in the sense of the third definition of "perish" in the OED to mean "destructive" (Arden ed. 121, n.59–60). Such a reading would, I believe, spoil the antithesis between "perishing" as "dying" and "increasing" as "growing" or "multiplying"— i.e., the poetic antithesis between death and life.

I wish to suggest, therefore, that in act 4, scene 2, of *Cymbeline,* Arviragus's wish for a divorce of the elder tree from the vine should be understood as an original Shakespearean *countertopos* to the elm and the vine. Although the scene begins with Imogen's complaint of sickness, the savage boys see her as a physician who has kept them well through her knowledge of the medicinal qualities of plants or pot-herbs:

> *Guid.* But his neat cookery! he cut our roots in characters,
> And sauced our broths, as Juno had been sick,
> And he her dieter.
> *Arv.*   Nobly he yokes [or *marries*]
> A smiling with a sigh; as if the sigh
> Was that it was, for not being such a smile;
> The smile mocking the sigh, that it would fly
> From so divine a temple, to commix
> With winds that sailors rail at.
>
> (49–56)

There is a sharply drawn antithesis here between sighing and smiling, which will then be transformed by Guiderius into two basic qualities of human life, grief and patience, and finally by Arviragus into the emblematic form of these qualities, the elder tree (death) and the vine (life). In fact, we are warned to look for an emblematic meaning in the passage when Guiderius says "he cut our roots in characters," since the word "characters" can mean both letters and visual images or emblems (see Arden ed. 120, n.49–51).

Guiderius continues the contrast between sighs and smiles as follows:

> *Guid.*   I do note
> That grief and patience, rooted in them both,
> Mingle their spurs together.
> *Arv.*   Grow patience!
> And let the stinking-elder, grief, untwine
> His perishing root, with the increasing vine!
>
> (4.2.56–60)

At this point the villain Cloten, who has caused much of Imogen's grief, enters in search of her and is beheaded by Guiderius in what we may understand to be an act of judicious pruning of at least one of the lateral roots (spurs) of grief.

Indeed Cloten's headless corpse soon becomes the central image of a theatrical Shakespearean emblem in 4.2. Awakening from her counterfeit sleep of death, Imogen shrinks back from the flower-strewn body next to her. But instead of screaming, she interprets what she sees in the form of a *subscriptio* to an emblem: "These flowers are like the pleasures of the world; / This bloody man, the care on't" (296–97), or human grief. Wither's emblem on Hercules' choice makes the same association visually between flowers, pleasure, and death (bk. 1, 22). The audience sees Imogen herself still next to the supine corpse but presumably sitting up, or alive and growing still—the stage image of "increasing" patience confronting death and grief.

To return to the earlier lines on the marriage of patience with the elder tree (4.2.56–60), we should note that Shakespeare is not only referring here to a personification of forbearance and long-suffering endurance such as Viola envisions with her famous description in *Twelfth Night,* "She sat like Patience on a monument, / Smiling at grief" (2.4.114–15), and such as Imogen acts out in act 4, scene 2. Guiderius and Arviragus are also speaking of a plant, for in *Cymbeline,* patience seems to mean two different things at the same time: forbearance and an edible plant or docke (rhubarb) called *Rumex patientia.* The bark and roots of patience and the elder were used both as purgatives and as healing poultices, although the herbalist John Gerarde warns that the elder purges "not without trouble and hurt to the stomacke."[19] Of patience, he tells us that,

> The Monkes Rubarbe is called in Latine *Rumex satiuus,* and *Patientia,* or Patience, which worde is borrowed of the French, who call this herbe *Pacience:* after whom the Dutch men name this pot herbe also *Patientie:* of some *Rhabarbarum Monachorum,* or Monkes Rubarbe: bicause as it should seeme some Monke or other haue vsed the roote heereof instead of Rubarbe. (1597, 314)

If powdered and added to wine, patience may also be used to ease internal illnesses. According to Gerarde: "The decoction of the rootes of Monkes Rubarbe is drunke against the bloudie flixe, the laske, the wambling of the stomacke which commeth of choler: and also against the stinging of serpents as *Dioscorides* writes" (1597, 314). The plant patience can, therefore, be the exact opposite from a purge, acting instead like a soothing dose of Pepto-Bismol, so to speak, and an efficacious remedy as well against the sting of a serpent or against evil itself.

The "stinking-elder," on the other hand, is associated with the betrayal, the despair, and the subsequent suicide of Judas, as Edward Dowden notes in his 1903 edition of *Cymbeline.* Dowden also points out that, "Pliny names elder props as suitable for vines, but does not name the elder as a living tree for vine-support," and that "Gerarde mentions 'stinking' in his description of the elder."[20] In fact Gerarde does state that "the leaues consist of fiue or six particular ones fastened to one rib, like those of the Walnut tree, but eucry particular one is lesser, nicked in the

edges, and of a ranke and stinking smell" (1233). But even more interesting
for this discussion is Gerarde's later description of the jagged elder, which
is identical to the common elder tree except for the leaves, "which doth so
much disguise the tree and put it out of knowledge, that no man would
take it for a kinde of Elder, vntil he had smelt thereunto, which will quickly
shew from whence he is descended" (1597, 1234). We may remember that
the lustful Cloten also gave forth a bad odor, a fact that the courtiers
mention twice in *Cymbeline*. In 1.3, the First Lord advises Cloten to
change his shirt after his swordplay with Posthumus, since "the violence
of action hath made you reek as a sacrifice: where air comes out, air comes
in: there's none abroad so wholesome as that you vent" (1–4). The Second
Lord comments later in 2.1 that Cloten, who desires to marry his step-
sister Imogen, smells "like a fool" (16), and thus further associates the
wicked Queen's son with a traitorous "stinking-elder" that must be un-
twined from the roots of the fruitful vine or Imogen.

We know, of course, that Shakespeare was aware of the tradition that
Judas had hanged himself on a elder tree, since he punned on this very bit
of arcane information in the early comedy *Love's Labor's Lost*. Holofernes tells Berowne to "Begin, sir, you are my elder," to which Berowne
replies, "Well follow'd: Judas was hang'd on an elder" (5.2.605–6). In
Cymbeline, therefore, the reference to the elder is another of many carefully sown allusions to the approaching birth and sacrifice of Christ, whose
resurrection will overcome the grief of believers and will serve as a
promise of the life to come. Yet perhaps we should note as well that the
scholarly Gerarde did his best to dispell this popular myth of the elder tree
in his entry for the Arbor Iuda, which he said "may be called in English
Iudas tree, whereon *Iudas* did hang himselfe, and not vpon the Elder tree,
as it is suide" (1597, 1240).[21]

Unfortunately, none of these herbal metaphors is of any use to the love-
sick Imogen, whose illness increases to the point where she finally decides
to take some of the Queen's medicine that Pisanio has given her. Although
Imogen then appears to die from what her stepmother had intended to be a
deadly poison, soon afterwards the heroine revives in imitation both of
Christ and of the pruned grapevine, once the drug wears off.

In *Cymbeline* the false marriage described by Arviragus between smiles
and sighs, the vine and the elder tree, is of course ultimately superseded
by the true marriage of the elm and the vine in 5.5. When Posthumus and
Imogen embrace, the husband invites his bride to "Hang there like fruit,
my soul, / 'Till the tree die" (263–64). Thus Shakespeare may possibly be
the first dramatic poet to literalize the metaphor through a stage embrace,
although Demetz mistakenly credits the German dramatist Heinrich von
Kleist in *The Prince of Homburg* with being the first to use this emblematic stage image:

the topos is transformed by the instincts of the playwright into pure theatrical effect and leads up to what early nineteenth-century stage technique considers a tableau. On the wooden quandrangle of the stage the Prince is transformed, as it were, into an elm by putting one of his arms around the Princess' body like a supporting branch . . . ; and Natalie, for her part, fully aware of this essentially connubial gesture, clings like the vine to his breast. . . . At this intense moment, the literary topos has abruptly been changed into pure pantomime, which speaks through ritual gestures rather than with mere words. (1958, 531)

All very well, but I would have to argue that von Kleist—probably, like most German romantics, an admiring reader of Shakespeare—could have discovered his theatrical literalization of the elm and vine *topos* in the English bard's *Cymbeline*. Here Posthumus is self-consciously the supporting elm and says so in "mere words," while Imogen is the fruitful vine who, at this point, rather fiercely clings to him.

We still must deal, however, with the problem of Imogen's masculine disguise, which gives a strange cast to this Jacobean stage literalization of the marriage topos. I want to suggest that Shakespeare may have arranged his visual image very deliberately in order to say something new about marriage itself. The emblem he gives us onstage is no longer that of woman as a clinging vine, no matter how fruitful, but of woman as an *equal* who has the strength and fortitude to sustain the elm after it dies, even as the tree now supports the vine. Indeed the sight of two men embracing onstage would normally suggest to a Renaissance audience not marriage but *friendship*.

The source for this transvaluation of the marriage *topos* into a symbol of friendship was the widely read *Emblemata* (1531) by Andrea Alciati (Demetz 1958, 526). Alciati's Emblem 160, which is based on the motto "Amicitia etiam post mortem durans," or "Friendship outlasting death," depicts a fruitful vine supported by the branches of a dying elm (1621 ed., 676–79). The Latin verse reads as follows:

Arentem senio, nudam quoque frondibus vlmum
   Complexa est viridi vitis opaca coma:
Agnoscitque vices natura, & grata parenti
   Officii reddit mutua iura suo.
Exemploque monet, tales nos quaerere amicos,
   Quos neque disiungat foedere summa dies.

(The elm withering because of old age, and bare of leaves,
the shady foliage of the green grape-vine has embraced.
It acknowledges the changes of nature, and grateful to its parent
renders the mutual rights of service, and by its own
example it advises us to seek such friends
as the last day, death would not separate from the pact of friendship.)[22]

16   ANDREAE ALCIATI

Amicitia etiam poſt mor-
tem durans.

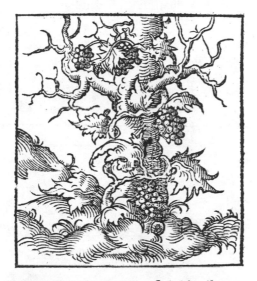

Arentem ſenio, nudam quoq; frondibus ulmum
Complexa eſt uiridi uitis opaca coma.
Agnoſcitq; uices naturæ, et grata parenti
Officij reddit mutua iura ſuo.
Exemploq; monet, tales nos quærere amicos,
Quos neque diſiungat fœdere ſumma dies.

The elm and the vine as friendship enduring after death, from Andrea Alciati,
***Emblemata* (Paris: Wechel, 1534), 16. Reprinted by permission of the Folger Shake-**
speare Library (PN 6349 A8 1534b Cage).

The German Protestant emblematist Joachim Camerarius, correctly observing that Alciati had borrowed his idea from both the *Greek Anthology* and Catullus, included a similar emblem in his own *Symbolorum et Emblematvm ex re Herbaria Desumtorum Centuria una Collecta* of 1559 (with many later editions) under the motto "Amicus Post Mortem."[23] His *subscriptio* reads "Quamlibet arenti vitis tamen haeret in ulmo: / Sic quoque post mortem verus amicus amat," which Henry Green translates,

"Yet as it pleases the vine clings to the withered elm, / So also after death the true friend loves."[24]

In England this distinctly humanist emblem of friendship first appeared in the 1586 edition of Geffrey Whitney's *A Choice of Emblemes,* a book almost certainly known to Shakespeare. Whitney's *inscriptio,* or motto, is "Amicitia, etiam post mortem durans" ("Friendship, even after death enduring"). The *pictura* illustrates a fruitful vine embracing a leafless elm, while the *subscriptio* reads as follows:

> A Withered Elme, whose boughes weare bare of leaues
> And sappe, was sunke with age into the roote:

Joachim Camerarius's elm and vine emblem, from the *Symbola et Emblemata* (Nuremberg, 1590), Emblem 34, bk. 1, 44. Reprinted by permission of the Folger Shakespeare Library.

A fruictefull vine, vnto her bodie cleaues,
Whose grapes did hange, from toppe vnto the foote:
   And when the Elme, was rotten, drie, and dead,
   His braunches still, the vine abowt it spread.

Which showes, wee shoulde be linck'de with such a frende,
  That might reuiue, and helpe when wee bee oulde:
And when wee stoope, and drawe vnto our ende,
Our staggering state, to helpe for to vphoulde:
   Yea, when wee shall be like a sencelesse block,
   That for our sakes, will still imbrace our stock.[25]

Whitney's emblem reverses the sexes of the elm and the vine, making the elm female and the vine male, probably to emphasize the friendship aspect of his version and to dissociate the vine from the idea of a fruitful wife. This new masculine vine could be either a faithful human friend, or even Christ as spiritual friend, or both. The reader makes his own associations.

Shakespeare's stage image of two males embracing takes Whitney's sexual reversal into account but still fundamentally retains the elm as the husband and the vine as the wife. At the same time, gender becomes curiously inconsesquential. The audience knows that the true Imogen is not a man, although the actor playing the role of Imogen is indeed a male. By means of such multiplied ambiguities, Shakespeare forces his audience to see through his provocative stage image in order to interpret it for themselves, just as the Protestant emblematists (and Catholic emblematists as well) expected their often borrowed mottos and *picturas* to be understood in the light of their newly written verses or *subscriptiones*. As Huston Diehl argues,

> English emblem books . . . reinforce the Protestant belief in the necessity of interpretation and speak to the new concern for the epistemological process. They force their readers to confront the disparity between signifier and signified and at the same time to pursue the analogous relationship between disparate things, between image and the invisible thing it signifies. The emblematic image stimulates the reader to seek what is absent and invisible; it thus serves as an intermediary between the physical and the spiritual worlds. The enigmatic quality of the emblem enhances its functions as a sign. . . . The emblematic image insists on being translated and transformed.[26]

Even as Shakespeare calls our attention to a new Protestant marital relationship with the stage embrace of Posthumus and Imogen, his ambiguities of gender in the theatrical image also remind his audience of the analogy between marriage itself and the spousal union of Christ with His Church. Indeed the entire play, as others have pointed out, demands that we see through its words and action to the invisible event of the Nativity that is soon to occur.

Transformations of the elm and the vine image continue within the

An English *amicitia* emblem from Geffrey Whitney, *A Choice of Emblemes* (Leyden: Plantin, 1586), 62. Reprinted by permission of the Folger Shakespeare Library.

emblem tradition as well. Cesare Ripa, for example, includes a different variation of "Amicitia" in his enormously popular *Iconologia.* The *pictura* in the 1603 edition shows the wedded elm and vine further embraced by a lady in white. Ripa's explanation of what is now a *personification* rather than a visual symbol of friendship, recalls the conventional marriage of the dead elm and the living vine, and then summarizes commonplace attitudes of the Renaissance toward friendship. Since there is no full English edition of Ripa yet available, I will quote a translation of the entire passage:

> A lady dressed in white, but roughly, so as to show the shoulder and bare breast, pointing with the right hand to the heart, on which will be a motto in golden letters, thus: LONGE, ET PROPE [Far and Near]; and on the hem of the dress will be written, MORS, ET VITA [Death and Life]. She will be rumpled,

and on her head there will be a garland of myrtle and of pomegranate blossoms intertwined; on her forehead will be written: HEIMS, AESTAS (Winter, Summer).

She will be rumpled, and with the left arm she will hold a dead elm tree, which will be encircled by a living vine. Friendship, according to Aristotle, is a mutual, express and reciprocal benevolence guided by virtue and by reason among men who have similar backgrounds and characters. The white and rough vestment is the simple candidness of spirit, by which true love is seen to be far removed from any sort of deceit or artful smoothness.

She shows the left shoulder and bare breast, attaching to the heart the motto, *Longe, & prope,* because the true friend, whether near by or far from the beloved person, is never separated in his heart; and in spite of the passage of time and fortune, he is always ready to live and die for the sake of friendship, and this is what the mottos on the hem of the dress and the forehead signify. But if it [friendship] is feigned, then, at the slightest change of fortune, you will see it vanish like the morning dew. Being rumpled, and having the garland of myrtle with the pomegranate blossoms, shows that the fruit of love and of the inner union reconciles and spreads abroad the sweet odor of its example of honorable actions, and *this without vanity of pompous show, under which very often adulation is born* [italics added], the enemy of this virtue.

She is depicted barefoot, likewise, to show readiness, or speed, and that in the service of the friend one should not prize comforts: as Ovid says on the art of love: *Si rota defuerit, tu pede carpe viam* [If wheels are lacking, make your way on foot]. Finally, she embraces a dead elm encircled by a living vine, in order to make it known that friendship begun in prosperity ought to endure always, and that the greater need should be friendship more than ever, if one remembers that there is no friend so useless that he does not know how to find some way or other to pay the obligations of friendship.[27]

All this sounds like a description of Imogen herself. And Ripa's contrast between friendship and "adulation" or adoration is equally significant in the light of both Posthumus's and Imogen's early insistence in *Cymbeline* that they adore one another as divinities rather than knowing, trusting, and loving one another as true friends.

Since the word "friend" when applied to a woman often meant "mistress" to the Jacobeans, Posthumus pompously informs his companions in Rome—then considered by Protestants to be the center of religious idolatry—that, "I profess myself her / adorer, not her friend" (1.5.65–66). This worshipful attitude would seem to be a shaky foundation for a happy marriage. Imogen is similarly foolish when she believes Iachimo's flattering description of Posthumus in 1.7: "He sits 'mongst men like a descended god; / He hath a kind of honour sets him off, / More than mortal seeming" (169–71). Moreover, she later becomes grotesquely absurd when she compares the corpse of Cloten, which she mistakes for that of Posthumus, to Mercury, Mars, Hercules, and even to Jove. The shrewd Italian tempter Iachimo was quite right in suspecting that Posthumus and Imogen did not yet have a mature understanding of one another or of marriage itself: "I have spoke this," says Iachimo, "to know if your

Cesare Ripa's version of "Amicitia" in *Iconologia* (Rome: Lepido, 1603), 16. Re-printed by permission of the Folger Shakespeare Library.

affiance / Were *deeply rooted*" (1.7.163–64; italics added), which it clearly was not. During the course of the play, therefore, the idolatrous lovers must die to one another and to their own immature selves before they can be reborn into the true matrimony symbolized by the embrace of the elm and vine.

Echoing the beautiful "love is strong as death" passage in The Song of Songs 7:6, Shakespeare's contemporary, the Dutch emblematist Otto van Veen also includes a version of Alciati's emblem on friendship in his multilingual *Amorvm Emblemata or Emblemes of Love*. Van Veen's motto is "Loue after death," while his *subscriptio* or verse assures us that,

> The vyne doth still embrace the elme by age ore-past,
> Which did in former tyme those feeble stalks vphold,

The elm and the vine from Otto van Veen, *Emblemes of Loue* (Antwerp, 1608), 245. Reprinted by permission of the Folger Shakespeare Library.

And constantly remaynes with it now beeing old,
Loue is not kild by death, that after death doth last.[28]

The *pictura* of the emblem shows a dying man at the base of the withered elm, an arrow in his heart; but—he is tenderly supported by the divine archer himself: Amor. Although the notion of a supportive friendship up to and after death should certainly be understood on the literal level, van Veen's emblem again reminds us that the *topos* extends to the realm of theology as well. In this sense, the true friend referred to in all the *Amicitia* emblems is both an earthly friend who will care for our children after we have died and a spiritual friend, Christ or the Love God Himself, who will uplift our souls in the life to come.

Shakespeare seems to combine all of these meanings in his verbal allusion to the elm and the vine *topos* in *Cymbeline* and in his visual literalization of the image onstage. The fact that Imogen, or the bride, is still dressed as a boy when the spouses embrace serves to emphasize the need for a faithful Platonic *friendship* between man and wife, in addition to the conventional feelings of romantic love and sexual desire. It suggests as well that marriage is a coupling between social equals who pledge mutual support up to and after death, although the husband, of course, always remains technically "head" of the Christian household, while the wife is the "heart."

Jeanne Addison Roberts has recently expressed a similar interpretation of Shakespeare's enlightened view of matrimony in her analysis of *The Taming of the Shrew* as a work very probably indebted to the image of another popular Renaissance marriage *topos,* the hermaphrodite, which derives from Ovid's *Metamorphoses.*[29] There is in fact a Protestant emblem by Mathias Holzwart (emblem 35 with the motto "Amor coniugalis") that combines the elm and the vine image with a matrimonial couple depicted as an hermaphrodite and praises the wife as "partner in joy and sorrow."[30] In any case, Posthumus in act 5 consciously relinquishes his former role in the play—that of idolater and jealous husband. Even though he still believes Imogen has been unfaithful to him, he generously forgives her "For wrying but a little" (5.1.5). To be sure, magnanimity toward a friend is emotionally much less difficult than magnanimity toward a straying sexual partner, and it was one of the virtues commonly taught to men of honor. Yet Posthumus is more than magnanimous here; he offers *all* of himself as a sacrifice to love, in imitation of the Savior soon to be born and in imitation of the dying elm that still supports the vine: "I'll die / For thee, O Imogen, even for whom my life / Is, every breath, a death" (5.1.25–27).

The original inspiration for Shakespeare's variation of the marriage *topos* to include mutuality and friendship may have come, like so much else in the canon, from Ovid's *Metamorphoses.* Like Catullus, Ovid also

EMBLEMA. XXXV.

Amor coniugalis.

Vxor lætitiæ consors simul atq; doloris,
Tesine me feriant tela cruenta uelim.
Tesine me rapiant optem crudelia fata,
Et mea mors soluat membra repente necans.
Vt, quæ iunxit amor communi fœdere lecti,
Vrna etiam iungat corpora bina leuis,
Ossaq; tumba olim uenerandi testis amoris
Iuncta eadem simili conditione tegat.

S 3

A hermaphrodite with the elm and the vine, from Mathias Holzwart, *Emblematum Tyrocinia* (Strassburg, 1581), sig. s3. Reprinted by permission of the Huntington Library.

mentions the marriage of the elm and the vine. In the story of Pomona and the love-sick viticulturist Vertumnus, the poet writes,

> There was an elm tree opposite, a lovely sight to see, with its bunches of shining grapes, and this the god praised, and its companion vine no less. 'But,' he said, 'if this tree trunk stood by itself, and was not wedded to the vine, it would be of no interest to anybody, except for its leaves. Moreover, the vine is supported by the elm to which it has been united, whereas if it had not been so married, it would lie trailing on the ground.'[31]

In answer to the self-serving youths of Catullus's "Greek Epithalamium," Ovid reminds us here of the entire equation that, if the unsupported vine is of no interest to anyone, neither is the unadorned withered elm. The freedom of bachelorhood is as sterile and useless as perpetual virginity. Marriage is the natural and fruitful state for mature men and women in the garden of the world, as Protestant clerics never tired of pointing out during Shakespeare's lifetime.[32]

Furthermore, friendship as the basis for a good marriage was an equally important sixteenth-century Protestant theme that Shakespeare appears to emphasize in *Cymbeline*. Despite all their subsequent troubles, Posthumus and Imogen, friends since childhood, have freely chosen one another in defiance of the king and have entered into a marriage of mutual love. According to Robert Cleaver, writing in 1598, "Mutuall loue, hauing his beginning of godlinesse and true vertue, maketh the husband and wife not to be too sharpe sighted in spying into one anothers faults: but that many things either they marke not, or if they marke them, they couer them with loue."[33] Although Posthumus ignores the first part of Cleaver's advice and does spy on Imogen, an amazing quality of love ultimately saves the marriage of Shakespeare's young couple, who mature before our eyes from idolatrous lovers of the Petrarchan mode into ideal, patient, and forgiving Protestant spouses.[34]

Imogen herself reveals no precise turning point in her understanding of marital love, as does Posthumus in his repentance scene. Nevertheless, by the end of *Cymbeline,* she is as magnanimous toward the husband who ordered her death as he has finally been toward her imagined infidelity. She recognizes Posthumus dressed as an invading Roman soldier and forgives this obvious political betrayal. She forgives as well his earlier personal betrayal of marital trust and friendship, treacheries that are analogous to the archetypal spiritual betrayal of Christ by Judas. Indeed it is very doubtful that in real life any woman could be so forgiving. In a similar manner, although Posthumus at first does not recognize his bride at all in her masculine disguise, he does at last see her as both his physical wife and as his forgiving spiritual *friend,* who will adorn his trunk with greenery and fruit for the rest of his life and beyond.

Dressed in male clothing, Imogen is no longer merely a clinging female vine supported by her "lord" (or husband-farmer), who has self-right-eously—and correctly, according to the usual agricultural metaphor of marriage—assumed life and death rights over her. She is finally accepted in public as a human and living symbol of divine friendship and of Posthumus's own immortal soul. Thus, Shakespeare, with the help of Ovid, Alciati, and the Protestant theologians of his time, seems to have arrived here at a poetic criticism of the hidden agricultural metaphor in the term "husband" itself as applied to human life and has substituted the notion of mutually supportive friendship as a superior ideal for matrimony. Only God has the rights of a gardener or husbandman over human affairs.

Moreover, since marriage was itself a popular metaphor of the rela-tionship between the king and his country, the political ramifications of this subtle metamorphosis in *Cymbeline* of the old agricultural metaphor, with its insinuation of dependency and of life and death rights of the husband over the wife for the sake of fruitfulness, to a metaphor of mutually supportive friendship in the political life of the nation, are as-tonishing. As we have seen, vegetation symbolism in general was widely used to signify rebirth and reform, according to Ladner (1961, 303–22), and there can be no doubt that the poet Shakespeare was fully aware of the political aspects of the elm and the vine *topos*. He had already used the motif in his previous Jacobean play *Macbeth* (c.1606) to contrast the tentative relationship between Duncan and the newcomer Macbeth with the enduring relationship between Duncan and his true heir, Banquo, the ancestor of James I of England. In act 1, Duncan receives Macbeth's homage formally and without embracing him: "Welcome hither! / I have begun to plant thee, and will labor to make thee full of growing." To his kinsman, however, the royal husbandman is considerably more effusive: "Noble Banquo," he says, "That hast no less deserv'd, nor must be known / No less to have done so, let me infold thee / And hold thee to my heart." Accepting his role as the fruitful vine supported by the elm, Banquo gracefully replies, "There if I grow, / The harvest is your own" (1.4.27–33). In the tragedy of *Macbeth*, the subject must accept the submissive role of a wife to the royal husbandman.[35]

But in *Cymbeline* the embrace of Posthumus and Imogen, now sym-bolizing, as I have suggested, mutual support and the friendship of equals, is the last we hear or see of the elm and the vine in this play. Reconciled in act 5 with his two wrongly banished courtiers Belarius and Posthumus, Cymbeline first substitutes a greeting of human equality for the agri-cultural metaphor in his reinstatement of Belarius: "Thou art my *brother;* so we'll hold thee ever" (5.5.399–400; italics added). The king then accepts the previously despised Posthumus into the royal family with the words, "We'll learn our freeness of a son-in-law: / Pardon's the word to all"

(5.5.422–23). "Freeness" here means generosity in forgiveness, which is quite different from either pruning or harvesting and suggests the possibility of a new kind of political rule corresponding to the Protestant ideal of a good Christian marriage. In tracts of the period, the husband is exhorted to be a leader and a teacher, rather than a tyrant, while the wife is now considered to be a willing "Helper" in the formation of a well-governed household (Cleaver 1598, 159). Well-governed households, in turn, were understood to be analogous to well-governed kingdoms.

Cymbeline ends with a royal proclamation of peaceful union between man and wife, peace between the king and those he has exiled, peace between Britain and Rome, and peace between heaven and earth. As the king himself announces, "Never was a war did cease / (Ere bloody hands were wash'd) with such a peace" (5.5.485–86).

What should now be clear at this stage of our iconographic study of *Cymbeline* is that the symbolic meanings of Shakespeare's vegetation imagery rather closely parallel what we have already discovered in respect to the major bird imagery in the play. The dramatist doubles his poetic means of signification in keeping with the familiar Renaissance model of an intelligible universe that reflects its divine creator-artist and is so designed that all the parts correspond to one another. Different aspects of the natural world can therefore have the same symbolic meaning. Within this complex artistic system of echoes, the act of pruning the branches and lateral roots of the royal cedar as a method of personal and social reform directly parallels the molting and penitential bath of the high-flying eagle and the sacrificial immolation of the phoenix. The subsequent renewal of the tree and its shoots is analogous to the renewal of the eagle's feathers and to the rebirth of the phoenix from its own ashes; and, finally, the companionate marriage of the elm and the vine is a reflection of a similar marriage between crows, which symbolizes faithfulness between spouses, political consensus, and universal concord. We will continue to hear similar thematic echoes in Shakespeare's symbolic use of animals and minerals in *Cymbeline*.

Notes

1. Mats Rydén, *Shakespearean Plant Names: Identifications and Interpretations* (Stockholm: Almquist & Wiksell International, 1978), 21.

2. See William Shakespeare, *Cymbeline,* ed. J. M. Nosworthy, Arden Edition (London: Methuen, 1955), lxxxi.

3. R. Van den Broek, *The Myth of the Phoenix: According to Classical and Early Christian Traditions* (Leiden: E. J. Brill, 1972), 308.

4. Ibid.

5. *The Phoenix Nest* (1593), ed. Hyder Edward Rollins (Cambridge, Mass.: Harvard University Press, 1931), 10.

6. Gerhart B. Ladner, "Vegetation Symbolism and the Concept of Renaissance," in *Essays in Honor of Erwin Panofsky,* 2 vols., ed. Millard Meiss (New York: New York University Press, 1961), 1, 303; hereafter referred to parenthetically. I am grateful to Douglas L. Peterson for calling this essay to my attention. In n.23, 150, of his *Time, Tide, and Tempest* (San Marino, Calif.: The Huntington Library, 1973), Peterson suggests that "Cloten's beheading may symbolically announce the public phase of the play's renewing action." William Barry Thorne also introduces the idea of regeneration as of utmost importance to *Cymbeline* but does not provide an extended analysis of the *topos* in his *"Cymbeline:* 'Lopp'd Branches' and the Concept of Regeneration," *Shakespeare Quarterly* 20 (1969): 143–59.

7. See Rose Jeffries Peebles, "The Dry Tree: Symbol of Death," in *Vassar Medieval Studies,* ed. Christobel Forsyth Fiske (New Haven: Yale University Press, 1923), 74, and Esther Casier Quinn, *The Quest of Seth for the Oil of Life* (Chicago and London: The University of Chicago Press, 1962), 88–90. Samuel C. Chew observes that "In the 'Hatfield Seasons' [tapestry] Justice stands between a tree in leaf and a withered tree." See *The Virtues Reconciled; An Iconographic Study* (Toronto: The University of Toronto Press, 1947), 95. See also Alan R. Young, "A Note on the Tournament Impresas in *Pericles,"* *Shakespeare Quarterly* 36 (1985): 453–56, especially 454 n.6, for actual Elizabethan tournament impresas that made use of the *topos.*

8. See Gerhart B. Ladner, *The Idea of Reform* (New York: Harper & Row, 1959), 20; hereafter referred to parenthetically.

9. See George Wither, *A Collection of Emblemes, Ancient and Modern* (London, 1635), 217; cited hereafter parenthetically.

10. Mehl, "Emblems in English Renaissance Drama," *Renaissance Drama* 2 (1962), 46.

11. Arden edition of *Cymbeline,* 177 n.263–64.

12. See Peter Demetz, "The Elm and the Vine: Notes Toward the History of a Marriage Topos," *PMLA* 73 (1958): 521–22; hereafter referred to parenthetically. I would like to add here the name of Sir John Davies to Demetz's list of English poets in the Renaissance who made use of the elm and vine *topos.* In his "Epithalamion," Davies has Euterpe sing, "Longe maye you Joye such sympathy of Loves, / as doth betwine the Elm and Vine remayne" (1975, 204, ll. 65–66), and in his *Orchestra* (1975, 105), we find the following verse (56) that gives cosmological significance to the *topos:*

What makes the vine about the elm to dance
With turnings windings and embracements round?
What makes the loadstone to the north advance
His subtile point, as if from thence he found
His chief attractive virtue to redound?
Kind nature first doth cause all things to love;
Love makes them dance and in just order move.

See *The Poems of Sir John Davies,* ed. Robert Krueger (Oxford: Clarendon Press, 1975).

13. *The Greek Anthology,* 5 vols., trans. W. R. Paton, The Loeb Classical Library (London, 1917), vol. 3, 121–23.

14. *The Poems of Catullus,* trans. F. W. Cornish, The Loeb Classical Library (New York, 1918), 89.

15. The relationship is briefly footnoted by G. K. Hunter in the Arden edition of *All's Well.* See 9 n.104–5; 10 n.126–27; and 12 n.148. See also my "Sacred and Sexual Motifs in *All's Well That Ends Well,*" *Renaissance Quarterly* 42 (Spring 1989): 33–59.

16. Desiderius Erasmus, *A Modest Meane to Marriage,* trans. N. L. (London: Henrie Denham, 1568), sig. B vii.

17. Glynne Wickham, "Riddle and Emblem: A Study in the Dramatic Structure of *Cymbeline,*" in *English Renaissance Studies: Presented to Dame Helen Gardner in honour of her 70th Birthday,* ed. John Carey (Oxford: The Clarendon Press, 1980), 111.

18. See Ben Jonson, "Hymenai," in *Inigo Jones: The Theatre of the Stuart Court,* 2 vols., ed. Stephen Orgel and Roy Strong (Berkeley: The University of California Press, 1973), vol. 1, 113, lines 778–86.

19. John Gerarde, *The Herball or Generall Historie of Plantes* (London: John Norton, 1597), 1235; hereafter referred to parenthetically.

20. William Shakespeare, *Cymbeline,* ed. Edward Dowden (London: Methuen, 1903), 130 n.59 and n.58.

21. Robert Graves notes in *The White Goddess* the importance of the elder to the Celtic tree alphabet and its associations with witchcraft, evil, and bad luck:

> The thirteenth tree is the elder, a waterside tree associated with witches, which keeps its fruit well into December. It is an old British superstition that a child laid in an elderwood cradle will pine away or be pinched black and blue by the fairies—the traditional wood for cradles is the birch, the tree of inception, which drives away evil spirits. And in Ireland elder sticks, rather than ashen ones, are used by witches as magic horses. Although the flowers and inner bark of the elder have always been famous for their therapeutic qualities, the scent of an elder plantation was formerly held to cause death and disease. So unlucky is the elder that in Langland's *Piers Plowman,* Judas is made to hang himself on an elder tree. Spenser couples the elder with the funereal cypress, and T. Scot writes in his *Philomythie* (1616):
>
>> The cursèd elder and the fatal yew
>> With witch [rowan] and nightshade in their shadows grew.
>
> King William Rufus was killed by an archer posted under an elder. The elder is also said to have been the Crucifixion tree, and the elder leaf shape of the funerary flints in megalithic long-barrows suggest that its association with death is long-standing. In English folklore to burn logs of elder 'brings the Devil into the house'.

See *The White Goddess,* amended and enl. ed. (New York: Farrar, Straus and Giroux, 1966), 185.

22. See Peter Daly, Virginia W. Callahan, and Simon Cuttler, eds., *Andreas Alciatus: Index Emblematicus,* 2 vols. (Toronto: University of Toronto Press, 1985), vol. 1: Emblem 161.

23. Joachim Camerarius, *Symbolorum et Emblematum* (Nuremberg, 1590), bk. 1, 36.

24. Henry Green, *Shakespeare and the Emblem Writers* (London: Trübner & Co., 1870), 308.

25. Geffrey Whitney, *A Choice of Emblemes* (Leyden: Christopher Plantin, 1586), 62.

26. See Huston Diehl, "Graven Images: Protestant Emblem Books in En-

gland," *Renaissance Quarterly* 39 (1986): 61. In fact, however, it is difficult for the modern scholar to distinguish between Catholic and Protestant emblematists when looking only at their emblems, and we must also remember that all emblems require careful interpretation. They are all variations of this or that classical or biblical theme. We would do well to remember as well that Andrea Alciati, father of the emblem book, was a renowned lawyer and author of a famous study on the continuing problems in the interpretation of legal texts.

27. Cesare Ripa, *Iconologia* (Rome: Lepido, 1603), 16. Translated for the author by Roger T. Simonds.

28. Otto van Veen, *Amorvm Emblemata or Emblemes of Love* (Antwerp, 1608), 244–45.

29. See Jeanne Addison Roberts, "Horses and Hermaphrodites: Metamorphoses in *The Taming of the Shrew,*" *Shakespeare Quarterly* 34 (1983): 159–80.

30. See Mathias Holtzwart, *Emblematum Tyrocinia: sive Picta Poesis latinogermanica* (Strassburg: Bernard Jobin, 1581), sig. s3.

31. Ovid, *Metamorphoses,* trans. Mary Innes (Baltimore, Md.: Penguin Books, 1955), bk. 14, 329.

32. See Henry Smith, "A Preparative to Marriage," *The Sermons of Maister Henrie Smith* (London: Peter Short for Thomas Man, 1594), 1–3; Lawrence Stone, *The Family, Sex and Marriage in England 1500–1800,* (New York, 1977), 135–36; and Mary Beth Rose, "Moral Conceptions of Sexual Love in Elizabethan Comedy," *Renaissance Drama* 15 (1984): 16–19.

33. Robert Cleaver, *A Godly Forme of Householde Government* . . . (London: Felix Kingston, for Thomas Man, 1598), 161; hereafter referred to parenthetically.

34. In respect to what Posthumus calls "the woman's part" in marriage, Robert Cleaver says that "she was ordeined as a *Helper,* and not as a hinderer" (1598, 159). He then argues "that women are as men are, reasonable creatures, and haue flexible wittes, both to good and euill, the which with vse, discretion, and good counsell, may be altered and turned. And although there be some euill and lewde women, yet that doth no more prooue the malice of their nature, then of men, and therefore the more ridiculous and foolish are they, that haue inveighed against the whole sexe for a few euill: and haue not with like furie vituperated and dispraised all mankind, because part of them are theeues, murtherers, and such like wicked liuers" (1598, 160).

35. I wish to express my appreciation to Ann Pasternak Slater for calling my attention to the presence of the elm and vine motif in *Macbeth,* to Margaret Mikesell for a bibliography of marriage manuals, and to Virginia W. Callahan for information on Alciati's version of the elm and the vine topos.

8

Animals, Minerals, and Rituals

The second nature of the lion is that, although he has fallen asleep, his eyes keep watch for him, for they remain open. In the Song of Songs the betrothed bears witness, saying, "I sleep but my heart is awake."

—Physiologus

Even minerals have symbolic significance within the Renaissance Neoplatonic system of correspondences between the sensory world and the intellectual world. I shall begin this chapter with an analysis of the possible moral implications of the diamond ring given by Imogen as a wedding token to Posthumus and of the gold bracelet he presents to her during a touching postmarital ritual before they part. Imogen clearly gives away the epitome of herself with the ring, but Posthumus presents her in exchange with untried gold in a form of jewelry that he himself understands to be symbolic of servitude.

In addition, Shakespeare employs certain animals as symbols in the tragicomedy. Cloten, for example, is often called an ass by the lords who attend him. But we can quickly sum up the significance of that lowly creature with one pithy sentence from Edward Topsell:

the which beast is intituled or phrased with many epithites among Poets; as slow, burthen-bearing, back-bearing, vile, cart-drawing, mill-labouring, sluggish, crooked, vulgar, slow-paced, long-eared, blockish, braying, ydle, devil-hayred, filthy, saddle-bearer, slow-foot four-foot, vnsauoury, and a beast of miserable condition; beside many other such titles in the Greeke.[1]

All these epithets add up to the famous Apuleian symbol of the ass as the lower nature of man in *The Golden Ass,* although ironically the ass is also the bearer of divinity (in this case Isis), and it becomes the consort of Beauty (Titania) in *A Midsummer Night's Dream.*

In the chapter on primitivism in *Cymbeline,* I have already discussed (1) the animals of prey, the wolves and foxes, which are commonly associated with Wild Men, and (2) the hunters' usual quarry, consisting of such sacrificial animals as the deer and the lamb. I have also pointed out earlier that the boar is a common symbol of unrestrained lust.[2] This significance explains why a corrupted Posthumus imagines Iachimo in Imogen's bed as "a full-acorn'd boar, a German one," that "Cried 'O!' and mounted" (2.4.168–69). Therefore, I shall limit my discussion in the second part of this section to a consideration of the lion, the fierce royal beast associated with Posthumus, and its relationship to the gentle lamb, with special attention to the dramatic rituals attending these important animal allusions in *Cymbeline*.

A Gold Bracelet of Bondage and a Diamond Ring of Virtue

In a brief ritual scene before Posthumus goes into exile, Imogen gives her husband a valuable wedding present to remind him of the bride he leaves behind:

> Look here, love;
> This diamond was my mother's; take it, heart;
> But keep it till you woo another wife,
> When Imogen is dead.
>
> (1.2.42–45)

Posthumus replies, as he slips the ring on his finger, "Remain, remain thou here, / While sense can keep it on" (1.2.48–49). He then presents Imogen with a gold bracelet. Although the scene is often cited by scholars as a betrothal, the couple must already be married at this time. The First Gentleman says they are (1.1.7); Jupiter later states that "in our temple was he [Posthumus] married" (5.4.105–6); and Posthumus himself comments here that, "As I my poor self did exchange for you / To your so infinite loss; so in our trifles / I still win of you" (1.2.50–52). The ceremonial exchange of gifts now witnessed by the audience is meant to further bind the bride and groom together though love tokens, but what Posthumus considers to be a mere "trifle" once belonged to Imogen's deceased mother and is a diamond ring symbolizing, as we shall see, the rare qualities of goodness, beauty, and indestructible virtue. Imogen's gift thus represents a complete emotional commitment on her part. It is indeed of considerably more spiritual as well as monetary value than what Posthumus bestows on her.

Posthumus's gift is a gold bracelet, which he places on Imogen's arm as a outward sign not of her individual value but of his (as good as gold) and of her current bondage to him:

> For my sake wear this,
> It is a manacle of love, I'll place it
> Upon this fairest prisoner.

(1.2.53–54)

In this way, Posthumus announces his personal possession of Imogen through their marriage, a conventional but rather commercial view of matrimony and a view that does not take into account the new Protestant ideal of mutuality and love. He reduces his bride to a piece of goods he has just purchased with gold. Later on, when—as a result of the infamous wager—both the bracelet and the woman are devalued by Iachimo in public, Posthumus believes Imogen's diamond ring to have lost its value as well and parts with it willingly. Such monetary rituals as the making of wagers and the settling of debts destroy the essence of a delicate love ritual originally intended to join Imogen and Posthumus forever.

The ideal Protestant marriage betrayed by Posthumus's commercialism and by his later irrational jealousy is clearly described in an emblem by George Wither, who borrowed the Latin mottos and engravings for his *Collection of Emblemes* (1635) from two earlier emblem books, the *Nucleus emblematum* (1611) and *Selectorum emblematum* (1613) by Gabriel Rollenhagen.[3] Since, by the early seventeenth century, the modern notion of a companionate marriage appears to have been widely accepted among Protestants, Wither's borrowed engraving (originally by Crispin van de Passe) depicts not an exchange of gifts between husband and wife but a ritual washing of one another's hands by the newlyweds. According to the emblem's English motto, "*Where* Lovers *fitly matched be,* / *In* mutuall-duties, *they agree.*" Thus no one is a prisoner of anyone else in this late version of Alciati's *amicitia* emblem, which we will remember had originally depicted the embrace of the elm and the vine. Wither's verses read as follows:

> Most *Lovers,* minde their *Penny,* or their *Pleasure;*
> Or, painted *Honors;* and, they all things measure,
> Not as they are, but as they helpfull seeme,
> In compassing those toyes, they most esteeme.
>   Though many wish to gaine a faithfull *Friend,*
> They seldome seeke one, for the noblest end:
> Nor know they (should they finde what they had sought)
> How *Friendship* should be manag'd, as it ought.
> Such, as good *Husbands* covet, or good *Wives*
> (The deare companions of most happy lives)
> Wrong Courses take to gaine them; yet contemne
> Their honest love, who rightly counsell them;
> And, lest, they unawares the Marke may hit,
> They blinde their *judgements,* and befoole their *wit.*

Newlyweds wash each other's hands as a representation of mutuality in marriage. From George Wither's *A Collection of Emblemes* (1635). The engraving is by Crispin van de Passe. Reprinted by permission of the Folger Shakespeare Library (STC 25900c), 162.

I have already suggested in my discussion of the elm and the vine *topos* that friendship and equality between husband and wife were what Shakespeare had in mind as the proper marital relationship between Imogen and Posthumus, rather than the physical and economic possession of the wife by a jealous husband. But Wither argues above that this ideal does not occur when young people, obsessed with sex, gold, and social position, fail to see love as a state of giving rather than a state of taking. The emblem continues:

> He, that will finde a *Friend,* must seeke out one
> To exercise unfeigned *love* upon;
> And, *mutuall-duties,* must both yield, and take,
> Not for himself, but, for his *Friendship* sake.

Such, as doe rightly *marry,* neither be
With *Dowries* caught, nor wooe a *Pedigree;*
Nor, merely come together, when they wed,
To reape the youthfull pleasures of the Bed:
But, seeke that fitnesse, and that *Sympathy,*
Which maketh up the perfect'st *Amity.*
    A *paire,* so match'd: *Like Hands that wash each other,*
    As mutuall-helpes, will sweetly live together.[4]

The word "friend" now applies properly to a spouse rather than to a mistress. However, at this early stage of their relationship in the play, instead of establishing such an adult friendship with his former childhood playmate, Posthumus enslaves Imogen with his gift of a golden manacle and merely accepts as his due her pledge of incorruptible virtue.

Commercialism in love was also remarked upon by the emblematist Otto van Veen in his adaptation of Ovid's "Auro conciliatvr amor." Under the motto "Love bought and sold," we find the following epigram:

    Loue iustly may complayn, and great abuse relate,
    In seeing loue to bee somtymes for treasure sold,
    As thogh high prysed loue were no more woorth then gold,
    And marchants might it sell at ordinary rate.[5]

It is almost as bad to make wagers involving gold and a diamond ring on the chastity of one's love as does Posthumus.

Unlike a diamond, gold can be adulterated by the addition of foreign substances, making it necessary for goldsmiths to test the value of the metal before buying it. And the value of Posthumus, which is in fact severely tested within the tragicomedy, is for a while found wanting. He is very easily corrupted by Iachimo's sexual insinuations and loses faith in Imogen's chastity on the basis of slight circumstantial evidence and verbal innuendo. We might remember especially the Italian courtier's sly insinuation that, "If you buy ladies' flesh at a million a dram, you cannot preserve it from tainting" (1.5.131–33).

Many Renaissance emblems compare the problem of adulterated gold with human behavior. Claude Paradin, for example, discusses the need to try or test faith, just as gold is tried by the goldsmith before he purchases the metal. Paradin's *inscriptio* is "Sic spectanda fides" ("So is faith to be tried"). The *pictura* shows the hand of God holding a gold coin, while according to the *subscriptio,*

    The goodnes of gold is not onely tryed by ringing, but also by the touchstone; so the triall of godlines and faith is to bee made not of wordes onely, but also by the action & performance of the deedes.[6]

Posthumus at first fails this test by not physically defending his wife's honor against any and all accusations of impurity, as we would expect a chivalric gentleman to do since his own honor is also at the stake. It seems obvious that a husband without faith in his wife's chastity is already a cuckold in his own mind and in the eyes of others. Psychologically, of course, Posthumus's failure in faith seems to indicate a pathetic lack of belief that he is lovable.

Geffrey Whitney uses the same motto and the same woodcut for his version of the gold and faith emblem. The verse reads,

> The touche doth trye, the fine, and purest goulde;
>   And not the sound, or els the goodly showe.
> So, if mennes wayes, and vertues, wee behoulde,
> The worthy men, wee by their workes, shall knowe,
>   But gallant lookes, and outward showes beguile,
>   And ofte are clokes to cogitacions vile.[7]

Again the acts a man performs are what characterize him, not his words. A faithful man shows his faith through deeds. To this commonplace Whitney adds the suggestion of hypocrisy. Although Posthumus boasts loudly of his bride's beauty and chastity in *Cymbeline,* instead of defending her against assault and proving his own moral quality, he sends an aquaintance to test her faithfulness to him.

In his *Collection of Emblemes,* Wither also discusses this problem of gold, a metal that should represent excellence and goodness but often does not. Under the motto "All is not Gold, *which makes a show; But, what the* Touchstone *findeth so,"* the emblematist teaches the following moral on friendship in the first part of his verse:

> When Silver *Medalls,* or some coynes of *Gold.*
>   Are by the *Gold-smith* either bought or sold,
>   Hee doth not only search them with his *Eye,*
>   But by the *Scale,* their *weight* will also trie;
> Or, by the *Touchstone,* or the *test,* assay
> The truenesse of them, and their just *Alay.*
> Now, by their warinesse, who thus proceed,
> Wee fairely are admonished, to heed
> The faithfulnesse of him wee make our *Friend;*
> And, on whose love wee purpose to depend:
> Or else, when wee a *Iewell* thinke to get,
> Wee may bee cheated by a *Counterfet.*

(1635, 233)

Since I shall discuss the deceiving of the visual sense further in the next chapter, suffice it to say here that in *Cymbeline,* Imogen trusts far too

Crispin van de Passe's emblem of testing gold for its purity. From George Wither, *A Collection of Emblemes* (1635), 233. Reprinted by permission of the Folger Shakespeare Library (STC 25900c).

much in Posthumus, who has not yet been tried in any way as a grown man, and by extension, she overly trusts Iachimo who visits her in the guise of Posthumus's "friend"—a counterfeit indeed. Because of his excessive pride, Posthumus removes Imogen's diamond ring from his finger in Rome and wagers against her wifely virtue the very symbol of that virtue. As witnesses of this act of betrayal, we see clearly that, despite all the hyperbolic praise of Posthumus we have heard from the First Gentleman and from Imogen, we should heed Wither's next moral, which is both conventional and generally correct as the world goes:

> All is not *Gold* that glisters; Otherwhile,
> The *Tincture* is so good, it may beguile
> The cunningst eye: But, bring it to the *Touch,*
> And, then, you find the value not so much.
> Some, keepe the *Tincture,* brooking likewise, well

An ordinarie *Touch;* but, yeeld a *Smell,*
Which will discover it, if you apply
Vnto your *Nose,* that piece of *Chymistrie.*
Sometime, when there's enough to give content,
In *Colour* the *Touch,* and in the *Scent;*
The *Bulke,* is more than answers *Gold* in *weight,*
And, proves it a sophisticall deceit.
Nay, some, is fully that which you desire,
In all these *Properties;* and, till the fire
Hath made *assayes,* you'l thinke you might be bold
To pawne your life, it had been *Ophir-gold:*
    But, to bee false, the *Metall's* then descride;
    And, such are many *Friends,* when they are tride.

(1635, 233)

On seeing the bracelet stolen from Imogen by Iachimo, Posthumus docs not recognize in it the image of himself as false gold but rather the image of his bride as debased and thus a counterfeit: "The vows of women / Of no more bondage be to where they are made / Than they arc to their virtues, which is nothing" (2.4.110–12). He then reasons further that if the female is false gold, so is the fruit of her womb: "Some coiner with his tools / Made me a counterfeit: yet my mother seem'd / The Dian of that time: so doth my wife / The nonpareil of this" (2.4.157–59). Scratch Posthumus at this point in his life, and one can smell rotten Cloten, or alloy.

Fortunately, however, that which is true gold (moral excellence) can be separated from the dross when the metal is "tried" or melted down. In the words of Sir John Davies,

If ought can teach vs ought, *Afflictions* lookes,
    (Making vs looke into our selues so neare)
    Teach vs to *know ourselues,* beyond all bookes,
    Or all the learned *Schooles* that euer were.

This *Mistresse* lately pluckt me by the Eare,
    And many a golden lesson hath me taught;
    Hath made my *Senses* quick and Reason cleare,
    Reformed my Will, and rectified my Thought;

So do the *Winds and Thunders* cleanse the Aire,
    So working Seas settle and purge the wine;
    So lopt and pruned Trees do florish faire;
    So doth the fire the drossie Gold refine.[8]

The action of the play finally separates and saves the true gold in Posthumus, who not only repents his foolish behavior toward Imogen but also becomes emotionally ready to atone for it by his own death:

For Imogen's dear life take mine; and though
'Tis not so dear, yet 'tis a life; you coin'd it.

Tween man and man they weigh not every stamp;
Though light, take pieces for the figure's sake.

(5.4.22–26)

Posthumus now realizes that he, not Imogen, is mostly alloy, and she is true gold. And, as E. M. W. Tillyard points out, in alchemy (the art of transformations), "Gold was king of metals, the sum of all metallic virtues; and alchemically it was a mixture of the elements in a perfect proportion. And the *aurum potabile* of alchemy was the link between the perfect metal and perfect health in the patient."[9] Once Posthumus is tried by the fire of jealousy, which results in loss, but then eventually "tempers" his emotions, he becomes the virtuous man he was always meant to be.

Imogen, on the other hand, bestows her diamond ring on Posthumus not as a symbol of his bondage to her but as a reminder of her beauty and goodness and of the durability of her virtue. This jewel was believed to be incorruptible, that is, as something to be treasured and not to be wagered or risked in any way. In fact, Stephen Batman states in *Batman Vppon Bartholome* that the diamond or "ADamas is a little stone of Inde: . . . Nothing ouercommeth it, neither iron nor fire, and also it heateth neuer: for of the Greekes it is called, a vertue that maye not be daunted. . . . Dioscorides saith, that it is called a Precious stone of reconciliation and of loue."[10] A diamond ring has even further intellectual significance because of its beauty within a gold setting. Indeed a charming emblem by Gilles Corrozet illustrates just such a ring under the Platonic *inscriptio* "Beaulté compaigne de bonté" ("Beauty the companion of goodness"). According to the *subscriptio,*

Comme la pierre precieuse
Est à l'Anneau d'or bien conioinete,
Ainsi la beaulté gracieuse
Doibt estre acuecq' la bonté ioinete.

(Just as the precious stone
Is to the gold ring well conjoined,
So gracious beauty
Should be with goodness joined.)[11]

Goodness and beauty are obviously well conjoined in Imogen, who even in disguise calls herself Fidele or faithfulness.

Through the diamond, once again we find Imogen associated by Shakespeare with a well known symbol both of Christ and of the immortality of the human soul. E. P. Evans reminds us that the diamond shines in the dark like Christ; for according to Isaiah, "The people that walked in darkness have seen a great light; they that dwell in the land of the shadow of death, upon them hath the light shined."[12] Physiologus, the major

Beaulté compaigne de bonté.

Comme la pierre precieuse,
Eſt à l'Anneau d'or bien conioincte:
Ainſi la beaulté gracieuse
Doibt eſtræ auecq' la bonté ioincte

A diamond mounted on a gold ring symbolizes "Beauty, the companion of goodness" in Gilles Corrozet's *Hecatomgraphie* (Paris: Denys Ianot, 1543), sig. f. M verso. Reprinted by permission of the Folger Shakespeare Library (PQ 1607 C6 1543 Cage).

source for medieval bestiaries and most Renaissance nature emblems, further reports

> that iron does not prevail against it, that is, death does not rule it. He destroyed death and trampled it under foot as the Apostle bore witness, saying, "Death is swallowed up in victory. Where is thy struggle, Death? Where is thy sting?" [I Cor. 15:55]. Nor can fire do anything to this rock, meaning the devil who with his fiery darts inflames every land and the lustful, drunken, wrathful cities. Of them Isaiah says, "The land lies desolate, your cities are burned with fire" [Is.

1:7]. "The Lord Jesus Christ killed him with the breath of his mouth" [II Thes. 2:8]. No other stone harms it, that is, no man at all nor any creature can stand against him. "All things were made through him, and without him nothing was made" [John 1:3].[13]

It follows that those people who are most like Christ in the world actually seem—like the diamond—to contain some of His divine essence, a belief that does appear to be true of Imogen, despite her immaturity and all too human imperfections.

The most complete Renaissance emblem in English on the symbolism of the diamond may be found once again in Wither's *Collection* of 1635. Under the motto "*True* Vertue, *firme, will always bide, By whatsoever* suffrings *tride,*" we see an engraving by van de Passe of the hand of God holding a hammer and striking a diamond, which has been placed on an anvil. The verse explains the diamond *topos:*

> This is a well-knowne *Figure,* signifying,
>   A man, whose *Vertues* will abide the trying:
>   For, by the nature of the *Diamond stone,*
> (Which, *Violence,* can no way worke upon)
> That *Patience,* and *long-suffering* is intended,
> Which will not bee with *Injuries* offended;
> Nor yeeld to any base dejectednesse,
> Although some bruising *Pow'r,* the same opresse;
> Or, such hard *streights,* as theirs, that hamm'rings feele,
> Betwixt an *Anvile,* and a *sledge* of Steele.

Such a diamond is given to Posthumus by Imogen to promise that she will be as much like that virtuous stone as is possible for a human to be. Wither also compares the diamond to Christ.

>   None ever had a perfect *Vertue,* yet,
> But, that most *Pretious-stone,* which God hath set
> On his right hand, in *beaming-Majestie,*
> Vpon the *Ring* of blest E T E R N I T I E.
> And, this, is that impenitrable *Stone,*
> The *Serpent* could not leave impression on,
> (Nor signe of any *Path-way*) by temptations,
> Or, by the pow'r of sly insinuations:
> Which wondrous *Mysterie* was of those *five,*
> Whose depth King *Solomon* could never dive.

The emblem ends with a prayer for the moral improvement of the poet himself through Christ:

>   Good *God!* vouchsafe, ev'n for that *Diamond-*sake,
> That, I may of his *pretiousnesse,* partake,
> In all my *Trialls;* make mee alwayes able

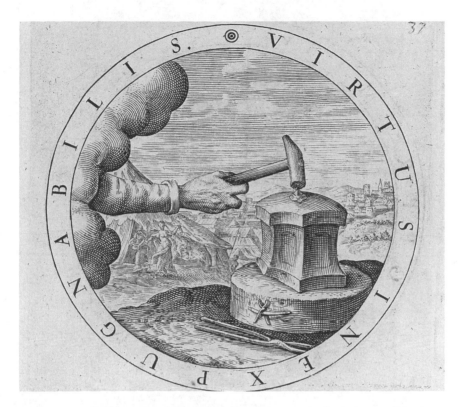

Crispin van de Passe's engraving of the diamond as a figure for indestructible virtue in George Wither's *A Collection of Emblemes* **(1635), 171. Reprinted by permission of the Folger Shakespeare Library (STC 25900c).**

To bide them, with a minde impenitrable,
How hard, or oft so'ere, those *hamm'rings* bee,
Wherewith *Afflictions* must *new fashion mee*.
And, as the common *Diamonds* polish'd are,
By their owne dust; so, let my *errours* weare
   Each other out; And, when that I am pure,
Give mee the *Lustre, Lord,* that will endure.

(1635, 171)

Although based on a different metaphor, this emblem is much like the Second Lord's prayer for Imogen: "The heavens hold firm / The walls of thy dear honour, keep unshak'd / That temple, thy fair mind, that thou mayst stand, / T'enjoy thy banish'd lord and this great land!" (2.1.61–64). Hence it would seem that Imogen's diamond ring was far more precious than Posthumus imagined when he removed it from his finger in the house of Philario.

Nec igni,nec ferro cedit.

Bipennis hinc,fax inde viuum ignem vomens,
Nexum adamãte suo decuſſat annulũ probè.
Fortis animus,conſtans'que,victor omnium,
Despuit intrepidus pericula & ſæuas cruces.

D 5　　　　　Venter,

Emblem 51 by Hadrianus Junius states that the diamond "yields neither to fire nor to the sword" (Antwerp: Plantin, 1565), 57. Reprinted by permission of the Folger Shakespeare Library (PN 6349 J8 1565a Cage).

In addition, Imogen may even have given it to her new husband as a protective talisman, for the diamond also symbolizes "A courage always unwavering," according to Guy de Tervarent, who quotes Valeriano as stating, "The diamond is the image of that virtue of courage by which one surmounts adversities while suffering them, and so that the favorable course of events leaves you unchanged."[14] A diamond ring became, therefore, the "device" of both the Medici and Este families in Italy because the stone was believed to have "the marvellous power of freeing the spirit of those who carry it from all vain fear and of teaching them to respond to arrogant Fortune."[15] Emblem 51 of Hadrianus Junius reflects this same widespread belief in the diamond as a protective talisman that gives courage to the wearer. The *inscriptio,* taken from Physiologus, is "Nec igni, nec ferro cedit" ("It yields neither to fire nor to the sword"), while the *subscriptio* states,

> Bipennis hinc, fax inde viuum ignem vomens,
>   Nexum adamante suo decussat annulum probè.
> Fortis animus, constansque, victor omnium,
>   Despuit intrepidus pericula et saeuas cruces.

> (Here a double axe, here a torch spewing forth living fire,
>   Criss-cross the binding ring with its fine diamond.
> A strong spirit, steadfast, victor over all,
>   fearlessly repulses perils and savage torments.)[16]

Once Posthumus has impetuously given the ring away, he must find such courage within himself to survive the loss of Imogen and his now ambivalent position in the war between Britain and Rome.

The Second Birth of the Lion's Whelp

According to the First Gentleman in *Cymbeline,* Imogen's bridegroom is the one remaining son of a renowned warrior family called the Leonati, a surname awarded them as a result of the extraordinary courage displayed by the father in battles against the invading army of Julius Caesar. Posthumus's father

> Was call'd Sicilius, who did join his honour
> Against the Romans with Cassibelan,
> But had his titles by Tenantius, whom
> He served with glory and admired success:
> So gain'd the sur-addition Leonatus:
> And had (besides this gentleman in question)
> Two other sons, who in the wars o' th' time
> Died with their swords in hand. For which their father,

Then old, and fond of issue, took such sorrow
That he quit being; and his gentle lady,
Big of this gentleman (our theme) deceas'd
As he was born. The king he takes the babe
To his protection, calls him Posthumus Leonatus,
Breeds him, and makes him of his bed-chamber,
Puts to him all the learnings that his time
Could make him the receiver, of which he took,
As we do air, fast as 'twas minister'd,
And in's spring became a harvest.

(1.1.29–46)

The name "Posthumus" refers literally to the fact that the child was born after the death of his father Sicilius, a situation further complicated by the death of his mother in childbirth. However, there are suggestions in this name as well of a poetic reference by Shakespeare to the spiritual rebirth of Posthumus after the "death" of his former vengeful self much later in the tragicomedy. The young man metaphorically succeeds himself as one reborn after the death of the old Adam within.

His Latin surname Leonatus means lion's whelp, a key term that emerges significantly in Jupiter's oracle: "When as a lion's whelp shall, to himself unknown, without seeking find, and be embrac'd by a piece of tender air . . . then shall Posthumus end his miseries, Britain be fortunate, and flourish in peace and plenty" (5.4.138–45). Although the First Gentleman and Imogen praise Posthumus to the skies for his accomplishments as a young courtier, at the beginning of the play he is still unknown to himself. Not only has he no remembrances of his own family, but he also has no inkling yet of his innate spiritual potential for transcending the conventional honor code of his times. In fact, Posthumus responds at first very conventionally to the slander of Imogen; he becomes murderously jealous and condemns his wife to death without ever hearing her side of the story. Later, however, he woefully condemns himself to death for such foolishness. Thus achievement of self-knowledge in the context of this particular play means to accept oneself humbly in the manner of Socrates as a person ignorant of the truth, then in the manner of a proto-Christian as a sinner like all the rest of humanity, and finally as a poor fallen creature with no special rights to judge the morality of others. Posthumus must painfully learn to forgive others as he hopes in turn to be forgiven by God for his moral arrogance.

The story of Posthumus's spiritual growth in *Cymbeline* parallels much of the legendary lore surrounding his totem animal. First, the lion is a solar animal that gives its name to the sign of the zodiac called Leo. Topsell, whose material on the beasts derives from Konrad Gesner, informs us that,

Edward Topsell's depiction of the lion (borrowed from Konrad Gesner) in *The Historie of the Four-footed Beastes* (London: William Jaggard, 1607), 457. Reprinted by permission of the Folger Shakespeare Library (STC 24123).

> When the sun comes to that sign [Leo], the vehement heat of the sun burns the earth and dries up the rivers. And because the lion is also of a hot nature and seems to partake of the substance and quantity of the sun, he has that place in the heavens. In heat and force, the lion excels all other beasts, as the sun does all other stars.[17]

This information warns us that the lion's whelp will be hot headed, fiery of temper, and intemperate if once provoked to wrath. Second, the lion is extremely intelligent, a fact that accords with the First Gentleman's claim that Posthumus was an apt student as a boy in Cymbeline's court. Third, the lion epitomizes courage and ferocity, which is why it is so often associated with royalty. Although we do indeed see Posthumus display courage on the battlefield, unfortunately we also see him act with ill-considered ferocity toward his innocent bride. Fourth, the lion is extremely proud, "resembling in all things a princely majesty," according to Topsell (ed. South, 1981, 129), and it is obviously this quality of Posthumus's nature that must be humbled. On the other hand, the lion is not easily angered insists the Cambridge *Bestiary;* he becomes violent only if he is first wounded:

> Any decent human ought to pay attention to this. For men do get angry when they are not wounded, and they oppress the innocent although the law of Christ bids them to let even the guilty go free. (White 1960, 9)

The above difference between himself and the lion must be learned by Posthumus, and fortunately it is.

In addition, like the eagle, the lion has excellent sight. Topsell reports that "They sleep with their eyes open" (ed. South, 1981, 127), a characteristic that equates the Lion with Christ, according to the Cambridge *Bestiary:*

> In this very way, Our Lord also, while sleeping in the body, was buried after being crucified—yet his Godhead was awake. As it is said in the *Song of Songs,* 'I am asleep and my heart is awake', or, in the Psalm, 'Behold, he that keepeth Israel shall neither slumber nor sleep.' (White 1960, 8).

Physiologus, who is the source of all the above, adds that "Jacob, blessing his son Judah, said, 'Judah is a lion's whelp' " (Curley 1979, 3). Hence Shakespeare associates not only Imogen with Christ in *Cymbeline* but also Posthumus Leonatus in his role as the lion's whelp. This unconscious *imitatio Christi* on the part of both Imogen and Posthumus throughout the play foreshadows "the monstrous birth" soon to take place, even as it also reminds us of the innate human potential to understand Beauty, Truth, Goodness, and Justice through Reason, or our ability to strive to become a little more like divinity and less like beasts during our brief life on earth.

That man's ascent to godliness was a possibility accepted by Renaissance Platonists can be seen in the following passage from *The Courtiers Academie* by Count Haniball Romei of Ferrara:

> Whereupon, calling unto him [Adam], he (the divine artificer) said "Live, O Adam, in what life pleaseth thee best and take unto thyself those gifts which thou esteemest most dear." From this so liberal a grant had our free will its original, so that it is in our power to live like a plant, a living creature, like a man, and lastly like an angel; for if a man addict himself only to feeding and nourishment he becometh a plant, if to things sensual he is a brute beast, if to things reasonable and civil he groweth a celestial creature; but if he exalt the beautiful gift of his mind to things invisible and divine he transformeth himself into an angel and, to conclude, becometh the son of God."[18]

This courtier's manual was translated into English in 1598 by "I. K." Romei's ideas derive from Cicero, from Pico de la Mirandola's "Oration on the Dignity of Man," and from Juan Luis Vives' "Fable About Man." The latter describes man as an actor in the great theater of the world striving to win the applause of the gods:

> He would change himself so as to appear under the mask of a plant, acting a simple life without any power of sensation. Soon after, he withdrew and returned on the stage as a moral satirist, brought into the shapes of a thousand wild beasts: namely the angry and raging lion, the rapacious and devouring wolf, the fierce and wild boar, the cunning little fox, the lustful and filthy sow, the

timid hare, the envious dog, the stupid donkey. After doing this, he was out of sight for a short time; then the curtain was drawn back and he returned a man, prudent, just, faithful, human, kindly, and friendly, who went about the cities with the others, held the authority and obeyed in turn, cared for the public interest and welfare, and was finally in every way a political and social being.[19]

Vives's important fable was also the source of Calderón de la Barca's *auto* "El gran teatro del mundo" and his tragicomedy *La vida es sueño.* I am certain that the Elizabethans knew it well since their work is full of references to the world as a theater metaphor, and the Globe Theatre itself literalized the *topos.* Vives's reference to man playing the parts of brute beasts on the stage derives from the Roman mimes in which animals symbolized human passions (cf. Cicero *De oratore* ii.59–60).[20]

As we have seen, however, brute beasts were often the symbolic teachers for Renaissance men and women of the higher goals of humanity as well. Topsell, for example, questions, "Why should any man living fall to do evil against his conscience or at the temptation of the Devil seeing that a lion will never yield?" (ed. South, 1981, 4). Yet it is just here that Posthumus is least like the lion, since he fails the test of conscience when he accepts Iachimo's vicious slander as a truth to be acted upon. For Shakespeare, the question of Free Will is clearly at issue in Posthumus's fall from grace, and the playwright's answer appears to be thoroughly Augustinian. St. Augustine believed that since the Fall, men and women have been incapable of choosing the right action, that is, of exercising their Free Will correctly; hence the only possibility of salvation lies through Divine Mercy or Grace. But Grace must be asked for by a truly penitent sinner, one who has come to know himself and his own moral failings that make him as guilty as everyone else. When Posthumus does at last ask for forgiveness, he is immediately rewarded by the descent of a merciful Jupiter.

Curiously enough, the lion is also symbolic of this very Divine Mercy in that he was widely believed to spare those he defeated. According to the Cambridge *Bestiary,* "The compassion of lions . . . is clear from innumerable examples—for they spare the prostrate; they allow such captives as they come across to go back to their own country; they prey on men rather than on women, and they do not kill children except when they are very hungry" (White 1960, 9). Topsell agrees with this lore, pointing out that "The clemency of lions is worthy of commendation and to be wondered at in beasts, for if one prostrates himself unto them as if in petition for his life, they often spare him, except in extremity of famine" (ed. South, 1981, 133). Likewise in *Cymbeline,* Posthumus Leonatus spares Iachimo after defeating him on the battlefield and then spares him again in 5.5 with the words, "The power that I have on you, is to spare you: / The malice towards you, to forgive you" (419–20).

De Tervarent adds that as a symbol of Divine Mercy the lion becomes a common attribute of justice in iconography (1958, 86). For example, the throne of Solomon had two lions on the armrests (I Kings 10:19) to indicate that justice could always be found before it. In imitation of Solomon's throne, James I of England also dispensed his justice from a throne with lions carved on the armrests. In the tragicomedy, Shakespeare's King Cymbeline finally learns royal mercy from Posthumus Leonatus, and, at the end of the tragicomedy, he too dispenses merciful justice by pardoning everyone and proclaiming a general peace in the land.

For Physiologus, however, the most important aspect of the lion concerns its strange origins:

> when the lioness has given birth to her whelp, she brings it forth dead. And she guards it for three days until its sire arrives on the third day and, breathing into its face on the third day, he awakens it. Thus did the almighty Father of all awaken from the dead on the third day the first born of every creature [cf. Col. 1:15]. Jacob, therefore, spoke well, "Judah is a lion's whelp; who has awakened him?" [Gen. 49.9]. (Curley 1979, 4)

The *Bestiary* quotes Jacob prophesying as well that, " 'He shall sleep like a lion, and the lion's whelp shall be raised' " (White 1960, 9). Likewise in *Cymbeline,* Posthumus sleeps like the lion with his spiritual eyes open in 5.5, at which time he has a vision of both his lost family and of Jupiter, who promises to raise him to good fortune. Although a despairing Posthumus had at first yearned for death in order to atone for the supposed murder of Imogen, the quarrelsome ghost of his father breathes new life into him and evokes Jupiter to do the same. The lion is therefore a symbol, like the phoenix, of resurrection.

E. P. Evans cites numerous examples in the decorations of medieval churches throughout Europe of this scene of the lion breathing life into its whelps, or roaring over them as some mythographers insisted it did, as a symbol of the resurrection (84–85). He adds that

> At a somewhat later period the lion, as a symbol of Resurrection, was sculptured on public buildings of a secular character and on private dwellings; it was also engraved on pieces of armour and especially on helmets, often with the legend *Domine vivifica me secundum verbum tuum,* or some other appropriate device, expressive of the hope of the warrior that, if slain in battle, he might be raised up on the last day. (1969, 85)

Early theologians, moreover, explain the association between St. Mark the Evangelist and his attribute the lion as deriving from the importance of the Resurrection scene in the Gospel of St. Mark, which was usually read at Eastertide (Evans 1969, 85). Indeed allusions to this resurrection myth of the lion are so widespread in the visual and verbal ecclesiastical arts of the

Middle Ages and the Renaissance that there can be little doubt that Shakespeare's audience knew all about the lion's whelp raised from the dead by its father's breath or roar as an analogy to the moment when "God the Father by His immense power called to life His Son on the third day" (Durand, quoted in Evans 1969, 85).

In act 5, scene 4 of *Cymbeline,* Shakespeare concocts a strange pagan ritual of evocation to give dramatic form to the lion myth as it pertains to the life of Posthumus, who is now condemned to die the following day. We have already heard Iachimo refer to sleep as the "ape of death," so that when Posthumus falls asleep on stage in act 5, we can easily equate his unconsciousness with a kind of death not unlike that of Imogen's deathlike sleep in the Welsh mountains. Thomas Sackville had compared sleep with death in the line, "Heavy Sleepe, the cosin of Death," while Samuel Daniel had found an even closer relationship between the two, since for him, sleep was "brother to Death." According to Samuel C. Chew, the classical source of the metaphor is "Seneca's *Hercules Furiens* (line 1069) where Sleep is 'frater durae languide Mortis.' "[21] In any case, Posthumus is asleep, or as we would say today, "dead to the world" in 5.4, although his spiritual eyes are finally open.

At this liminal moment, the ghosts of Posthumus's long dead relatives enter, accompanied by solemn music, and they surround the sleeping man. The use of ancestral ghosts to conjure up a god or an action was, of course, a standard convention in the tragedies of Seneca, whose work Shakespeare undoubtedly studied as a schoolboy. In this case, the ghosts "circle Posthumus round as he lies sleeping" and chant to Jupiter one by one, in hopes of luring the deity down to earth. The father, Sicilius, demands that Jupiter, "Thy crystal window ope; look out; / no longer exercise / Upon a valiant race thy harsh / and potent injuries" (5.4.81–84). The mother reminds the god of his own justice, arguing that since her "son is good," he should not be suffering such miseries; while Posthumus's two brothers, displaying their bloody war wounds, threaten—with typical youthful extravagance—to rebel against Jupiter's rule if the god does not descend to help the last remaining Leonatus: "Help, Jupiter, or we appeal, / and from thy justice fly" (5.4.91–92). In this extraordinary play concerned with personal, social, and political reformation, it seems that even the deity must now reform himself or lose his position of authority.

The theatrical effect on an audience of the invocation of a god by music, by the slow circular dance of the ghosts in imitation of planetary motions and by the rhythms of vocal incantation, is stunning. Almost at once the god descends from the "heavens" on the back of his eagle and throws down a thunderbolt, which in itself has several important implications. First, the sound of thunder is like the bass voice of an organ pipe. Alonzo makes this association in act 3 of *The Tempest:* "and the thunder, / That deep and dreadful organ pipe. . . . It did bass my trespass" (3.97–99). He refers to the roar of the portative organ (often played by angels in Renaissance paintings) that calls sinners to justice, since it can play all the notes of "World Harmony."[22] Second, the bolt of lightning may signify, according to Carl Jung, "a sudden, unexpected, and overpowering change of psychic condition." In his discussion of this strange transformational power of lightning, Jung quotes the religious thinker Jakob Boehme, who wrote, "if I could in my Flesh comprehend the Flash, which I very well see and know how it is, I could clarify or transfigure my Body therewith, so that it would shine with a bright light and glory. And then it would no more resemble and be conformed to the bestial Body, but to the angels of God."[23] Such a complete transformation within a living man is obviously an impossibility, but in *Cymbeline* at least a partial change of psychic condition does occur within the sleeping Posthumus because of the lightning bolt. Not surprisingly, Jupiter then promises a change in fortune for the penitent.

In the context of Posthumus's dream vision, Jupiter's thunder corresponds to the fatherly lion's roar that will revive the lion's whelp in the play. Indeed Sicilius reminds the god of his neglected paternal duties:

I died whilst in the womb he stay'd,
    attending Nature's law:
Whose father then (as men report
    thou orphans' father art)
Thou shouldst have been, and shielded him
    from this earth-vexing smart.

(5.4.37–42)

But, in keeping with the lion myth, Jupiter tells the earthly father to "Be content, / Your low-laid son our godhead will uplift" (5.4.102–3). At this point the lion's whelp will undergo his second birth now that new life has been supernaturally breathed into him by the roar of the thunderbolt. We may also note that Sicilius describes the god's breath as follows: "He came in thunder; his celestial breath / Was sulphurous to smell" (5.4.114–15), making it possible for us to interpret the first part of Jupiter's written oracle a little more accurately than does the Roman Soothsayer at the end of the play with his somewhat forced Latin pun on the word "mulier" to refer to Imogen as air. The oracle begins, "When as a lion's whelp shall, to himself unknown, without seeking find, and be embrac'd by a piece of tender air" (5.4.138–40), which a Christian audience of the period would immediately understand as being embraced by a supernatural spirit, since spirits were then thought to be made of air. The Soothsayer's interpretation is partially correct, however, in that Imogen's spiritual qualities cannot be denied, and she does later embrace Posthumus physically. But now asleep, the lion's whelp is unknown to himself or unconscious; although he did not search for his dead family, their ghosts appear to plead on his behalf; and finally Posthumus Leonatus is miraculously embraced by the sulphurous breath or life-giving air of Jupiter, loving father of orphans.

Another legendary characteristic of the lion is the belief that he always sleeps with his eyes open, which is why stone lions often guard the entrances to medieval and Renaissance churches. Physiologus says that open-eyed sleep was also true of Christ, who "physically slept on the cross, but his divine nature always keeps watch in the right hand of the Father [cf. Matt. 26:64]" (Curley 1979, 4). In a like manner, Posthumus sleeps physically but keeps his inner eyes open to visions of divinity.

The hero's sleep of death is a necessary prelude for this miracle of spiritual renewal to occur in *Cymbeline*. According to a popular Neo-platonic belief, the soul could actually leave the body at times to commune with the airy spirit world in a state of ecstasy, but then it had to return to the body once more in order to "understand" its own spiritual nature through the five senses. Christopher Goodman describes this kind of out-of-body experience in *The Fall of Man* (1616):

> Though the present condition of man be earthly, made of the earth, feeds on the earth, and is dissolved to the earth, and therefore the soul doth less discover herself by her proper actions than doth the material body; yet it is not unknown to philosophy that there is an ecstasis of the soul, wherein she is carried in a trance, wholly and only intending the intellectual functions, while the body lies dead like a carcass, without breath sense motion or nourishment, only as a pledge to assure us of the soul's return. (quoted by Tillyard 1959, 77)

Such an experience during sleep was apparently a common part of initiation rites for the mystery religions of antiquity. However, according to Renaissance Neoplatonic writers, unless the ecstasy is then translated into sensory experience, the soul cannot gain knowledge of itself and its nature and must remain an unenlightened prisoner within the body. As Tillyard reminds us, John Donne refers to this very paradox in his poem *The Ecstasy:*

> So must pure lovers' souls descend
>   To affections and to faculties
> Which sense may reach and apprehend;
>   Else a great prince in prison lies.
>
> (1959, 77)

Without self knowledge, the imprisoned soul cannot gain salvation.

Perhaps this essentially Aristotelian belief that sense must inform the intelligence or soul lies behind the remarkable emphasis on the senses that Shakespeare imparts to Posthumus's extra-sensory dream vision. The ghosts introduce the sound of music and their vocal lamentations, to say nothing of the vision of their very presence onstage to the dreamer's and our senses. Jupiter brings down the sight of himself on his eagle, the sound and flash of his thunderbolt, and the sulphurous smell of his breath. Although there appears to be no direct reference to taste in this scene, the sense of touch is not forgotten, since the deity leaves a tablet on Posthumus's breast for the penitent to handle and read after he awakens and to carry away with him because it reminds him mysteriously of his own life.

Speaking of the use of music in Shakespeare's plays in general, R. W. Ingram remarks that

> The vision scenes are reminiscent of archaic dumbshows. They may read as though they are dead on the printed page, but on the stage, clothed in sound— especially music—and spectacle they come to life. Their musical parts are vital and only when judged solely as poetry do they suffer. The slackening in poetic quality or feeling is compensated for by the music and the theatrical effects of the shows accompanying them, by the emotional impact of pomp, mystery, and music. Librettos are rarely of much poetic worth because they are not meant to stand alone, and the vision scenes are very much like short librettos.[24]

Through a combination of such ritualized music, dance, and poetry in *Cymbeline,* Shakespeare brings the pagan underworld up to and heaven down to the stage level, or to earth, and dramatically realizes in Jupiter's descent the prophecy of Psalm 102:17–20:

> He will regard the prayer of the destitute,
>   and not despise their prayer.
> This shall be written for the generation to come: and the
>   people which shall be created shall praise the Lord.
> For he hath looked down from the height of his sanctuary;
>   from heaven did the Lord behold the earth;
> To hear the groaning of the prisoner; to loose those that
>   are appointed to death.

After the vision, a messenger appears and tells Posthumus's gaoler to "Knock off his manacles, bring your prisoner to the king" (5.4.193–94). Meanwhile Imogen has—through disguise—escaped her own imprisonment to both the Queen and to Posthumus, who from now on must see her as his "friend" rather than as his manacled bond-servant.

I have argued elsewhere that the descent of Jupiter in *Cymbeline* is a deliberate Shakespearean analogue to the immanent descent of Christ.[25] Since the name of the Christian God could not by law be spoken on the English stage during the early seventeenth century, "Jove" was, and still is, a standard English euphemism for the deity. Even in Catholic Italy, Dante referred to Christ as "supreme Jove, who for us on earth was crucified," and Petrarch evoked his God as "eternal Jove" (Evans 1969, 309–10). According to Jean Seznec, moreover, the Italian humanist Mutianus Rufus wrote to a friend, "You, since Jupiter, the best and greatest god, is propitious to you, may despise lesser gods in silence. When I say Jupiter, understand me to mean Christ and the true God."[26] Therefore, Renaissance audiences would surely have recognized the Christian significance of the descending Jupiter in Posthumus's theatrical dream vision.

The very fact that Jupiter descends on the back of an eagle further reinforces the Christian allusion. According to Sicilius,

> the holy eagle,
> Stoop'd, as to foot us: his ascension is
> More sweet than our blest fields: his royal bird
> Prunes the immortal wing, and cloys his beak,
> As when his god is pleased.

$$(5.4.115-19)$$

The suggestion here seems to be that Christ's ascension to Heaven will prove sweeter for humanity than the pagan promise of an afterlife for heroes in the Elysian Fields. In any case, the Renaissance ornithographer Ulisse Aldrovandi asserts firmly in 1599 that the eagle itself is a symbol of Christ. Aldrovandi cites as his source St. Ambrose, who pointed out three major similarities between Christ and the bird that flies higher than any other: (1) as the eagle eats snakes, Christ conquers the devil; (2) as the eagle protects its nest, Christ hovers defensively over the church; and (3) as the eagle pushes its young out of the nest if they cannot stare directly at the sun, Christ turns away from those who are lacking in faith.[27]

However, the god Jupiter has other dramatic functions in the play besides theatrically prefiguring the birth of Christ and fulfilling the myth of the lion's breath in respect to Posthumus, the lion's whelp. First, he represents Divine Providence, or purposeful fate, since he controls the lives of everyone in the play and ultimately brings together all the irrational elements of its many interweaving plots. Second, he symbolizes the theological concept of Divine Grace in that he forgives the repentant sinner and thus provides an example of mercy to Posthumus, who in turn provides an example to Cymbeline. Third, he signifies Divine Justice. He allows Cloten to be killed and the wicked Queen to die of despair after her son's disappearance, thereby alloting them the same deaths they had wished for Posthumus and Imogen. Fourth, he appears as a liberator— freeing Posthumus from his bonds, Imogen from her idealization of human love, the Wild Boys from their cave of ignorance, Belarius from his disgrace and banishment, and Cymbeline from his mistaken view of the world. Finally, as I have stated above, he demonstrates to the senses of the audience (through his miraculous descent) the doctrine of Christ's Incarnation.

The Triumph of the Lamb Over the Lion

Returning to the image of Posthumus as a lion, we must also recall Imogen's own association of herself with a sacrificial lamb. When she learns that Posthumus has ordered Pisanio to murder her, she begs the servant to "Prithee, despatch: / The lamb entreats the butcher. Where's thy knife?" (3.4.97–98). But Pisanio refuses to perform the rite of sacrifice since he knows that an immoral order need not and should not be obeyed. Even without dying, however, Imogen ultimately manages to overcome the lion's intemperate rage. According to a French emblem by Gilles Corrozet, humility is what finally allows the helpless lamb to triumph over the pride and ferocity of the lion. Under the motto "Triumphe de humilité" ("Triumph of humility"), Corrozet's verse states,

> Vn doulx Aigneau soubz son pied tient
> Le Lyon des bestes le prince.
> Humilité maistre, & vince
> Les plus grands, que terre soustient.

> (A sweet Lamb holds under his foot
> the Lion, prince of beasts.
> Humility masters and conquers
> the greatest ones that earth sustains.)[28]

As we have seen earlier, Imogen first learns humility herself by serving as a cook for Wild Men and later as a page to the Roman Lucius, her country's enemy. Posthumus learns humility, too, by repenting of his violence toward Imogen and then by changing into the clothes of a simple peasant to help the Wild Men fight off the Romans invading Britain.

Theatrically the tragicomedy constantly emphasizes humility rather than pride as an important character trait for those who wish to enjoy love in the form of Anteros or the love of virtue. Indeed the play functions in the theater as a type of shared initiation rite designed to shock lovers and courtiers (both on and offstage) with an astonishing revelation of humble human mortality when face to face with divine immortality. This is the same self-knowledge that Marsyas finally gains when flayed by Apollo during Ovid's cruel Dionysian ritual in *The Metamorphoses*.

In this chapter I have discussed the refining of Posthumus through the fire of suffering, as gold is tried in the furnace to separate the pure metal from alloys. The experience purges him of pride and teaches him that a wife is not a bond-maid to be boasted of and wagered on but a dear friend to be cherished. I have also pointed to the significance of the diamond ring as a symbol of Imogen's incorruptible virtue, as representative of the

Triumphe de humilité.

Vn doulx Aigneau foubz fon pied tient
Le Lyon des beftes le prince.
Humilité maiftriæ, & vince
Les plus grands, que terre fouftient.

Pride bows to Humility in Gilles Corrozet, *Hecatomgraphie* (Paris: Denys Ianot, 1543), sig. F ii verso. Reprinted by permission of the Folger Shakespeare Library (PQ 1607 C6 a543 Cage).

conjoining of beauty and goodness in such a virtuous person, and as a protective talisman of courage for the banished Posthumus. In *Cymbeline,* however, the postmarital bestowal of gifts between husband and wife is a maimed ritual of love, not only because it is interrupted by Cymbeline's entrance in a state of fury but also because Posthumus's view of its meaning and of the value of the exchanged tokens is a distorted one.

In addition, I have explained the myth of the lion and its relevance to

Posthumus as Leonatus, the lion's whelp who is twice born according to Physiologus. As part of the hero's rite of initiation into a mystery religion, Jupiter plays the role of the paternal lion and breathes new life into the sleeping hero. This action echoes symbolically the Christian doctrines of Redemption and Resurrection. However, the human lion must first relinquish his excessive pride and allow himself to be overcome by the humility of the sacrificial lamb, who is innocent and always willing to be slaughtered for the sake of her beloved, a ritual that does not take place in *Cymbeline*.

Notes

1. Edward Topsell, *The Historie of Fovre-footed Beastes* (London: William Jaggard, 1607), 20–21.

2. See Beryl Rowland, *Blind Beasts: Chaucer's Animal World* (Kent, Ohio: The Kent State University Press, 1971), 80.

3. See Peter Daly, *Emblem Theory: Recent German Contributions to the Characterization of the Emblem Genre* (Nendeln, Liechtenstein: KTO Press, 1979), 19.

4. George Wither, *A Collection of Emblemes, Ancient and Moderne* (London, 1635), 162; hereafter cited parenthetically.

5. Otto van Veen, *Emblemes of Love* (Antwerp, 1608), 128–29.

6. Claude Paradin, *The Heroicall Devises of M. Claudius Paradin (1591),* A Photoreproduction with an Introduction by John Doebler (Delmar, N.Y.: Scholars' Facsimiles & Reprints, 1984), 213.

7. Geffrey Whitney, *A Choice of Emblemes* (Leiden: Christopher Plantin, 1586), 139.

8. Sir John Davies, *Nosce teipsum* (London: Richard Field, 1599), 7.

9. See E. M. W. Tillyard, *The Elizabethan World Picture: A Study of the Idea of Order in the Age of Shakespeare, Donne and Milton* (London: Chatto and Windus, 1943), 65; hereafter cited parenthetically. Although this work probably should have been called "Notes on the World View of Renaissance Neoplatonists and Poets" rather than implying that it would be a report on all Elizabethan thought, it remains an extremely useful little book despite the recent criticism of it by Jonathan Dollimore and his Marxist followers.

10. See Stephan Batman, trans., *Batman vppon Bartholome, his Booke De Proprietatibus Rerum* (London: Thomas East, 1582), sig. 255ᵛ.

11. Gilles Corrozet, *Hecatomgraphie* (Paris: Denys Ianot, 1543), sig. Mv. Translation by Roger T. Simonds.

12. See E. P. Evans, *Animal Symbolism in Ecclesiastical Architecture* (1896; reprint Detroit: Gale Research Company, 1969), 45; hereafter cited parenthetically.

13. See *Physiologus,* trans. Michael J. Curley (Austin: University of Texas Press, 1979), 64; hereafter to be cited parenthetically.

14. See Guy De Tervarent, *Attributs et symboles dans l'art profane 1450–1600* (Geneva: Librairie E. Droz, 1958), 147–48, col. 1. Translation by Roger T. Simonds.

15. Ibid.

16. Hadrianus Junius, *Emblemata* (Antwerp: Christopher Plantin, 1565), 57.

17. See *Topsell's Histories of Beasts* ed. Malcolm South (Chicago: Nelson Hall, 1981), 140; hereafter to be cited parenthetically. For other information on Renaissance lion lore, see Dale B. J. Randall, "A Glimpse of Leontes Through an Onamastic Lens," *Shakespeare Jahrbuch* (1988); 123–29.

18. Quoted by Tillyard, 68. But since Tillyard mistakenly assigns the passage to the chapter "On Beauty" rather than to the chapter "Of humane Loue," where it is actually found, see also Count Haniball Romei, *The Courtiers Academie,* trans. I. K. (London: Valentine Sims, 1598), sigs. G4 and G4v.

19. Juan Luis Vives, "A Fable About Man," trans. Nancy Lenkeith, in *The Renaissance Philosophy of Man,* ed. Ernst Cassirer, Paul Oskar Kristeller, and John Herman Randall, Jr. (Chicago: The University of Chicago Press, 1948), 389.

20. Ibid., n.4.

21. See Samuel C. Chew, *The Pilgrimage of Life* (New Haven: Yale University Press, 1962), 234–35. See also S. Viswanathan, "Sleep and Death: The Twins in Shakespeare," *Comparative Drama* 13 (1979): 49–64.

22. See Leo Spitzer's comprehensive study *Classical and Christian Ideas of World Harmony* (Baltimore: Johns Hopkins University Press, 1963).

23. See C. G. Jung, *The Archetypes and the Collective Unconscious,* trans. R. F. C. Hull (New York: Pantheon Books, 1959), 295. Jung also writes that "Lactantius (*Works,* trans. by Fletcher, I, p. 470) says '. . . the light of the descending God may be manifest in all the world as lightning.' This refers to Luke 17:24: '. . . as the lightning that lighteneth . . . so shall the Son of Man be in his day.' " See *Archetypes,* 295, n.7.

24. See R. W. Ingram, "Musical Pauses and the Vision Scenes in Shakespeare's Last Plays," in *Pacific Coast Studies in Shakespeare,* ed. Waldo F. McNeir and Thelma N. Greenfield (Eugene: University of Oregon Books, 1966), 243.

25. See Peggy Muñoz Simonds, "Jupiter, His Eagle, and BBC-TV," *Shakespeare on Film Newsletter* 10 (December 1985): 3.

26. Jean Seznec, *The Survival of the Pagan Gods,* trans. Barbara F. Sessions (New York: Pantheon Books, Inc., 1953), 99 n.72.

27. Ulisse Aldrovandi, *Ornithologiae hoc est de avibus historiae,* 3 vols. (Bononiae: Franciscum de Francis Senensem, 1599), vol. 1, 66.

28. See Corrozet, sig. Fiiv. Translated by Roger T. Simonds.

9

The Five Senses and the Limits of Perception

Sense outsides knows, the Soule through all things sees,
Sense circumstance, she doth the substance view;
Sense sees the barke, but she the life of trees;
Sense heares the sounds, but she the Concords true.
                                    —Sir John Davies, *Nosce Teipsum*

One of the most popular *topoi* in the arts of both the Middle Ages and the
Renaissance was the visual representation or literary description of the
five senses, which were viewed with considerable suspicion at first.[1]
Medieval Christians believed that the Capital Sins attacked the human
soul through the five senses, which must be guarded, therefore, like the
gates of a city or a citadel against impure sensory stimulation. According
to Carl Nordenfalk,

> The distrustful attitude of the Church towards the Senses is perhaps most
> strikingly expressed in the Sacrament of Extreme Unction. This consisted in
> anointing the sense organs by which the dying man may have sinned, so that, to
> quote a Sacramentary from Oignies, described by the Benedictine travellers
> Martene and Durand, "the stains which through the Five Senses and weakness
> of mind and body might adhere to them, thanks to this spiritual medicine and
> the grace of God might be purged."[2]

The senses were primarily associated in medieval thought with the distrac-
tions of love, a correspondence that continued into later Neoplatonism
with certain important revisions.

Ficino, who carefully distinguished between lust (Eros) and love (Anteros), associated the senses of smell, taste, and touch, with lust alone.
These lower senses, he explained, were of no real use to the philosopher.
On the other hand, he considered the senses of seeing and hearing to be
the means by which we perceive and enjoy beauty, which inspires us in
turn to true love and leads us ultimately to divinity.

> When we say "love," understand "the desire for beauty." For this is the
> definition of love among all philosophers. Beauty is a certain grace which most

300

often originates above all in a harmony of several things. It is three-fold. For from the harmony of several virtues in souls there is a grace; from the harmony of several colors and lines in bodies a grace arises; likewise there is a very great grace in sounds from the harmony of several tones. Beauty, therefore is three-fold: of souls, of bodies, and of sounds. That of souls is known through the intellect; that of bodies is perceived through the eyes; that of sounds is perceived only through the ears. . . . What need is there for smell? What need is there for taste, or touch? These senses perceive odors, flavors, heat, cold, softness and hardness, and similar things. None of these is human beauty since they are simple forms, whereas the beauty of the human body requires a harmony of different parts. Love regards the enjoyment of beauty as its end. That pertains only to the intellect, to seeing and to hearing. Love, therefore, is limited to these three; an appetite which follows the other senses is not called Love, but lust or madness.[3]

This profound shift of attitude toward the senses of seeing and hearing by Ficino and his followers is of paramount importance to the development of Renaissance art and music, which were often designed to inspire the viewer or the listener through sensory stimulation to desire intellectual beauty or virtue itself.

True Platonism, of course, distrusted the data of *all* the five senses. Plato makes this clear in Book VII of *The Republic* through the Parable of the Cave. Here the soul or mind is shown figuratively to reside within a dark cave, which is analogous to the body. Since the soul receives information only through the imperfect senses, any knowledge it acquires can be no more than opinion in this situation. Only through learning to reason about the eternal Ideas without recourse to the senses can the soul escape from its dark prison and achieve enlightenment. As David Summers points out, Plato's "definition of the relation between reason and sense had the broadest and deepest influence, and largely on his authority it was assumed and believed that no wisdom, or even knowledge, was to be found in the realm of sense. Precisely because it showed us most about this realm, sight was most often deceived, since what it showed us was always fleeting and incomplete; and when catalogues of the deceptions of the senses were drawn up, deceptions of sight always far outnumbered those of the other senses."[4] The senses provided us with no more than shadows in contrast to the reality of Forms or innate Ideas.

Plato's pupil Aristotle disagreed, however, arguing that the soul did not contain innate ideas and that it could only reason about the information it received through sensory perceptions in terms of the common sense, which integrated all the perceptions. "To the functions of the common sense besides the perception of general and special qualities, belongs the perception of sensation itself. . . . The distinction between the sensations of different senses, too, is made by the common sense. Finally, the coordination of the sense-organs' rest, which takes place during sleep, results from the suspension of the common sense."[5]

Renaissance Neoplatonists attempted to combine these two incompatible views. Therefore, in an explanation of the "truth" of perspective in art, which is achieved through sensory deception, Lomazzo argues from Aristotle, St. Thomas and other scholastics, as follows:

> But if any man shall object, that the images doe not represent naturall & artificiall thinges to the *eie*, but to the *vnderstanding* and to the *memory*, I reply, that it is true that the finall ende of *images* is the vnderstanding, but the *eie* is the immediate, according to that of *Aristotle, there is nothing in the vnderstanding, which was not first in the sense:* and so it must needes be, that before these images can come to our vnderstanding, they bee first in the eie: that is, they must first be seene.[6]

Lomazzo attempts here to save the sense of vision from Plato's criticism so that artists can exploit it as a vehicle of truth, much as Shakespeare saves the sense of hearing—also often deceived or inadequately used—in *Cymbeline* so that poets and musicians can exploit it as a vehicle of truth.

In any case, the problem of the senses as easily duped and yet as necessary sources of information for the soul was constantly debated during the Renaissance and depicted through the various arts in England. In the visual arts, for example, tapestries illustrating personifications of the five senses with their attributes may still be seen today at the Elizabethan country houses Haddon Hall and Hardwick Hall in Derbyshire, while symbols of the five senses were also sculpted in plaster on the ceiling of the Long Gallery in Blickling Hall, Norfolk, a magnificent stately home built for Sir Henry Hobart, Lord Chief Justice to James I.

In English poetry of the Renaissance, Edmund Spenser adopted the medieval viewpoint in *The Faerie Queene* that the five senses were analogous to the gates of a castle and that they must be guarded against invasion by "lawlesse lustes, corrupt enuies, / And couetous aspectes (II.xi.8)."[7] Spenser describes the "House of Alma," or the body as the house of the soul, in Book II, canto xi:

> But in a body, which doth freely yeeld
>   His partes to reasons rule obedient,
> And letteth her that ought the scepter weeld,
>   All happy peace and goodly gouernment
>   Is setled there in sure establishment;
> There *Alma* like a virgin Queene most bright,
>   Doth florish in all beautie excellent:
>   And to her guestes doth bounteous banket dight,
> Attempted goodly well for health and for delight.

> (verse 2)

But war is waged by the vices against the five bulwarks of the castle, particularly against sight and hearing. The first gate is entered with ease by "Beautie, and money" (verse 9), while the second is soon breached by

Slaunderous reproches, and fowle infamies,
Leasings, backbytings, and vaine-glorious crakes,
Bad counsels, prayses, and false flatteries.

                                                                    (verse 10)

Of special interest to students of *Cymbeline* is that among the assailers of
the bulwark of smell in *The Faerie Queene* are "Puttockes, all in plumes
arayd" (verse 11), which tells us that Cloten's bird, the puttock, was itself a
symbol of the bad odor that the dramatic character himself is said to emit.
However, for Spenser, as for medieval commentators, touch is the most
heinous and dangerous of all the senses because of its association with
sexuality and other lower bodily functions.

Sir John Davies is less suspicious of the senses in his *Nosce Teipsum*
(Know Thyself), a philosophical poem on the order of Alexander Pope's
later *Essay on Man*. Although—like most poets of the period—a Neo-
platonist at heart, Davies argues the popular Aristotelian and scholastic
doctrine that the soul can gain knowledge of the world and thus of its own
different nature only through judicious use of the senses. In this poem, the
soul is once again likened to a queen, but to a queen imprisoned:

Yet in the Bodies prison so she lyes,
  As through the bodies windowes she must looke,
  Her diuerse powers of *Sense* to exercise,
  By gathering Notes out of the *Worlds* great Booke.

Nor can her selfe discourse, or iudge of ought,
  But what the sense Collects and home doth bring;
  And yet the power of her discoursing thought,
  From these Collections, is a Diuerse thing.[8]

For Davies, the senses represent a great power to be used by the reasonable soul in its study of God's creation, knowledge of which should lead
eventually to an understanding of God Himself.

This power is Sense, which from abroad doth bring
  The *colour, tast*, and *touch*, and *sent* and *sound*,
  The *quantitie*, and *shape* of euery thing,
  Within th' earths Center, or heauens Circle found.

This Power in parts made fit, fit objects takes,
  Yet not the things, but Formes of things receiues;
  As when a Seale in Waxe impression makes,
  The print therein, but not it selfe, it leaues.

And though things sensible be numberlesse,
  But onely fiue the *Senses* Organs bee;
  And in those fiue All things their Formes expresse,
  Which we can *touche, tast, feele*, or *heare*, or *see*.

> These are the windowes, through the which she viewes
>   The *light of knowledge,* which is lifes load-starre;
>   And yet whiles she these spectacles doth vse,
>   Oft worldly things seeme greater then they are.

(1599, 41)

In this last verse, Davies admits to the problem of "seeming" in the soul's effort to understand the information provided her by the five senses. This same dichotomy between appearance and reality, of course, is what worried Plato from the very beginning.

Like Ficino, Davies believes that the organs of sight and hearing provide important information for the mind, while the lower senses of taste, smell, and feeling principally serve the body. The poet's analysis of sight and hearing are, therefore, well worth reproducing here as fairly typical of Neoplatonic thought during the Renaissance. In respect to sight, Davies expounds as follows:

> *First* the two *Eyes,* which haue the *Seeing* power,
>   Stand as one watchman, Spie, or Sentinell,
>   Being plac'd aloft within the Heads high Tower;
>   And though both see, yet both but one thing tell.
>
> These Mirrors take into their little space,
>   The formes of *Moone* and *Sunne,* and euery *Starre,*
>   Of euery Bodie, and of euery place,
>   Which with the worlds wide Armes embraced are.

(1599, 42)

Then he pauses to remind us of the "eyes of the mind," which will outlast the eyes of the body and which have a different goal.

> Yet their best obiect, and their noblest vse,
>   Hereafter in another world will bee,
>   When God in them shall heauenly light infuse,
>   That face to face they may their *Maker* see.

On the other hand, our bodily eyes are significant, too,

> Here are they guides, which do the Bodie leade;
>   Which else would stumble in eternall night;
>   Here in this world they do much knowledge *reade,*
>   And are the Casements which admit most light;
>
> They are her farthest reaching Instrument,
>   Yet they no beames vnto their Obiects send,
>   But all the rayes are from their Obiects sent,
>   And in the *Eyes* with pointed Angles end.

If th' obiects be farre off, the rayes do meete
  In a sharpe point, and so things seeme but small;
  If they be neere, their rayes do spread and fleete,
  And make broade points, that things seeme great withall.

Lastly, Nine things to *Sight* required are,
  The *power* to see, the *light* the *visible* thing,
  Being not too *small,* too *thinne,* too *nigh,* too *farre,*
  Cleere space, and *time* the forme distinct to bring.

Thus see we how the *Soule* doth vse the Eyes,
  As Instruments of her quicke power of sight;
  Hence do th' Arts *Opticke,* and faire *painting* rise;
  Painting which doth all gentle minds delight.

                                                    (1599, 42–43)

Here Davies brings us back to Lomazzo's defense of the artistic use of perspective, in this case to serve the intellectual needs of "gentle minds."

The sense of hearing also has its part to play as an agent for the imprisoned soul, that "she her prison may with pleasure beare / Having such prospects All the world to view" (1599, 44). After a detailed description of the labyrinth of the inner ear in terms of a "maze," Davies discusses hearing as the most morally sensitive means of perception:

It is the slowest, yet the daintiest *Sense,*
  For euen the *eares* of such as haue no skill,
  Perceiue a discord, and conceiue Offence,
  And knowing not what is good, yet find the ill.

And though this *Sense* first gentle *Musicke* found,
  Her proper object is *the speech of men;*
  But that speech chiefly, which Gods herrulds found,
  When their Tongs vtter, what his Spirit did pen.

                                                    (1599, 44)

Davies refers here to the Bible, which Protestants believed must be regularly listened to as well as read silently by the worshipper. Since the word of God must enter the human ear to be most effective, this Protestant aspect of hearing will be of considerable importance to our understanding of *Cymbeline.*

Unlike Spenser, Davies has great respect for the sense of touche or "Feeling," which he likens both to a spider's web, an interesting metaphor for the nervous system, and to the root of a tree or plant.

Lastly the Feeling power, which is Lifes roote,
  Through euery living part it selfe doth shed,
  By *sinewes,* which extend from head to foote,
  And like a Net all ore the bodie spred.

Much like a subtill Spider, which doth sit
In middle of her Web, which spreadeth wide,
If ought do touch the vtmost threed of it,
She feeles it instantly on euery side.

(1599, 45)

In *Cymbeline,* when the king learns of his queen's treachery, he exclaims, "O my daughter, / That it was folly in me, thou mayst say, / And prove it in thy *feeling*" (5.566–68; italics added). At this point, Cymbeline believes the Queen to have poisoned Imogen in accordance with the confession he has just heard reported by Cornelius. Since the root of Imogen's life has supposedly been poisoned, she has experienced the pain of such a death through her sense of feeling, or so her father now believes.

George Chapman, another prominent contemporary of Shakespeare, also wrote on the five senses, employing the *topos* of the "banquet of the senses" in his 1595 narrative poem *Ovids Banquet of Sence.* Louise Vinge believes this controversial work to be concerned with the role of the senses in artistic creation, in this case, the creation of *The Art of Love,* because the poem describes the poet Ovid's sensual enjoyment of the charms of his muse and mistress Corinna after she emerges naked from a bathing pool in the emperor's garden. As Vinge summarizes the poem,

> He hears her singing, he smells her ointments, he sees her through the hedge. He tastes her kiss, and is finally allowed to let his hand touch her breast. The central point of the poem is the continuous discussion of how these experiences influence his creative powers as a poet, and how the two lovers mutually influence each other in a mystical union, for which the sensuous experiences form the necessary basis and the result of which will be the creation of a poem.[9]

The only problem with an aesthetic interpretation such as this of Chapman's poem is that Vinge fails to consider the type of art work that results from so much sensory gratification. Ovid's *The Art of Love* is an amusing didactic poem of instruction for lovers in the techniques of wanton Eros; the love it celebrates is adultery; and it ends appropriately with a description of the various positions for successful intercourse.

Within the poem, Ovid as satiric *persona* reveals the typical misogyny of the libertine when he claims, first, that all women are by nature wantons and then provides a catalog of famous nymphomaniacs, and, second, that women enjoy being raped. Such a poem might well be written after the sensual experiences Chapman describes of the voyeur Ovid, not only gazing lasciviously on beauty bare—like Actaeon from behind the bushes—but then tasting and touching as well. The author of *The Art of Love,* according to Chapman in his *Banquet of Sence,* has here gone sliding down the ladder of the senses in the garden of love instead of climbing upward to sight and hearing and finally experiencing a communion of souls with his muse and mistress. Thus Chapman's poem can only be a satire on sensory love. And, needless to say, after writing his famous mock handbook on seduction, *The Art of Love,* Ovid himself soon felt called upon to follow it with a mock recantation entitled *Remedia Amoris,* as Chapman well knew.

The Renaissance sonneteers, who also praise their muse's sensual charms, usually begin with a positive attitude toward sensory inspiration, but in the end, most admit that they must ultimately free their art from such images in order to reveal divine truth and divine love to the intellect through poetry.[10]

In addition, there was an extremely popular Renaissance play on the five senses, which Vinge also summarizes in detail (1975, 98–103). Entitled *Lingua,* it appeared in at least six different editions between 1607 and 1657. A comedy on the efforts of the tongue to be considered one of the senses, *Lingua* contains colorful masques praising and displaying the qualities and attributes of each of the five senses. Of special interest is the fact that Auditus is appointed "Lord Intelligencer to Psyche her majesty" (Vinge 1975, 99), although Sight is finally crowned as the most important of the senses.

Shakespeare himself has a great deal to say about the five senses in his narrative poem *Venus and Adonis* (1593) and all of it apparently positive, except that the poem—like Chapman's *Banquet of Sence*—is also a satire on physical love that is doomed to end with the death of the beloved. Irony is thus paramount in all Venus's sensory descriptions of Adonis's beauty. Perhaps more to the point, therefore, is Sonnet 141:

In faith I do not love thee with mine eyes,
For they in thee a thousand errors note;
But 'tis my heart that loves what they despise,
Who in despite of view is pleased to dote.
Nor are mine ears with thy tongue's tune delighted;
Nor tender feeling to base touches prone,
Nor taste, nor smell, desire to be invited
To any sensual feast with thee alone.
But my five wits, nor my five senses can
Dissuade one foolish heart from serving thee,
Who leaves unswayed the likeness of a man,
Thy proud heart's slave and vassal wretch to be.
  Only my plague thus far I count my gain,
  That she that makes me sin awards me pain.[11]

Stephen Booth has extensively explored the multiple ambiguities of this poem, which seems to pose an antithesis between what the senses report and what the speaker actually feels or knows.[12] The profound Shakespearean distrust expressed in the *Sonnets* of sensory information, or at least of our ability to interpret it correctly, derives from Plato and is also found throughout *Cymbeline*. In the play, only the sense of hearing offers real hope to a confused and sinful group of people. Yet hearing is the very sense that got them all into so much trouble in the first place.

Shakespeare's contemporary Francis Bacon, a practicing lawyer, not surprisingly employs a courtroom metaphor in respect to the senses. He argues that the information they supply must always be put on trial by reason and imagination before being accepted as true: "sense sends all kinds of images over to imagination for reason to judge of; and reason again when it has made its judgment and selection, sends them over to imagination before the decree can be put in execution."[13]

In this chapter I shall discuss the failure of sight and hearing to provide accurate knowledge of the world to Imogen, Posthumus, Cymbeline, and Iachimo, and the ways in which hearing ultimately saves them from their folly.

"Mine eyes were not in fault, for she was beautiful."

The most striking example of the failure of vision in *Cymbeline* is surely the king's uncritical love for his Queen, Imogen's wicked stepmother. Attracted by her outward beauty, Cymbeline marries a vicious and ambitious woman, whose bad counsel nearly destroys the kingdom. Even after he learns of her attempt to murder Imogen and of her hatred for his own person, which she also planned to destroy, Cymbeline still believes that her beauty must have indicated inner goodness:

> Mine eyes
> Were not in fault, for she was beautiful:
> Mine ears that heard her flattery, nor my heart
> That thought her like her seeming. It had been vicious
> To have mistrusted her.
>
> (5.5.62–66)

Nevertheless he finally does admit that indeed his love was "folly" (67).

Shakespeare's mistrust of outward beauty as a mask hiding inward corruption is later echoed in an emblem by George Wither. The *inscriptio* states that "Deformitie, *within may bee,* / *Where outward* Beauties *we doe see.*" The *pictura* shows an old and ugly woman holding the mask of a beautiful young woman before her wrinkled face. The *subscriptio* exhorts us to

> Looke well, I pray, upon this *Beldame,* here,
>   For, in her *habit,* though shee gay appeare,

You, through her youthfull *vizard,* may espy
Shee's of an old *Edition,* by her *Eye:*
And, by her wainscot face, it may bee seene,
Shee might your *Grandams* first *dry nurse* have been.

After this comic introduction to the "Loathly Lady," Wither explains the moral of the picture by Crispin van de Passe:

This is an *Emblem,* fitly shaddowing those,
Who making faire, and honest outward showes,
Are inwardly deform'd; and, nothing such,
As they to be suppos'd, have strived much.
They chuse their *words* and play well-acted *parts,*
But, hide most loathsome projects in their hearts;
And, when you think sweet *Friendship* to embrace,
Some ugly *Treason,* meets you in the face.

Wither then decries the painted faces of such "old Wantons" and similar false religious shows by hypocrites.

Take heed of such as these; and, (if you may)
Before you trust them, track them in their way.
Observe their footsteps, in their private *path:*
For, these (as 'tis beleev'd, the *Devill* hath)
Have *cloven feet;* that is, *two wayes* they goe;
One for their *ends,* and tother for a *show.*[14]

Cymbeline's Queen is a personification of just such a hypocrite, although no mention is made in the play of "cloven feet."

In act 1 she pretends to befriend Imogen and Posthumus, but instead she sees to it that Cymbeline discovers the two spouses together in the garden. She pretends to supply a good medicine to Pisanio, but actually she provides that which she believes to be a deadly poison. She encourages Cloten to pursue Imogen, although she knows that the princess has properly married Posthumus with Pisanio as witness: "the remembrancer of her to hold / The hand-fast to her lord" (1.6.77–78). She plots to put Cloten on the throne after the death of her husband, whom she will slowly kill by poison, and she advises the king to cease paying tribute to Rome, which causes a nearly disastrous war for Britain. Only the mysterious disappearance of her son Cloten can overcome her in the end. She sickens, goes mad with the despair she has wished for others, then confesses her evil deeds to Cornelius on her death-bed. Her only repentance is that her evil plots have failed. But her beautiful exterior has revealed nothing of this corrupt interior mind to her besotted husband during her lifetime.

Imogen makes the most direct comment on the inability of human beings to interpret correctly what they see: "Our very eyes / Are some-

George Wither's figure of Hypocrisy as engraved by Crispin van de Passe in *A Collection of Emblemes* (1635). Reprinted by permission of the Folger Shakespeare Library (STC 25900c, 229).

times like our judgements, blind" (4.2.301–02). However, she too is a victim of her own defective eyesight when she believes the headless corpse of Cloten to be Posthumus only on the basis of the clothes it wears, or of outward appearance, and even her reason fails her when, in 5.5., she accuses Pisanio of having tried to poison her. Likewise, Posthumus is unable to recognize Imogen dressed as a boy—once again a matter of deceptive outward appearance. Even the Wild Men, who intuitively recognize Imogen's value, are deceived by the appearance of death in sleep and provide a touching funeral for the boy they assume to have died. Nor does Cymbeline immediately recognize his old counsclor Belarius in the guise of a Wild Man. As Sir John Davies puts it,

> But in this life no *Soule* the truth can know
>   So perfectly, as it hath power to do,

If then perfection be not found below,
An high place must make her mount thereto.

(Nosce Teipsum 1599, 57)

Since partial blindness to reality is endemic to the human condition, true knowledge will always be lacking to those who depend on their eyes alone.

More serious is the fact that the sight of beauty does not always lead the soul upward. When Iachimo sees Imogen's nude beauty in the bedchamber scene, he must struggle against a strong desire to touch her, that is, a desire to descend to the satisfaction of his lowest sense. This, however, would awaken her and spoil his scheme. When Cloten sees Imogen's beauty, he wants to "penetrate" her, to rape the body that his eyes have made him desire. In both cases, sight has awakened the lower nature of the man rather than leading him to love, as Ficino hoped it would. The result is that Imogen—like so many Shakespearean heroines—must eventually disguise her beauty in order to survive in a world ruled by masculine lust.

As Plato taught, only intuitive reason, the eye of the mind that finally begins to see clearly as physical sight declines, is capable of approaching reality. Summers reminds us that, for Plato,

> The data of sense—and especially of sight—are . . . phantasms, appearances of things in the light, in themselves without truth, even perhaps illusive and chimerical. In writers who held this view, pagan or Christian, images that might seem to us to reveal keen observation in painting or poetry were treated as 'phantasms,' as examples of the untrustworthiness of sense, and, either implicitly or explicitly, as evidence of the difficulty of obtaining any knowledge, wisdom, or salvation in this world.[15]

Yet in all fairness, we must also recall that in the *Timaeus* (47), Plato particularly lauds the sense of sight because it allows us to see the measured order of the sun, the stars and the planets. Our sight of the heavens has caused such benefits as the invention of mathematics, our understanding of time, and philosophy itself. The issue really is the proper use of our sense of vision. According to Plato, "the god invented and gave us vision in order that we might observe the circuits of intelligence in the heaven and profit by them for the revolutions of our own thought, which are akin to them, though ours be troubled and they are unperturbed; and that, by learning to know them and acquiring the power to compute them rightly according to nature, we might reproduce the perfectly unerring revolutions of the god and reduce to settled order the wandering motions in ourselves."[16]

In an interesting discussion of "Sexual Disguise in *Cymbeline,*" Nancy K. Hayles has argued that,

In the scenes where Imogen is in disguise, the characters' understanding of the underlying relationships comes, not from sensory perception and reasoning, but from intuition of a more irrational, mysterious kind. Indeed, the power of intuition to penetrate appearances and reveal the underlying reality is the chief interest in these scenes. Until the meeting with Lucius, everyone Imogen sees (and Imogen herself) is in disguise: the disguises emphasize that she cannot possibly understand the significance of events through sensory perception alone.[17]

I agree in general with Hayles's point; however, her use of the word "irrational" suggests that hers is not a Renaissance but a nineteenth-century Romantic viewpoint, which emphasizes "emotional intuition" and denies the usefulness of "logical intuition." Such Romantic distortions appear continually in modern Shakespearean scholarship and tend to obscure much of what Shakespeare and his contempories were actually implying through their art. In fact, the highest type of knowledge recognized by Plato in Book VI of *The Republic* is immediate "logical intuition" or insight in contrast to ordinary deduction or reasoning from assumptions, but this has nothing to do with the emotions or irrationality. "Reason" for Plato and his followers is always intellectual and can be defined very simply as the mental intuition of latent or inherent relationships, mathematical and otherwise. Like Sophocles in *Oedipus Rex,* Shakespeare demonstrates this kind of intuitive reasoning metaphorically in dramatic scenes involving the recognition or lack of recognition of family relationships among humans. For example, the Wild Boys in *Cymbeline* are using reason, not emotion, when they intuit their natural kinship with the page Fidele; Cymbeline is using his native reason when, although he firmly believes Imogen to be dead, he recognizes his daughter's particular "tune" in the speech of Fidele; but Posthumus is still depending only on his five senses and his emotions when he does not recognize his own relationship to the pageboy in 5.5 and thus behaves irrationally or violently toward Fidele.

For the Platonists, the eyes of the mind can indeed perceive the inner man or woman; they can see through disguises or misleading outer appearances to the truth. Such logically intuitive perceptions are then recorded in the heart, which was believed in antiquity and during the Middle Ages to be the seat of both thought and wisdom—not the center of the emotions, as we think of the heart today. According to the thirteenth century poet Rustico di Filippo, "I have heard that man cannot live nor endure at all without his heart; but I live without it, and yet I do not lose my color nor my knowledge nor thought."[18] By the time of the Renaissance, however, the heart was generally spoken of in love poetry as equivalent to the soul or to the spiritual self of the lover, who could exchange his heart (soul) with his beloved through a kiss (Perella 1969, 120). Yet the soul itself was partly reason, according to the Platonists. Therefore, although intuition may be mysterious, it is always reasonable for Neoplatonic Renaissance writers and capable of penetrating intellectually the outer apppearances to the logic within another person. As Sir John Davies stated in *Nosce Teipsum,* "The Soule through all things sees" (1599, 19), although the senses perceive only outer appearances. Surely this was what Shakespeare was also implying about the heart versus the five senses in Sonnet 141.

To descend from the high art of that exquisite poem to the explicit statement of a Whitney emblem entitled "Interiora vide" ("See within"), may be painful but possibly helpful at this point in our consideration of Renaissance attitudes toward the visual sense. Whitney warns us,

> Though outwarde thinges, doe trimme, & braue, appeare,
>   And sights at first, doe aunswere thie desire,
> Yet inwarde partes, if that they shine not cleare,
> Suspecte the same, and back in time retire:
>   For inwardlie, such deadlie foes maie lurke,
>   As when wee trust, maie our destruction worke.
>
> Though bewtie rare, bee farre and neare renoum'de,
> Though Natures giftes, and fortunes doe excell:
> Yet, if the minde, with heinous crimes abounde,
> And nothing good with in the same doe dwell:
>   Regarde it not, shonne the outward showe,
>   Vntill, thou doe the inwarde vertues knowe.[19]

Through such logical intuition, Posthumus, in at least one moment of true reason, describes the Imogen he remembers as a "temple of Virtue" (5.5.220–21), in contrast to his previous emotional insistence that she was faithless. Imogen's outward beauty does in fact enclose inner goodness, and Posthumus has actually known this in his heart all along. Metaphorically speaking, whether disguised or even ruined by age, the body of a virtuous person still houses Truth, Beauty, Goodness, and Justice, as a temple always houses within itself the spiritual meaning of a religion.

Although Posthumus only occasionally intuits this well, he—rather than Imogen—manages in the play to transcend his limited physical eyesight and become a visionary. He, like the savage Caliban in *The Tempest,* sees in dreams that the heavens do open and drop blessings upon him, despite his unworthiness. Shakespeare appears to suggest by this that anyone prepared to submit himself or herself to the divine will may experience such prophetic visions through the eyes of the mind. This is the real irony of the First Gaoler's comment to Posthumus in 5.4 that "you know not which way you shall go" (177–78) after death. Having been told by Jupiter that he will "end his miseries," Posthumus insists that he does indeed know which way he shall go. The First Gaoler replies with the familiar *momento mori* emblem of a skull: "Your death has eyes in's head then: I have not seen him so pictur'd" (180–81). However, Shakespeare's hero, who has just recently escaped from the dark cave of the body through his dream vision, is not referring to physical eyes or to the sense of sight but to the inner eyes of the mind: "I tell thee, fellow, there are none want eyes to direct them the way I am going, but such as wink, and will not use them" (187–89). Just as the cave dwellers in Plato's *Republic* call the condemned prisoner "blind," who has escaped from the senses into the light of reason and then has returned to show others the way, so the Gaoler accuses Posthumus of "blindness" (5.4.192) as he leads this now enlightened prisoner apparently to his execution.

"No More . . . Offend Our Hearing": The Ear in *Cymbeline*

Similar problems occur with the sense of hearing. But, once again, Plato has explained in the *Timaeus* why the gods presented humanity with the gift of hearing, a sense that can be so easily abused. With our ears, he says, we perceive human speech (a necessity of philosophy) and music (the cause of inner harmony):

> harmony, whose motions are akin to the revolutions of the soul within us, has been given by the Muses to him whose commerce with them is guided by intelligence, not for the sake of irrational pleasure (which is now thought to be its utility), but as an ally against the inward discord that has come into the revolution of the soul, to bring it into order and consonance with itself. Rhythm also was succour bestowed upon us by the same hands to the same intent, because in the most part of us our condition is lacking in measure and poor in grace.[20]

Thus the human condition requires the sense of hearing to restore measure into behavior and harmony into the soul.

In a provocative essay on aural imagery in *Othello,* John N. Wall calls our attention to "the act of hearing and its attendant agent, the human ear . . . as a significant motif of action"[21] in many of Shakespeare's plays. His observation that the moral seduction of Shakespeare's characters is often accomplished onstage through auditory means should not of course surprise us, since Genesis records that hearing was the very first of man's five senses to be corrupted by the tempting words, or persuasive aural poison, of the serpent. Although Wall concentrates his analysis on the pseudosexual nature of auditory corruption in *Othello,* his remarks on Shakespeare's use of the ear metaphor can be applied equally well to *Cymbeline* in which a noble husband's ear is also poisoned against his innocent wife by deliberate calumny. In *Cymbeline,* however, the playwright goes beyond dramatizing the tragic fall of a good man seduced into irrational violence by a conventional vice figure adept at verbal persuasion. Here Shakespeare demonstrates as well that verbal and musical sound can elevate, even save, the human soul, when it is sufficiently harmonious and properly directed toward moral ends. By the use of the god Jupiter in his deus ex machina scene (5.4), Shakespeare suggests, moreover, a means by which justice may ultimately prevail against the dangers of auditory seduction.

As I have noted earlier, the plot of *Cymbeline* could easily end in disaster like that of *Othello,* but just when it seems that the play will evolve into a tragedy for both Britain and the royal family, Jupiter descends to Shakespeare's *theatrum mundi* and throws a thunderbolt at the Ghosts of the hero's ancestors as they try to intercede for Posthumus with incantations and prayers. Jupiter's first words bring instant silence to the stage: "No more, you petty spirits of region low / Offend our hearing: hush!" (5.4.93–94). To understand the significance of this command, we need to know that Jupiter was for the Jacobeans not only a symbol of godhead and divine justice[22] but also a symbol of the necessary virtue of listening carefully to both sides of any question or accusation. Listening to both sides is clearly the only practical means by which human beings can protect themselves and those they love against slander in a corrupt and fallen world.

A descending Jupiter strikingly similar to Shakespeare's deus ex machina appears in the popular *Emblemata* of 1565, with many later editions, by the Dutch physician Hadrianus Junius. This emblem may help us to clarify both the meaning of the line "No more . . . Offend our hearing" and the overall significance of Shakespeare's emphasis on the sense of hearing in *Cymbeline* as well. Under the motto "Princeps ne cui aures seruas praebeat" ("Let a Prince not furnish slavish ears to anyone"), the woodcut for Emblem 48 depicts Jupiter, armed with lightning bolts, descending on the back of an eagle to the natural world. The verse reads as follows:

Sublimem aere Iouis statua, patula aure carente,
   Sacrarat Minoia Creta.
Principis est, regnum dextra moderatis habena,
   Seruam ne cui commodet aurem.

(A statue of Jove high in the air, lacking an open ear,
   Minoan Crete had dedicated.
It is characteristic of a Prince, moderating his kingdom
   with skillful rein,
Not to lend a slavish ear to anyone.)[23]

The emblem derives in general from the classical antiflattery *topos*,[24] a commonplace warning in varying forms to rulers that they should beware of what courtiers tell them, but it is also intimately concerned with the problem of justice in the western world.

Junius provides a lengthy commentary on the significance of the emblem to his own times. The motto, he says,

> is taken from Plutarch's book on Isis . . . where he speaks thus. In Crete there was a statue of Jove without ears: by which symbol the artificer wished to suggest that a prince, or whoever has authority over all, ought not to give his ears in servitude to anyone, that is, to so accommodate the other's wishes as to make his ears seem to be the other's possessions, and to put the latter in a position to abuse their compliance.

Aside from the immediate application to *Cymbeline* of this advice, we may also be reminded here of Caesar's princely command to Mark Antony to "come on my right hand, for this ear is deaf" (1.4.213) when he desires his lieutenant's opinion of Cassius in *Julius Caesar;* of that same Mark Antony's later insidious request to the populus to "lend me your ears" (3.2.73); and of Regan's cold observation in *King Lear* that her father is "apt to have his ears abus'd" (2.4.306–7).

Junius continues his explanation in typical Renaissance scholarly fashion with similar statements from other ancient sources of wisdom:

> Nothing is more pernicious than that the prince should leave his ears open to everything: as Marcellinus proclaims in book 16 of his work on Constantine the Great, casting aspersions of turpitude on that great Emperor; against which fault the same author in book 18 cites a famous saying and maxim of Julianus, his cousin, who (he declared) was steadfast in his duties as one who distinguishes the just and the unjust: and he attaches a laudable anecdote by way of example, which is as follows: when Numerius, rector of the province of Narbonne, was accused of embezzling public funds, he easily explained away the basis of the charge by reference to his accounts, but the orator Cephidius bitterly opposed the man's innocence and, deprived of documentary evidence, he exclaimed: "No one would ever be found guilty, if denial were sufficient." Julianus wisely replied, "And who then will be found innocent, if accusation were sufficient?"

This sound legal advice from the past is obviously applicable to much of *Cymbeline,* a play in which accusation alone is too often sufficient for instant condemnation. Junius concludes his commentary on Emblem 48 by reminding his readers that "Alexander of Macedon acted accordingly when he covered one ear with a hand in order to keep it in reserve for the defendant."[25] As we know, Alexander claimed paternity from Jupiter Ammon, the very same god commemorated by the statue in Crete and the ruling deity of Shakespeare's tragicomedy.

The widespread popularity during the sixteenth century of the Junius

Princeps ne cui aures feruas præbeat.

Sublimem ære Iouis ftatuã, patula aure carentĕ,
Sacrarat Minoïa Creta.
Principis eft, regnum dextra moderãtis habena,
Seruam ne cui commodet aurem.

Amo-

A descending Jupiter teaches us to keep one ear reserved for the defense in Emblem 48 of Hadrianus Junius's *Emblemata* (Antwerp, 1565), 54. Reprinted by permission of the Folger Shakespeare Library (PN 6349 J8 1565 copy 2 Cage).

Emblemata suggests (1) that the visual image of the descending Jupiter as a symbol of the need for listening to both sides of a dispute and (2) that the accompanying historical examples for princes to follow were both generally familiar to Jacobean poets and audiences, especially since Junius lived for some years in England. Even the clergyman Stephen Batman, ostensibly so critical of pagan beliefs in his *Golden Boke of the Leaden Gods* (1577), an English adaptation of Cartari, describes Jupiter as having no ears: "his want of Eares declare him to be indifferent unto all, not harkening more to one than to an other."[26]

Justice Demands Keeping One Ear Open for the Defense

The principal characters in *Cymbeline*—the king, Posthumus, Imogen, and even Iachimo—could all have profited from obeying the motto of Junius's Emblem 48: "Let a Prince not furnish slavish ears to anyone." After hearing untruths, or exaggerated truths in the case of Iachimo, all four make serious mistakes and suffer for them because they do not keep one ear reserved for the other side of the question. What follows is a review of the aural aspects of the action.

The play opens to scenes of family and political discord in Britain. We soon learn that Cymbeline has already banished true virtue from his kingdom after listening to slander brought to his unguarded ears by jealous courtiers against his faithful knight Belarius. Thus, from the beginning, the king is left without wise counsel. We learn as well that the affronted Belarius has then kidnapped the two young sons of Cymbeline and transported them into exile with him, hoping to bring them up as honest men in a state of nature, far from the artifices, calumny, and deceptions of the court. During act 3, when the warlike talents of Belarius and the boys are about to be called upon for the defense of the kingdom against Roman invaders, Belarius finally informs the princes of his own unmerited disgrace and banishment: "My fault being nothing . . . But that two villains, whose false oaths prevail'd / Before my perfect honour, swore to Cymbeline / I was confederate with the Romans" (3.3.65–68). Unfortunately for Britain, in this instance Cymbeline had ears only for the prosecution.

Second, Cymbeline listens uncritically to bad advice on both family and state affairs from his beautiful second wife, who knows how to flatter him. At the Queen's instigation, he banishes his new son-in-law Posthumus, a young man he has brought up himself and whose fundamental virtue he knows well. Cymbeline thus leaves his daughter Imogen unprotected and vulnerable to the rapacious attentions of the Queen's lustful, unintelligent, and foul-smelling son Cloten. The Queen's hidden goal in persuading Cymbeline to banish Posthumus as "poison" to the royal "blood" (1.2.60) is to secure her own son's position as heir apparent to the throne. Also, at the Queen's verbal instigation, Cymbeline refuses to pay the usual tribute to Rome, thus refusing to "render unto Caesar the things which are Caesar's" (Matt. 22:21) and plunging his already unhappy kingdom into the further discord of war. Not until the last act does the unwary king finally realize that his power has been used and his ears abused by the Queen through adept verbal flattery. He claims that "It had been vicious / To have mistrusted her" (5.5.65–66), but then he begs pathetically, "Heaven mend all!" (5.5.68).

It is heaven indeed that must come to the aid of the royal family and the British kingdom, both endangered by a foolish king who characteristically gives ear only to one side of any question. Shakespeare's *A Winter's Tale* also requires that the gods directly intervene to tell erring human beings how to untangle their false beliefs, suggesting that the playwright was deeply concerned with this problem of the difficulties of correctly interpreting sensory information during his final years.

In *Cymbeline* the exiled bridegroom Posthumus, once away from the civilizing influence of Imogen, allows his ears to be poisoned as well against his nearest relative, his wife, by an equally greedy and unscrupulous person, and he rules the kingdom of his mind thereafter with an emotional abandon and heedlessness similar to the misrule of Cymbeline in Britain. In Italy, an excessively proud Posthumus is first tempted aurally by the subtle courtier Iachimo into accepting a wager on the chastity of his princess. Then he is convinced by Iachimo's use of circumstantial evidence, his verbal insinuation of sexual dalliance with Imogen, and a false oath that Imogen has in fact been unfaithful. Posthumus immediately succumbs to a fit of passion. Without allowing his bride an opportunity to reply to such vicious slander, the young husband sends a letter to his servant Pisanio, ordering him to murder the princess in revenge for her supposed adultery. In so doing, Posthumus violates the legal principle of keeping one ear open for the defense, as he ultimately begins to realize:

> You married ones,
> If each of you should take this course, how many
> Must murder wives much better than themselves
> For wrying but a little?
>
> (5.1.2–5)

Fortunately, the servant Pisanio has a better memory of the general wisdom of the times than has his master, and he does not obey this unjust command to kill. Only after seeing the bloody cloth in act 5 does Posthumus realize that he has ordered his servant to commit an evil act.

"O Pisanio, / Every good servant does not all commands: / No bond but to do just ones" (5.1.5–7).

Instead of obeying the orders in Posthumus's letter, Pisanio suspects calumny at once and cries out in terms of the ear metaphor,

> O master, what a strange *infection*
> Is fall'n into thy *ear!* What false Italian
> (As *poisonous tongu'd* as handed) hath prevail'd
> On thy *too ready hearing?* Disloyal? No.
>
> (3.2.3–6; italics added)

Since Posthumus has failed to reserve an ear for the defense, Pisanio, like Belarius, must now betray his master in order to save an heir to the throne.

Imogen, on the other hand, at first displays true princeliness in her refusal to listen to Iachimo's calumny against Posthumus and to his sly suggestion that she ought to be revenged on her allegedly unfaithful husband:

> Reveng'd!
> How should I be reveng'd? If this be true,
> (As I have such a heart that *both mine ears*
> *Must not in haste abuse*) if it be true,
> How should I be reveng'd?
>
> (1.7.128–32; italics added)

Apparently a reader of Plutarch and of emblem books, like most literate people of Shakespeare's time, she is concerned that *both* her ears should not listen to accusations against Posthumus, whom she has promised to love. Imogen's response is also reminiscent of an emblem inspired by Ovid from Otto van Veen's collection *Emblemes of Loue* (1608). Under the *inscriptio* "Loue often deaf," we see the engraving of Fame blowing a trumpet at Cupid, who covers his ears with his hands. The *subscriptio* informs us that

> Whatever fame brutes foorth which tendeth to disgrace,
> Of loues deer prysed loue; hee not endures to heare,
> But makes himself bee deaf by stopping either eare,
> To shew hee will not giue to ill opinion place.[27]

In the play, Iachimo then graciously offers himself as a willing instrument for her sexual vengeance. "I dedicate myself to your sweet pleasure" (1.7.136), he says; to which an astonished Imogen replies in anger, "Away, I do *condemn mine ears,* that have / So long attended thee" (1.7.141–42). She not only refuses to judge Posthumus at this point but also—unlike her father—condemns her own ears for listening to the insinuations of Iachimo, whose true motives are now all too apparent: "If thou wert

A M O R V M.

Love should refuse to listen to any slander against the beloved by Fame in Otto van Veen's *Emblemes of Loue* (Antwerp, 1608), 67. Reprinted by permission of the Folger Shakespeare Library (STC 24627a.5 copy 1).

honourable, / Thou wouldst have told this tale for virtue, not / For such an end thou seek'st, as base, as strange" (1.7.142–44).

Despite her wise resistance to obvious calumny, however, Imogen's ear is as easily penetrated by flattery as were both her father's ears, although—in this case—it is the hyperbolic *praise* of her beloved by Iachimo that does the trick. Iachimo, using words that anticipate the true later descent of Jupiter, falsely says of Posthumus that "He sits 'mongst men like a descended god; / He hath a kind of honour sets him off, / More than a mortal seeming" (1.7.168–71). Since Imogen, the epitome of innocent faith, cannot believe Posthumus has any mortal weaknesses, she falls instant prey to the flattering suggestion that he has immortal virtues. Her defenses once penetrated by this sly approach, she further believes

Iachimo when he says he had only been testing her loyalty through his attempts to seduce her, and she now makes her ear a willing slave to his words. First, she naively forgives his previous abuse of her hearing: "All's well, sir: take my power i' th' court for yours" (1.7.179). Next, she agrees to protect Iachimo's trunk of supposed valuables in her bedchamber, "and pawn mine honour for their safety, since / My lord hath interest in them" (1.7.194–95). Her honor is indeed pawned by this error, an error in judgment that has an ironic parallel in 4.2, when Imogen mistakes Cloten's headless *trunk* for that of Posthumus and then eulogizes its godlike beauty. In accepting Iachimo's deceptive trunk in 1.7, however, she allows him, through a crass appeal to her uncritical love for Posthumus, to achieve in a moment what Cloten fails to attain through hired music—a complete change of affection and facile admission (hidden within the trunk) into the private apartments of Britain's most chaste princess. The trunk, usually a container for treasure, thus becomes a symbol of vice hidden within a deceptive exterior.[28]

The ear metaphor is particularly noticeable in 3.2, when Pisanio gives Imogen a letter from Posthumus falsely telling her to meet her husband in Milford-Haven. Shakespeare had earlier used the situation of being duped by false words in a letter in the Gloucester plot in *King Lear,* a play that also blends the problem of sight/insight with that of hearing and believing false information. In *Cymbeline,* Imogen begs Pisanio to inform her at once of the distance she must travel to meet Posthumus: "say, and speak thick, / (Love's counsellor should *fill the bores of hearing,* / To the smothering of the sense)" (3.2.58–59; italics added). She would be deaf to any words that do not concern her husband; both her ears are slaves to love and to love alone. But, of course, the words in the letter she has just received are as much a trap as Iachimo's trunk, since Pisanio has been ordered by Posthumus in another letter to kill Imogen during the journey. In 3.4 Pisanio finally shows his mistress the letter expressing Posthumus's true feelings toward his wife, and she, in immediate and hopeless despair, pleads with the servant to fulfill his master's orders at once and to kill her. Life no longer has any value, since love's spoken vows have been proven false and love's written promise of a reunion has been a lie.

In dealing with both Iachimo and Posthumus, Imogen has failed to keep one ear open to the *prosecution,* just as Cymbeline and Posthumus have consistently refused to listen to the *defense*. Her resulting disillusionment with Posthumus then fallaciously leads to a general disillusionment with all men who must be liars as well:

> *Pisanio:*   Good Madam, *hear* me.
> *Imogen:* True honest men, being *heard* like false Aeneas,
>   Were in his time thought false: and Sinon's weeping

> Did scandal many a holy tear, took pity
> From most true wretchedness: so thou, Posthumus,
> Wilt lay the leaven on all proper men:
> Goodly and gallant shall be false and perjur'd
> From thy great fail.
>
> > (3.4.58–65; italics added)

Her response is much like that of Posthumus; once he has decided on Imogen's guilt, he condemns all females as whores. And, as prone to impulsive action as both Cymbeline and Posthumus, Imogen yearns for annihilation at once, without waiting to discover why Posthumus has come to believe her false. She merely assumes that an Italian whore has wounded his pride through her infidelity, thus causing him to believe that his wife is the same kind of woman.

Shakespeare continues his use of ear imagery in this scene. Once Pisanio succeeds in quieting Imogen's pleas for death, he again begs her to "*Hear* me with patience" (3.4.114):

> *Imogen:*   Talk thy tongue weary, *speak:*
> I have *heard* I am a strumpet, and *mine ear,*
> Therein false struck, can take no greater wound,
> Nor tent, to bottom that. But speak.
>
> > (3.4.114–17; italics added)

Pisanio then presents his plan, which will gain time for them to disabuse Posthumus's ear, so thoroughly poisoned by Iachimo's calumny, and also to disabuse Imogen's ear, now equally poisoned by the letters of Posthumus himself. Pisanio advises her to disguise herself as a page and to serve the Roman Lucius, thus contriving to live near Posthumus so that "Report should render him hourly to *your ear* / As truly as he moves" (3.4.152–53; italics mine). Pisanio assures her that the musicality of her own voice will undoubtedly gain her service with the honorable Roman Lucius, "If that his head have *ear* in music" (3.4.177).

Proceeding to Milford-Haven as the page Fidele (Faithful *in extremis*), Imogen meets Belarius and her younger brothers, none of whom she recognizes, and she joins them in their mountain cave. Their natural goodness convinces her at last that one must not always believe what one hears from others but must always keep an ear in reserve for the other side. "These are kind creatures," she observes. "Gods what lies I have heard! / Our courtiers say all's savage but at court; / Experience, O, thou disprov'st report!" (4.2.32–34).

There is a curious additional irony to this problem of the aural seduction of the three princely characters in *Cymbeline*—the king through flattery, Posthumus through Iachimo's slander of Imogen, and Imogen through overpraise of her husband and false words of love. Iachimo, the apparent villain of the play and certainly a direct theatrical descendant of Iago and the medieval vice figure,[29] informs us in 5.5 that he, too, has been seduced through the ear, in this instance by Posthumus's foolish boasting of Imogen's beauty and constancy at a banquet in Italy:

> This Posthumus,
> Most like a noble lord in love and one
> That had a royal lover, took his hint,
> And (not dispraising whom we prais'd, therein
> He was as calm as virtue) he began
> His mistress' picture, which, by his tongue, being made,
> And then a mind put in't, either our brags
> Were crak'd of kitchen-trulls, or his description
> Prov'd us unspeaking sots.
>
> (5.5.170–78)

Posthumus's glowing report of Imogen's charms during what must have been little more than a stag party, challenges the male pride of his listeners and excites the lascivious interest of Iachimo in Imogen.[30] As a number of students of *Cymbeline* have observed, Posthumus's boast is similar to Collatine's public vaunting of the chaste beauty of his wife in Shakespeare's narrative poem *The Rape of Lucrece,* and, of course, Iachimo does indeed compare himself to Tarquin when he emerges from the trunk in Imogen's bedchamber. Later, this same Italian courtier explains to Cymbeline that his fall into temptation was directly caused by Posthumus's glowing description: "Your daughter's chastity (there it begins)— / He spoke of her, as Dian had hot dreams / And she alone were cold" (5.5.179–81).

Warnings against publicizing love in this way were very common in Shakespeare's time. For example. Van Veen's *Emblemes of Loue* contains a verse under the motto "Loue's secresie is in silence," which reads

> Both by the peach and goos is silence signifyed,
> The louer must in loue to silence be enclynd,
> For speaking of his loue bewrayes the louers mynd,
> But silence vs'd in loue doth make it vnespyed.

The engraving depicts a goose with a stone in its beak beside Amor, who is holding a peach branch in his right hand while placing his left forefinger to his lips.[31] According to Peter M. Daly, who has done an extensive study of this emblem,

> The finger signal, today a commonplace for silence, has, however, an interesting history, which is relevant in this context. Harpocrates, god of mystical silence, was always depicted making this gesture. Later the same gesture was applied to Hermes who guides the souls from the world of appearances. In his *Metamorphoses* Ovid transferred the finger sign for silence to love, and the

fifteenth commandment in the *Ars Amatoria* enjoins silence on the lover. Van Veen derived his emblem, or at least an important quotation that accompanies the *pictura,* from the *Ars Amatoria:*

> Praecipue Cytherea iubet sua sacra taceri:
> Admoneo, veniat ne quis ad illa loquax
>
> (II, 607 f.)[32]

Love then, for both Ovid and van Veen, is a sacred mystery that must be shrouded in silence.

But why is Amor holding a peach branch? Plutarch reports that the peach tree is "sacred to Isis, because its fruit resembles the heart and its leaf the tongue, speech being the most divine of all man's powers" (Daly 1979, 105). Hence Alciati's Emblem 30 uses the peach branch to depict "wisdom in the heart" and "vigour of speech." Valeriano insists that the tree is sacred not only to Isis but to Harpocrates as well, and therefore it became an Egyptian hieroglyph for silence. Thus Daly explains the meaning of van Veen's use of the peach branch as follows: "The communication (leaves) of the secrets of the heart (peaches) is forbidden by Cupid's warning finger, which reinforces the connotation of peach with silence, already present through the association of the tree with Harpocrates" (1979, 106). The goose with the stone in its beak "indicates the need for watchfulness and silence, since love is surrounded by dangers" (Daly 1979, 107), a moral deriving from Pliny's report in his *Natural History* that geese prudently carry stones in their beaks during dangerous moments when they have to avoid their usual loud cackling (Daly 1979, 106). Long associated with the goddess Aphrodite, the goose also symbolizes love itself (Daly 1979, 118, n.67).

Unlike the prudent geese, however, Posthumus communicated secrets about his love during the most dangerous of situations—a bachelors' party. In his analysis of aural imagery in *Othello,* Wall argues that "Othello's ear and Iago's tongue become displaced organs of generation, and Iago is revealed as the Moor's aural-sexual partner. Iago's words thus become the seed that impregnates Othello's mind through his ear so that it will produce the 'monstrous birth' of sexual jealousy, or the 'green-eyed monster'" (1979, 361). In *Cymbeline,* Shakespeare ironically precedes the impregnation of Posthumus's ear with the seed of sexual jealousy by Posthumus's own unwitting impregnation of Iachimo's ear with the seeds of wounded male pride and lust, and thus the monstrous wager scheme is born. On the other hand, as Wall also reminds us, "The Incarnation is . . . datable from the time when Mary, who conceived the divine Word and bore him into the World, heard the Word of God borne by his angelic spokesman" (1979, 366). The ear can conceive peace and harmony as well as murder.

The Four Redemptive Functions of Sound

Thus far we have seen that in Shakespeare's dramatic vision the temple of the mind can be penetrated rather easily through the ear. Aural poison works in *Cymbeline,* as in *Othello,* to corrupt human reason, to unbridle passion, and to lead the characters into acts of violence or desperation. Yet, Pisanio's mention of Lucius as a possible savior for Imogen, "if that his head have ear in music" (3.4.176), reminds us that the sense of hearing can also lead to salvation. The Roman Lucius is indeed moved by Imogen's musical voice to "father" the unhappy page Fidele (4.2.395). He then reminds Imogen (and the audience) of the doctrine of the Fortunate Fall, which assumes an ultimate redemptive purpose in the tragic history of the world: "Be cheerful; wipe thine eyes: / Some falls are means the happier to arise" (4.2.402–3).

Indeed sound appears to have four redemptive functions in *Cymbeline.* First, through the measured verse and music of prayer and ritualized magic, it can attract benevolent influences down into the *theatrum mundi* from the supernatural world. Second, prophetic words of happy events to come can both heal despair and renew human courage in the face of psychological disillusionment and physical death. Third, verbal good news about a "lost one found" can heal a broken heart, and finally, music—including songs of praise and thanksgiving—can help to heal the division between heaven and earth that began with the first poisoned ear in the Garden of Eden. These functions of sound are entirely in accord with Christian doctrine, despite the pagan form they take in the tragicomedy.

Neoplatonists believed during the Renaissance that music not only soothes the savage breast but that it has a definite influence on the deity as well. As Frances Yates has pointed out, music and incantation were understood to have magical powers of invoking heavenly influences through analogy with the assumed powers of the *Orphica,* a collection of hymns thought to have been composed by the mythological poet-musician Orpheus:

> Ficino used to sing the Orphic songs accompanying himself probably on a *lira da braccio.* They were set to some kind of simple monodic music which Ficino believed echoed the musical notes emitted by the planetary spheres, to form that music of the spheres of which Pythagoras spoke. Thus one could sing Sun hymns, or Jupiter hymns, or Venus hymns attuned to those planets, and this, being reinforced by the invocation of their names and powers, was a way of drawing down their influence.[33]

Indeed Jupiter does descend into the world of *Cymbeline* to dispense his grace and to announce his providential plan in answer to formal prayer and to ritual incantations accompanied by music and dance.

It is generally accepted by scholars that lines 11 through 28 in 5.4 constitute a formal prayer of penitence by Posthumus and an allusion to the basic Christian contract between man and God implicit in the Lord's Prayer: "Forgive us our debts, as we forgive our debtors." The sound of these repentant words, coupled with the measured verse and solemn music of the Ghosts during Posthumus's succeeding dream vision, reach the divine ears and immediately evoke the appearance of Jupiter on his eagle. The opposite occurs in the tragedy of *King Lear* when the protagonist informs his daughter, "I do not bid the thunder-bearer shoot, / Nor tell tales of thee to high-judging Jove" (2.4.227–28). In *Cymbeline*, the god Jupiter—who "could be called Providence," according to Vincenzo Cartari, "because he saw to it that the world would proceed smoothly along its ordained course"[34]—brings down to earth both a verbal and a written promise of salvation for Posthumus, Imogen, Cymbeline, and Britain. In fact, Jupiter responds to the prayers of the Ghosts for their descendant's well-being, a pagan ritual, with the Christian doctrine of Grace, as Robert G. Hunter and Homer D. Swander have convincingly demonstrated:[35] "Whom best I love, I cross; to make my gift, / The more delay'd delighted" (5.4.101–2). Thus, although Jupiter quiets the Ghosts with a thunderbolt and a stern, "No more, you petty spirits of region low / Offend our hearing: hush!" (5.4.93–94) because he does not wish to hear any further "special pleading" or ignorant criticism of his purposes, he also freely promises happiness to their offspring Posthumus, or to the one born after death.

Jupiter's real purpose in descending is to bring good news to human ears. In fact, Shakespeare's deus ex machina is so determined to be taken seriously, and to be understood as "real" in a world of false appearances, as I have prevously stated, that he leaves behind a prophetic tablet that will be clearly discernible to the senses of Posthumus when he awakens from his sleep. But words require interpretation. Since Posthumus cannot exactly decipher the prophetic message of this "rare" book, which he reads aloud to the audience, he calls it a "senseless speaking or a speaking such / As sense cannot untie" (4.4.148–49), thus pointing directly to the supersensory nature of reason and particularly of human knowledge about the divine. Indeed it takes the special talents of a soothsayer, with an ear accustomed to prophetic oracles, to decipher Jupiter's message somewhat accurately in the last scene of the play. The prophecy not only predicts reunion and happiness for the British royal family but also a new era of peace for the world. For Posthumus in 5.4, however, " 'Tis still a dream: or else such stuff as madmen / Tongue and brain not" (146–47); although his spirits are sufficiently renewed by the vision to allow him now to jest about death with his Gaoler.

At this point a messenger enters with a brisk order that Posthumus be unshackled and escorted to the king. "Thou bring'st good news," says Posthumus, "I am call'd to be made free" (5.4.195–96), an allusion to the central messge of the Gospels and to St. Paul (Gal. 5:1): "Stand fast, therefore, in the liberty wherewith Christ hath made us free, and be not entangled again with the yoke of bondage." In keeping with Jupiter's promise, 5.5 becomes a veritable motet of good news, as one voice after another reports the truth at last, reminding us of the words of St. John the Evangelist, whose symbol was the eagle (a bird referred to many times in *Cymbeline*): "And ye shall know the truth and the truth shall make you free" (John 8:32).

Cornelius announces that the wicked Queen is dead and that she confessed her evil deeds before she died. When Cymbeline asks, "Heard you all this, her women?" (5.5.61), they corroborate the physician's testimony in chorus. And now Cymbeline even deigns to lend an ear to Imogen (still disguised as Fidele) when she asks him "To give me *hearing*" (5.5.116); italics added), which he has previously refused to do. When he also grants her request to hear Iachimo's explanation of the diamond ring won from Posthumus, out pours the good news of Imogen's true virtue from her only accuser of vice. Then Cymbeline recognizes his lost daughter by the musical sound of her voice, and he exclaims, "The tune of Imogen!" (5.5.238). Finally, all tales are properly told by the various characters of earlier events in the play, and with such overwhelmingly happy results that the king at one point exclaims, "When shall I *hear* all through?" (5.5.383; italics mine).

All this good news of resurrection and redeemed innocence is a dramatic analogy to the providential spreading of the good news of the Gospels prophesied by St. Paul in Romans. In a recent essay on the providential view of history as it was still being argued in early seventeenth-century England, Lila Geller cites John Speed's *Theatre of the Empire of Great Britain* (1611):

> The Apostle himself saith [Rom. 10:18], that the sound of the Gospell went thorow the earth, and was heard unto the ends of the world; which his saying cannot more fitly bee applied to any other Nation than unto us of Britaine, whose Land by the Almightie is so placed in the terrestriall globe, that thereby it is termed of the ancient, the Ends of the Earth, and deemed to be situated in another world.[36]

This identification of St. Paul's prophecy with Britain, information gleaned by Speed from "the earliest extant British historian,"[37] Gildas, seems very pertinent to the last scene of *Cymbeline*, during which Jupiter's prophecy is fulfilled. At this point, Imogen speaks of having "got two worlds" (5.5.375), and the Soothsayer hails the happy rejoining of the Roman eagle "with the radiant Cymbeline, / Which shines here in the

West" (5.5.476–77). This reunion between Rome and Britain has been identified by Geller and many others as the Pax Augustus necessary for the Incarnation to take place.[38] Since the play is so deeply concerned with hearing and with the problem of faith, perhaps Shakespeare himself was thinking of the Epistle to the Romans when he composed *Cymbeline:*

> But the righteousness which is of faith speaketh on this wise, Say not in thine heart, Who shall ascend unto heaven? (that is, to bring Christ down *from above*):
> Or, Who shall descend into the deep? (that is, to bring up Christ again from the dead.)
> But what saith it? The word is nigh thee, *even* in thy mouth, and in thy heart: that is, the word of faith, which we preach.
> (Romans 10:6–8)

St. Paul then adds in verse 17 that "faith cometh by hearing and hearing by the word of God."

On the other hand, St. Paul also remarks in the famous passage of 1 Corinthians 13:12 on the limitations of the visual sense in this world: "now we see through a glass darkly." Although the "word" may now be heard at last, human sight will not be redeemed until after death. For this reason, when Imogen awakens from her deathlike sleep, she is still human, and she correctly observes that "Our very eyes / Are sometimes like our judgements, blind" (4.2.301–2). She then promptly mistakes the body of Cloten, dressed in the garments Posthumus had worn on his last day at court, for the body of Posthumus himself. In 5.5 Posthumus likewise fails to recognize Imogen dressed as the page Fidele, despite his earlier conversion. Refusing to hear her words of comfort, he knocks her down for intruding on his theatrical expression of grief for the loss of his beloved wife. Thus, although all losses are ultimately restored in this tragicomedy, Shakespeare does not suggest for one moment that the Incarnation and widespread acceptance of the New Dispensation will of themselves make men perfect in this life. We still live in a fallen world where, as Feste wistfully reminds us in *Twelfth Night,* "the rain it raineth everyday" (5.1.392).

Nevertheless, if calumny was the seed of a green-eyed monster and of death in the earlier play *Othello,* in *Cymbeline* truth and the good news that the king's three children are still alive engender joy for all listeners. Cymbeline's exclamation, "O, what am I? / A mother to the birth of three? Ne'er mother / Rejoic'd deliverance more" (5.5.369–71), reverses the ugly sexual connotations of ear imagery in *Othello* with spiritual connotations of rebirth and salvation. It also plainly answers Brabantio's rejection of verbal comfort in *Othello* when he says, "But words are words; I never yet did hear / That the bruis'd heart was pierced through the ear" (1.3.218–19).

Shakespeare tells us clearly in *Cymbeline* that words can indeed relieve the pain and infection of a bruised heart. Although Brabantio loses his daughter in *Othello,* Cymbeline finally opens his ears to good news of his three missing children, and all that first was lost through slander is happily restored to him through truth.

The fourth and final redemptive function of sound in *Cymbeline* is the hymn of praise and thanksgiving that now rises to the ears of the deity. Renaissance poets considered the Psalms of David to be the highest form of their art.[39] These intense spiritual poems from the ancient world begin, of course, with the advice not to walk "in the counsel of the ungodly," continue with prayers to be heard by the deity ("Give ear to my words, O Lord") and with confessions of personal unworthiness, and at length they culminate in a series of thanksgivings, most of which begin with the exhortation, "Praise ye the Lord." In *Cymbeline,* if special pleading and complaints of divine injustice have previously offended the hearing of Jupiter, his divine ears will now surely open to the last speech of the king:

> Laud we the gods,
> And let our crooked smokes climb to their nostrils
> From our blest altars. Publish we this peace
> To all our subjects.
>
> (5.5.477–80)

And, as we know, this very complex tragicomedy comes to a final close with the joyous word "peace," which should remind us at once of the cherubim on the ceiling of Imogen's bedchamber, singing in silence, "Glory to God in the highest, and on earth peace, good will to men."

Shakespeare has intimated in *Cymbeline* that the discordant tragedy of the ear's corruption in Eden through listening to the lies of a false counselor, an archetype brilliantly dramatized in *Othello,* may be transposed by means of another dramatic genre into what Dante had previously termed a divine comedy. The metamorphosis is accomplished here through prayers and music reaching the ears of divinity, through the incarnation of Jupiter, and finally through human beings listening to the resulting good news and responding appropriately to it. In *Cymbeline,* the Roman visionary Philarmonus proclaims an inspired eulogy to the higher properties of the sense of hearing: "The fingers of the powers above do tune / The harmony of this peace" (5.5.467–68), thus finally resolving the imagery concerned with "ears" and "hearing" into the harmonious music of the spheres.

Notes

1. For a survey of the five senses in art, see Samuel C. Chew, *The Pilgrimage of Life* (New Haven, Conn.: Yale University Press, 1962), 192–95.

2. Carl Nordenfalk, "The Five Senses in Late Medieval and Renaissance Art," *Journal of the Warburg and Courtauld Institutes* 48 (1985): 3.

3. See Marsilio Ficino, *Commentary on Plato's "Symposium on Love,"* trans. Sears Jayne (Dallas, Texas: Spring Publications, Inc., 1985), 40–41.

4. David Summers, *The Judgment of Sense: Renaissance Naturalism and the Rise of Aesthetics* (Cambridge: Cambridge University Press, 1987), 42.

5. See Louise Vinge, *The Five Senses: Studies in a Literary Tradition* (Lund, Sweden: Liber Laromedal, 1975), 20; hereafter cited parenthetically.

6. P. Lomazzo, *A Tracte containing the Artes of curious Paintinge.* trans. R. Haydocke (Oxford: Joseph Barnes for R. H., 1598), 180.

7. All quotations from Edmund Spenser's *The Faerie Queene* are from the Yale Edition, ed. Thomas P. Roche, Jr., with the assistance of C. Patrick O'Donnell, Jr. (New Haven: Yale University Press, 1981).

8. See Sir John Davies, *Nosce Tiepsum* (London: Richard Field, 1599), 14–15; hereafter cited parenthetically. See also T. S. Eliot, "Sir John Davies," in *On Poetry and Poets* (New York: Farrar, Straus and Cudahy, 1957), 149–55.

9. See Chapman, *Ouids Banquet of Sence* (London: I. R. for Richard Smith, 1595). See also Louise Vinge, "Chapman's *Ovids Banquet of Sence.* Its Sources and Theme," *Journal of the Warburg and Courtauld Institutes* 38 (1975): 234–57; and Rhoda M. Ribner, "The Compasse of This Curious Frame: Chapman's *Ovids Banquet of Sence* and the Emblematic Tradition," *Studies in the Renaissance* 17 (1970): 233–58.

10. See Peggy Muñoz Simonds, "Eros and Anteros in Shakespeare's Sonnets 153 and 154,"*Spenser Studies* 7 (1987): 261–86, and 311–22.

11. From Stephen Booth, *Shakespeare's Sonnets* (New Haven: Yale University Press, 1977), 120.

12. Ibid., 485–91.

13. *Works of Francis Bacon,* ed. James Spedding, R. Ellis, and D. Heath (London, 1857–1874), vol. 4, 405–6. See also Roger T. Simonds, "Bacon's Legal Learning: Its Influence on His Philosophical Ideas," *Acta Conventus Neo-Latini Sanctandreani,* ed. I. D. McFarlane, (Binghamton, N.Y.: Medieval & Renaissance Texts & Studies, 1986), 493–501.

14. See George Wither, *A Collection of Emblemes* (London, 1635), 229.

15. Summers, 43.

16. See Francis MacDonald Cornford, *Plato's Cosmology: The 'Timaeus' of Plato translated with a running commentary* (London: Routledge & Kegan Paul Ltd., 1937), 158.

17. See Nancy K. Hayles, "Sexual Disguise in *Cymbeline,*" *Modern Language Quarterly* 41 (1980): 239. For a brilliant, if more traditional, discussion of disguise in *Cymbeline,* see John Scott Colley, "Disguise and New Guise in *Cymbeline,*" *Shakespeare Studies* 7 (1974): 233–52.

18. See Nicolas J. Perella, *The Kiss Sacred and Profane* (Berkeley: The University of California Press, 1969), 95.

19. Geffrey Whitney, *A Choice of Emblemes* (Leiden: Christopher Plantin, 1586), 69.

20. Cornford, 158–59.

21. See John N. Wall, "Shakespeare's Aural Act: The Metaphor of the Ear in *Othello,*" *Shakespeare Quarterly* 30 (1979): 358–66, 359. Ear and hearing imagery actually pervades the dramatic works of Shakespeare. The center of *Hamlet,* for example, is the dumb show in which the king's ear is literally poisoned while he sleeps in the orchard (a parallel to the Garden of Eden myth); King Lear, like

Cymbeline, will not listen to his true counselors; and Gloucester is easily corrupted by false accusations against his good child. The list goes on and on.

22. See Richard Lynche, *The Fountaine of Ancient Fiction* (London, 1599; reprint. New York & London: Garland Publishing, 1976). Lynche states that Jupiter was for the ancients "the only and especiall god that had the power to befriend or prosper the estates of men here below, or to plague & scourge them with crosses, miseries, and mortalities," and that "The Platonickes vnderstand by Iupiter the soule of the world, and that diuine spirit, through whose mightinesse all things whatsoeuer first receiued their being, and still ioiously increase and flourish in their instant continuance: and such powerfull spirit and commander they entearmed by the name of god" (sigs. Iii and Iiiᵛ).

23. Hadrianus Junius, *Emblemata* (Antwerp: Christopher Plantin, 1565), 54. English translation by Virginia W. Callahan.

24. For a study of the problem of flattery in Renaissance courts, see my "Freedom of Speech and the Emblem Tradition," in *Acta Conventus Neo-Latini Sanctandreani,* ed. I. D. McFarlane (Binghamton, N.Y.: Medieval & Renaissance Texts & Studies, 1986), 605–16.

25. Junius, 139–40. English translation by Roger T. Simonds of the following Latin text: "Desumptum est ex Plutarcho, libro de Iside saepius anteacitato, ubi sic ait. In Creta Iouis fuit status, auribus mutila: quo symbola innuere voluit artifex, principem & qui ius in omnes habeat, non debere alicui aures suas mancipio dare, hoc est, ita accommodare ut ab illo possessae videantur, ut que illarum obsequio abuti queat. Nihil perniciosius est quàm quòd aures in omne patentes princeps habeat: id quod Marcellinus lib. 16 de Constantino Caesare praedicat, turpem tanto Imperatori maculam adspergens; contrà quàm praeclarum acroama & elogium Iuliano lib. 18 idem tribuit ilius patrueli, quo praedicat eum personarum indeclinabilem iusti iniustique fuisse distinctorem: addito & documenti vice exemplo laudabili, quod huiusmodi est: nam cùm Numerius, prouinciae Narbonensis rector, peculatus insimulatus, rationibus crimen obiectum facilè dilueret, ac Cephidius orator hominis innocentiam acerrimè oppugnaret, inopsque documentorum exclamaret: Neminem quemquam nocentem fore, si infitiari sufficeret: Iulianus sapienter ex tempore subiecit, Ecquis tandem innocens erit, si accusasse sufficiet? Non alienum hinc est Alexandri Macedonis factum, altera manu opposita aurem obstruentis, ut reo seruaretur integra."

26. Stephen Batman, *The Golden Boke of the Leaden Gods* (London, 1577; reprint. New York & London: Garland Publishing, 1976), 1.

27. Otto van Veen, *Amorvm emblemata, or Emblemes of Loue* (Antwerp, 1608), 66–67.

28. For a brilliant study of outer appearance and inner content in terms of the Alcibiades box, see Barbara J. Baines, "Shakespeare's Plays and the Erasmian Box," *Renaissance Papers* (1981): 33–44.

29. See Bernard Spivack, *Shakespeare and the Allegory of Evil* (New York: Columbia University Press, 1598), and Robert Grams Hunter, *Shakespeare and the Comedy of Forgiveness* (New York: Columbia University Press, 1965), 79.

30. Noted by Catherine Gira, "Shakespeare's Venus Figures and Renaissance Tradition," *Studies in Iconography* 4 (1978): 101.

31. Van Veen, 70–71.

32. See Peter M. Daly, *Emblem Theory: Recent German Contributions to the Characterization of the Emblem Genre* (Nendeln, Liechtenstein: KTO Press, 1979), 104.

33. See Frances Yates, *Giordano Bruno and the Hermetic Tradition* (London:

Routledge & Kegan Paul, 1964), 78. R. J. Clements points out that George Wither called music "the handmaid of the Lord" in his *A Collection of Emblemes* (1635); see Robert J. Clements, *Picta Poesis: Literary and Humanistic Theory in Renaissance Emblem Books* (Rome: Edizioni di Storia e Letteratura, 1960), 83. Of course, Shakespeare himself provided an extensive discussion of the Pythagorean powers of music and of the unheard harmony of the spheres in the love scene between Jessica and Lorenzo in *The Merchant of Venice* (5.1.54–86).

34. Vincenzo Cartari, *Le imagini degli dei degli Antichi* (Venice: Vincentio Valgrisi, 1571), 131. Translation by Roger T. Simonds.

35. See Robert Grams Hunter, *Shakespeare and the Comedy of Forgiveness* (New York: Columbia University Press, 1965), 184, and Homer D. Swander, "*Cymbeline:* Religious Idea and Dramatic Design," in *Pacific Coast Studies in Shakespeare,* ed. Waldo McNeir and Thelma N. Greenfield (Eugene: University of Oregon Books, 1966), 256–57.

36. See Lila Geller, "*Cymbeline* and the Imagery of Covenant Theology," *Studies in English Literature* 20 (1980): 245.

37. Ibid.

38. Ibid., 243.

39. See Barbara Lewalski, *Protestant Poetics and the Seventeenth Century Religious Lyric* (Princeton, N.J.: Princeton University Press, 1979), 39–53. I am grateful to Stella P. Revard for directing me to this excellent discussion of the importance of the Psalms to Protestant poets in England.

10

Conclusion: The Tempered Music of Orpheus

Orpheus with his lute made trees,
And the mountain tops that freeze,
    Bow themselves when he did sing.
To his music, plants and flowers
Ever sprung, as sun and showers,
    There had made a lasting spring.

Every thing that heard him play,
Even the billows of the sea.
    Hung their heads, and then lay by.
In sweet music is such art,
Killing care and grief of heart,
    Fall asleep, or hearing die.
          —*King Henry VIII* (3.1.3–14)

We are now finally ready to answer Samuel Johnson's complaint about "incongruity" in *Cymbeline*. That which holds together all of the apparently incongruous images from nature and mythology in the tragicomedy is quite simply the Neoplatonic–Pythagorean cosmology of Shakespeare's era, the widely held belief in an integrated universe ruled by cosmic harmony or divine concord. Within this philosophy, apparently disparate images and metaphors can be seen to echo one another thematically and without any contradiction at all. Not everyone in England accepted the harmonist theory as true, to be sure, especially during the early seventeenth century when "science" and philosophical scepticism were calling so much in doubt, but a belief in this theory of the universe was still generally shared by the majority of Shakespeare's literary contemporaries, as we can see by their poetic and political writings.[1] Although Shakespeare himself was subtly challenging and revising certain traditional metaphors about life, as I noted earlier in my discussion of the elm and the vine *topos,* his dramatic works are still seen by Renaissance scholars today as probably the richest mine of harmonist statements available since the first appearance of Plato's *Timaeus*. Although we must always keep in mind that what Shakespeare's characters say onstage cannot be necessarily assumed to represent the personal beliefs of the dramatist, my own position is that Shakespeare was very much a harmonist, because the theory (1) was so attractive to the poetic sensibility and (2) was such an important element of the Platonist tradition he had inherited from the great English poets who preceded him.

In any case, Shakespeare's characters Philarmonus and Cymbeline are clearly harmonists in their political thought, as we have just observed in the previous chapter. Once the characters in *Cymbeline* are psychologically in tune with themselves and socially in tune with each other, men and women can at last live in tune with the gods, at which point universal peace or concord reigns. The same is true of the other three Shakespearean tragicomedies. As Catherine M. Dunne has indicated,

Pericles, Cymbeline, The Winter's Tale, and especially *The Tempest* reveal a world which operates largely according to Neoplatonic principles. This world is like a gigantic instrument upon which the gods play. When it is in tune, there is peace and harmony; when it is "dis-tempered", or out of tune, there is discord and disorder. And the final transformation and reconciliation of the characters is frequently effected by music, just as it is usually paralleled or symbolized by changes in the physical universe and in the accompanying music.[2]

In our tragicomedy, King Cymbeline hears "the tune of Imogen" (5.5.238), a form of *musica humana* that echoes the harmony of the spheres or the *musica mundana,* to use the familiar terminology of Boethius, and he enters into a state of concord with his family and with Rome. After Philarmonus rejoices that "The fingers of the powers above do tune / the harmony of this peace" (5.5.467–70), Cymbeline leads the entire company offstage to sing hymns of thanksgiving and praise to the gods who have restored to him all that was earlier lost through discord.

We should note here that "the tune of Imogen" is also understood earlier by the Wild Boy Arviragus to echo the unheard cosmic harmony when he observes of her *persona* Fidele, "How angel-like he sings!" (4.2.48).[3] Even an untutored savage responds to beautiful singing, as Macrobius pointed out in his commentary on Cicero's *Somnium Scipionis:*

Every soul in the world is allured by musical sounds so that not only those who are more refined in their habits, but all the barbarous peoples as well, have adopted songs by which they are inflamed with courage or wooed to pleasure; for the soul carries with it into the body a memory of the music which it knew in the sky, and is so captivated by its charm that there is no breast so cruel or savage as not to be gripped by the spell of such an appeal.[4]

In addition, the phoenix, to which Imogen is compared by Iachimo, was said by Lactantius (lines 45–50 in *The Phoenix*) to have a sweeter song than any other bird, and the poet likens its warbling to the music of the lute (Hollander 1961, 55). These and similar musical references in *Cymbeline* have, of course, been iconographically prefigured by the elaborate cosmic ceiling of singing cherubim in Imogen's bedchamber, a motif repeated in the harmonies of the last scene of the play.

In contrast to the harmonies in the late tragicomedies, Shakespeare's earlier histories and tragedies abound with references to personal and political discord. John Hollander calls our attention specifically to act 5 of *Richard II*, when a defeated and repentant king confesses,

> And here have I the daintiness of ear
> To check time broke in a disordered string,
> But for the concord of my state and time
> Had not the ear to hear my true time broke.

> (5.5.45–48)

According to Hollander, the "disordered string" is Richard himself, "an emblem of the unruled, unruly state," (1961, 148). Likewise, Shakespeare's Henry VI is pathetically unable to tune the nobility of his commonwealth to the harmonies of the ideal state as described in *Henry V*:

> For government, though high and low and lower,
> Put into parts, doth keep in one consent,
> Congreeing in a full and natural close,
> Like music.

> (1.2.180–83)

Ideas like the above of political concord can be found in most of the Jacobean court masques, all of which conclude with a dance uniting the audience and the actors in a musical and measured imitation of the natural union between heaven and earth through cosmic harmony.[5] As James Daly points out, during the Renaissance it was commonly believed that "Music was the result of an order dictated by reason"; and "It followed that political order sprang from a constitutive harmony of classes, a variety in wealth, social position, and function. . . . The king's job is the coordination and balancing of the different social sounds, so that all together make harmony, and he does this by good laws, wise ministers, etc."[6] In respect to individuals, Hollander observes that, "The notion of the soul as a *harmonia* or proportionate distribution of unlike parts accommodated itself equally well to the musical metaphor and to the same kind of interpretation of it as was given in the myth of heavenly music" (1961, 31).

Without an understanding of the pervasive harmonist theory in the play, it is very difficult for modern readers of *Cymbeline* to grasp, for example, why the Queen and Cloten are thought to be evil in advising the king to refuse the customary payment of tribute to Rome. Today we tend to admire the nationalist fervor of Cloten, even though it results in the discord of war and in many deaths on the battlefield. But alliances between states, like the agreement between Britain and pagan Rome in *Cymbeline,* were commonly understood during Shakespeare's time to reflect or echo cosmic harmony, a binding together of man with man as the heavenly bodies were bound together in their cosmic dance under divine law. In fact, Horapollo's *Hieroglyphics* of 1505 cites the lyre as the obvious symbol of a political leader who unites people since "the lyre preserves the unity of its sounds" (quoted in Hollander 1961, 48). Thus, Alciati's Emblem 10, which is dedicated to the Duke of Milan, depicts a lute lying on a couch for its protection. Under the inscriptio "Foedera" ("Alliances"), the subscriptio reads as follows.

> Hanc citharam, à lembi quae forma halieutica fertur,
>   Vendicat et propriam Musa Latina sibi,
> Accipe Dux: placeat nostrum hoc tibi tempore munus,
>   Quo nova cum sociis foedera inire paras.
> Difficile est, nisi docto homini, tot tendere chordas;
>   Unaque si fuerit non bene tenta fides,
> Ruptave (quod facile est) perit omnis gratia conchae,
>   Illeque praecellens cantus, ineptus erit.
> Sic Itali coeunt proceres in foedera: concors
>   Nil est quod timeas, si tibi constet amor.
> At si aliquis desciscat (uti plerumque videamus)
>   In nihilum illa omnis solvitur harmonia.

> (Accept, Duke, this lute, which is said to derive its form from a fishing boat,
>   And which the Latin Muse claims as her own.
> May this gift of ours be pleasing to you at this time, as you prepare to enter
>   upon new alliances with your allies.
> It is difficult, unless a man is skilled, to tune so many strings.
> And if one string is not well tuned, or is broken—which can easily happen—
>   the entire pleasantness of the shell perishes; and that excellent music will be
>   ineffectual.
> Thus the leaders of Italy are joining together in alliances. There is nothing for
>   you to fear, if harmonious love for you continues;
> but if anyone withdraws—as we often see—the entire harmony is reduced to
>   nothing.)[7]

When Britain withdraws from its alliance with the Roman Empire in *Cymbeline,* the entire harmony of the Augustan *pax romana* is also temporarily put out of tune.

Hollander has shown as well that many emblems and poems on music pertaining to human love, the body politic, and the motion of the planets followed Alciati's treatment of the subject, so that the lute or lyre became a particularly important symbolic indicator of pyschological and political harmony during the Renaissance. "It was by and large most common to

6   ANDREAE ALCIATI

Fœdera.

Hãc cithará à lembi quæ forma halieutica fertur,
   Vendicat & propriam Mufa latina fibi,
Accipe Dux,placeat noftrũ hoc tibi tẽpore munus,
   Quo noua cum focijs fœdera inire paras.
Difficile eft,nifi docto homini,tot tendere chordas,
   Vnáq; fi fuerit non bene tenta fides,
Ruptáue (qd' facile eft) perit omnis gratia cõchæ,
   Illeq; præcellens cantus,ineptus erit.
Sic Itali coëunt proceres in fœdera,concors,
   Nil eft quod timeas,fi tibi conftet amor.
At fi aliquis defcifcat (uti plcrunque uidemus)
   . In nihilum illa omnis foluitur harmonia.

Emblem 10 by Andrea Alciati, *Emblemata* (Paris: Wechel, 1534), 6, depicts a lute as a symbol of political alliance, but the verse warns that a single broken string can destroy its harmony. Reprinted by permission of the Folger Shakespeare Library (PN 6349 A8 1534b Cage).

allow the strings to represent abstract 'harmony' and 'order' [like that of the Great Chain of Being] by typifying musical harmoniousness and ordered tuning. Thus the Platonic notion of the World-Soul (as well as the individual psyche) considered as a tuning, or *harmonia,* finds figurative expression in the image of the World-Lyre, or the stringed instrument of the human soul" (Hollander 1961, 44). However, the influence of music could extend in either direction, leading either upward or downward. In *Othello,* Iago warns that he will destroy the harmony of love and marriage when he says, "I'll set down the pegs that make this music" (2.1.200), meaning that he will untune the soul of Othello and make a beast of him. As far as the inspirational influence of the individual soul or the well-tuned microcosm on the greater world is concerned, Chapman describes in *Ouids Banquet of Sence* the uplifting effect of lute music in conjunction with the human voice when Corinna bursts into song in the garden:

O that as man is cald a little world
The world might shrink into a little man,
To heare the notes about this Garden hurld,
That skill desperst in tunes so Orphean
  Might not be lost in smiting stocks and trees
That have no eares; but growne as it began
  Spred theyr renounes, as far as *Phoebus* sees
Through earths dull vaines: that shee like heauen might moue,
In ceaseless Musick, and be fill'd with loue.[8]

In contrast to a world filled with love because of music, the effect of a broken lute string is devastating for it symbolizes a broken heart, a broken promise in love, or a broken agreement in the realm of politics. To take one illustration, Mary F. S. Hervey has demonstrated that the key to our understanding of Holbein's famous painting of "The Ambassadors" is not the startling anamorphic image of a skull, which is simply Holbein's (Hollow Bones) signature and possibly a warning for the future of international relations,[9] but rather the broken string on the lute that represents world harmony all out of tune.[10] The painting is thus an emblem of the fact that someone (probably the Duke of Milan) has broken a political agreement, although it apparently also expresses the hope through its many symbols of the humanizing Liberal Arts and Sciences and the portraits of France's leading ambassadors, Jean de Dinteville and Bishop Georges de Selve, that the lute can be repaired by the ambassadors meeting with equally prominent and reasonable statesmen of other countries to form a new alliance.

In this elaborate system of echoing and reechoing world harmonies, the individual could easily become discordant by allowing his humors to get out of balance, as Posthumus in *Cymbeline* allows the emotions of jealousy and wrath to overcome the rest of his psyche. Yet he too may be restored to harmony if he will allow his intellect (usually symbolized by Mercury) to regain control over his passions, an event that does not occur until late in the play. Emblematist Geffrey Whitney discusses this very problem in an emblem depicting Mercury repairing a lute, while in the background, a man plays on a lute and Natura dances to his tune. The motto states, "Industria naturam corrigit" ("Industry corrects nature"); while according to the verse,

The Lute, whose sounde doth most delighte the eare,
   Was caste aside, and lack'd bothe stringes, and frettes:
Whereby, no worthe within it did appeare,
Mercvrivs came, and it in order settes:
   Which being tun'de, such Harmonie did lende,
That Poëttes write, the trees their toppes did bende.

Euen so, the man on whome doth Nature froune,
Whereby, he liues dispis'd of euerie wighte,
Industrie yet, maie bringe him to renoune,
And diligence, maie make the crooked righte:
   Then haue no doubt, for arte maie nature helpe.
   Thinke howe the beare doth forme her vgly whelpe.[11]

Or for that matter, think how the lion breathes new life on the third day
into its whelp and inspires its rebirth through the art of a bass roar. All
such metaphors echo one another, according to the harmonist theory.
Similarly, human psychology can be restored to harmony through repentance and/or therapeutic music, after which a person's situation in the
world will also improve. Even families broken apart by internal discord
can regain lost harmony, as Shakespeare demonstrates in all four of his
final tragicomedies.

In fact, the happy family was itself a primary symbol of cosmic harmony. According to James Daly, it "provided the pattern for both larger
and smaller political and social relationships, and was an essential part of
the human cosmology, a reflection of the harmony of other images in the
system" (1979, 6). For this reason, the marriage *topos* of the elm and the
vine acquires such importance in *Cymbeline* as a metaphor intimately
related to cosmic harmony.

Morality based on universal laws was an implicit part of the harmonist
theory as well. Hence Cloten's immoral intent toward Imogen is probably
the reason why she does not hear or respond to his dawn serenade in act 1.
Ironically, although an *aubade* is among other things an invocation to the
sun or to Apollo, who is the opposite from Dionysos, god of darkness,
sexuality, and passion, Cloten naively invokes the god of light and reason
to help him accomplish dark ends. Yet, considerably more serious moral
infractions than that of sexual lust in the play are (1) Imogen's disobedience toward her father and king, a disobedience that directly destroys
both the family and the national harmony, and (2) the servant Pisanio's
disobedience of his master's order to kill a bride thought to be wanton.
James Daly tells us, however, that in the harmonist system, only *moral*
commands had to be obeyed, and we know that neither the king's command to Imogen to marry the lout Cloten and thereby give him access to
the throne nor Posthumus's command to Pisanio to kill Imogen were
moral. Harmonist "analogies reinforced obedience only to lawful or moral

Induſtria naturam corrigit.

Ad D. H. Wh. patruelis mei F.

T H E Lute, whoſe ſounde doth moſt delighte the eare,
Was caſte aſide, and lack'de bothe ſtringes, and frettes:
Whereby, no worthe within it did appeare,
M E R C V R I V S came, and it in order ſettes:
   Which being tun'de, ſuche Harmonie did lende,
   That Poëttes write, the trees theire toppes did bende.

Euen ſo, the man on whome dothe Nature froune,
Whereby, he liues diſpiſd of euerie wighte,
Induſtrie yet, maie bringe him to renoume,
And diligence, maie make the crooked righte:
   Then haue no doubt, for arte maie nature helpe.
   Thinke howe the beare doth forme her vglye whelpe.

Ouid. Epiſt. 15.

Si mihi difficilis formam natura negauit;
Ingenio forma damna rependo mea.

Infor-

Mercury (intellect) repairs a broken lute representing harmony in Geffrey Whitney's
***A Choice of Emblemes* (Leyden, 1586), 92. Reprinted by permission of the Folger**
Shakespeare Library (STC 25437.8).

actions—and the system was confident that people knew which actions were lawful and moral" (Daly 1979, 30, n.53). In fact, one actually had the moral duty to *disobey* bad commands, even though the ideal of harmony would then suffer for a while as a result of the hierarchical breakdown. As Posthumus admits, "Every good servant does not all commands: / No bond, but to do just ones" (5.1.6–7).

The restoration of lost harmony in persons and communities was achieved by means similar to those used by musicians to retune their instruments. For the individual to restore or maintain harmony within himself, he must "temper" or tune his various humors to one another as the strings of a lute are tuned to a chosen scale. However, we must also note that during the Renaissance "harmony" did not mean the consonance of a chord as it does today but the tonal relationship of each note of a scale to each of the others. According to Boethius, such tuning meant in human terms, "that which unites the incorporeal activity of the reason with the body . . . a certain mutual adaptation and as it were a tempering of high and low sounds into a single consonance" (quoted in Hollander 1961, 25). A tempering of this sort amounted to the realization of Aristotle's notion of desirable moderation in human thought, feeling, and behavior in contrast to the disastrous continuance in a discordant state of distemper or intemperance.

Thus the virtue of temperance became perhaps the most important in human society of all Plato's cardinal virtues, for without it one may be courageous but certainly neither just nor wise. Indeed James J. Yoch, Jr., has argued persuasively that temperance is the basic theme of all Renaissance tragicomedies:

> These dramas of passion leading to orderly conclusions . . . draw on several antique sources to enrich the personal theme of temperance and to extend its scope by implication or by statement into politics. In Italy the hope for a happy ending despite the appearance of chaos was a matter of belief central both to princely and ecclesiastical systems. . . . The optimistic transformations from sorrow to joy for the good and from vice to virtue for the bad depend on the principle of moderation both in the characters and in the authors of Renaissance tragicomedies.[12]

Yet, there must be discernable inner and outer reform before such fine tuning can be achieved.

Cymbeline and other Renaissance tragicomedies not only insist on temperance as the virtue most needed by the characters, but these plays are even more significantly calls to personal, political, and spiritual reform. They were written to echo the harmony of the spheres in the theater through their music and poetry, to remind the audience of the harmonious beauty of the Golden Age before man's fall from grace, i.e., to evoke a psychological experience of Platonic "recollection," and to inspire the audience with a longing for this lost ideal world. Although we may laugh today at the unreality of the happy endings in such plays, we also leave the theater with a strong feeling of dissatisfaction with the present state of the inner and outer affairs to which we must return. One who, like Iachimo, has actually entered into the Temple of the Graces will never again be quite happy in any other environment. Thus the tragicomic playwright demands something from us in return for the "unbelievable" entertainment and the "touches of sweet harmony" he has provided in the theater. Through reminding us of the pleasurable ideal of concord after the tension of discord, he also insists that we strive to reform our own inner lives to be more in harmony with his Orphic vision of earthly potential, of matter interpenetrated by divinity, and that we further strive to reform our social and political systems to reflect the measure and harmony of the planetary dance and the unheard song of the planets and the cherubim. Finally, he gives us hope that the ideal may just possibly become real in the world, at least for short periods of time, as he has made it real on the stage.

The true central theme of tragicomedy is, therefore, nothing less than *reformation,* a theme that echoes and reechoes in *Cymbeline* by means of Shakespeare's bird, animal, vegetable, mineral, and musical symbols as well as through the mimetic action of the characters onstage.

All that I have said here about the harmonist theory and its relationship

Emblem 18 in *The Mirrour of Maiestie* (1618) sums up much of the harmonist theory. Reprinted by permission of the Folger Shakespeare Library (PN 6349 M6, 35).

to humanity can be summed up by Emblem 18 in *The Mirrour of Maiestie*. Like most of the other emblems referred to in this study, this emblem is not for one moment a source for Shakespeare's thought or poetry but is offered as an illustrative parallel to the harmonist universe implied in *Cymbeline*. Under a woodcut of a lady playing the lute and literally surrounded by a circle of listening ears, we find the following verse:

> As busie Bees vnto their Hiue doe swarme,
> So do's th' attractive power of *Musicke* charme
> All *Eares* with silent rapture: nay, it can
> Wilde *Reason* re-contract, diuorc'd from man.
> *Birds* in their warblings imitate the *Spheares:*
> This sings the *Treble,* that the *Tenour* beares:
> *Beasts* haue with listning to a Shepheards lay,
> Forgot to feed, and so haue pin'd away:
> *Brookes* that creepe through each flowr-befretted field,
> In their harmonious murmurs, musicke yeeld:
> Yea, senseless *stones* at the old *Poets* song,
> Themselues in heapes did so together throng,
> That to high beauteous structures they did swell
> Without the helpe of *hand,* or vse of *skill:*
> This *Harmony* in t'humane *Fabricke* steales:
> And is the sinewes of all Common-weales. [13]

Cymbeline's commonwealth is ultimately tuned to such harmony through his practice in act 5 of royal mercy or, in legal terms, of equity.

Orpheus and the Tuning of the Inner and Outer Man

We have noted earlier that the figure of Orpheus is a barely suppressed presence in all Shakespeare's final tragicomedies. As David Armitage puts it, "The Orpheus who haunts the romances is a composite figure, a cluster of associations which can be seen accumulating across Shakespeare's work."[14] But what exactly is the demigod's significance within the context of these plays, especially since the tragicomedies restore all losses, while Orpheus is unsuccessful in restoring Eurydice to mortal life in most versions of his myth? To my knowledge, none of those scholars discovering Orpheus as a phantom presence in Shakespeare's later works has yet offered a satisfactory explanation. Even Cody, who claims that pastorals contain an Orphic rite of some sort, is not particularly clear as to what that ritual might be. The purpose of this section, therefore, is to attempt at the very least a suggestion of the Renaissance meaning of Shakespeare's Orphic allusions in *Cymbeline*.

In general, Orpheus played many roles for Renaissance Neoplatonists.

First, he was a passionate lover and one cruelly separated from the beautiful woman he adored, as Petrarch is separated from Laura, and as Posthumus is separated from Imogen. His music and poetry celebrate both the beauty of his beloved and his emotional grief at the early loss of such beauty to death. As poet and musician, Orpheus laments the shortness of life and love and the ephemeral quality of the very sensory pleasure that inspires his art in the first place. Thus, despite his Apollonian sources, he is best known for his Dionysian *furor* or passionate love. In a 1595 Elizabethan poem by R. B. called *Orpheus, His Journey to Hell, and his musicke to the Ghosts, for the regaining of faire Euridice his Love, and new spoused Wife,* the poet has Orpheus furiously blame Eurydice for dying on their wedding day before they have consummated their love. He complains that he cannot renew "her now decaying beautie,"[15] and in his later song to charm Cerberus, he further laments "How Loues effect is an vnconstant thing" (sig. C2), the implication being that there is little value in loving mortal beauty that is so soon destroyed. Yet his love is so overwhelming that he attempts the fearful journey to Hades to save Eurydice from final oblivion. Lyre in hand, the musical child of Apollo bravely enters the dark subterranean realm of Dionysos, the underworld of the passions from which he hopes to rescue beauty through his song.

There are as many explanations for the failure of Orpheus's quest as there are versions of the myth, but I have found R. B.'s interpretation particularly suggestive for our understanding of *Cymbeline* since it emphasizes the singer's passionate love and uncontrolled personal emotions in contrast to his artistic control in song. Orpheus's song to Pluto, explaining his presence alive in Hades, consists of eleven verses, each ending with the Virgilian refrain so dear to the Neoplatonists, "Quod Amor vincit omnia" ("Love conquers all"). A typical verse reads as follows:

> Thus loue that enters at the eie,
>   And slyely steales downe to the heart:
> There doth ingender fantasie,
>   Whose issue breeds, or joy, or smart,
> Perforce enforces all to say,
>   *Quod Amor vincit omnia.*
>
> (R. B. 1595, sig. D^v)

As Virgil had pointed out, passionate love overcomes everyone, both man and god. Agreeing with Orpheus's statement, Pluto allows him to lead Eurydice back to earth but with the injunction that the poet may not "see" her, or have any sensory information about her, until they are safely out of Hades.

> But if fond jealousie should make him doubt,
>   And he looke back to see his Loues sweet face:

Before he be from his vast kingdome out,
　And past the fatall limits of that place.
Then should his wife be snatch'd away againe,
　And he should nere the like good turne obtaine.

(sig. D3)

In other words, Pluto apparently understands the power of human passion
to undermine faith and to cause doubt. As a fallible human being, Orpheus
at some point will have to demand sensory proof that the figure behind him
is really Eurydice. His passion for her will cause him to succumb to doubt
and the temptation to know.

Eurydice is then given heavily veiled to Orpheus so that he cannot see
her eyes and reassure himself of her love, nor can the lovers speak to one
another during the journey toward light. But, unlike Mozart's later successful Orpheus, Tamino in *The Magic Flute,* R. B.'s Orpheus, who has
already lost Eurydice once to death, fears that she will be "vnconstant" a
second time and breaks the taboo because of his passionate jealousy.

But longer can he not forbeare to see,
　if she did follow him along or no:
Such was the effect of burning jealousie,
　that would not let him any further goe,
Before he had satisfi'd his longing mind,
In looking if his louer were behind.

(sig. D3ᵛ)

Just as in *Cymbeline,* jealous love here leads to doubt, although in this
poem Eurydice is lost forever, while Imogen is restored by Providence to
Posthumus. Returning alone to earth, Orpheus transforms his songs of
love and lamentation into satirical invectives against deceitful women, all
of whom, he says, are sure to be fickle to their lovers. Other men,
impressed by this new satiric art, leave their wives to join Orpheus in a life
of celibacy. Furious at this male desertion of imperial love, the women
then decide to kill Orpheus since "He was an enemie vnto their gender"
(sig. Dᵛ). Orpheus's subsequent death and dismemberment by Maenads
becomes a celebration of the usual Dionysian ritual or bloody "passion,"
in this case a celebration quite appropriate for one who has acted out the
passion of jealousy even in the underworld. The story appears to symbolize that the Apollonian poet-musician must fully suffer through the
Dionysian passion in order to understand divine beauty as eternal and
contrary to the mortal beauty originally praised in his art. Thus Robert
Fludd's illustration of the Temple of Harmony pays homage to both types
of music, the lute songs of Apollo and the pipes of Pan or Dionysos.

In contrast to Orpheus as passionate lover, the second traditional role of
the legendary poet-musician was that of "the civilizer," who softens the

Robert Fludd's Temple of Harmony includes the music of both Apollo and Pan. From *Ultriusque Cosmi Historia* by permission of the Folger Shakespeare Library (BD 500 F4 1617c Cage, 168).

hearts of primitive people.[16] According to Boccaccio, "he makes wild beasts gentle, that is to say bloody and rapacious men whom eloquence often recalls to gentleness and humanity" (quoted in Warden 1982, 90). Landino goes even further to say that Orpheus brings Wild Men in from the forest to live together in communities ruled by law, " 'and this is precisely what the poets meant when they said that Orpheus could make the wild beasts tame with his lyre, make the rocks and woods move and halt streams in their courses; that he could with his sweet speech bring to civilization men who were insensitive to virtue as though made of stone and who were crazed and maddened by the pleasures of the body' " (quoted in Warden 1982, 90). John Warden tells us that Orpheus is there-fore the teacher of *humanitas,* which Ficino defines as "the capacity for love" (1982, 91). For Ficino, Orpheus becomes not only a gifted teacher but also an artist, "who looks within himself to discover the harmony of the cosmos and by artistry leads others to an understanding and beyond" (Warden 1982, 90). Above all, the poet leads man to the love of his fellows through his cilivizing influence.

The third role of Orpheus is that of theologian. The Greeks had believed that the mystery religions were created by Orpheus, and Renaissance thinkers later believed that it was he who taught the mysteries to Pythagoras and Plato. As a poet, Orpheus characteristically sings of the creation of the world, of how love came into being within chaos, and of the essential "unity and singleness of the cosmos" (Warden 1982, 92). His lyre with its seven strings represents the seven known planets and thus is a symbol for cosmic harmony, since "mathematically the intervals of the Orphic lyre are the structured basis of the entire visible universe and of the human soul. It offers an assurance on the relationship between microcosm and macrocosm. Man, by exploring his own interior space, finds a structure in the microcosm identical with that of the macrocosm. He finds the lyre within himself and 'explicates' it, as Cusanus put it" (Warden 1982, 93). Above all, Orpheus the theologian taught humanity to love God as the ultimate source of all truth and beauty.

Indeed the Middle Ages had actually considered Orpheus to be even more than a theologian, seeing him as a prefiguration of Christ and as a mythological personage to be used as a pictorial symbol of Christ in art. According to John B. Friedman, "In search of an iconography for Christ, the psychopomp, early Christian artisans turned to the pictorial vocabulary of paganism. There they found one figure who seemed not too unlike their new savior in attitudes and who, moreover, had to some degree been sanctified as a spokesman for monotheism in literature. This person was Orpheus."[17] The poet-musician also had the status of a prophet for Christians, since the Greeks had reported that his head continued singing after his death and was installed by Apollo in a temple on Lesbos as an oracle, i.e., as an intermediary between man and the gods.

This means, of course, that inspired poets who follow in the footsteps of Orpheus can also explain the ways of God to man. For example, Shakespeare's Jupiter may seem to be only a theatrical illusion to us, but his oracle concerned with Posthumus turns out to be true within the play. Likewise, the dramatic poet's promise through Jupiter that suffering will lead to joy for all men and nations who seek humbly to achieve harmony, just as Posthumus does in the play, may be understood by the audience to be a true Orphic prophecy. In fact, we have heard the same prophecy before in the final lines of Guarini's *Il pastor fido:* "True joy is a thing / That springs from Vertue after suffering" (Guarini, 411). Needless to say, the claim of prophetic powers is an exalted one for poets to make, but it was taken up once more in the nineteenth century by the Romantics, as we know, at least by those poets who were influenced by Neoplatonism. Moreover, we should remember at this point that during Shakespeare's final years as a practicing poet in the theater, and like his poetic predecessor Edmund Spenser and his successor John Milton, the dramatist was continually prophesying happy prosperity for his countrymen—but only if they endeavored to keep their lives in tune with the unheard music of the spheres. Those who provoked discord, in contrast, would be appropriately punished, and such troublemakers could actually include present rulers, as we see among the *dramatis personae* of *The Tempest,* for example. If I am correct in all this, Shakespeare is himself that faintly perceived ghost of Orpheus noticed by Armitage in the final tragicomedies, and our recognition of this hint of Orphic magic in the poet's repertory is probably as close as we will ever come to Shakespeare's view of himself as an artist.

The fourth, and most important, role of Orpheus was precisely that of the inspired poet and "the self-conscious artist" (Warden 1982, 99), whose magic redeems nature or the sensible world by reshaping its forms. Like a creator god, the creative artist gives intellectual and emotional meaning to natural life, suffering, and death. As for Orpheus, who was born in the Golden Age, he was—like Christ—from the very beginning made of finer stuff than ordinary people, as R. B. reminds us in *Orpheus, His Journey to Hell:*

In this contented time was *Orpheus* borne,
    compos'd of purer metal than a man:
Made mortall by the Gods in Natures scorne,
    that earth might witness how the heavens can
Inclose in Elementall shapes celestiall thinges,
Whose life from quintescence of heauen springs.

(sig. B^v)

Like a creator god, the artist also encloses celestial truths in elemental shapes and "gives to aery nothing / A local habitation and a name" (*MND* 5.1.16–17). Thus, in Renaissance Italy, as Charles Segal writes, "The dominant tone [of the Orpheus myth] is not so much tragic loss as the celebration of poetry, music, and beauty as the guide to the truly civilized life. Politan [Poliziano], for example, whose *Orfeo* is a dramatized reworking of Virgil and Ovid, pays relatively little attention to the failure of Orpheus. His hero is an idealized artist. Like Ovid, Politan has Eurydice exonerate Orpheus and complain only of 'the too great love that has undone us both' *('l troppo amore n'ha disfatti ambedua')*."[18]

To imitate or to continue God's act of artistic creation, the poet must, according to Ficino, "Begin by considering thyself" (Warden 1982, 100) or begin by obeying the ancient command of Apollo to "Know thyself!" This involves a careful looking within oneself to find divinity. It also involves some kind of penitential or purification rite to harmonize the outer man with the inner man, that is, an act of reshaping the self or a *reformation*. Ficino taught that, since "Love is the power that produces harmony in all things," the artist must somehow "achieve a state of love" (Warden 1982, 102) before his skill can be used effectively. For the Renaissance, therefore, love is the key to understanding all the secrets of the universe. Says Ficino, "All parts of the world, because they are the works of a single creative artist, and, as components of the same construct, are all alike in their essence and manner of existence, are bound together each with each by a sort of mutual affection, so that love can properly be called the perpetual knot or link of the universe" (quoted in Warden 1982, 102). This idea, which derives from Plato's *Symposium* integrates easily with the Christian notion of charity. The artist, through his passion combined with his technical skill and control, "brings about a state of love by imposing order and shape; as one who loves and suffers he is privileged to be filled with the *furor amatorius* which leads the mind beyond understanding to the vision of divine beauty and to a state of joy" (Warden 1982, 103).

The Orphic voice is, therefore, the voice of a mature artist who has first suffered loss and has learned to understand transformation through death, then to recognize an eternal Adonis in the living flower and an ever fleeing Daphne in the tree. Orpheus brings us news from the other side of the veil of life by singing praises to the continual rebirth of life and love into the mutable forms of nature. Indeed the twentieth-century poet Rainer Maria Rilke seriously questions in *Sonnets to Orpheus* if this mysterious poet-god belongs to the living or the dead:

> Does he belong here? No, out of both
> realms his wide nature grew.
> More knowing would he bend the willows' branches
> who has experienced the willows' roots.[19]

(Pt. I, Sonnet 6, v. 1)

By the time Shakespeare began to write his Orphic tragicomedies, he had certainly "experienced the willows' roots" and was now ready to tell us about them and the order they represent.

Leo Spitzer explains historically that, "According to the Pythagoreans, it was cosmic order which was identifiable with music; according to the Christian philosophers, it was love and in the *ordo amoris* of Augustine we have evidently a blend of the Pagan and the Christian themes: henceforth 'order' is love."[20] This was true for Shakespeare and for the later Rilke as well. The notion also lies behind van Veen's emblem "All depends vpon loue" in which the *subscriptio* tells us,

The litle God of loue transpearseth with his dartes
The heauens and eke the earth in musicall accord,
For without loue it were a chaos of discord,
Thats fastned now in one of well conioyned partes.[21]

In *Cymbeline,* Shakespeare's renewal of marital love between Posthumus and Imogen is thus essential to the harmonious ending of the play. Without it, there could be no final concord or world peace in preparation for the birth of Christ or the God of Love. Nevertheless, it is the dramatist, or the inspired poet, who arranges these things on the stage of the Globe Theatre.

The profound Renaissance belief in the power of art to redeem natural beauty from inconstancy or mutability and to eternize it though giving it a

A M O R V M.

Otto van Veen's "All depends upon Loue" insists it is love that makes harmony in the world. From *Emblemes of Loue* (Antwerp, 1608), 35, and reprinted by permission of the Folger Shakespeare Library (STC 24627a.5 copy 1).

new form was, of course, widely accepted in Shakespeare's time. We can find, for example, an interesting illustration of the notion in Nicholas Reusner's emblem entitled "Musicae et Poëticae vis" ("The Power of Music and Poetry"). According to the verse:

Terribiles Orpheus tigres, rabidosques leones,
    Et volucres cantu leniit, atque feras.
Saxa sono blandae mouit testudinis alter
    Amphion: Thebas dum struit abque manu.
Scilicet agrestes animos, hominesque feroces
    Molliit: et populos imbuit arte rudes:
Quos blanda flexit prece comiter; eloquioque:
    Et quos ius docuit, iustitiamque sequi.
Musica sic multum, multum divina Poësis,
    Concentu numeris conueniente, valet.
Si vox est, canta: genius si, carmina salta:
    Commoda sed vitae carmina, grata Deo.
Carminibus mentes, mulcentur cantibus aures:
    Fontibus aetheriis vtraque vena fluit.

(Orpheus tamed terrible tigers, raging lions
    and wild birds also by his singing.
Amphion, likewise, moved stones with the sound of his alluring lyre, when he
    built Thebes without using his hands.
That is, he civilized rustic spirits and wild men, and he instructed ignorant
    people by his art.
He moved them with friendly enticements and eloquence, and he taught them
    to follow law and justice.
Thus Music, like divine Poetry, has great strength through the harmonious
    cooperation in its measures.
If you have a voice, sing! If the spirit moves you, dance the song.
    But fit the song to life, give thanks to God.
Minds are charmed by the songs, ears by the singing.
    Each stream flows from heavenly fountains.)[22]

Although the humanist Reusner emphasizes Orpheus as "civilizer" in this emblem, his point that the arts of music and poetry bring heaven and earth together through mutual creativity seems very significant. Life provides the materials for art; art reshapes or transforms these materials to reflect divine harmony in terms that humans can understand intellectually and then integrate into their personal and social lives.

Conscience as the Orphic Lyre Within

It is well known that for Renaissance Protestants, the god to be dis-covered within, or the orphic lyre belonging to all men and women, was invariably the conscience, that Socratic *daemon* that teaches the dif-

Orpheus brings harmony into nature through his music and poetry. From Nicholas Reusner, *Emblemata* (Frankfurt, 1581), 129. Reprinted by permission of the Folger Shakespeare Library (PN 6349 R4 1581 Cage).

ference between right and wrong to the soul. The word "conscience," which appears nine times in *Cymbeline,* should be understood here primarily as the Orphic guide pointing the way upward to light and to reformation. Indeed this resonant tragicomedy pits outer appearances and values (including the honor code) against the inner knowledge of conscience, which recognizes morality or immorality even in other people. It seems clear then that the fundamental dramatic conflict in the play is expressed most succinctly by Iachimo when he removes Imogen's gold bracelet from her arm and says, " 'Tis mine, and this will witness outwardly, / As strongly as the conscience does within, / To the madding of her lord" (2.2.35–37). Iachimo reckons here that Posthumus, like most people, will choose the misleading sensory phenomenon over the voice of his conscience, which is his latent inner knowledge of Imogen's true virtue. Like R. B.'s passionate lover Orpheus, Posthumus will want sensory rather than spiritual knowledge about his wife. Also like Orpheus, Posthumus has a "gift of the gods" in Imogen, but his lack of faith in his own conscience or inner knowledge of virtue causes him to lose her to an illusion fostered by Iachimo's demonic art.

The notion of the conscience as a provider of inner knowledge about the good or evil in others may seem very odd today, but this is one of the ways Shakespeare uses the term in *Cymbeline*. The physician's conscience, for instance, warns him against the evil intentions of the hypocritical Queen:

> But I beseech your grace, without offence
> (My conscience bids me ask) wherefore you have
> Commanded of me these most poisonous compounds,
> Which are the movers of a languishing death:
> But though slow, deadly.

(1.6.6–10)

Even though the Queen assures him that she means no harm to human beings, Cornelius mistrusts her enough to substitute his own drugs for hers. In contrast, Imogen immediately trusts the Wild Boys, conventional symbols for savagery, when she first meets them, because she recognizes the virtuous quality of people living in harmony with the dictates of their conscience.

>   Great men
> That had a court no bigger than this cave,
> That did attend themselves, and had the virtue
> Which their own conscience seal'd them, laying by
> That nothing-gift of differing multitudes,
> Could not out-peer these twain.

(3.7.54–59)

Unfortunately, however, she forgets her early conscientious mistrust of Iachimo as soon as he begins to flatter her lord; while, on the other hand, she firmly expects Pisanio to recognize her own inner virtue through the voice of his personal conscience: "I false? Thy conscience witness" (3.4.47). Similarly, the First Gaoler's sympathy for Posthumus in act 5 is also based on knowledge obtained from his conscience: "on my conscience, there are verier knaves desire to live, for all he be a Roman . . . I would we were all of one mind, and one mind good" (4.202–3, and 205–6).

In addition, Shakespeare uses the word "conscience" in *Cymbeline* in its more usual sense of an inner knowledge of one's own personal innocence or guilt.[23] In act 3, Belarius exclaims, "O Cymbeline, heaven and my conscience knows / Thou didst unjustly banish me" (3.99–100). A repentant Posthumus imprisoned in act 5 yearns to atone for his supposed crime against Imogen with the line, "My conscience, thou art fetter'd / More than my shanks and wrists: you good gods, give me / The penitent instrument to pick that bolt, / Then free for ever" (4.8–11). He now understands that the irreligious mandate of the honor code to kill an adulterous wife is obviously in direct conflict with the now stronger command of the conscience to forgive. Even Iachimo is finally bowed by the weight of a guilty conscience in this play: "But now my heavy conscience sinks my knee, / As then your force did. Take that life, beseech you, / Which I so often owe" (5.414–16). Shakespeare appears to suggest here that persons who are in tune with the cosmic harmony can hear the inner voice of conscience, while others apparently can not. A traumatic confrontation with a loved one's death often opens the ear to the god or lyre within.

The mythical Orpheus was required to come face to face with the fact of death, an experience that altered his songs from reflections of divine harmony to artistically controlled lamentations, or to the human expression of grief through poetry and music. In *Cymbeline,* Posthumus's sight of the bloody cloth sent him by Pisanio as proof of Imogen's death is a similar encounter with mortality, one that shocks him into an understanding of the finality of death for the body and into spiritual repentance for his immoral order of Imogen's murder. Posthumus's grief is expressed through his desire for atonement, which is to say, that he too wishes to die or to descend into the underworld in search of his beloved. Instead the underworld—in the persons of his ghostly relatives—comes up to him and evokes a happy prophecy for the future from Jupiter. The prophecy comes true in *Cymbeline,* however, only because Posthumus recognizes the need for conscientious inner reform: "To shame the guise o' th' world, I will begin, / The fashion less without, and more within" (5.1.32–33).

This stripping off of outer fashion, protective armor, and the recognizable signs of aristocracy by the hero, as I have suggested before, resembles the mythic flaying of Marsyas and symbolizes Posthumus's conscious sacrifice of worldly position, fame, and honor on the altars of the gods. His humble search for a sacrificial death on the battlefield and his subsequent dream-vision then constitute his Orphic rite of initiation to the inward spiritual level of existence where a divinely prophesied happy ending can take place. Posthumus's eventual good fortune provides us in the end with an understanding of Platonic meaning that has perhaps been explained most elegantly by Joseph Campbell:

> The happy ending of the fairy tale, the myth, and the divine comedy of the soul, is to be read, not as a contradiction, but as a transcendence of the universal

tragedy of man [his mortality]. The objective world remains what it was, but, because of a shift of emphasis within the subject, is beheld as though transformed. Where formerly life and death contended, now enduring being is made manifest—as indifferent to the accidents of time as water boiling in a pot is to the destiny of a bubble, or as the cosmos to the appearance and disappearance of a galaxy of stars.[24]

Such a transcendent vision is, of course, the essential stuff of Renaissance tragicomedy and the final artistic objective of the Orphic poet, who must himself have passed first through a flaying by Apollo in order to know his own limitations and to receive divine inspiration for his art. According to Edgar Wind, "The torture of the mortal by the god who inspires him was a central theme in the revival of ancient mysteries" during the Renaissance.[25]

Moreover, as Wind also reminds us, the tale of Cupid and Psyche by Apuleius, or the mythic archetype hidden within *Cymbeline,* is the most elaborate variation of such stories dealing with the divine torture of initiates before they are granted the joy of wisdom, and "the ordeals suffered by Psyche to regain Amor were understood as stages of a mystical initiation" (1968, 175). Thus Imogen's loss of Posthumus, her descent into a cave and later into a deathlike sleep constitute her own initiation into the mysteries, as we have seen earlier.

The Orphic mysteries are associated with other characters in *Cymbeline* as well. For example, Belarius has—like the medieval Sir Orfeo—stripped off his courtier's garments in his own act of sacrificial flaying and has gone to live in the wilderness as a Wild Man long before the play opens. He marries Euriphile, who has gone into exile with him and whose name may be an allusion to Eurydice; when she dies, her passing is marked by the music of what Belarius calls his "ingenious instrument" (4.2.186). We hear the "solemn music" of this same instrument in the play just after Guiderius announces that he has tossed Cloten's head into the river. If this act is an allusion to the death of Orpheus, as most scholars believe it is, then the mysterious instrument itself must be an allusion to Orpheus's lyre, which, as Shakespeare says elsewhere, "was strung with poet's sinews" (*TGV* 3.3.1). The third and final sounding of Belarius's "ingenious instrument" to announce Fidele's death is, therefore, a reminder of how music can console us in times of loss and grief and aid us in emotionally transcending the objective fact of death.

Orpheus's Music, "Killing care and grief of heart"

The apparent death of Imogen in act 4 of *Cymbeline* is followed by a touching funeral ceremony made especially notable by the second famous song in the play, in this case a dirge.

Fear no more the heat o' th' sun,
  Nor the furious winter's rages,
Thou thy worldly task has done,
  Home art gone and ta'en thy wages.
Golden lads and girls all must,
As chimney-sweepers, come to dust.

(4.2.258–63)

Perhaps the saddest line of all is the reminder in the song that "All lovers young, all lovers must / Consign to thee and come to dust" (274–75). The dirge is spoken to the corpse of Fidele by the Wild Boys, Guiderius and Arviragus, to comfort the soul of the deceased.

It is important to notice that the dirge is spoken rather than sung, after the following exchange between the Wild Boys:

Arv.   Be't so:
    And let us, Polydore, though now our voices
    Have got the mannish crack, sing him to th' ground,
    As once to our mother: use like note and words,
    Save that Euriphile [Eurydice?] must be Fidele.
Gui. Cadwal,
    I cannot sing: I'll weep, and word it with thee;
    For notes of sorrow *out of tune* are worse
    Than priests and fanes that lie.
Arv.   We'll speak it then.

(4.2. 234–42; my emphasis)

Although some critics have suggested that speech rather than song was required because Shakespeare's company was lacking boy soprano voices at the time *Cymbeline* was produced, this unlikely invention has been challenged by G. K. Hunter, who points out that similar dirges were spoken rather than sung in both *The Spanish Tragedy* and John Marston's *Antonio's Revenge*.[26] After discovering the body of his son in *The Spanish Tragedy* (2.2), Hieronimo states, "Ile say his dirge, singing fits not this case." Even more similar to *Cymbeline,* is the exchange between Pandulpho, Antonio, and Alberto in act 4, scene 2, of *Antonio's Revenge* (1599) preceding the burial of Feliche:

Ant. Wilt sing a dirge, boy?
Pan. No; no song; 'twill be vile out of tune.
Alb. Indeed he's hoarse; the poor boy's voice is crack'd.
Pan. Why, coz, why should it not be hoarse and crack'd,
    When all the strings of nature's symphony
    Are crack'd and jar? Why should his voice keep tune,
    When there's no music in the breast of man?
    I'll say an honest antic rhyme I have:
    Help me, good sorrow-mates, to give him grave.[26]

Hunter proposes that the spoken dirge seems to have been "an effective theatrical convention" considered by dramatists to be more sincere than one that is sung.[28]

In the light of our knowledge of the cosmic harmony theory, however, "sincerity" has little to do with it. The mourners in all three instances are emotionally suffering from grief, a passion that will crack their voices and spoil or untune the comforting effect of a ritual song addressed to the deceased. The dirge, as an attempt to return harmony to nature and to human souls after life's most traumatic event, must not be out of tune in any way. Passion or emotion is forbidden during an Orphic rite of resignation to the death of natural beauty whose essence still remains alive in the intellectual world.

In *The Untuning of the Sky,* Hollander quotes a lyric by Thomas Campion that illustrates how even the poet's heart can break [become out of tune] at the expression of grief by his muse:

> When to her lute Corrina sings,
> Her voice revives the leaden strings,
> And doth in highest noates appeare,
> As any challeng'd eccho cleere;
> But when she doth of mourning speake,
> Ev'n with her sighes the strings do breake.
> And as her lute doth live or die,
> Led by her passion, so must I,
> For when of pleasure she doth sing,
> My thoughts enjoy a sodaine spring,
> But if she doth of sorrow speake,
> Ev'n from my hart the strings doe break.
>
> (1961, 204)

Typically, Corrina does not sing of grief but rather speaks her sorrow as do Guiderius and Arviragus in *Cymbeline*. Only the demigod Orpheus could control his musical lamentations sufficiently to sing them in tune and thereby overcome through his magic the resistance of the underworld to a rebirth into nature.

The most significant aspect of the poet-musician Orpheus, therefore, is that his tempered and tuneful art, or reformation of nature, offers consolation to mortals for their ultimate return to the dust. Claude Paradin states as much in his emblem on music. Under the *inscriptio* "In sibilo aura tenuis" ("In the muttering of the gentle aire") and the *pictura* of a harp, Paradin writes that,

> Musicke is of it[s] owne nature an enimie to melancholy, and therefore is able to qualifie any furie that riseth of a vehement melancholie. Wherefore she is able also to driue away heauines, and dulnesse, which proceed of blacke choler, being ouerwhelmed and suffocate with flegme. With the which one hath recorded that once he saw a man sore troubled, and so sound and fast on sleepe,

that you could by no meanes get a word of him, but onely by a harpe sounding in his eares, at the pleasant harmonie whereof, he lifting vp his head, laughed, & answered to their demands. Which thing is an argument that there is no small affinitie betwixt Musicke and the soule.

After such a musical tempering of the individual melancholy soul, Paradin adds that a harmonious social effect can be expected as well. He claims that, "as in Musicke of different voices there is made tunable musicke, so of men also that are of one minde there may be made a consent of contrary natures and manners, which God accepteth aboue all other things that may be obserued or kept."[29] Although similar allusions to the ideal brotherhood of man are found in *Cymbeline,* not until the harmonious finale of the play does the king begin to address his social inferiors as "brother," realizing at last that if death is the great equalizer, the art of a good life must also include a recognition of the fundamental equality of man, despite existing and politically necessary social hierarchies.

The Orphic obligation to console humanity, no matter what losses the poet himself has suffered, is referred to in R. B.'s *Orphevs, His Journey to Hell.* While in the underworld, the poet-musician plays and sings for the tortured sinners of antiquity, and his divine music makes their sufferings to "surcease" (sig. C3 verso). Since Ovid implies a similar cessation of torture for the sinners in his version of the Orpheus's descent, this same obligation to comfort the audience, as we shall now see, was assumed by the composers of Renaissance tragicomedies.

To conclude this study of *Cymbeline,* we must return to the aesthetic problem of defining its tragicomic genre, which means treading once again on a sacrosanct principle of modern literary criticism in order to ask what effect the dramatist wishes his play to have on the audience. What is the author's aesthetic intent? Guarini provides us with the answer in a clear statement of the emotional aim of tragicomedy, a peculiarly Orphic genre. He states in his *Compendio* that in such plays the artistic intent is

> to imitate through the *mise en scène* a contrived action which combines all the tragic and comic elements which can believably and decorously coexist, regulated within the frame-work of a unified dramatic form whose aim is to purge with delight the sadness of the audience. In such a way that Imitation—the "technical" objective—is a mixed one, because it represents a combination of tragic and comic elements. Whereas Purgation—the "overall" objective—is a single one because it reduces this combination of elements to one basic concept: the liberation of the audience from melancholy.[30]

The Orphic poet thus makes us confront our foolishness and our mortality, but at the same time he liberates us from our sadness at loss through death by dramatizing the happy ending that awaits the virtuous on the other side of the bloody veil.

In this way, tragicomedy attempts through its special music to lead the audience upward to what Campbell describes as "a transcendence of the universal tragedy of man." We will not be purged of pity and fear, as Aristotle required of tragedy, but purged through tragicomedy of the existential melancholy that lies at the heart of the human condition. To achieve a state of spiritual delight in his audience, the writer of tragicomedy must first temper his own soul and then, through his poetic art, transform the information of sense into intelligence. This is to say that his music must make stones feel and trees move. For the stony hearts and wooden minds of an average audience to be charmed away from weeping over the inevitable end of life, they must be taught by art to follow faithfully the tuneful harmony of Tamino's magic flute or Orpheus's lyre through all the natural elements of this world and up to the higher intellectual world, which the senses have only dimly reflectd heretofore. This then is the Platonic quest for wisdom fulfilled by art, rather than by philosophy alone.

According to Segal, Orphic poetry is particularly concerned with metamorphosis and changes both upward and downward in the characters of a tale are possible. In Ovid, he says,

> True Orphic song crosses the boundaries betwen matter and spirit in an upward direction: it brings life and sensitivity where before there was only inert matter. The enraged Bacchantes and the foolish Midas undergo downward meta-mor-phosis, from human to bestial or plant forms. The deity presiding over these latter changes is not Olympian Apollo, protector of Orpheus, but the god of the drunken revel, Bacchus, whose Maenads destroy Orpheus, his half-bestial com-panion Silenus, and the goat-footed god of the wild countryside, Pan. Over against the ever-present possibility of human degradation to bestiality in this world of sudden, arbitrary change and unstable identity, therefore, stand this Apollonian-Orphic poetry and its upward movement from matter to spirit, from lifeless stone or tree to human sensitivity.[31]

However, in Renaissance tragicomedy, the Orphic spirit results in a *reconciliation* between Apollo and Bacchus rather than in a continued opposition. Both deities are ultimately necessary for humanity to achieve happiness through wisdom, as Plato implies in *The Symposium* and as Renaissance art reiterates over and over again. In the words of Richard Cody, "the power of Orphic song sways Hades and survives death as a voice in which the Apolline and Bacchic are one. They are always the indivisible brothers, says Ficino; both are exactly the same."[32]

Theoretically then, the audience must be enticed by the magical experience of tragicomedy not only to feel love but to think about it or reason about it as well in order to understand fully the nature of its highest form:

The beautiful Orpheus chimneypiece in Haddon Hall, Derbyshire, an Elizabethan country house. Photograph by Peggy Muñoz Simonds.

caritas. Pico de la Mirandola emphasizes the dual roles of feeling and reason to the attaining of enlightenment in typical harmonist terms: "if through moral philosophy the forces of our passions have by fitting agreement become so intent on harmony that they can sing together in undisturbed concord, and if through dialectic our reason has moved progressively in a rhythmical measure, then we shall be stirred by the frenzy of the Muses and drink the heavenly harmony with our inmost hearing."[33]

In *Cymbeline,* Shakespeare dramatizes the process of that Platonic journey to intellectual enlightenment, which dispels human melancholy, by first immersing us in the sufferings caused by Eros, bewildered sufferings with no apparent meaning and epitomized by Imogen's complaints of her blindness in respect to the future: "I see before me, man: nor here, nor here, Nor what ensues but have a fog in them, / That I cannot look through" (3.2.79–81). Second, the dramatist demonstrates through the action of the play that personal reformation from the love of terrestrial Eros to the love of virtue or Anteros and the willingness to sacrifice oneself in atonement for the past will finally lead to a vision of divinity, then to rebirth and a second chance. Finally, like Orpheus, Shakespeare liberates us from melancholy by leading us upward through the dense fog of mistaken identities typical of comedy and mistaken purposes typical of tragedy to a series of joyful resurrections, recognitions, and reunions. The process results in harmony and peace within the family, within the kingdom of Britain, and finally throughout the world.

Notes

1. The major work on the harmonist theory and its poetic applications is John Hollander, *The Untuning of the Sky: Ideas of Music in English Poetry, 1500–1700* (Princeton, N.J.: Princeton University Press, 1961). See also S. K. Heninger, Jr., *Touches of Sweet Harmony: Pythagorean Cosmology and Renaissance Poetics* (San Marino, Calif.: The Huntington Library, 1974); Leo Spitzer, *Classical and Christian Ideas of World Harmony* (Baltimore: Johns Hopkins University Press, 1963); and E. M. W. Tillyard, *The Elizabethan World Picture: A Study of the Idea of Order in the Age of Shakespeare, Donne and Milton* (London: Chatto and Windus, 1943).

2. See Catherine M. Dunne, "The Function of Music in Shakespeare's Romances," *Shakespeare Quarterly* 20 (Autumn 1969): 394.

3. Noted by Dunne, 398.

4. Quoted in Hollander, 30. *The Untuning of the Sky* will be cited hereafter parenthetically.

5. See Sir John Davies, *Orchestra: or a poem of dauncing* (London: I. Robarts for N. Ling, 1596), in which the universal harmony is imaged as a measured courtly dance of the spheres.

6. See James Daly, "Cosmic Harmony and Political Thinking in Early Stuart England," *Transactions of the American Philosophical Society* 69 (October 1979): 13.

7. Peter M. Daly, Virginia W. Callahan, and Simon Cuttler, eds., *Andreas Alciatus: Index Emblematicus,* 2 vols. (Toronto: University of Toronto Press, 1985), vol. 1: Emblem 10.

8. See George Chapman, *Ovid's Banquet of Sence* (London: I. R. for Richard Smith, 1595), sig. B3ᵛ.

9. See William S. Heckscher, "Shakespeare in his Relationship to the Visual Arts" in *Art and Literature: Studies in Relationship,* ed. Egon Verhayen (Durham, N.C.: Duke University Press, 1985), 383: "A skull taken literally is a 'hollow bone' and thus a punning allusion to the artist's name, 'hohl Bein'." Heckscher cites as his source for this observation Erwin Panofsky, "Galileo as a Critic of the Arts: Aesthetic Attitude and Scientific Thought," *Isis* 47: 6.

10. See Mary F. S. Hervey, *Holbein's "Ambassadors": The Picture and the Men* (London: George Bell and Sons, 1900), 228–31.

11. Geffrey Whitney, *A Choice of Emblemes* (Leiden: Christopher Plantin, 1586), 92.

12. James J. Yoch, Jr., "The Renaissance Dramatization of Temperance: The Italian Revival of Tragicomedy and *The Faithful Shepherdess,*" in *Renaissance Tragicomedy: Explorations in Genre and Politics,* ed. Nancy Klein Maguire (New York: AMS Press, 1987), 124.

13. *The Mirrour of Maiestie: or, The Badges of Honovr* (1618), facsimile copy, ed. Henry Green and James Croston (London: Trubner & Co., 1870), sig. F2.

14. See Armitage, "The Dismemberment of Orpheus: Mythic Elements in Shakespeare's Romances," *Shakespeare Survey* 39 (1986): 123.

15. R. B., *Orpheus His Journey to Hell, and his Musicke to the Ghosts, for the regaining of faire Euridice his Love, and new spoused Wife* (London: Richard Johns, 1595), sig. B3; cited hereafter parenthetically.

16. See John Warden, "Orpheus and Ficino," in *Orpheus: the Metamorphoses of a Myth,* ed. John Warden (Toronto: University of Toronto Press, 1982), 89–91; cited hereafter parenthetically.

17. See John B. Friedman, *Orpheus in the Middle Ages* (Cambridge, Mass.: Harvard University Press, 1970), 39.

18. See Charles Segal, *Orpheus: The Myth of the Poet* (Baltimore Md.: Johns Hopkins University Press, 1989), 169.

19. Rilke, *Sonnets to Orpheus* trans. M. D. Herter Norton (New York: W. W. Norton, 1942), 27.

20. Spitzer, 20.

21. Otto van Veen, *Amorvm Emblemata or Emblemes of Loue* (Antwerp: Venalia apud auctorem, 1608), 34–35.

22. Nicholas Reusner, *Emblemata* (Frankfort, 1581), bk. 3, 129–130. Translation by Roger T. Simonds.

23. For more information on the conscience, see my essay "Some Images of the Conscience in Emblem Literature," in *Acta Conventus Neo-Latini Guelpherbytani,* ed. Stella P. Revard, Fidel Radle, and Mario A. Di Cesare (Binghamton, N.Y.: Medieval and Renaissance Texts & Studies, 1988), 315–30.

24. Joseph Campbell, *The Hero with a Thousand Faces,* 2d ed. (Princeton N.J.: Princeton University Press, 1968), 28.

25. See Edgar Wind, *Pagan Mysteries in the Renaissance,* 2d ed. (New York: W. W. Norton & Co., 1968), 175; hereafter cited parenthetically.

26. See G. K. Hunter, "The Spoken Dirge in Kyd, Marston, and Shakespeare: A Background to *Cymbeline,*" *Notes and Queries* n.s. 11 (1964): 146–47.

27. John Marston, *Antonio's Revenge,* ed. G. K. Hunter, Regents Renaissance Drama Series (Lincoln: University of Nebraska Press, 1965).

28. Hunter, "The Spoken Dirge," 147.

29. See *The Heroicall Devises of M. Claudius Paradin* (1591), a Photoreproduction with an Introduction by John Doebler (Delmar, N.Y.: Scholars Facsimiles & Reprints, 1984), 121–23.

30. Quoted in David L. Hirst, *Tragicomedy,* The Critical Idiom 43 (London and New York: Methuen, 1984), 5–6.

31. Segal, 28.

32. See Richard Cody, *The Landscape of the Mind* (Oxford: The Clarendon Press, 1969), 34.

33. Pico de la Mirandola, "Oration on the Dignity of Man," trans. Elizabeth Livermoore Forbes, in *The Renaissance Philosophy of Man,* ed. Ernst Cassirer, et al. (Chicago: The University of Chicago Press, 1948), 234.

Select Bibliography

Abartis, Caesarea. *The Tragicomic Construction of "Cymbeline" and "The Winter's Tale."* Salzburg: Institut für Englische Sprache und Literatur Universität Salzburg, 1977.

Aelian. *On the Characteristics of Animals.* 3 vols. Translated by A. F. Scholfield. Loeb Classical Library, 1958.

Aesop. *Fables of Aesop According to Sir Roger L'Estrange.* New York: Dover Publications, 1967.

Alciati, Andrea. *Emblemata.* Antwerp: Christopher Plantin, 1577.

———. *Emblemata cum commentariis.* Padua, 1621.

Aldrovandi, Ulisse. *Aldrovandi on Chickens: The Ornithology of Ulisse Aldrovandi (1600), Volume II, Book XIV.* Translated by L. R. Lind. Norman: University of Oklahoma Press, 1963.

———. *Ornithologiae hoc est de avibus historiae.* 3 vols. Bononiae: Franciscum de Francis Senensem, 1599.

Allen, Michael J. B. "The Chase: The Development of a Renaissance Theme." *Comparative Literature* 20 (1968): 301–12.

Apuleius, Lucius. *The XI Bookes of the "Golden Ass" conteigning the Metamorphosie of Lucius Apuleius.* Translated by William Adlington. London: William How, for Abraham Veale, 1571.

Armitage, David. "The Dismemberment of Orpheus: Mythic Elements in Shakespeare's Romances." *Shakespeare Survey* 39 (1986): 123–33.

Axton, Marie. *The Queen's Two Bodies: Drama and the Elizabethan Succession.* London: Royal Historical Society, 1977.

Bacon, Francis: *Fables of the Ancients.* Edited by Dr. Shaw. London: J. Cundee, 1803.

———. *Works of Francis Bacon.* Vol. 4. Edited by James Spedding, R. Ellis, and D. Heath. London, 1857–1874.

Baines, Barbara J. "Shakespeare's Plays and the Erasmian Box." *Renaissance Papers* (1981): 33–44.

Baldwin, T. W. *William Shakspere's Small Latine & lesse Greeke.* 2 vols. Urbana: University of Illinois Press, 1944.

Barber, C. L. *Shakespeare's Festive Comedy: A Study of Dramatic Form and Its Relation to Social Custom.* Princeton, N.J.: Princeton University Press, 1959.

Barkan, Leonard. "Diana and Actaeon: The Myth as Synthesis." *English Literary Renaissance* 10 (1980): 317–59.

———. *The Gods Made Flesh: Metamorphosis & the Pursuit of Paganism.* New Haven and London: Yale University Press, 1986.

Basford, Katherine. *The Green Man.* Ipswich: D. S. Brewer Ltd., 1978.

Batman, Stephen. *Batman vppon Bartholome, his Booke De Proprietatibus Rerum.* London: Thomas East, 1582.

———. *The Golden Boke of the Leaden Gods.* 1577. Reprint. New York & London: Garland Publishing, 1976.

Beard, Geoffrey, *Decorative Plasterwork in Great Britain.* London: Phaidon, 1975.

Bergeron, David. *English Civic Pageantry 1558–1642.* London: Edward Arnold, 1971.

———. *Shakespeare's Romances and the Royal Family.* Lawrence, Kansas: University Press of Kansas, 1985.

Bernheimer, Richard. *Wild Men in the Middle Ages: A Study in Art, Sentiment, and Demonology.* Cambridge: Harvard University Press, 1952.

Berry, Edward. *Shakespeare's Comic Rites.* Cambridge: Cambridge University Press, 1984.

Blake, William. *The Poetical Works of William Blake.* Edited by John Sampson. London: Oxford University Press, 1914.

Boccaccio, Giovanni. *The Decameron* (1353). Translated by John Payne. New York: Modern Library, n.d.

Bocchi, Achille. *Symbolicarum Qvaestionvm . . . Libri Quinque.* Bologna, 1555.

Bono, Barbara. *Literary Transvaluation: From Vergilian Epic to Shakespearean Tragicomedy.* Berkeley, Cal.: University of California Press, 1984.

The Book of Common Prayer 1559. Edited by John E. Booty. Charlottesville: University Press of Virginia, 1976.

Booth, Stephen, ed. *Shakespeare's Sonnets.* New Haven: Yale University Press, 1977.

Bowra, C. M. "Orpheus and Eurydice." *The Classical Quarterly,* n.s. 2 (1952): 113–26.

Brockbank, J. Philip. "History and Historiography in *Cymbeline.*" *Shakespeare Survey* 11 (1958): 42–49.

Broek, Roelof Van den. *The Myth of the Phoenix: According to Classical and Early Christian Traditions.* Leiden: E. J. Brill, 1972.

Callahan, Virginia W. "Ramifications of the Nut Tree Fable." In *Acta Conventus Neo-Latini Turonensis,* edited by Jean-Claude Margolin, 197–204. Paris, 1980.

Campbell, Joseph. *The Hero with a Thousand Faces.* 2d ed. Princeton: Princeton University Press, 1968.

Camerarius, Joachim. *Symbolarum et Emblematum.* Nuremberg, 1590.

———. *Symbolarum et Emblematum.* 2d ed. Nuremberg: Voegelinianis, 1605.

Carr, Joan. "*Cymbeline* and the Validity of Myth." *Studies in Philology* 75 (1978): 316–30.

Cartari, Vincenzo. *Le imagini degli dei degli Antichi.* Venice: Vincentio Valgrisi, 1571.

Catullus. *The Poems of Catullus.* Translated by F. W. Cornish. The Loeb Classical Library, 1918.

Cescinsky, Herbert. *English Furniture from Gothic to Sheraton.* 2d ed. Garden City, N.Y.: Garden City Publishing Co., 1937.

Chapman, George. *Ouid's Banquet of Sence.* London: I. R. for Richard Smith, 1595.

Chew, Samuel C. *The Pilgrimage of Life*. New Haven: Yale University Press, 1692.

———. "Richard Verstegan and the *Amorvm Emblemata* of Otho van Veen." *The Huntington Library Quarterly* 8 (1944–45): 192–99.

———. *The Virtues Reconciled: An Iconographic Study*. Toronto: University of Toronto Press, 1947.

Cleaver, Robert. *A Godly Forme of Householde Government: for the Ordering of Private Families*. London: Felix Kingston, for Thomas Man, 1598.

Clements, Robert J. *Picta Poesis: Literary and Humanistic Theory in Renaissance Emblem Books*. Rome: Edizioni di Storia e Letteratura, 1960.

Clubb, Louise George. *Italian Drama in Shakespeare's Time*. New Haven and London: Yale University Press, 1989.

———. "The making of the pastoral play: Italian experiments between 1573 and 1590." In *Petrarch to Pirandello,* edited by Julius Molinaro, 46–72. Toronto: University of Toronto Press, 1973.

Cody, Richard. *The Landscape of the Mind: Pastoralism and Platonic Theory in Tasso's "Aminta" and Shakespeare's Early Comedies*. Oxford: The Clarendon Press, 1969.

Cohen, Walter. "The Politics of Golden Age Spanish Tragicomedy." In *Renaissance Tragicomedy. See* Maguire 1987.

Colley, John Scott. "Disguise and New Guise in *Cymbeline*." *Shakespeare Studies* 7 (1974): 233–52.

Collier, John P. *The History of English Dramatic Poetry in the Time of Shakespeare*. London, 1831.

Colonna, Francesco. *Hypnerotomachia. The Strife of Loue in a Dreame*. 1592. Reprint. New York and London: Garland Publishing, Inc., 1976.

Combe, Thomas. *The Theater of Fine Devices*. London: Richard Field, 1614.

Cope, Jackson. *The Theater and the Dream: From Metaphor to Form in Renaissance Drama*. Baltimore: Johns Hopkins University Press, 1973.

Corbett, Margery, and R. W. Lightbown. *The comely frontispiece: The Emblematic Title-page in England, 1550–1660*. London: Routledge and Kegan Paul, 1979.

Cornford, Francis MacDonald. *Plato's Cosmology: The 'Timaeus' of Plato translated with a running commentary*. London: Routledge & Kegan Paul Ltd., 1937.

Corrozet, Gilles. *Hecatomgraphie*. Paris: Denys Ianot, 1543.

Crundell, H. W. "Shakespeare, Lyly, and Aesop." *Notes & Queries* 168 (1935): 312.

Curley, Michael J., trans. *Physiologus*. Austin: University of Texas Press, 1979.

Daly, James. "Cosmic Harmony and Political Thinking in Early Stuart England." *Transactions of the American Philosophical Society* 69 (October 1979): 3–41.

Daly, Peter. *Emblem Theory: Recent German Contributions to the Characterization of the Emblem Genre*. Nendeln, Liechtenstein: KTO Press, 1979.

———. *Literature in the Light of the Emblem*. Toronto: University of Toronto Press, 1979.

———. "Of Macbeth, Martlets and other 'Fowles of Heauen.'" *Mosaic* 12 (Fall 1978): 23–46.

———. "Alciato's 'Emblem Concordiae Symbolum': A Medusa's Mirror for Rulers?" *German Life and Letters* 41 (July 1988): 349–62.

———. "Shakespeare and the Emblem: The Use of Evidence and Analogy in Establishing Iconographic and Emblematic Effects in the Plays." In *Shakespeare and the Emblem: Studies in Renaissance Iconography and Iconology*, edited by Tibor Fabiny, 117–86. Szeged: Attila Jószef University Press, 1984.

Daly, Peter M., Virginia W. Callahan, and Simon Cuttler, eds. *Index Emblematicus: Andreas Alciatus*. 2 vols. Toronto: University of Toronto Press, 1985.

Dante Alighieri. *The Divine Comedy*. Translated by Dorothy L. Sayers and Barbara Reynolds. Baltimore: Penguin Books, 1962.

Davies, Sir John. *Nosce Teipsum*. London: Richard Field, 1599.

———. *Orchestra: or a poeme of dauncing*. London: I. A. Robarts for N. Ling, 1596.

———. *The Poems of Sir John Davies*. Edited by Robert Krueger. Oxford: Clarendon Press, 1975.

Davies of Hereford, John. *The Holy Roode, or Christs Crosse: Containing Christ Crucified, described in speaking-picture*. London: John Windet for Nathaniel Butter, 1609.

———. *Wittes Pilgrimage*. In *The Complete Works of John Davies of Hereford*, vol. 2, edited by Alexander B. Grosart. Edinburgh: Edinburgh University Press, 1878.

De Armas, Frederick A. *The Return of Astraea: An Astral-Imperial Myth in Calderón*. Lexington: University Press of Kentucky, 1986.

De Jongh, E. "Erotica in Vogelperspectief." *Simiolus* 3 (1968–69): 22–74.

Demetz, Peter. "The Elm and the Vine: Notes Toward the History of a Marriage Topos." *PMLA* 73 (1958): 521–32.

Diehl, Huston. "Graven Images: Protestant Emblem Books in England." *Renaissance Quarterly* 39 (Spring 1986): 49–66.

Dixon, Mimi Still. "Tragicomic Recognitions: Medieval Miracles and Shakespearean Romance." In *Renaissance Tragicomedy. See* Maguire 1987.

Donaldson, Ian. *The Rapes of Lucretia: A Myth and its Transformations*. Oxford: Clarendon Press, 1982.

Donne, John. *The Complete Poetry of John Donne*. Edited by John T. Shawcross. New York: New York University Press, 1968.

Dudley, Edward, and Maximilian E. Novak, eds. *The Wild Man Within: An Image in Western Thought from the Renaissance to Romanticism*. London: Harry M. Snyder & Co., 1972.

Dunlop, Ian. *Palaces and Progresses of Elizabeth I*. London: Jonathan Cape, 1962.

Dunne, Catherine M. "The Function of Music in Shakespeare's Romances." *Shakespeare Quarterly* 20 (Autumn 1969): 391–405.

Economou, George. "Chaucer's Use of the Bird in the Cage Image in the *Canterbury Tales*." *Philological Quarterly* 54 (1975): 679–84.

Edgerton, Samuel Y., Jr. *The Renaissance Rediscovery of Linear Perspective*. New York: Basic Books, Inc., 1975.

Edwards, Ralph. *The Dictionary of English Furniture*. Rev. ed., 2 vols. London: Country Life Ltd., 1954.

Eliade, Mircea. *Myth and Reality*. Translated by Willard R. Trask. New York: Harper & Row, 1963.

————. *The Myth of the Eternal Return*. Translated by Willard R. Trask. New York: Pantheon Books, 1954.

————. *Myths, Rites, Symbols*. Edited by Wendell C. Beane and William G. Doty. New York: Harper Colophon Books, 1975.

Eliot, T. S. "Sir John Davies." In *On Poetry and Poets*, 149–55. New York: Farrar, Straus and Cudahy, 1957.

Empson, William. *Some Versions of the Pastoral*. London: Chatto & Windus, 1950.

Erasmus, Desiderius. *The Education of a Christian Prince*. Translated by Lester K. Born. New York: Columbia University Press, 1936.

————. *Enchiridion*. Translated and edited by Raymond Himelick. Bloomington: Indiana University Press, 1963.

————. *A Modest Meane to Marriage (Proci et Puellae)*. Translated by Nicholas Leigh. London: Henrie Denham, 1568.

Eriksen, Roy T. " 'Un certo amoroso mirtire': Shakespeare's 'The Phoenix and the Turtle' and Giordano Bruno's *De gli eroici furori*." *Spenser Studies* 2 (1981): 193–215.

E. P. Evans. *Animal Symbolism in Ecclesiastical Architecture*. 1896. Reprint. Detroit: Gale Research Co., 1969.

Farmer, Norman K., Jr. *Poets and the Visual Arts in Renaissance England*. Austin: University of Texas Press, 1984.

Felperin, Howard. *Shakespearean Romance*. Princeton, N.J.: Princeton University Press, 1965.

Ficino, Marsilio. *Commentary on Plato's "Symposium" on Love*. Translated by Sears Jayne. Dallas, Texas: Spring Publications, Inc., 1985.

————. *Ficino's Commentary on Plato's "Symposium"*. Translated by Sears R. Jayne. Columbia, Mo.: University of Missouri Press, 1944.

————. *Theologica platonica*. Translated by Abigail Young. Forthcoming.

Fludd, Robert. *Utriusque Cosmi Historia*. Oppenheim: Aere Johan-Theodore De Bry, Typus Hieronymi Galleri, 1617–1619.

Fowler, Alistair. *Triumphal Forms: Structural Patterns in Elizabethan Poetry*. Cambridge: Cambridge University Press, 1970.

Fraunce, Abraham. *The Third part of the Countesse of Pembroke's Iuychurch: Entitled Amintas Dale*. London: Thomas Woodcocke, 1592.

Freedberg, Sydney. "Titian and Marsyas." *FMR* 1 (1985): 51–67.

Friedman, John Block. *Orpheus in the Middle Ages*. Cambridge: Harvard University Press, 1970.

Frye, Northrop. *Anatomy of Criticism: Four Essays*. Princeton, N.J.: Princeton University Press, 1957.

————. *A Natural Perspective: The Development of Shakespearean Comedy and Romance*. New York: Columbia University Press, 1965.

Frye, Roland Mushat. *The Renaissance Hamlet: Issues and Responses in 1600*. Princeton, N.J.: Princeton University Press, 1984.

Fulgentius. *Fulgentius the Mythographer*. Trans. Leslie George Whitbread. Columbus: Ohio State University Press, 1971.

Garber, Marjorie. "Shakespeare and the Languages of Myth." *Mosaic* 10 (1977): 105–15.

Garrard, Mary D. *Artemisia Gentileschi: The Image of the Female Hero in Italian Baroque Art*. Princeton, N.J.: Princeton University Press, 1989.

Geller, Lila. "*Cymbeline* and the Imagery of Covenant Theology." *Studies in English Literature* 20 (1980): 241–55.

Generosa, Sister M. "Apuleius and *A Midsummer Night's Dream*: Analogue or Source, Which?" *Shakespeare Quarterly* 33 (1945: 198–204.

Gerarde [Gerard], John. *The Herball or Generall Historie of Plantes*. London: John Norton, 1597.

Gilman, Ernest. *The Curious Perspective: Literary and Pictorial Wit in the Seventeenth Century*. New Haven and London: Yale University Press, 1978.

Ginzburg, Carlo. "High and Low: The Theme of Forbidden Knowledge in the Sixteenth and Seventeenth Centuries." *Past and Present* 73 (November 1976): 28–41.

Gira, Catherine. "Shakespeare's Venus Figures and Renaissance Tradition." *Studies in Iconography* 4 (1978): 96–114.

Goldberg, Jonathan. *James I and the Politics of Literature*. Baltimore: Johns Hopkins University Press, 1983.

Goldsmith, Robert Hillis. "The Wild Man on the English Stage." *Modern Language Review* 53 (1958): 481–91.

Gombrich, Ernst. *Symbolic Images: Studies in the Art of the Renaissance*. London: Phaidon, 1972.

Graves, Robert. *The Greek Myths*. 2 vols. Baltimore: Penguin Books, 1955.

———. *The White Goddess*. Amended and enl. ed. New York: Farrar, Straus and Giroux, 1966.

The Greek Anthology. 5 vols. Translated by W. R. Paton. Loeb Classical Library, 1958.

Green, Henry. *Shakespeare and the Emblem Writers*. London: Trübner & Co., 1870.

Guarini, Giambattista *The Compendium of Tragicomic Poetry*. In *Literary Criticism from Plato to Dryden,* edited by Alan H. Gilbert. New York: American Book Company, 1940.

———. *Il pastor fido*. London: Giovanni Volfeo, 1591.

———. *Il pastor fido: or the Faithful Shepherd*. Translated by John Dymock. London: Simon Waterson, 1602.

———. *Il pastor fido*. Translated (1647) by Richard Fanshawe. Italian and English texts edited by J. H. Whitfield. Austin: University of Texas Press, 1976.

Hackenbroch, Yvonne. *English and other Needlework: Tapestries and Textiles in the Irwin Untermyer Collection*. London: Thames and Hudson, 1960.

Hayles, Nancy K. "Sexual Disguise in *Cymbeline*." *Modern Language Quarterly* 41 (1980): 231–47.

Harris, Bernard. " 'What's past is prologue': 'Cymbeline' and 'Henry VIII'." In *Later Shakespeare*. Stratford Upon-Avon Studies 8. London: Edward Arnold Ltd., 1966: 203–34.

Hartwig, Joan. *Shakespeare's Analogical Scene: Parody as Structural Syntax*. Lincoln and London: University of Nebraska Press, 1983.

———. *Shakespeare's Tragicomic Vision*. Baton Rouge: Louisiana State University Press, 1972.

Heckscher, William S. *Art and Literature: Studies in Relationship.* Edited by Egon Verheyen. Durham, N.C.: Duke University Press, 1985.

Held, Julius. *Rembrandt's Aristotle.* Princeton, N.J.: Princeton University Press, 1969.

Henkel, Arthur, and Albrecht Schöne, eds. *Emblemata.* Stuttgart: J. B. Metzlersche Verlagsbuchandlung, 1967.

Heninger, S. K., Jr. *The Cosmographical Glass: Renaissance Diagrams of the Universe.* San Marino, Calif.: The Huntington Library, 1977.

———. *Touches of Sweet Harmony: Pythagorean Cosmology and Renaissance Poetics.* San Marino, Calif.: The Huntington Library, 1974.

Herrick, Marvin T. *Tragicomedy: Its Origin and Development in Italy, France, and England.* Urbana: University of Illinois Press, 1955.

Hervey, Mary F. S. *Holbein's "Ambassadors": The Picture and the Men.* London: George Bell and Sons, 1900.

Heywood, Thomas. *Love's Mistress, or The Queen's Masque.* Edited by Raymond C. Shady. Salzburg: Institut für Englische Sprache und Literatur, 1977.

Hirsch, E. D., Jr. *Validity in Interpretation.* New Haven and London: Yale University Press, 1967.

Hirst, David L. *Tragicomedy.* The Critical Idiom 43. London and New York: Methuen, 1984.

Hollander, John. "Summer Day." *The New Yorker* (14 August 1989): 28.

———. *The Untuning of the Sky: Ideas of Music in English Poetry, 1500–1700.* Princeton, N.J.: Princeton University Press, 1961.

Holtzwart, Mathias. *Emblematum Tyrocinia: sive Picta Poesis latinogermanica.* Strassburg: Bernard Jobin, 1581.

Hunter, G. K., ed. The Arden Edition of Shakespeare's *All's Well That Ends Well.* London, Methuen 1959.

———. "The Spoken Dirge in Kyd, Marston, and Shakespeare: A Background to *Cymbeline.*" *Notes and Queries* n.s. 11 (1964): 146–47.

Hunter, Robert Grams. *Shakespeare and the Comedy of Forgiveness.* New York: Columbia University Press, 1965.

Husband, Timothy. *The Wild Man: Medieval Myth and Symbolism.* New York: Metropolitan Museum of Art, 1980.

Hutton, James. "Analogues of Shakespeare's Sonnets 153 and 154: Contributions to the History of a Theme." In *Essays on Renaissance Poetry,* edited by Rita Guerlac, 149–68. Ithaca, N.Y.: Cornell University Press, 1980.

Ingram, R. W. "Musical Pauses and the Vision Scenes in Shakespeare's Last Plays." In *Pacific Coast Studies in Shakespeare,* edited by Waldo F. McNeir and Thelma N. Greenfield, 234–47. Eugene: University of Oregon Books, 1966.

Jaeger, Ronald. "A Biblical Allusion in Shakespeare's Sonnet 154." *Notes and Queries,* n.s. 19 (1981): 125.

James I. *The Workes of the Most High and Mightie, Prince Iames.* London: Robert Barker and Iohn Bill, 1616.

Jonson, Ben. *Ben Jonson.* 11 vols. Edited by C. H. Herford, Percy and Evelyn Simpson. Oxford: Clarendon Press, 1925–52.

———. "Hymenai." In *Inigo Jones: The Theatre of the Stuart Court.* 2 vols.

Edited by Stephen Orgel and Roy Strong, vol. 1, 105–13. Berkeley: University of California Press, 1973.

———. *The Workes of Ben Jonson*. London: Will Stansby, 1616.

Jung, C. G. *The Archetypes and the Collective Unconscious*. Translated by R. F. C. Hull. New York: Pantheon Books, 1959.

Junius, Hadrianus. *Emblemata*. Antwerp: Christopher Plantin, 1565.

Kantorowitz, Ernst H. *The King's Two Bodies: A Study in Medieval Political Theology*. Princeton, N.J.: Princeton University Press, 1957.

Kerenyi, C. "Prolegomena." In *Essays on a Science of Mythology*. By C. G. Jung and C. Kerenyi. Translated by R. F. C. Hull. Princeton: Princeton University Press, 1969.

King, John N. *Tudor Royal Iconography: Literature and Art in an Age of Religious Crisis*. Princeton, N.J.: Princeton University Press, 1989.

Kirsch, Arthur C. "*Cymbeline* and Coterie Dramaturgy." *English Literary History* 34 (1967): 285–306.

———. *Jacobean Dramatic Perspectives*. Charlottesville: University Press of Virginia, 1972.

———. *Shakespeare and the Experience of Love*. Cambridge: Cambridge University Press, 1981.

Knapp, Peggy Ann. "The Orphic Vision of Pericles." *Texas Studies in Literature and Language* 15 (1973–74): 615–26.

Knight, G. Wilson. *The Crown of Life*. Oxford: The Clarendon Press, 1947.

———. *The Shakespearean Tempest*. 3d ed. London: Methuen, 1953.

Ladner, Gerhart B. *The Idea of Reform*. New York: Harper & Row, 1959.

———. "Vegetation Symbolism and the Concept of Renaissance." In *Essays in Honor of Erwin Panofsky*. 2 vols. Edited by Millard Meiss. New York: New York University Press, 1961.

Lewalski, Barbara. *Protestant Poetics and the Seventeenth Century Religious Lyric*. Princeton, N.J.: Princeton University Press, 1979.

Linche [Lynche], Richard. *The Fountaine of Ancient Fiction*. London: Adam Islip, 1599.

———. *The Fountaine of Ancient Fiction*. 1599. Reprint. New York & London: Garland Publishing, 1976.

Loewenstein, Joseph. "Guarini and the Presence of Genre." In *Renaissance Tragicomedy*. See Maguire 1987.

Lomazzo, Giovanni Paolo. *A Tracte containing the Artes of curious Paintinge*. Translated by Richard Haydocke. Oxford: Joseph Barnes for R. H., 1598.

Lovejoy, Arthur O., and George Boas. *Primitivism and Related Ideas in Antiquity*. 1935. Reprint. New York: Octagon Books, 1973.

Lloyd, Michael. "Cleopatra as Isis." *Shakespeare Survey* 12 (1959): 88–94.

MacDougall, Elisabeth B. "The Sleeping Nymph: Origins of a Humanist Fountain Type." *Art Bulletin* 57 (1975): 357–65.

Maguire, Nancy Klein, ed. *Renaissance Tragicomedy: Explorations in Genre and Politics*. New York: AMS Press, 1987.

Mandeville, Sir John. *The Travels of Sir John Mandeville*. 1356. Translated by C. W. R. D. Moseley. New York: Penguin Books, 1983.

Marcus, Leah S. *Puzzling Shakespeare: Local Reading and Its Discontents.* Berkeley: University of California Press, 1988.

Marston, John. *Antonio's Revenge.* Edited by G. K. Hunter. Lincoln: University of Nebraska Press, 1965.

Mazzeo, J. A. *Renaissance and Seventeenth-Century Studies.* New York: Columbia University Press, 1964.

McPeek, James A. "The Psyche Myth and *A Midsummer Night's Dream.*" *Shakespeare Quarterly* 33 (1982): 433–48.

Mehl, Dieter. "Emblems in Renaissance Drama." *Renaissance Drama* n.s. 2 (1969): 43–51.

Meiss, Millard. "Sleep in Venice: Ancient Myths and Renaissance Proclivities." In *The Painter's Choice: Problems in the Interpretation of Renaissance Art,* 212–39. New York: Harper and Row, 1976.

Merrill, Robert V. "Eros and Anteros." *Speculum* 19 (1944): 265–84.

Miola, Robert S. *Shakespeare's Rome.* Cambridge: Cambridge University Press, 1983.

The Mirrour of Maiestie: or, The Badges of Honovr. 1618. Edited by Henry Green and James Croston. Facsimile Copy. London: Trübner & Co., 1870.

Moffet, Robin. "*Cymbeline* and the Nativity." *Shakespeare Quarterly* 13 (1962): 207–18.

Moffit, John F. "Paul Klee's *Twittering Machine* and the Emblematic 'Birds-in-Bondage-Vile' Theme." *Studies in Iconography* 9 (1983): 135–74.

More, Sir Thomas. *Utopia.* Edited by Edward Surtz, S. J., and J. H. Hexter. New Haven: Yale University Press, 1965.

Mowat, Barbara. *The Dramaturgy of Shakespeare's Romances.* Athens: The University of Georgia Press, 1976.

———. "Lavinia's Message: Shakespeare and Myth." *Renaissance Papers* (1981): 55–69.

Neumann, Erich. *Amor and Psyche: The Psychic Development of the Feminine.* Translated by Ralph Mannheim. New York: Pantheon Books, 1956.

———. *The Great Mother.* 2d ed. Translated by Ralph Mannheim. Princeton, N.J.: Princeton University Press, 1963.

Nordenfalk, Carl. "The Five Senses in late Medieval and Renaissance Art." *Journal of the Warburg and Courtauld Institutes* 48 (1985): 1–22.

Ovid. *Metamorphoses.* Translated by Mary M. Innes. New York: Penguin Books, 1955.

Panofsky, Dora and Erwin. *Pandora's Box: The Changing Aspects of a Mythical Symbol.* New York: Pantheon Books, 1956.

Panofsky, Erwin. *The Iconography of Correggio's Camera Di San Paolo.* London: The Warburg Institute, 1961.

Paradin, Claude. *The Heroical Devises of M. Claudius Paradin (1591).* A photoreproduction with an Introduction by John Doebler. Delmar, N.Y.: Scholars' Facsimiles & Reprints, 1984.

Paster, Gail Kern. "'To Starve with Feeding': The City in *Coriolanus.*" *Shakespeare Studies* 11 (1978): 123–44.

Peebles, Rose Jeffries. "The Dry Tree: Symbol of Death." In *Vassar Medieval*

Studies, edited by Christobel Forsyth Fiske, 59–79. New Haven: Yale University Press, 1923.

Perella, Nicolas J. *The Kiss Sacred and Profane.* Berkeley: University of California Press, 1969.

Perry, Ben Edwin, ed. *Aesopica.* 2 vols. Urbana: University of Illinois, 1952.

———, ed. *Babrius and Phaedrus.* Loeb Classical Library, 1965.

Peterson, Douglas L. *Time, Tide, and Tempest: A Study of Shakespeare's Romances.* San Marino, Calif.: The Huntington Library, 1973.

Petowe, Henry. *England's Caesar. His Maiesties Most Royall Coronation.* London: John Windet for Mathew Law, 1603.

Petrarch, Francesco. *Petrarch's Lyric Poems: The 'Rime Sparse' and Other Lyrics.* Translated and edited by Robert M. Durling. Cambridge: Harvard University Press, 1976.

Phillips, Margaret Mann. *The 'Adages' of Erasmus: A Study with Translations.* Cambridge: Cambridge University Press, 1964.

The Phoenix Nest. 1593. Edited by Hyder Edward Rollins. Cambridge: Harvard University Press, 1931.

Pico de la Mirandola, Giovanni. "Oration on the Dignity of Man." Translated by Elizabeth Livermore Forbes. In *The Renaissance Philosophy of Man,* edited by Ernst Cassirer, et al., 223–54. Chicago: University of Chicago Press, 1948.

Pigler, Andor. *Barockthemen.* 2 vols. Budapest: Akadèmiai Kiadó, 1974.

Pinciss, G. M. "The Savage Man in Spenser, Shakesepare, and Renaissance English Drama." In *The Elizabethan Theatre* 8, edited by George R. Hibbard, 69–89. Port Credit, Ont.: P. D. Meany, 1982.

Planiscig, Leo. *Venezianische bildhauer der renaissance.* Vienna: A. Schroll, 1921.

Plato. *Plato: The Collected Dialogues.* Edited by Edith Hamilton and Huntington Cairns. 1963. Reprint. New York: Pantheon Books, 1966.

Plutarch. *The Philosophie, commonlie called, The Morals Written by the learned Philosopher Plutarch.* Translated by Philemon Holland. London: Arnold Hatfield, 1603.

Praz, Mario. *Studies in Seventeenth-Century Imagery.* 2 vols. London: The Warburg Institute, 1939.

Quinn, Esther Casier. *The Quest of Seth for the Oil of Life.* Chicago and London: University of Chicago Press, 1962.

R. B. *Orpheus His Journey to Hell, and his Musicke to the Ghosts, for the regaining of faire Euridice his Love, and new spoused Wife.* London: Richard Johns, 1595.

R. E. S. " 'Landscape with Sylvia and Satyrs'—Domenichino." In *The Age of Correggio and the Carraci: Emilian Painting of the Sixteenth and Seventeenth Centuries.* Washington, D.C.: National Gallery of Art, 1986.

Randall, Dale B. J. "A Glimpse of Leontes Through an Onamastic Lens." *Shakespeare Jahrbuch* (1988): 123–29.

Rees, Roger. "Posthumus in *Cymbeline.*" In *Players of Shakespeare 1: Essays in Shakespearean Performance by Twelve Players with the Royal Shakespeare Company,* edited by Philip Brockbank, 139–52. 1985. Reprint. Cambridge: Cambridge University Press, 1988.

Reich, Herman. "Zur Quelle des 'Cymbelin'."*Shakespeare Jahrbuch* 41 (1905): 177–81.

Remington, Preston. *English Domestic Needlework.* New York: Metropolitan Museum of Art, 1945.

Reusner, Nicholas. *Emblemata.* Frankfort, 1581.

Revard, Stella P. " 'L'Allegro' and 'Il Penseroso': Classical Tradition and Renaissance Mythography." *PMLA* 101 (1986): 338–50.

Ribner, Rhoda M. "The Compasse of This Curious Frame: *Ovids Banquet of Sence* and the Emblematic Tradition." *Studies in the Renaissance* 17 (1970): 233–58.

Rilke, Rainer Maria. *Sonnets to Orpheus.* Trans. M. D. Herter Norton. New York: W. W. Norton, 1942.

Ripa, Cesare. *Iconologia.* Rome: Lepido, 1603.

———. *Iconologia.* 1611. Reprint. New York: Garland Publications, 1976.

Ristine, Frank Humphrey. *English Tragicomedy: Its Origin and History.* New York: Columbia University Press, 1910.

Roberts, Jeanne Addison. "Horses and Hermaphrodites: Metamorphoses in *The Taming of the Shrew.*" *Shakespeare Quarterly* 34 (1983): 159–380.

Roche, Thomas P., Jr. "How Petrarchan Is Shakespere?" In *Shakespeare's Art from a Comparative Perspective,* edited by Wendall M. Aycock, 147–64. Lubbock: Texas Tech Press, 1981.

Romei, Count Haniball. *The Courtiers Academie.* Translated by I. K. London: Valentine Sims, 1598.

Rose, Mary Beth. "Moral Conceptions of Sexual Love in Elizabethan Comedy." *Renaissance Drama* 15 (1984): 1–29.

Rowland, Beryl. *Birds with Human Souls.* Knoxville: University of Tennessee Press, 1978.

———. *Blind Beasts: Chaucer's Animal World.* Kent, Ohio: Kent State University Press, 1971.

Russell, Daniel. "Alciati's Emblems in Renaissance France." *Renaissance Quarterly* 34 (Winter 1981): 534–54.

Rydén, Mats. *Shakespearean Plant Names: Identifications and Interpretations.* Stockholm: Almquist & Wiksell International, 1978.

Sambucus, Johannes. *Emblemata, et Aliqvot.* 4th ed. Antwerp: Christopher Plantin, 1576.

Schlam, Carl. *Cupid and Psyche: Apuleius and the Monuments.* University Park, Penn.: American Philological Association, 1976.

The Search for Alexander: An Exhibition. New York: Little, Brown, 1980.

Segal, Charles. *Orpheus: The Myth of the Poet.* Baltimore: Johns Hopkins University Press, 1989.

Sellin, Peter R. "The Hidden God: Reformation Awe in Renaissance English Literature." In *The Darker Vision of the Renaissance,* edited by Robert S. Kinsman, 147–96. Berkeley: University of California Press, 1974.

Sexton, Joyce H. *The Slandered Woman in Shakespeare.* Victoria, B.C.: University of Victoria Press, 1978.

Seznec, Jean. *The Survival of the Pagan Gods: The Mythological Tradition and Its*

Place in Renaissance Humanism and Art. Translated by Barbara F. Sessions. New York: Pantheon Books, 1953.

Shakespeare, William. *Cymbeline.* Edited by Edward Dowden. London: Methuen, 1903.

———. *Cymbeline.* Edited by J. M. Nosworthy. London: Methuen, 1955.

———. *The Riverside Shakespeare.* Edited by G. Blakemore Evans. Boston: Houghton Mifflin, 1974.

Siemon, James Edward. "Noble Virtue in *Cymbeline.*" In *Shakespeare Survey* 29 (1976): 51–61.

Simonds, Peggy Muñoz. "Eros and Anteros in Shakespeare's Sonnets 153 and 154. An Iconographical Study." *Spenser Studies* 7 (1987): 261–86 and 311–22.

———. "Freedom of Speech and the Emblem Tradition." In *Acta Conventus Neo-Latini Sanctandreani,* edited by I. D. McFarlane, 605–16. Binghamton, N.Y.: Medieval & Renaissance Texts & Studies, 1986.

———. "The Iconography of Primitivism in *Cymbeline.*" *Renaissance Drama* 16 (1985): 95–120.

———. "Jupiter, His Eagle, and BBC-TV." *Shakespeare on Film Newsletter* 10 (December 1985): 3.

———. " 'Killing care and grief of heart': Orpheus and Shakespeare." *Renaissance Papers* (1990): 79–90.

———. "The Marriage Topos in *Cymbeline:* Shakespeare's Variations on a Classical Theme." *English Literary Renaissance* 19 (Winter 1989): 94–117.

———. " 'No more . . . Offend our hearing': Aural Imagery in *Cymbeline.*" *Texas Studies in Literature and Language* 24 (Summer 1982): 137–54.

———. "Sacred and Sexual Motifs in *All's Well That Ends Well.*" *Renaissance Quarterly* 42 (Spring 1989): 33–59.

———. "Some Emblematic Courtier *Topoi* in *Cymbeline.*" *Renaissance Papers* (1981): 97–112.

———. "Some Images of the Conscience in Emblem Literature." In *Acta Conventus Neo-Latini Guelpherbytani,* edited by Stella P. Revard, et al., 315–30. Binghamton, N.Y.: Medieval and Renaissance Texts & Studies, 1988.

———. "*The White Hotel:* A Sexual Satire." *Critique* 27 (Fall 1985): 51–63.

Simonds, Roger T. "Bacon's Legal Learning: Its Influence on His Philosophical Ideas." In *Acta Conventus Neo-Latini Sanctandreani,* edited by I. D. McFarlane, 493–501. Binghamton, N.Y.: Medieval & Renaissance Texts & Studies, 1986.

Smith, Bruce R. "Landscape with Figures: The Three Realms of Queen Elizabeth's Country-house Revels." *Renaissance Drama* n.s. 8 (1977): 57–115.

———. "Sermons in Stones: Shakespeare and Renaissance Sculpture." *Shakespeare Studies* 17 (1985): 1–23.

Smith, Henry. "A Preparative to Marriage." In *The Sermons of Maister Henrie Smith,* 1–38. London: Peter Short for Thomas Man, 1594.

Smith, Pauline M. *The Anti-Courtier Trend in Sixteenth Century French Literature.* Geneva: Libraire Droz, 1966.

Soellner, Rolf. "Shakespeare's *Lucrece* and the Garnier-Pembroke Connection." *Shakespeare Studies* 15 (1982): 1–20.

Speed, John. *The History of Great Britaine*. London: William Hall and John Beale, 1611.

Spenser, Edmund. *The Faerie Queene*. Edited by Thomas P. Roche, Jr., with the assistance of C. Patrick O'Donnell, Jr. 1978. Reprint. New Haven: Yale University Press, 1981.

Spitzer, Leo. *Classical and Christian Ideas of World Harmony*. Baltimore: Johns Hopkins University Press, 1963.

Spivack, Bernard. *Shakespeare and the Allegory of Evil*. New York: Columbia University Press, 1958.

Starnes, DeWitt T. "Shakespeare and Apuleius." *PMLA* 60 (1945): 1021–50.

Steadman, John M. "Chaucer's Eagle: A Contemplative Symbol." *PMLA* 75 (1960): 153–59.

———. *Nature into Myth: Medieval and Renaissance Moral Symbols*. Pittsburgh: Duquesne University Press, 1979.

Stone, Lawrence. *The Family, Sex and Marriage in England 1500–1800*. New York: Harper and Row, 1977.

Summers, David. *The Judgment of Sense: Renaissance Naturalism and the Rise of Aesthetics*. Cambridge: Cambridge University Press, 1987.

Swain, Margaret. *The Needlework of Mary Queen of Scots*. New York: Van Nostrand Reinhold Co., 1973.

Swander, Homer D. "*Cymbeline:* Religious Ideas and Dramatic Design." In *Pacific Coast Studies in Shakespeare,* edited by Waldo McNeir and Thelma N. Greenfield, 248–62. Eugene: University of Oregon Books, 1966.

Tasso, Torquato. *Aminta: Fávola Boschereccia*. London: Giovanni Volfeo, 1591.

———. *Amyntas*. Trans. Leigh Hunt. In *The Genius of the Italian Theater,* edited by Eric Bentley. New York: Mentor Books, 1964.

———. *Tasso's Dialogues: A Selection*. Trans. Carnes Lord and Dain A. Trafton. Berkeley: University of California Press, 1982.

Tatum, James. *Apuleius and "The Golden Ass": Eleven Books of Metamorphoses*. Ithaca and London: Cornell University Press, 1979.

Taylor, Michael. "The Pastoral Reckoning in 'Cymbeline'." *Shakespeare Survey* 36 (1983): 97–106.

Tervarent, Guy de. *Attributs et symboles dans l'art profane 1450–1600*. Geneva: Libraire E. Droz, 1958.

———. "Eros and Anteros: Or Reciprocal Love in Ancient and Renaissance Art." *Journal of the Warburg and Courtauld Institutes* 28 (1965): 205–8.

Thiébaux, Marcelle. *The Stag of Love: The Chase in Medieval Literature*. Ithaca and London: Cornell University Press, 1974.

Thompson, Ann. "Philomel in 'Titus Andronicus' and 'Cymbeline'." *Shakespeare Survey* 31 (1978): 23–32.

Thomson, W. G. *A History of Tapestry, from the Earliest Times to the Present Day*. 3d ed. Edited and revised by F. P. and E. S. Thomson. London: EP Publishing Ltd., 1973.

Thorne, William Barry. "*Cymbeline:* 'Lopp'd Branches' and the Concept of Regeneration." *Shakespeare Quarterly* 20 (1969): 143–59.

Tillyard, E. M. W. *The Elizabethan World Picture: A Study of the Idea of Order in the Age of Shakespeare, Donne and Milton*. London: Chatto and Windus, 1943.

Tobin, J. M. *Shakespeare's Favorite Novel: A Study of "The Golden Asse" as Prime Source*. Lanham, Md.: University Press of America, 1984.

Topsell, Edward. *The Fowles of Heauen or History of Birdes*. Edited by Thomas P. Harrison and F. David Hoeniger. Austin: University of Texas Press, 1972.

———. *The Historie of Foure-footed Beastes*. London: William Jaggard, 1607.

———. *Topsell's Histories of Beasts*. Edited by Malcolm South. Chicago: Nelson-Hall, 1981.

Traversi, Derek. *Shakespeare: The Last Phase*. Stanford: Stanford University Press, 1952.

Trinkaus, Charles. *In Our Image and Likeness: Humanity and Divinity in Italian Humanist Thought*. 2 vols. London: Constable & Co., Ltd., 1970.

Turbervile, George. *Turbervile's Booke of Hunting*. 1576 reprint. Oxford: Clarendon Press, 1908.

Veen, Otto van. *Amorvm emblemata, or Emblemes of Loue*. Antwerp, 1608.

Vertova, Luisa. "Cupid and Psyche in Renaissance Painting Before Raphael." *Journal of the Warburg and Courtauld Institutes* 42 (1979): 104–21.

Vinge, Louise. "Chapman's *Ovids Banquet of Sence*. Its Sources and Theme." *Journal of the Warburg and Courtauld Institutes* 38 (1975): 234–57.

———. *The Five Senses: Studies in a Literary Tradition*. Lund, Sweden: Liber Laromedal, 1975.

Virgil. *The Aeneid*. Translated by W. F. Jackson Knight. Baltimore: Penguin Books, 1956.

Viswanathan, S. "Sleep and Death: The Twins in Shakespeare." *Comparative Drama* 13 (1979): 49–64.

Vives, Juan Luis. "A Fable About Man." Translated by Nancy Lenkeith. In *The Renaissance Philosophy of Man*, edited by Ernst Cassirer, et al., 387–93. Chicago: University of Chicago Press, 1948.

Waith, Eugene M. *The Pattern of Tragicomedy in Beaumont and Fletcher*. New Haven: Yale University Press, 1952.

Wall, John N. "Shakespeare's Aural Art: The Metaphor of the Ear in *Othello*." *Shakespeare Quarterly* 30 (1979): 358–66.

Warden, John, ed. *Orpheus: The Metamorphoses of a Myth*. Toronto: University of Toronto Press, 1982.

Welles, Elizabeth Basset, trans. "Poliziano's *Orfeo*." *La Fusta* 4 (1979): 100–20.

Whitney, Geffrey. *A Choice of Emblemes*. Leiden: Christopher Plantin, 1586.

White, T. H., ed. *The Bestiary: A Book of Beasts*. New York: G. P. Putnam's Sons, 1954.

Wickham, Glynne. "Riddle and Emblem: A Study in the Dramatic Structure of *Cymbeline*." In *English Renaissance Studies: Presented to Dame Helen Gardner on her 70th Birthday*. Edited by John Carey, 94–113. Oxford: Clarendon Press, 1980.

Wind, Edgar. *Pagan Mysteries in the Renaissance: An Exploration of Philosophical and Mystical Sources of Iconography in Renaissance Art*. 2d ed, rev. and enl. New York: W. W. Norton, 1968.

Wither, George. *A Collection of Emblemes, Ancient and Modern*. London, 1635.

Wittkower, Rufolf. "Eagle and Serpent." *Journal of the Warburg Institute* 2 (1938–39): 293–325.

Wood, John Philip. *The Peerage of Scotland*. 2 vols. Edinburgh: George Ramsay and Co., 1813.

Yates, Frances. *Giordano Bruno and the Hermetic Tradition*. London: Routledge & Kegan Paul, 1964.

————. *Shakespeare's Last Plays: A New Approach*. London: Routledge and Kegan Paul, 1975.

Yoch, James J., Jr. "The Limits of Sensuality: Pastoral Wildernesses, Tasso's *Aminta* and the Gardens of Ferrara." *Forum Italicum* (Spring–Fall 1982): 60–81.

————. "The Renaissance Dramatization of Temperance: The Italian Revival of Tragicomedy and *The Faithful Shepherdess*." In *Renaissance Tragicomedy. See* Maguire 1987.

————. "Subjecting the Landscape in Pageants and Shakespearean Pastorals." In *Pageantry in the Shakespearean Theater*, edited by David M. Bergeron, 194–219. Athens, Ga.: University of Georgia Press, 1985.

Young, Alan R. "A Note on the Tournament Impresas in *Pericles*." *Shakespeare Quarterly* 36 (1985): 453–56.

Index

Actaeon, 103–8, 151
Adam, 48, 190, 199; old clothes of, 215
Adlington, William, 89
Aelian, 174–75
Aesop, 38, 144, 188; "The Nightingale," 144; "the ravished tree," 182
Air, as element, 98
Alberti, Leone Battista, 193
Alcestis, 52, 56
Alciati, Andrea, 21, 38, 195; against astrologers, 215–17, 219; on concord, 210–12; on courtiers, 171–74; on the empty head, 186–88; on Eros and Anteros, 47, 63 nn. 28 and 29, 111–16, 141–45; on friendship, 256–57, 274; on harmony, 337–38; on hope, 176–77; on the kite, 204; on the peach tree, 325; on "the ravished tree," 183–84
Aldrovandi, Ulisse, 206, 215, 220, 295
Alexander of Macedon, 172, 316
Allegory, 67, 80; of the soul's journey, 83
Allusions, classical, 68
Amazons, 111
Ambiguity, 16
Ambrose, St., 72, 209, 295
Amicitia, personification of, 260–61. *See also* Friendship
Amor, 41; as desire for beauty, 44; as god of love in contrast to Cupid's lust, 84, 88–89, 119, 264; Imogen as, 148–49, 324–25
Andirons, 96, 109–19
Androgyny, 100, 127, 235
Animals: ape, 198, 200, 205; ass, 78–92, 105, 272; bat, 174–75; boar, 56, 273; elephant, 22; foxes and wolves, 137, 140, 186; lamb, 151, 296–98; lion, 164, 166, 285–98, 340; as moral symbols, 199, 272–98; snakes, 18–20; women as wild animals, 39

Anne, Queen, 193, 230
Anteros. *See* Eros and Anteros
Antipater, 250
Aphrodite, *Anadyomene* 98, 126–27; 325. *See also* Venus
Apollo: and Coronis, 203; as father of Orpheus, 345–46, 348–49; flaying of Marsyas, 73; laurel of, 111, 229; opposite from Dionysos, 340; as patron god of poetry, 356; priest of, 55; as shepherd, 33, 53–54; reconciled with Dionysos, 90, 360; rites of, 56–60
Appearance versus reality, theme of, 83, 213, 304, 322
Apuleius, Lucius, 32, 58, 64 n.42; Cupid and Psyche, 78–92; *The Golden Ass,* 98, 105, 119, 272, 356. *See also* Neoplatonism
Araldi, Alessandro, 102
Archaeology, literary, 21
Argumentum emblematicum, 143, 181
Ariadne, as sleeping woman, 68, 119–29
Aristippus, 172
Aristotle, 172; on dramatic structure and unities, 29–30; on the senses, 293, 301–3, 342; on tragedy, 360
Armitage, David, 56, 64 n.40, 344, 349
Arms and armor, 22, 57, 155, 220, 355
Art, 58; as ape of Nature, 198, 200; funerary, 83, 122, 124, 210, 251; as instruction, 102; as political weapon, 73–75; as quest for wisdom, 360
Artist, as Orpheus, 349–52. *See also* Orpheus
Atonement, 40, 60, 228
Augustine, St., 72, 195 n.4, 289
Augustus Caesar, 21, 44, 101, 149, 152, 233, 235
Axton, Marie, 97

Bacchus, 120. *See also* Dionysos